UNDERSTANDING
CONTEMPORARY
RUSSIA

UNDERSTANDING

Introductions to the States and Regions of the Contemporary World

Donald L. Gordon, series editor

Understanding Contemporary Africa, 4th edition
edited by April A. Gordon and Donald L. Gordon

Understanding Contemporary Asia Pacific
edited by Katherine Palmer Kaup

Understanding the Contemporary Caribbean
edited by Richard S. Hillman and Thomas J. D'Agostino

Understanding Contemporary China, 3rd edition
edited by Robert E. Gamer

Understanding Contemporary India
edited by Sumit Ganguly and Neil DeVotta

Understanding Contemporary Latin America, 3rd edition
edited by Richard S. Hillman

Understanding the Contemporary Middle East, 3rd edition
edited by Jillian Schwedler and Deborah J. Gerner

Understanding Contemporary Russia
edited by Michael L. Bressler

UNDERSTANDING CONTEMPORARY RUSSIA

edited by
Michael L. Bressler

LYNNE
RIENNER
PUBLISHERS

BOULDER
LONDON

Published in the United States of America in 2009 by
Lynne Rienner Publishers, Inc.
1800 30th Street, Boulder, Colorado 80301
www.rienner.com

and in the United Kingdom by
Lynne Rienner Publishers, Inc.
3 Henrietta Street, Covent Garden, London WC2E 8LU

Library of Congress Cataloging-in-Publication Data
Understanding contemporary Russia / edited by Michael L. Bressler.
    p. cm. — (Understanding)
Includes bibliographical references and index.
ISBN 978-1-58826-586-9 (hardcover : alk. paper)
ISBN 978-1-58826-561-6 (pbk. : alk. paper)
    1. Russia (Federation)—Politics and government—1991–   2. Russia
(Federation)—Economic conditions—1991–   3. Russia (Federation)—Social
conditions—1991–   4. Russia (Federation)—Civilization. I. Bressler,
Michael L., 1962–
    JN6695.U53 2008
    947.086—dc22
                                                                    2008014892

British Cataloguing in Publication Data
A Cataloguing in Publication record for this book
is available from the British Library.

Printed and bound in the United States of America

The paper used in this publication meets the requirements
∞ of the American National Standard for Permanence of
Paper for Printed Library Materials Z39.48-1992.

5 4 3 2 1

Contents

Illustrations

▓ Figures

▓ Photographs

Acknowledgments

One of the great rewards of this project has been the opportunity to work with so many talented people. I am most grateful to the authors for the time and energy they devoted to this endeavor. Their willingness to share their expertise with a new generation of students is a high mark of their commitment to their fields. Much gratitude is owed as well to Lynne Rienner and her wonderful staff. Professionals of the highest order, they were helpful, supportive, and enthusiastic from start to finish.

I would also like to thank the Furman University staff members whose efforts helped make this book possible. They include Department of Political Science assistant Carol Whitmire, who scanned a number of the photos that appear in the book, and reference librarian Laura Baker and her assistant Derrick Stewart, who enthusiastically located and delivered scores of books and articles, often at a moment's notice. Thanks must go, too, to Kevin Burkhill and Anne Ankcorn of the University of Birmingham's School of Geography, Earth, and Environmental Sciences for preparing the maps that appear in Chapter 2.

To series editor and colleague Don Gordon I owe a special debt. Don and his wife, April, set a high standard for the series with their publication of *Understanding Contemporary Africa* in 1992. Now in its fourth edition, that book remains the premier text in its field. Without Don's vision and discernment, *Understanding Contemporary Russia* never would have gotten off the ground. Ever supportive, he has been a reliable source of advice and encouragement. Another special thank you must go to Furman University president David Shi, who provided funding to complete the project.

Thanks are also in order for the chair of my department, Brent Nelsen, who allowed me to hire Furman student Kaleb McMichen as a research assistant through the department's PS Fellows program, funds for which are provided by a generous anonymous donor. Kaleb, a talented young man with a keen, critical mind, served as a second set of eyes in the editing process. The "student's perspective" he provided helped make this a better book.

    I would like to thank, too, Alexandra Baker of the Russian Department at Middlebury College and Lynne deBenedette of the Department of Slavic Languages at Brown University for their help on certain critical points of editing. Thanks go as well to Furman colleagues Danielle Vinson, Glen Halva-Neubauer, Cleve Fraser, and Kate Kaup for their constant encouragement. My family deserves special thanks for their steadfast support and assistance. To them I am especially grateful.

    Finally, given the nature of this volume and its primary audience, I think it necessary to thank several professors from my own undergraduate experience at Ohio State whose fascination with Russia became my own. More than two decades later their dedication to teaching and learning continues to inspire me. To each I owe sincere thanks: Philip Stewart in Political Science; Michael Curran in History; George Demko in Geography; Warren Eason in Economics; Gretchen Trimble, Jerry Ervin, Father Mateja Matejic, George Kalbouss, and Jerzy Krzyzanowski in Slavic Languages and Literatures; and Jan Adams, Mark Piwinsky, and Dolores Brzycki in International Studies. This volume is dedicated to them.

—*Michael L. Bressler*

UNDERSTANDING
CONTEMPORARY
RUSSIA

1

Introduction

Michael L. Bressler

During the Cold War, Russia's standing as a superpower (then the Soviet Union) ensured that it would be the primary focus of foreign policy makers in the West and a ready source of headlines for news organizations around the world. With the loss of its superpower status following the Soviet system's collapse in 1991, Russia was no longer the principal concern of Western foreign policy. Throughout the 1990s, interest in Russia declined, so much so that just a few years ago a number of US experts on Russia expressed their concerns about the future of Russian studies in the United States (see Hanson and Ruble 2005).

Of late, however, Russia has reclaimed at least a part of its former status as a result of its growing economy, its expanding influence in energy markets, and its increasing assertiveness in foreign policy. Indicative of Russia's return to center stage was *Time* magazine's choice of President Vladimir Putin as its 2007 "Person of the Year." Just a few years ago, with Russia's economy and society in decline, many observers questioned its importance in global affairs. With energy prices reaching record levels and Russia's economy rebounding, few question its significance now.

Although public awareness of Russia's importance seems to be increasing, this does not necessarily reflect a deeper knowledge or understanding of the country and its people. This seems especially true of those who have no memory of either the Cold War or the Soviet Union or of a time when the "Russians" dominated our news and focused our attention. For this younger generation, Russia waits to be discovered anew. *Understanding Contemporary Russia* is designed specifically to aid in this discovery and to promote the study and exploration of a country that continues to intrigue all who encounter it.

Almost twice the size of the United States and occupying nearly a third of the immense Eurasian landmass, Russia is by far the largest country in the world. A diverse land of harsh tundra, vast forests, rugged mountains, semiarid expanses, and seemingly endless steppes, Russia is graced not only by incredible natural beauty but also considerable natural wealth. As is the case around the world, the impulse in Russia to exploit its seemingly limitless stores of natural resources (including oil, gas, minerals, metals, and timber) poses a constant threat to the health of a natural environment that includes such wonders as Lake Baikal and the Ob and Yenisey rivers.

A country on such a scale, so varied in its ecologies and landscapes, must also be diverse in its peoples and cultures. Even though nearly 80 percent of its population is ethnically Russian, Russia is home to nearly 160 other officially recognized ethnic groups. Religiously, the country is also diverse. Although Russian Orthodoxy dominates among believers, Islam is Russia's second largest religion. Buddhism, Judaism, various forms of Western Christianity, and a number of traditional ethnic faiths also have adherents. At the same time, as one legacy of the communist era, nearly a third of the population is made up of nonbelievers.

In considering the many links between Russia's past and its present, one is struck by the centrality of its relationship with the West. For more than three hundred years the more modern West has posed a significant challenge to Russia. Although Russia's leaders have tended to view the question primarily in military and economic terms, more often than not the challenge from the West has been social and political. On occasion Russia has responded effectively, as it did under Peter the Great, the first Russian leader who sought to reduce the West's lead in science and technology. Frequently, however, Russia has fallen short in its efforts, at times with catastrophic results. Imperial Russia's ruin in 1917 and the Soviet Union's demise in 1991 are perhaps best understood as failures of two different Russian systems (one tsarist and one communist) to cope with the challenge of the West. Not long after the Soviet system's collapse, Boris Yeltsin's launching of "shock therapy" represented yet another attempt to modernize and transform a country that was lagging far behind the West.

As much as the West has influenced Russia, so too has Russia influenced the West. During much of the nineteenth and twentieth centuries Russians played a central role in transforming the arts through their music (for instance, Alexander Borodin and Igor Stravinsky), dance (Sergei Diaghilev and the Ballets Russes), literature (numerous authors, including Lev Tolstoy and Anton Chekhov), painting (for example, abstract artist and theorist Vasily Kandinsky), and theater (Konstantin Stanislavsky and the Moscow Art Theater).

Russia's contributions in the sciences and social sciences were also great in such fields as psychology (by Ivan Pavlov, whose work on conditioned responses earned him a Nobel Prize), chemistry (by Dmitri Mendeleev, who developed the periodic law and the first comprehensive periodic table), and mathematics (by Nikolai Lobachevsky, one of the founders of non-Euclidean geometry). During the communist era the Soviet Union ushered in the space age by beating the United States into outer space not once but twice: by launching the first artificial satellite, *Sputnik 1,* in 1957, and by completing the first successful manned space flight, by cosmonaut Yuri Gagarin, in 1961. Although the Soviets never managed to put a man or woman on the moon, early success in their space program spurred their Cold War rival, the United States, into action. Thus, even as Russia has struggled and sometimes failed in its efforts to meet the challenges posed by a more modern West, its influence on the West and the world has been both real and substantial.

From their first encounters with the Russians several centuries ago, Western elites have tended to distort Russian realities, sometimes idealizing the country and at other times demonizing it. These Western views of Russia, Martin Malia (1999) argues, have often reflected political and socioeconomic currents inside the West as much as they have conditions inside Russia. When Russia seems to look more like the West, regardless of what is actually going on inside the country, relations between Russia and the West have grown warm. When Russia appears to diverge from the West, however, Western perceptions change and relations cool.

As its relationship continues to evolve with the West, Russia faces a number of challenges, not least of which is the transformation of its political and economic systems. Nearly two decades after the Soviet system's collapse Russia is still finding its way, at times seemingly converging with the West and at times apparently moving away from it. A number of other questions also demand Russia's attention, each defying simple solutions: holding together a multiethnic, multiconfessional society; coping with a public health crisis that threatens the long-term viability of the Russian state and its people; dealing with the many negative effects of environmental degradation; and reforming a corrupt bureaucracy. The question of Russian identity also looms large in the policies of ruling elites who, much to the dismay of many observers in the West, seem increasingly convinced that Russia must strike out on a uniquely "Russian" course in its political, economic, and social development.

Understanding another country and appreciating the many challenges facing it is hard work. How easy it is, Malia (1999) reminds us, to allow our own interests and fears to influence what we grasp and perceive. Undoubtedly, this is true of any relationship between peoples of different histories and cultures. The authors of this volume have endeavored to provide a fair appraisal of contemporary Russia and a thoughtful assessment of where the country is, how it got there, and where it might be going. We hope the reader will gain a greater understanding of a country that has long struggled to find its place in the world and to be at peace with itself.

* * *

This book is the result of a collaborative effort by eleven scholars who have devoted much of their lives to the study of things Russian. During the recruitment of authors for this project, the near universal reaction was that the publication of such a volume was long overdue. Interdisciplinary in design, *Understanding Contemporary Russia* is intended primarily for use as a core text in introductory Russian survey courses. The authors do not assume an in-depth knowledge or understanding of Russia on the part of the reader. Accordingly, the book is straightforward both in content and design. At the same time, the authors, by drawing on the best research in their fields, have resisted the temptation to be simplistic in their approaches. Although not an exhaustive survey, this book aims to provide students with a sophisticated yet accessible treatment of Russia. In this way, the authors hope to leave students with a finer appreciation of the many challenges facing Russia and its people.

This first chapter has provided a brief overview of the subject with special attention paid to Russia's relationship with the West. It is followed by detailed chapters on Russia's geography (Chapter 2) and history (Chapter 3), which taken together provide the foundation for the rest of the volume. Mindful of the many links between Russia's past and present, subsequent chapters examine the country's politics (Chapter 4) and economics (Chapter 5) as well as Russia's place in the international system (Chapter 6). From here the book considers some of the more important issues facing Russian society today: ethnicity and identity (Chapter 7), population and health (Chapter 8), the environment (Chapter 9), the role of women (Chapter 10), and religion (Chapter 11). No survey of Russia would be complete without a detailed examination of Russian literature and film (Chapter 12). Finally, in the closing chapter, the book reflects on where Russia has been and speculates about where it might be going.

■ A Note on Transliteration

Because the Russian language is rendered in Cyrillic letters, not in Latin script, the transliteration of Russian words poses a challenge to any editor. This volume generally follows the Library of Congress's transliteration scheme. In cases in which other forms are more common (such as Yeltsin, instead of El'tsin), the more common form is used. In instances in which Russian and English first names are essentially equivalent (such as the Russian "Aleksandr" and the English "Alexander") the English form is used. In cases in which Russian and English first names are not quite as close, either in pronunciation or transliteration (for example, the Russian "Mikhail" and the English "Michael"), the Russian form is used. With the exception of their use in bibliographic entries, diacritical marks (for soft signs and hard signs) are omitted.

▧ Bibliography

Hanson, Stephen E., and Blair A. Ruble. 2005. "Rebuilding Russian Studies." *Problems of Post-Communism* 52(3): 49–57.

Malia, Martin. 1999. *Russia Under Western Eyes: From the Bronze Horseman to the Lenin Mausoleum.* Cambridge, MA: Harvard University Press.

2

Russia:
A Geographic Preface

Denis J. B. Shaw

Independent since 1991, the Russian Federation is one the younger countries of the world. As a recognizable political entity, however, Russia has a far longer history. Prior to 1991 it was one of the fifteen republics that formed the Soviet Union, a superpower that challenged the United States for global supremacy. Officially a federation, the Union of Soviet Socialist Republics (USSR) was a highly centralized, Russian-dominated state in which the levers of power were firmly in the hands of the Communist Party leadership in Moscow. If observers in the West often incorrectly referred to the Soviet Union as "Russia," ethnic Russians tended to assume that they, of all the peoples of the USSR, were the ones who should take the political lead in their country.

That many ethnic Russians viewed the Soviet Union in this way was natural given that the USSR was built on the ruins of Imperial Russia. This empire, as its name suggests, was very much a Russian affair, ruled over by Russian emperors whose seat of power was in St. Petersburg, an entirely artificial city built by Peter the Great on the shores of the Gulf of Finland. Although St. Petersburg holds a prominent place in Russian history, it is in Moscow that one finds the origins of the modern Russian state more than five centuries ago. Thus, contemporary Russia, although in one sense new, rests upon well-established foundations. Two specific features of today's Russia relate directly to its imperial past. One is the country's multiethnic character. The other is its enormous territorial expanse.

■ The Imperial Heritage: Russian Territorial Expansion

Map 2.1 shows the location of the Russian Federation and its geographical relationship to the other fourteen states that, like Russia, were once part of

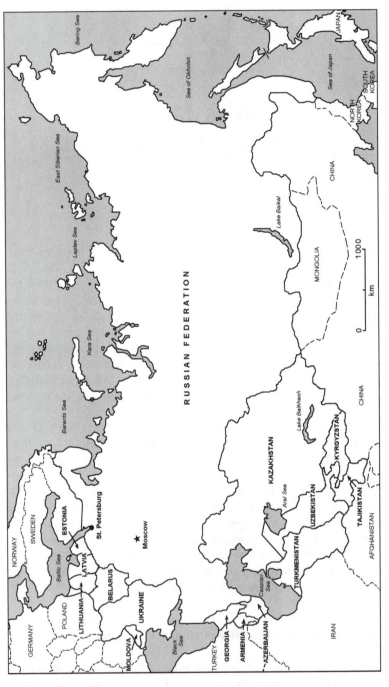

Map 2.1 The Russian Federation and the Soviet Successor States

the USSR. Despite its separation from these former Soviet republics, Russia easily remains the largest country in the world. With a territory of some 6.6 million square miles (17.1 million square kilometers), Russia is nearly 1.8 times the size of China, almost 1.9 times that of the United States, and 70 times the size of the United Kingdom. Its west-east expanse is particularly impressive, stretching over eleven time zones from the Baltic Sea bordering Poland in the west to the Bering Strait separating Asia and North America in the east. In the middle of the strait two islands, one belonging to Russia and the other to the United States, are less than three miles apart. The north-south axis is also great, extending from the polar regions of the far north to the semidesert lands bordering the Caspian Sea in the south. Geopolitically, this means that Russia is in close contact with several quite disparate cultural and political arenas: Central and Eastern Europe and the North Atlantic to the west; the Mediterranean basin to the southwest; the Middle East to the south; China and the Far East to the southeast; and the North Pacific and Arctic basin to the east and north. Accordingly, Russian foreign policy (as Allen Lynch shows in Chapter 6) must be equally complex.

Russia owes the vast size of its territory to its imperial past. At the beginning of the fourteenth century, the Muscovite state, out of which the Russian empire would eventually form, occupied only about 7,700 square miles of land (about the size of Massachusetts). From this territory, in what is now the center of European Russia, the grand princes of Moscow set out to absorb all the surrounding Russian cities and principalities, a feat more or less accomplished by the mid-sixteenth century. Muscovy continued to expand, partly through spontaneous colonization and settlement and partly through warfare and conquest. The princes of Moscow, who now called themselves "tsars" in imitation of the Roman Caesars, began occupying Siberia in the 1580s, establishing the first Russian settlement on the Pacific coast in 1649. Taking much of eastern Ukraine in the seventeenth century, they absorbed western and southern Ukraine, Belarus, and the present-day Baltic states during the eighteenth. The nineteenth century witnessed further territorial acquisitions, notably in the Transcaucasus region (now often referred to as the South Caucasus), Central Asia, and the Far East. At the same time, Russia gained additional land in the west. By 1917 the Russian empire occupied more than 7.7 million square miles of land (Map 2.2).

Like all imperial expansions, Russia's acquisition of territory witnessed great migrations and settlement, especially by the Russians themselves. Two kinds of environments proved particularly attractive to Russian migrants. The first were those that were similar to the original Russian homeland in the central East European plain, which is to say the mixed forest region and the more favorable parts of the coniferous forest belt to the north. Over time, Russians came to dominate these lands, which encompassed the eastern parts of the East European plain and the southern territories of Siberia. Only

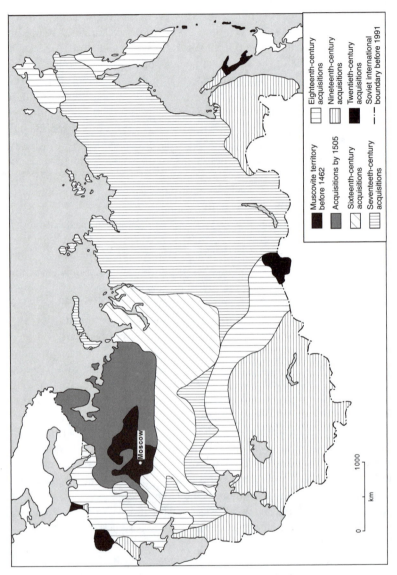

Map 2.2 Territorial Expansion

Muscovite territory before 1462

Acquisitions by 1505

Sixteenth-century acquisitions

Seventeenth-century acquisitions

Eighteenth-century acquisitions

Nineteenth-century acquisitions

Twentieth-century acquisitions

Soviet international boundary before 1991

Moscow

0   1000

km

in northern European Russia and northern Siberia, where conditions were harsher, did Russian settlement initially play a more limited role while that of the native peoples remained significant. Even here the Russians eventually began to settle in greater numbers because of the north's natural resource wealth. The second environment that proved attractive to Russian migrants consisted of steppe grasslands (with natural conditions similar to those of the American prairies) that stretched across central and southern Ukraine, southern European Russia, and southwestern Siberia. Russian and Ukrainian agricultural settlers eventually converted these grasslands into farmlands, pacifying or expelling the former nomadic inhabitants of these regions (Tatars, Kalmyks, and Bashkirs among others).

Beyond these regions of Russian migration and settlement, many territories of the empire proved less attractive to ethnic Russians. Among these were those with harsh environments, not only in the far north of European Russia and Siberia (with some exceptions as noted above) but also in the deserts of Central Asia. Less appealing, too, were territories already settled by non-Russian peoples. Such areas included what is now Moldova, the Baltic states of Estonia, Latvia, and Lithuania, the Transcaucasus states of Georgia, Armenia, and Azerbaijan, the oases and river valleys of Kazakhstan and the Central Asia states of Uzbekistan, Tajikistan, Turkmenistan, and Kyrgyzstan, and much of Ukraine and Belarus, whose peoples are closely related to the Russians both ethnically and culturally. Taken together, these regions constitute the fourteen non-Russian Soviet successor states, the borders of which, along with those of the current Russian Federation, were drawn and redrawn by the Soviet leadership over a period of several decades.

In defining these borders, the Soviet leaders allocated to Russia those territories that were predominantly ethnic Russian. They also assigned to Russia regions whose non-Russian populations were either numerically insignificant or located deep within Russia's interior, prohibiting the creation of their own separate republics. Consequently, what is now the Russian Federation was once a multiethnic republic of the USSR, a fact that, as this and later chapters will show, continues to exert great influence on Russia.

▉ Population and Settlement Distribution

A glance at Map 2.3 reveals the uneven distribution of Russia's population. Only about 21 percent of that population lives in either Siberia or the Far East, the regions lying to the east of the Ural Mountains, which account for nearly three-quarters of the country's territory (see Map 2.4). Map 2.3 also reveals a triangular-shaped wedge of more densely populated territory (with more than twenty-five persons per square kilometer on average), the base of

12

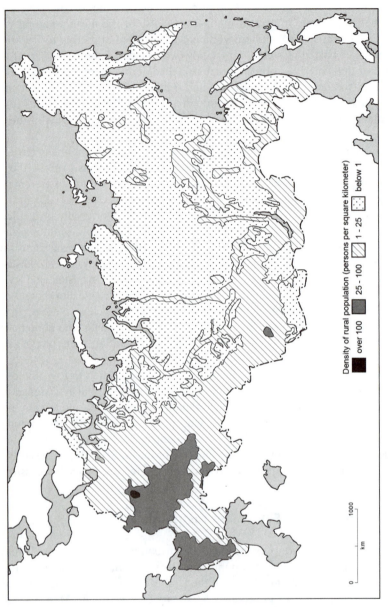

Density of rural population (persons per square kilometer)

over 100 25 - 100 1 - 25 below 1

Map 2.3 Population Density

1000

km

0

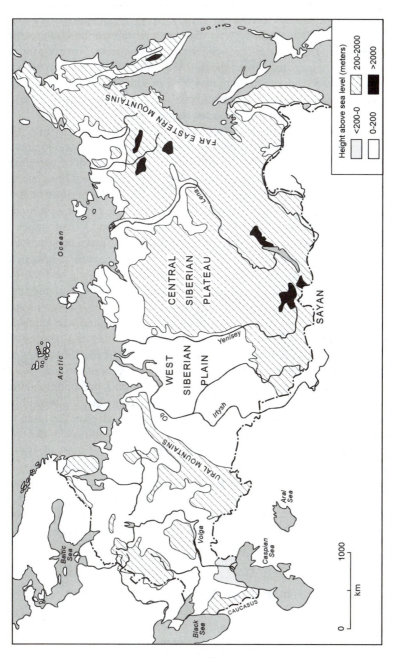

Map 2.4 Physical Features

which runs along the Ukrainian and Belarusian frontiers in the west and the apex of which points east toward the Urals. In sparsely populated Siberia and the Far East, population density typically is greater toward the south, particularly along the route of the Trans-Siberian Railway. Here, however, mountainous terrain greatly influences the detailed settlement geography, such as in the Altai and Sayan mountain ranges west of Lake Baikal where population density is low. In sum, in terms of population distribution, as opposed to territory, Russia is primarily a European country.

A number of implications flow from this basic geographical fact. The first is that the Russian Federation's socioeconomic center of gravity lies to the west of the Urals. As such, Russia's leaders inevitably will be concerned about events in Europe, relations with the European Union, and European attitudes toward Russia. In the past, many Europeans and a number of Russians have hoped that Russia might see its future as lying to the east, in developing the rich resources of Siberia and the Far East, and in cultivating its relations with China, Japan, and other Asian countries. Such a perspective is unrealistic, as Russia is bound to Europe by numerous economic, historical, and cultural ties. Important, too, is that vast areas of Siberia and the Far East, because of their harsh climates, are generally unattractive to migrants.

From this follows a second implication of Russia's geography: the spatial discrepancy between the more densely populated and economically active west and the sparsely populated but resource-laden east. During the Soviet period population and industrial activity west of the Urals grew relentlessly, increasing the demands made on the resources of the east. Soviet planners were persistent in their efforts to relocate both population and industry to the east, but with only limited success. Over time, the men in the Kremlin devoted increasing amounts of money to developing the often remote resources of the east, not only to support Soviet industry in the west but also to raise revenue for the state budget through exports abroad. By the 1980s, Siberia and the Far East accounted for about two-thirds of Soviet oil production (over 90 percent of Russian production) and an equivalent proportion of natural gas production (about three-quarters of Russian production). The east also supplied much of the country's coal. Today, Russia continues to rely on the resources of the east, with much of its current economic growth coming from the export of oil and natural gas.

▨ Climate, Settlement, and the Natural Environment

Why does Russia's population geography seem so at odds with the geography of the territory as a whole, with such a high proportion of the population concentrated in the west and south, with vast empty spaces in the east and north? Much of the answer to this question lies in the character of the country's natural environment.

The twin peaks of Mt. Elbrus in the North Caucasus.
Elbrus is Europe's highest mountain.

First, Russia's core lies relatively far to the north in the Northern Hemisphere, particularly in comparison with North America. At 55 degrees 45 minutes N, Moscow is north of Edmonton in Alberta, Canada, and at the same latitude as southern Hudson Bay. St. Petersburg, at 59 degrees 55 minutes N, lies just south of Anchorage, Alaska (61 degrees 13 minutes N), and closely parallels the southern boundary of Canada's Yukon Territory and Northwest Territories. In comparison with North America, Western Europe's northerly position is ameliorated by the moderating effects of the North Atlantic Drift, an ocean current that bathes the coast of Western Europe with relatively warm water originating in the Gulf of Mexico, the Caribbean, and adjacent maritime regions. Otherwise, Western Europe's climate would be much more severe than it is. But Russia, situated well to the east across the huge Eurasian landmass (the largest continuous landmass in the world), is largely shielded from such moderating maritime influences. Russia's terrain is also unhelpful in this respect. Although much of Russia is open to moist air masses from the Atlantic, it is also open to Arctic air from the north. By contrast, warm air masses traveling north from the Indian Ocean are largely blocked by the Himalayan and neighboring mountain ranges. Likewise, the potential moderating effects of air masses from the North Pacific on the climates of East Siberia and the Far East are largely nullified by mountainous terrain along the Pacific coast.

The overall result of these patterns is that most of Russia suffers from a harsh, continental climate with moderately warm summers and very cold winters. During the winter a high pressure zone that centers on southern Siberia influences much of the country (see Map 2.5). This gives rise to stable weather conditions with predominantly clear skies in mid-winter, causing temperatures to fall rapidly. Winter isotherms in the western half of the country tend to run north-south, meaning that average temperatures fall as one moves toward the east. The mean January temperature in Moscow, for instance, is 13.5 degrees Fahrenheit (–10.3 degrees Celsius), while that of Novosibirsk, at roughly the same latitude as Moscow but 1,700 miles to the east in West Siberia, is –2.2 degrees F (–19 degrees C). The lowest average winter temperatures are in northeastern Siberia (strictly speaking, in the northern part of the Far East) in the neighborhood of Verkhoyansk, which has a mean January temperature of –56 degrees F (–48.9 degrees C). Even though much of Russia's territory is covered by snow during the winter, snow cover may be insufficient to protect wintering crops from severe frosts, particularly in parts of the east.

In summer, low pressure centered in Central Asia greatly influences conditions across Russia (see Map 2.6). Isotherms tend to run east-west, meaning that average temperatures increase as one moves from north to south. The mean July temperature in Moscow, for example, is 64 degrees F (17.8 degrees C) while that at Sochi, 840 miles to the south on the Black Sea coast, is 72.8 degrees F (22.7 degrees C). Overall, the average temperature range and the degree of continentality both increase as one moves east. Thus at Moscow the difference between January and July mean temperatures is about 50 degrees F (28 degrees C), at Novosibirsk 68.4 degrees F (38 degrees C), and at Verkhoyansk 115.2 degrees F (64 degrees C).

Patterns of precipitation respond to the prevailing patterns of high and low pressure (see Map 2.7). Precipitation maxima tend to occur in the summer when the prevailing low pressure systems pull in moist air masses traveling in from the Atlantic. By contrast, high pressure during the winter tends to deflect cyclonic (or low pressure system) activity. Mean annual precipitation tends to fall as one moves from west to east, until, in East Siberia and the Far East, Pacific influences become apparent. This reduction in precipitation is particularly obvious in south European Russia and neighboring parts of Ukraine where drought is a frequent problem. In fact, near semi-desert conditions are present in the Volga Delta, close to the Caspian Sea, where the average annual precipitation in Astrakhan is only 7.5 inches (190.1 millimeters), compared to 22.6 inches (575 millimeters) in Moscow.

These broad geographical patterns of temperature and precipitation also help to define patterns of natural vegetation (natural zones or *biomes*). Unlike in North America, where such patterns are complicated by the presence

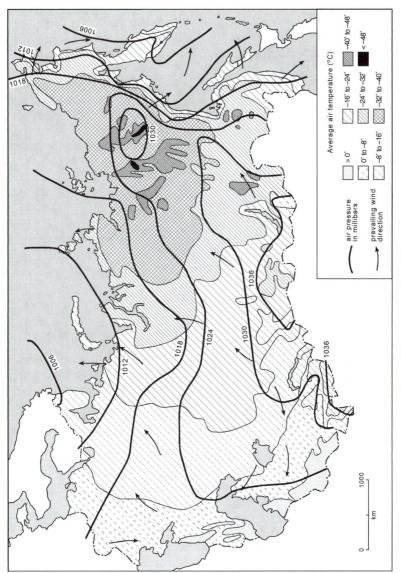

Map 2.5 January Weather Patterns

Average air temperature (°C)

> 0°   -16° to -24°   -40° to -48°
0° to -8°   -24° to -32°   < -48°
-8° to -16°   -32° to -40°

— air pressure in millibars
→ prevailing wind direction

1006
1012
1018
1030
1036
1018
1024
1030
1036
1012
1006
1036

0   1000
km

18

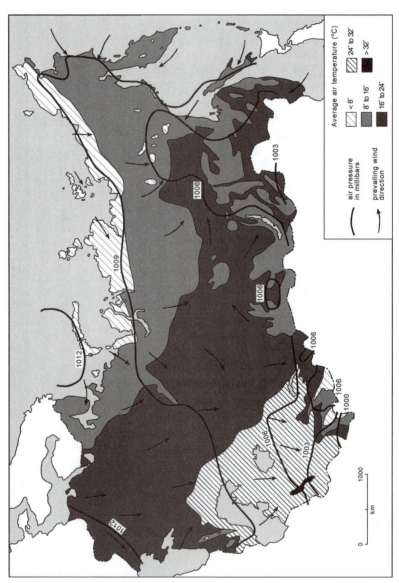

Map 2.6 July Weather Patterns

Average air temperature (°C)

< 8°   8° to 16°   16° to 24°   24° to 32°   > 32°

air pressure in millibars

prevailing wind direction

1012
1009
1006
1003
1006
1006
1006
1006
1000
1006
1003
1012

0   1000
km

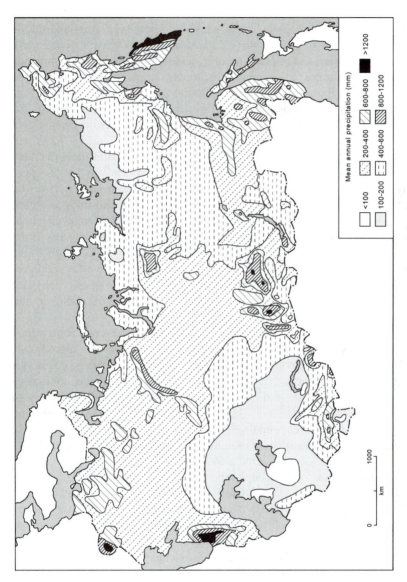

Map 2.7 Mean Annual Precipitation

Mean annual precipitation (mm)

<100
100–200
200–400
400–600
600–800
800–1200
>1200

0   1000
km

of the Appalachian Mountains in the east and the Western Cordilleras in the west (the most prominent of which are the Rocky Mountains), those in Russia are relatively straightforward, tending to run from west to east (see Map 2.8). The harshest conditions are in the north, in the tundra, an inhospitable land of swamp, moss, peat, lichen, scrub, and perennial grassland that is conducive neither to dense human settlement nor tree growth. Historically devoted to hunting and reindeer herding, and more recently to certain kinds of natural resources development, the tundra stretches along the Arctic coast from the Barents Sea in the west to the Bering Strait in the east. Further south is the boreal or coniferous forest belt, known as the taiga. In European Russia the taiga extends south to St. Petersburg before running on a southeasterly course toward Nizhnii Novgorod on the middle Volga and then eastward to the Urals. Most of Siberia and the Far East lie in the taiga zone. The taiga, too, is a harsh land with seemingly endless forests interspersed with vast expanses of swamp. Soils generally consist of poor acidic podzols (a grayish white, ashy soil), whose swampy conditions are often exacerbated by the presence of an iron-hard pan some half a meter (about 20 inches) below the surface, as well as by permafrost in many parts of the north and the east. Like the tundra, the taiga is not conducive to dense human settlement. Agriculture is confined to only the most favorable regions. In addition to hunting and reindeer herding, economic activities include the exploitation of various natural resources (energy, timber, and minerals).

South of the taiga, in European Russia, is the mixed forest zone, which constitutes the historic heartland of the Russian state. With a more favorable balance between average temperatures and moisture levels, conditions are more moderate here than in the taiga. A transitional zone, coniferous forests are predominant in the north, while deciduous woodlands are more common in the south. Historically, the mixed forest zone has been a region of agricultural settlement populated mainly by ethnic Russians, Belarusians, and Ukrainians, with a mixture of non-Slavic peoples in certain areas. Large industrial cities are also scattered across this territory.

As one moves south through the mixed forest zone, natural conditions become drier until forests are gradually confined to the better-watered river valleys. Eventually the forests disappear altogether, giving way to steppe grassland. This mixed landscape of forest and steppe is known, appropriately enough, as the forest-steppe and forms a belt 150 to 300 miles wide. In European Russia, the forest-steppe fringes the mixed forest to the north. In Siberia, however, it borders directly with the taiga and continues to run in an easterly direction until it is finally interrupted by the western slopes of the Altai Mountains. East of these mountains, forest-steppe and steppe characteristics occasionally reappear in the intervening basins.

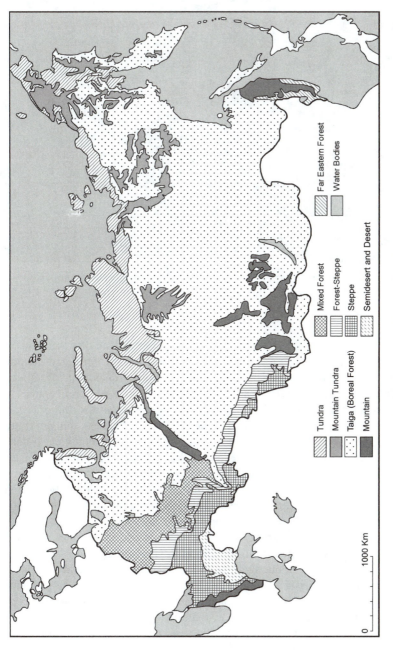

Map 2.8 Natural Vegetation Zones

Tundra

Mountain Tundra

Taiga (Boreal Forest)

Mountain

Mixed Forest

Forest-Steppe

Steppe

Semidesert and Desert

Far Eastern Forest

Water Bodies

1000 Km

0

BigStockPhoto.com; © Sergey Pristyazhnyuk

The vast boreal forests of the
taiga stretch across the length of Russia.

Like the mixed forest zone, the forest-steppe is one of transition, but this time between the mixed forest and the taiga to the north and the pure steppe to the south. Tree species are predominantly deciduous. Relatively fertile gray forest soils and other soil types characterize the forested areas, as in the southern parts of the mixed forest zone. By contrast, the grassland communities, which vary in species and decline in richness and variety toward the south, give rise to the famous chernozem or black earth soils, which are among the most fertile in the world. As such, the forest-steppe and steppe regions are Russia's breadbasket, and are thus highly significant from an agricultural point of view but also important for their major cities and industry. Although productive agriculturally, these regions suffer at times from drought, especially in the drier steppe toward the south.

Ultimately, the southern steppe shades into semidesert and then pure desert as moisture conditions deteriorate even further toward the south. Such natural zones lie mainly in former Soviet Kazakhstan and the Central Asian states to Russia's south. In Russia, only around the Volga Delta and the regions northeast of the Caspian Sea do semidesert conditions become apparent. Here the prevalence of evaporation over precipitation means that soil moisture movement is mainly upward, toward the upper horizons of soils. This leads to the concentration of salts and other minerals in these horizons to the detriment of fertility. Such impoverished soils support only depleted communities of xerophytic (or dryland) grasses, shrubs, and similar plants and can thus be used only to a limited degree for grazing and some resource-oriented economic activity.

Some Implications of Russia's Natural Environment

Not surprisingly, Russia's natural environment has a great impact on the country's economic and social development. Less than 8 percent of Russia's total territory is used for arable farming. Another 5 percent is devoted to livestock grazing. The remaining 87 percent is unfit for agriculture and as a result is largely devoid of significant human settlement. Most of the north and east is too cold and wet for farming; some parts of the south too dry. Even in the more favorable regions (largely corresponding with the mixed forest, forest-steppe, and steppe zones), natural conditions are often far from ideal. Thus, at the end of the Soviet era, Russia, with 76.2 percent of the USSR's territory, produced (by value) only 45.8 percent of its agricultural output.

In the mixed forest zone recent glaciation greatly affects agriculture in a number of areas. Earth and stones deposited by glaciers in these territories often interfere with natural drainage. Such features, combined with the many lakes, boulders, and marshes of these regions, form a serious barrier to agricultural settlement. In other parts of the mixed forest zone agriculture is also limited, such as in the sandy, poorly drained Meshchera Lowland southeast of Moscow, a region of pine and spruce forests and marshes. Other problems of the mixed forest zone include acidic soils, short growing seasons (only 130 days around Moscow, for example), and late spring–early autumn frosts. Further south, in the forest-steppe and steppe, conditions are better, with longer growing seasons and more fertile soils. Even in these zones, a number of problems can arise, including: drought, soil erosion, insect pests, disease, and, in the past, shortages of fuel and building materials. A number of studies suggest that agricultural output in Russia probably has always lagged behind that achieved in the more environmentally favored regions of the United States and Western Europe (Field 1968; Ioffe and Nefedova 1997, 31–33).

In the past, when agriculture played a central role in Russia's economy, underperformance meant that there was often little surplus available for any purpose other than subsistence. National economic development suffered accordingly and hence Russia lagged behind the West. Other factors, too, contributed to this situation. One was Russia's sheer size and location relative to the dynamic economies situated on either side of the North Atlantic and, more recently, the Pacific. Before the advent of railways, Russia's vast territories were especially difficult to cross and challenging to control. The building of railways, and later airports, only partially solved these problems as the distances between resources and markets remained vast.

Russia's relative cultural and political isolation also hindered its economic development. Before Peter the Great, the Orthodox faith largely shielded Russia from the West. Centuries later, under the communists, policies of economic autarky limited the Soviet Union's contact with the capitalist world. A heavy military burden and prevailing political and social structures, such as serfdom during the tsarist era and an increasingly complex and inflexible planned economy under Soviet rule, further impeded Russia's long-term development.

Not surprisingly, conditions in Russia, even in some of its more favored regions, can be quite different from those experienced in the United States and Western Europe. For instance, low population densities across much of rural Russia, coupled with decades of underinvestment in roads, public transportation, and other services, mean that isolation is a genuine problem in the countryside. During the 1970s, for example, fewer than half of all rural settlements in Yaroslavl Oblast, a region east of Moscow, lay within three kilometers (about two miles) of a bus route, while in nearby Kostroma Oblast the situation was even worse. In the relatively well-off Poltava Oblast in eastern Ukraine only about 11 percent of local roads had a hard surface (Pallot and Shaw 1981, 236–237). The difficulties of gaining access to most essential services, including health and education, were commensurately great. The situation is not much better today in many areas (Ioffe and Nefedova 1997, 26–31).

Spatial discrepancies between a populated west and a thinly populated but resource-rich east have also posed several challenges for Russian development. In an effort to exploit these resources, the Soviets tried to shift more of their economic activity to the east. This policy fell short of its goals, not only because of the cost of relocating industry to environmentally less favorable regions but also because of the sheer difficulty of persuading people to live there. Under Stalin, the latter problem was partially solved through forced labor and compulsory migration. After Stalin, the Kremlin relied on positive incentives such as higher wages and enhanced working conditions to encourage people to move east. This policy was expensive, however, and in any case less effective than had been hoped by the Soviet leaders. Despite this, the Soviets developed their more remote regions to a much greater extent than might have been possible, or deemed desirable, under capitalism.

In the post-Soviet era, economic contraction and a reduction in the subsidies that supported many kinds of northern and eastern development have greatly undermined the attractiveness of these regions for many migrants. As a result, many parts of Siberia and the Far East have experienced high levels of outmigration as people relocated to European Russia (Heleniak

1999). Some regions of the north, too, have seen a spectacular collapse in their population levels since the Soviet system's collapse in 1991.

■ Environment and Development

Since the arrival of modern science in their country during the eighteenth century, the Russians have had a deep interest not only in how to cope with the challenges posed by the natural environment but also in how nature might be modified in a rational way to meet national needs. In the nineteenth and early twentieth centuries Russian scientists made important advances in a range of environmental sciences (Graham 1993; Vucinich 1963).

Two characteristic features of Russian environmental science during this period were (1) the early realization of the close interrelationship between all aspects of the natural environment and human society, and (2) the highly practical nature of much scientific endeavor. Simplistic ideas about the environment and its deterministic influence over human social development, although taken seriously by a number of scientists in the West, never had much appeal in Russia. Instead, Russian scientists tended to believe that science, if applied correctly, could provide answers to a wide range of their country's environmental challenges (Pryde 1991).

The wise application of science, however, did not always sit well with the aspirations of those who held political power. Particularly during the Soviet era, science and the environment were often sacrificed to the ambitious economic and political goals of the men in the Kremlin, sometimes with catastrophic results. After Stalin's death in March 1953, attitudes toward nature slowly began to change as more attention was paid to conservation and environmental protection. Eventually, the Soviet leaders abandoned most of Stalin's grand schemes to transform nature. Even so, there were limits to how far and how fast the Soviet leaders would alter the course of policy. So strong was the desire to control nature that the last of the great transformation projects, the idea to divert part of the flow of western Siberian and northern European Russian rivers to the arid and drought-prone regions of Central Asia and southern European Russia, would not be dropped until the mid-1980s. Furthermore, given the highly centralized nature of the Soviet planned economy and its devotion to the sustained development of the country's military-industrial complex, it is difficult to see how the system might have been modified to pay more respect to the most basic of environmental concerns (Pryde 1991; Turnock 2001).

In the post-Soviet period the issue remains one of securing economic growth as far as possible while ensuring that environmental improvement occurs within the limits imposed by the need for all-around conservation. This is a difficult task, especially in the midst of economic transformation.

The temptation to sacrifice the environment to other concerns remains great, though for different reasons than under the communists. The hope, however faint, must be that Russia's leaders manage to secure the economic future of their people together with their environmental future, perhaps by building on Russian traditions in environmental science that long predate the communist era. As Philip Pryde explains in Chapter 9, however, Russia's leaders have not gone much beyond their own rhetoric in dealing with the environmental challenges facing their country.

■ The Imperial Heritage: Russia's Ethnic Geography

Part of Russia's heritage as a former imperial power is its multiethnic character. Unlike many countries where ethnic composition is impossible to determine from official statistics, in Russia a person's ethnicity is recorded at birth and then carefully copied into his or her official documents. Ethnicity is different from citizenship, which is a political designation that normally includes the right to carry the national passport when traveling abroad and may include the right to vote as well as other forms of political participation. By this definition, most residents of the Russian Federation are citizens of Russia regardless of their ethnicity. In theory, ethnicity relates to one's ancestry or lineage. Russia's careful recording of ethnicity provides a detailed picture of the country's ethnic structure (see Table 2.1 and Map 2.9).

Table 2.1 reveals that nearly 80 percent of Russia's population is ethnic Russian, down slightly from 1989, the year of the last Soviet census. In the 1989 census, ethnic Russians accounted for more than 80 percent of the Russian Republic's population. At the same time, they made up just over half of the Soviet Union's total population. Thus, one effect of the USSR's dissolution was to increase dramatically the preponderance of ethnic Russians within their own national territory. Despite this demographic and political change in circumstances, one in five of Russia's inhabitants (more than 29 million people comprising 159 officially recognized ethnic groups) are ethnically non-Russian. Notwithstanding the great number and diversity of Russia's minority peoples, most, with some exceptions, have lived alongside ethnic Russians for generations, speak Russian as their second language, and have otherwise adapted to Russian cultural norms. The spatial spread of ethnic Russians across Russia also means that they are the largest ethnic group in most areas, though again with some exceptions.

Among the largest non-Russian ethnic groups in the Federation are several who by ethnic designation derive from other former Soviet republics: Ukrainians, Armenians, Belarusians, Kazakhs, and Azerbaijanis. The Soviet period in particular witnessed considerable ethnic mixing as people moved between republics and regions, often in connection with economic policies of

Table 2.1 Ethnic Composition of the Russian Federation (numerically most significant ethnic groups)

	2002	Percent Total	1989	Percent Total	2002 Percent of 1989
Russian	115,889,107	79.83	119,865,946	81.53	96.68
Tatar	5,554,601	3.83	5,522,096	3.76	100.59
Ukrainian	2,942,961	2.03	4,362,872	2.97	67.45
Bashkir	1,673,389	1.15	1,345,273	0.91	124.39
Chuvash	1,637,094	1.13	1,773,645	1.21	92.30
Chechen	1,360,253	0.94	898,999	0.61	151.31
Armenian	1,130,491	0.78	532,390	0.36	212.34
Mordvin	843,350	0.58	1,072,939	0.73	78.60
Avar	814,473	0.56	544,016	0.37	149.71
Belarusians	807,970	0.56	1,206,222	0.82	66.98
Kazakh	653,962	0.45	635,865	0.43	102.85
Udmurt	636,906	0.44	714,833	0.49	89.10
Azerbaijani	621,840	0.43	335,889	0.23	185.13
Mari	604,298	0.42	643,698	0.44	93.88
German	597,212	0.41	842,295	0.57	70.90
Kabardinian	519,958	0.36	386,055	0.26	134.68
Ossetian	514,875	0.35	402,275	0.27	127.99
Dargin	510,156	0.35	353,348	0.24	144.38
Buryat	445,175	0.31	417,425	0.28	106.65
Yakut	443,852	0.30	380,242	0.26	116.73
Kumyk	422,409	0.29	277,163	0.19	152.40
Ingush	413,016	0.28	215,068	0.15	192.04
Lezgin	411,535	0.28	257,270	0.17	159.96
Komi	293,406	0.20	336,309	0.23	87.24
Tuvin	243,442	0.17	206,160	0.14	118.08
Others	5,181,000	3.57	3,493,576	2.38	148.30
Total	145,166,731	100.00	147,021,869	100.00	98.74

Sources: Goskomstat Rossii 2004; Goskomstat RSFSR 1990.

the era. Many of these people have stayed put since the Soviet Union's breakup in 1991, although further migration has occurred (as Timothy He-leniak explains in Chapter 8) in connection with the political and economic changes and upheavals of the postcommunist period.

Ethnically, Russia's peoples can be divided into several groups. The Russians, Ukrainians, and Belarusians are Slavs. Numerically predominant, they are found throughout the country. Turkic and related peoples include the Tatars, Bashkirs, and Chuvash who live in the regions between the middle Volga and the Urals. Others in this group are scattered across Siberia and the

28

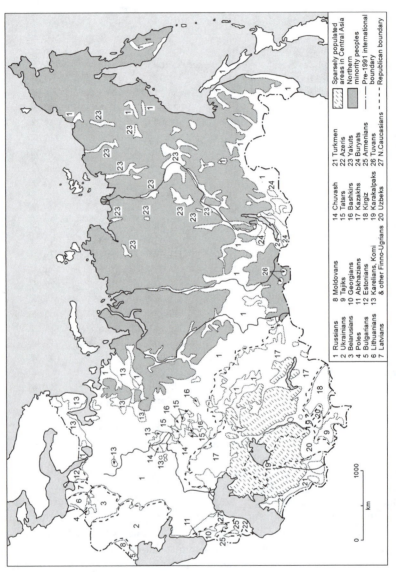

Map 2.9 Ethnic Groups in the Russian Federation and the Soviet Successor States

1 Russians	8 Moldovans	14 Chuvash	21 Turkmen
2 Ukrainians	9 Tajiks	15 Tatars	22 Azeris
3 Belarusians	10 Georgians	16 Bashkirs	23 Yakuts
4 Poles	11 Abkhazians	17 Kazakhs	24 Buryats
5 Bulgarians	12 Estonians	18 Kirgiz	25 Armenians
6 Lithuanians	13 Karelians, Komi	19 Karakalpaks	26 Tuvans
7 Latvians	& other Finno-Ugrians	20 Uzbeks	27 N.Caucasians

Sparsely populated areas in Central Asia

Northern minority peoples

Pre-1991 international boundary

———— Republican boundary

Far East (notably the Yakuts/Sakha in the northeast), as well as the North Caucasus (the Kumyks for example). The Caucasian peoples include the Chechens, Avars, Kabardinians, Dargins, Ingush, and Lezgins, all of whom live in the North Caucasus. By contrast, the ancestors of the Finno-Ugrian peoples lived on the East European plain before Slavic settlement. They include the Mordvins, Udmurts, and Mari, whose homes are along the middle Volga, the Komi of northeast European Russia, and the Karelians near the Finnish frontier. The Ossetians of the North Caucasus are an Iranian people, while the Buryats of East Siberia are of Mongol origin. The many peoples of the Russian north are also quite diverse, coming from a wide variety of ethnic backgrounds. Two other peoples are the Germans and Jews, both of which are officially designated as distinctive ethnic groups.

Early in the Soviet era the Bolshevik leadership established national homelands for a number of the country's ethnic groups. The most important of these homelands were the "union republics." Because only the most important ethnic groups could be represented by union republics, the Soviet leaders created lesser ethnic homelands within the territories of these republics. Eventually a hierarchy of units came into being based on the numerical significance of each group. In Russia these units have endured into the post-Soviet era. Now they are known as republics of the Russian Federation, autonomous oblasts (regions), and autonomous okrugs (districts), in descending order of importance. Their general locations within Russia are illustrated in Map 2.10. These ethnic units have specific rights and powers to uphold the cultural distinctiveness of their peoples. Thus, Russia is a federation of ethnic and nonethnic units. In Chapter 7, Katherine Graney examines in greater detail the effects of the Federation's multiethnic character on contemporary Russian politics and society.

▨ Conclusion

Although geography is not a simple deterministic force guaranteeing certain outcomes for a society, it does establish specific physical and demographic boundaries within which that society must operate. The Soviet Union failed in its attempt to develop and sustain a modern society in part because of its inability to come to terms with the main geographic legacies of the country's imperial past: the country's great territorial expanse and its multiethnic population. Contemporary Russia's prospects are also tied to this geographic inheritance. Those who govern Russia today can no more escape the realities of its physical size and location than they can safely ignore the practical implications of its multiethnic heritage.

Despite the great loss of territory that accompanied the USSR's collapse, Russia easily remains the largest country in the world. Located farther

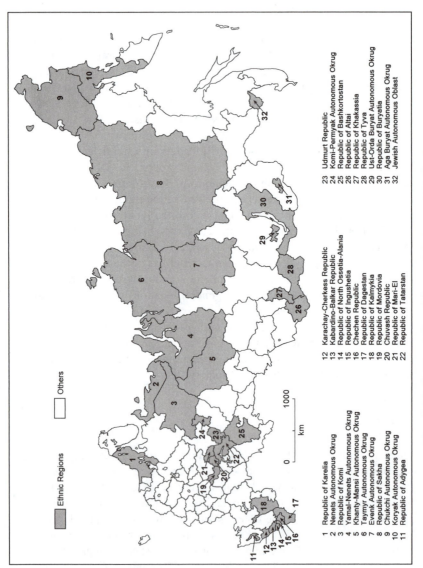

Map 2.10 National Republics and Autonomous Regions of the Russian Federation, Before December 1, 2005

Ethnic Regions

Others

km

0   1000

1   Republic of Karelia
2   Nenets Autonomous Okrug
3   Republic of Komi
4   Yamal-Nenets Autonomous Okrug
5   Khanty-Mansi Autonomous Okrug
6   Taymyr Autonomous Okrug
7   Evenk Autonomous Okrug
8   Republic of Sakha
9   Chukchi Autonomous Okrug
10 Koryak Autonomous Okrug
11 Republic of Adygea

12 Karachay-Cherkess Republic
13 Kabardino-Balkar Republic
14 Republic of North Ossetia-Alania
15 Republic of Ingushetia
16 Chechen Republic
17 Republic of Dagestan
18 Republic of Kalmykia
19 Republic of Mordovia
20 Chuvash Republic
21 Republic of Mari-El
22 Republic of Tatarstan

23 Udmurt Republic
24 Komi-Permyak Autonomous Okrug
25 Republic of Bashkortostan
26 Republic of Altai
27 Republic of Khakassia
28 Republic of Tyva
29 Ust-Orda Buryat Autonomous Okrug
30 Republic of Buryatia
31 Aga Buryat Autonomous Okrug
32 Jewish Autonomous Oblast

north than the continental United States, farther east than Western Europe, and walled off by mountains to the south and to the east, most of Russia's territory is far removed from the moderating influences of the world's great oceans. Although the country possesses vast stores of natural resources, the harsh environments in which most of these resources are located mean that Russia's natural wealth alone cannot ensure its long-term economic viability. The extent to which these resources are used efficiently and rationally will determine to a great extent how far Russia will advance as a society.

▨ Bibliography

Bradshaw, Michael, and Alison Stenning, eds. 2004. *East Central Europe and the Former Soviet Union: The Post-Socialist States.* Harlow, UK: Pearson Education.

Bremmer, Ian, and Ray Taras, eds. 1993. *Nations and Politics in the Soviet Successor States.* Cambridge, UK: Cambridge University Press.

Field, N. C. 1968. "Environmental Quality and Land Productivity: A Comparison of the Agricultural Land Base of the USSR and North America." *The Canadian Geographer* 12(1): 1–14.

Goskomstat Rossii. 2004. *Vserossiiskaia perepis' naseleniia 2002 goda* [The 2002 All-Russia population census]. http://www.perepis2002.ru/index.html?id=17.

Goskomstat RSFSR. 1990. *Natsional'nyi sostav naseleniia RSFSR: po dannym Vsesoiuznoi perepici naseleniia 1989 goda* [National composition of the population of the RSFSR: According to the data of the 1989 All-Union population census]. Moscow: Respublikanskii informatsionno-izdatel'skii tsentr.

Graham, Loren R. 1993. *Science in Russia and the Soviet Union: A Short History.* New York: Cambridge University Press.

Gwynne, Robert N., Thomas Klak, and Denis J. B. Shaw. 2003. *Alternative Capitalisms: Geographies of Emerging Regions.* London: Arnold.

Hanson, Philip, and Michael J. Bradshaw, eds. 2000. *Regional Economic Change in Russia.* Cheltenham, UK: Edward Elgar.

Heleniak, Timothy. 1999. "Out-Migration and Depopulation of the Russian North During the 1990s." *Post-Soviet Geography and Economics* 40(3): 155–205.

———. 2003a. "Geographical Aspects of Population Aging in the Russian Federation." *Eurasian Geography and Economics* 44(5): 325–347.

———. 2003b. "The 2002 Census in Russia: Preliminary Results." *Eurasian Geography and Economics* 44(6): 430–442.

Ioffe, Grigory, and Tatyana Nefedova. 1997. *Continuity and Change in Rural Russia: A Geographical Perspective.* Boulder, CO: Westview Press.

Kaiser, Robert J. 1994. *The Geography of Nationalism in Russia and the USSR.* Princeton, NJ: Princeton University Press.

Lydolph, Paul E. 1977. *Climates of the Soviet Union.* Vol. 7 of *World Survey of Climatology.* Amsterdam: Elsevier.

———. 1990. *Geography of the U.S.S.R.* 5th ed. Elkhart Lake, WI: Misty Valley.

Pallot, Judith, and Denis J. B. Shaw. 1981. *Planning in the Soviet Union.* London: Croom Helm.

Pryde, Philip R. 1991. *Environmental Management in the Soviet Union.* Cambridge, UK: Cambridge University Press.

Shaw, Denis J. B. 1999. *Russia in the Modern World: A New Geography.* Oxford, UK: Blackwell.

Shaw, Denis J. B., and Jonathan Oldfield. 1998. "The Natural Environment of the CIS in the Transition from Communism." *Post-Soviet Geography and Economics* 39(3): 164–177.

Thompson, Niobe. 2004. "Migration and Resettlement in Chukotka: A Research Note." *Eurasian Geography and Economics* 45(1): 73–81.

Turnock, David, ed. 2001. *Eastern Europe and the Former Soviet Union: Environment and Society.* London: Arnold.

Vucinich, Alexander. 1963. *Science in Russian Culture: A History to 1860.* London: Owen.

3

The Historical Context

Steven G. Marks

This chapter provides an overview of 1,300 years of Russian history and, where relevant, places it in the context of simultaneous European developments. Brief treatments of Kievan Rus, Mongol rule, and Muscovy are followed by a more detailed survey of the imperial and Soviet periods. The themes of this nation's history have been remarkably persistent from the Muscovite era onward. Many of these constants are related to its geographical sprawl, which raised the cost of communications, resource extraction, administration, and defense. The multiethnicity of the tsarist and Soviet empires amplified tensions and added to these costs. As if to compensate for its potential weakness in the face of always strong centrifugal forces, the Russian state's instinct was to aggressively impose its authority in what by the seventeenth century had already become the largest territorially unified polity on earth.

This near obsession with centralizing goes far to explain why the Russian state remained so long devoted to autocratic principles of governance. Combined with psychopathological factors, the centralizing tendency also helps to account for the violent and despotic willfulness of rulers such as Ivan the Terrible or Joseph Stalin. But the control sought by the government was elusive as it could not easily make its presence felt in a country of this size. A lament by the Soviet dictator Nikita Khrushchev illustrates this point:

> You'd think I, as [Communist Party] first secretary, could change anything in this country. Like hell I can! No matter what changes I propose and carry out, everything stays the same. Russia's like a tub full of dough, you put your hand in it, down to the bottom, and think you're the master of the

situation. When you first pull out your hand, a little hole remains, but then, before your very eyes, the dough expands into a spongy, puffy mass. That's what Russia is like! (quoted in Taubman 2003, 598)

To govern such a country, Khrushchev observed, a leader must be prepared to act ruthlessly.

To mobilize the people and resources of its immense domain, the central government also tended to rely on a social elite who were often the true power in the provinces and on the periphery. Inevitably, that elite exploited the population for their own benefit as well as the state's, and they could resist rather than facilitate government directives. Given the often improvised nature of these arrangements and the personalized nature of the ruler's authority, individual and patron-client relationships would play a more prominent role than institutionalized and nonarbitrary, regularized methods of governance (Hosking 2001).

In this setting the mass of the populace lacked a political voice and was often oppressed and impoverished. They went about their lives and managed as best they could, in the process creating a distinctive folk culture, but at times they rose up in rebellion, instances of which punctuate modern Russian history. Among the underlying causes of these rebellions were the often sudden changes forced on the nation by various rulers, who felt compelled to introduce radical reforms or policy shifts in order to reverse the government's perceived impotence in internal affairs, to strengthen territorial integrity, and to compete with other great powers. In an autocratic system, popular consultation was out of the question, and these measures were often unpopular, especially when they involved adopting Western innovations that made daily existence more difficult and seemed to threaten the Russian way of life.

That constant interaction with the rest of Europe is another enduring theme in Russian history. As all nations in the modern era, Russia had no choice but to come to grips with the powerful cultures of the West. It did so early on and more consistently than other nations outside of the West. The simultaneous receptivity and hostility that accompanied the relationship with Europe and the resulting struggle to define and maintain its identity gave shape to many features of the Russian past.

A chronology presenting key events in Russian history from 750 to 1991 appears on pages 83–86.

■ Kievan Rus, 750–1240

The early medieval Russian heartland was a far-flung territory reaching from the northern forests to the southern grasslands of the steppe. It was lightly populated, without organized government, and inhabited by a variety of nomadic and settled agrarian peoples, mainly Slavic, Baltic, Turkic, and Finnic groups. In the eighth and ninth centuries Swedish warrior-merchants—akin to the Vikings but termed Varangians in East European history—ventured into this territory in quest of slaves, furs, and other forest products to exchange at markets in Baghdad and Constantinople, the respective capitals of the Islamic Caliphate and the Byzantine Empire. In the early 900s they located their base of operations at Kiev on the Dnieper River, a site that was convenient for control of north-south movement between the Baltic and Black seas. A flourishing commerce with Arabs and Greeks ensued. By the end of the twelfth century, according to one reasonable estimate, Kiev's population reached between 36,000 and 50,000, which was comparable in size to medieval London and Paris (Martin 1995, 60–61).

The formation of a political structure that reflected the various ethnic and cultural crosscurrents in this region took shape over the succeeding centuries and came to be known as Kievan Rus. By the late tenth century, the Scandinavian warrior-elite had established a ruling dynasty and become slavicized through intermarriage with the local populace, but the ruler called himself a *kagan,* reflecting the influence of Turkic political notions. Kagan, or Prince, Vladimir (reigned from about 980 to 1015) converted to Orthodox Christianity some time around 988 in order to strengthen ties with the Byzantine Empire and gain religious sanction to legitimize his rule after overthrowing his brother.

The adoption of Eastern Orthodoxy was not just a matter of imitating a higher civilization, for it inspired a native cultural expression with some literary production and distinctive Russian styles of church architecture and icon painting. But the choice of Orthodoxy had long-lasting implications for the future insofar as it meant keeping Western culture at arm's length. This was not only because of the rejection of Latin and Catholicism that the choice entailed, but also because of Byzantine Christianity's endorsement of autocracy. Kievan Rus was far from an autocracy, but the Russian state's eventual evolution in this direction was in part justified by the historical experience of the Orthodox Church. By contrast the Roman Church and the secular rulers of the West were locked in a centuries-long rivalry that ultimately dampened monarchical power.

It is worth noting that other factors were at play that gave Kievan Rus the potential for developing along European lines. The social structure was similar to that of neighboring Poland and Hungary, or even pre-Carolingian northern France and Germany, with an aristocratic warrior-elite—the *boyars*—and tribute-paying, nominally free commoners rather than serfs (although there were also numerous slaves). One similarity with parts of Italy was the concentration of aristocrats and other elites in towns, which dominated the countryside and enjoyed wide autonomy.

Despite the cohesion offered by the establishment of the Riurikid dynasty (named after Riurik, the legendary founder) and conversion to Orthodoxy, the Rus polity fragmented as a result of internecine conflict among the many descendants of Vladimir, each with his own territorial power base. Attempts to maintain stability among the princes via rotational rule and seniority—a pattern possibly borrowed from the neighboring Turkic Khazar Khanate (a khanate being any political entity, such as a kingdom or principality, ruled by a khan)—failed, and subsequent centuries saw constant feuding and violent succession struggles, which split Kievan Rus into warring clans and rival principalities (e.g., Vladimir) or independent city-states, the most significant being Novgorod, which was closely linked to the Baltic trading world. The Kievan period came to an end with the Mongol invasion, which is when the divergence between Russia and most of the rest of Europe first becomes truly marked.

■ Mongol Rule, 1237–1400

The thirteenth century was the highpoint of nomadic horseback-warrior domination of the Eurasian grasslands. Under Genghis Khan, the Mongols created the largest empire the world had ever seen, unifying China, Central Asia, Afghanistan, Iran, Iraq, the Transcaucasus, and the Rus steppe—the latter conquered by Genghis's grandson Batu in 1237–1240. The Rus called them Tatars, after an altogether different Asian people, a term also applied to the fusion of Mongols and Turkic speakers who settled in parts of the region. Tatar khans were the factotums (or servants) through whom the Mongols ruled this distant part of their empire, and the Rus were their subjects. The Tatars (who converted to Islam in the next century) formed the Qipchak Khanate, or Golden Horde, with a capital at Sarai on the lower Volga River. Even so, Russian princes remained in charge locally and from the mid-fourteenth century were seen as sufficiently loyal to the system to be given responsibility for their own tribute collection.

Russian culture as inherited from Kiev continued to develop unabated by the Mongols, who were tolerant of the Orthodox Church (along with other religions). But in statecraft the Russian grand princes were now more oriented toward the East and absorbed bureaucratic practices from their Mongol and Tatar overlords (Ostrowski 1998). Scholars still debate the nature and extent of Mongol influence on Russian politics, but it likely augmented hierarchical and strong-arm tendencies rather than the opposite. The conquests, furthermore, caused a significant shift in the basis of Russian society. Russia lost its importance as a major trade route linking Europe and Asia, and agriculture became the mainstay of the economy. Accordingly, the wealth of princes and *boyars* came to derive from land ownership and rent paid by peasants instead of from international trade and urban dues as in the Kievan period. This was a striking contrast with Western Europe, where commerce and cities were now on the rise.

By the 1350s the Mongol domain was splitting into its component parts, often warring among themselves. This created a power vacuum exploited by the principality of Moscow, whose stone fortress, or Kremlin, was built in 1367–1368. Situated at a nexus of navigable river systems and at the intersection of forest and steppe, this town had emerged in the 1320s as the increasingly wealthy rival of the powerful principality of Vladimir-Suzdal and the successor to Kiev (although not in the south). Moscow maneuvered to convince the Tatars to give its prince, Ivan I (nicknamed "Kalita" or "Moneybag"; reigned 1325–1341), responsibility for tax and tribute collection among the Rus. Moscow also had close trade ties with Byzantium, and its authority was enhanced when it became the residence of the Orthodox Metropolitan of Kiev and all Rus in 1326 (by the 1450s the Turkish conquest of Byzantium allowed the Russian Orthodox Church to become virtually independent of Constantinople; in 1589 Moscow was elevated to an Orthodox Patriarchate). Several centuries of conflict with other cities and the remnants of the Golden Horde would follow, but by the early fifteenth century Moscow was supreme, the capital of a Russian kingdom known as Muscovy.

■ Muscovy, 1400–1700

The ambition of Grand Prince Ivan III (reigned 1462–1505) and his son Vasili III (reigned 1505–1533) was to assert Muscovite authority over all the former territories of Rus. They succeeded in central Russia and, to the northwest, in Novgorod and Pskov. Upon the coronation of Ivan IV, "the Terrible," in 1547, the Moscow grand princes adopted the title "Tsar," which derived from "Caesar" and made reference to the Byzantine autocrats and Mongol khans, and claimed parity with the German Holy Roman emperor. If the attendant belief that the tsar derived his powers from God was rooted in Byzantine thought, the more elaborate new royal ceremonies reflected growing cultural contacts with the West in the immediate post-Mongol era. Russian diplomats were received at European courts and began to discover Renaissance culture. The first Russian translations of Latin texts appeared, and in the fifteenth century Italian master craftsmen were brought to work in Moscow. Frequent conflict and contact with neighboring Poland-Lithuania (linked since 1386), which had absorbed Rus territories west of the Dnieper beginning in the Mongol period, both thwarted and furthered these efforts.

Yet Muscovy remained unique. The essence of the European sociopolitical system, for all the many differences country by country, lay in the formation of incorporated social estates and an increasingly dynamic urban and commercial sector. Nowhere did royal power survive unchallenged and unalloyed even where it was ostensibly absolutist in nature. In Russia, nothing like the European professional or mercantile middle class or the crafts guilds emerged. Compared to Western Europe, Russia's towns were small and lacked grants of special rights. And the Russian aristocracy was more or less subservient to the Kremlin, which gained the upper hand in part by distributing state lands to be held on condition of obligatory service and loyalty to the crown.

The Muscovite tsar ruled through this aristocracy, which over the course of several centuries became a service nobility formed from the scions of old princely and *boyar* clans or lesser elite families. The aristocracy led the cavalry-based military and staffed the upper ranks of the government, in return for which service they received landed estates called *pomeste*. Hence, these noblemen were known as *pomeshchiki* (the nobility as a whole was later called the *dvorianstvo*, or courtier class). Feuding within these groups had often led to destructive warfare, and the solution for the sake of class stability was to accept the tsar's absolutism and allow him to arbitrate among them by administering the complex *mestnichestvo* system, which doled out privileges to *boyars* according to strict accounting of their genealogies and seniority rankings (Kollmann 1987).

This is not to say that Russian absolutism was all-powerful, and some scholars emphasize the similarities between the Muscovite tsardom and the limited monarchies of Western Europe. The Kremlin's desired governmental control over social elites was somewhat neutralized by the de facto hereditary nature of the supposedly conditional grants of land made to aristocratic servitors, who routinely transferred them to their next of kin. And the nobility's multiplicity of regional attachments and ties of kinship and personal patronage imposed further limits on the powers of the tsar (Kivelson 1996; Kollmann 1997).

Nonetheless, the tsars succeeded in turning what was a messy political reality to their advantage. Increasingly from the fifteenth through the seventeenth centuries they made themselves autocrats in fact as well as theory, a desire that only grew as the Russian government witnessed on its borders the rising power of absolutist Sweden and the weakness of Poland, where the nobility succeeded in enfeebling the monarchy.

Few alternatives to these arrangements existed in a nation of this size without modern technologies of social control. Reliance on noblemen for police and bureaucratic functions meant that although central institutions of government were all-powerful, at the local level authority was in the hands of strongmen who could act arbitrarily, and the exploitative practice of "feeding" off the land (*kormlenie*) was and would long remain the norm in a country unable to properly fund its own local administration. This gave rise to the most enduring feature of Russian administrative history, which was that institutions of government were always most highly developed at the center, while at the local level the country suffered from their weak presence. Throughout Russia's history, this would perpetually stymie the assertion of central authority and almost preclude responsive governance.

Also in this period, the legal condition of the peasantry in Russia slowly deteriorated into serfdom, in line with its fate elsewhere in Eastern Europe, but out of synch with Western Europe, where by the late Middle Ages bondage had disappeared. As Marshall Poe puts it, the Muscovite tsar nationalized land and labor and parceled them out to the noble elite, who could then exploit the peasants on their estates both for their own benefit and to collect taxes and recruit soldiers as required by the Kremlin (Poe 2003, 54–55). This may have been seen as the only practical solution in a large country with a low population density, but inevitably peasants sought to escape their oppression by fleeing to the unsettled borderlands (where some mingled with non-Slavic peoples of the southern frontier and merged to form seminomadic Cossack communities only later integrated into the Russian empire). The state responded to peasant flight with legislation that by the 1590s further restricted whatever rights peasants had once had to move from the land. These rights were eliminated altogether in the next century.

For the majority that stayed put, this arrangement was perhaps not quite as bad as it sounds. As Peter Kolchin has shown, even at the peak of serfdom in the eighteenth century the peasants had more autonomy than did their African equivalents on the plantations of the southern United States, where the ratio of slaves to masters was low and the latter intervened frequently in the lives of the former (Kolchin 1987). In Russia, the lords were vastly outnumbered by peasants, who, if not household servants, came into contact with their owners infrequently (although that is not to deny that serious abuses took place. Also, many petty landlords had smaller numbers of serfs, which made for regular interaction between these two groups). The peasant village commune, or *mir,* was itself responsible for doling out labor obligations and dues. By periodically repartitioning the land in accordance with the size of peasant households, a basic minimum was guaranteed to all.

The Russian peasants' standard of living, furthermore, even into the nineteenth century compared favorably with that of the rural lower classes in various parts of Western Europe, including Ireland and Scotland (Pipes 1974, 151–152). In much of the country, but especially where soil conditions were unfavorable for profitable farming, peasants could pay dues to their landlords in place of labor, and a surprising level of handicrafts production was achieved. In some instances peasants became extremely wealthy by this means and purchased their way out of bondage. But in the long run the institution of serfdom, which affected the majority of the Russian populace, left a bitter legacy of peasant resentment toward the elite, hindered the development of notions of private property, and retarded the economic development potential of the nation.

The trend in this period was toward consolidation and resolution of conflict among the elite, but the situation of the royal court in the late sixteenth and early seventeenth centuries plunged Muscovy into crisis, violence, and near ruin. Ivan the Terrible ruled between 1533 and 1584, inflicting terror on his kingdom in his last two decades. A full explanation still eludes us, but Ivan was clearly continuing the efforts of his predecessors to tighten his rein on the *boyars,* some of whom were thought to be dangerously envious of the liberties of the Polish aristocracy. The tsar also desired to combat independently minded factions within the Orthodox Church, victory over which would bring vast landholdings into the control of the state treasury. But apparently wracked with the pain and torments of physical and mental disease, Ivan fomented an orgy of violence against suspect parts of the population. Entire aristocratic families (and many commoners as well) were brutally murdered or deported into the interior, operations carried out by Ivan's horseback death squads, the so-called *oprichniki.*

Not long after Ivan's death the country was plunged into the Time of Troubles (1598–1613), a decade and a half of civil war. The war was sparked by famine and a succession struggle that followed the dying out of the Riurikid dynasty, but its underlying cause was the rage felt by peasants, Cossacks, soldiers, and ethnic minorities at their loss of status, excessive taxation, or serfdom. Separate Polish, Swedish, and Turkish-backed Tatar military invasions threatened the existence of the Muscovite state, but Russian forces were eventually able to coalesce and expel them. In 1613 a Council of the Land, or Zemskii sobor, convened at which townsfolk, soldiers, and Cossacks influenced the outcome of the *boyars'* election of a new monarch. They chose Mikhail Romanov, a relative of the deceased tsar, whose dynasty would remain on the throne for the next three centuries. In accordance with past practices, the *boyar* elite reconstituted the autocracy as the best insurance of their own interests against potential internal upheavals and foreign threats.

The reigns of the first two Romanov tsars, Mikhail and his son and successor Alexei (reigned 1613–1645 and 1645–1676 respectively), laid the basis for the successes and difficulties faced by the next generation under Alexei's son Peter the Great. The trends of the Muscovite past continued as the state further expanded its prerogatives over the nation. For fiscal and military purposes the peasants were finally and fully bound to the land. Political centralization was manifested in the steady, if haphazard, expansion of bureaucratic departments called *prikazy* to oversee the affairs of state. The *prikazy* were hindered by overlapping and ill-defined jurisdictions, but nonetheless were all too efficient for those who felt new tax pressures or regulations imposed by Moscow. One result was a mass antigovernment revolt of peasants, ethnic minorities, and Don Cossacks on the southern steppe led by Stenka Razin in 1670–1671.

One component of the Razin Rebellion was a fear of change that threatened Russian traditions in the late Muscovite period. The seventeenth century was the time when full-fledged contact with the West resumed in Russia after a hiatus of many centuries. The great naval powers of England and Holland had established trade contacts in the far north at Arkhangelsk in the previous century, and merchants were followed in the 1600s by increasing numbers of mercenaries, who served as military advisers and regimental commanders in the Russian army. Some among the Russian elite were attracted by Western technology, dress, culture, and manners, fascinations furthered by the acquisition of parts of Ukraine in the 1650s and 1660s, which became a conduit for the flow of Polish and other European cultural influences. The number of "Europeanized" Russian aristocrats was still small as there were no institutions by which the new ideas might penetrate deep into the culture: no universities or public theaters, and the sole printing press in all of Muscovy was controlled by the Orthodox Church. Nonetheless, cultural norms and above all the intellectual monopoly of the church were challenged by the allure of Western theological and secular ideas.

What commenced was a broad-based cultural conflict. The necessity of adopting Western political and military notions for strategic reasons and the irresistible appeal Western culture had for some influential clerics and statesmen contributed to a long-festering and often violent schism within the Orthodox Church between the official hierarchy and a large group of sectarians known as Old Believers. But suspicions of the new ways were also held by many others in the society.

Despite these tensions, and for all the inadequacies of the seventeenth-century Muscovite political system, this tsardom functioned well enough to acquire a continent-sized territory. In the sixteenth century Moscow had expanded south and southeast into the Black Earth Zone of the steppe, and across the Volga, where in 1552 the Tatar capital of Kazan was subjugated (celebrated by the construction of St. Basil's Cathedral near the Kremlin). Thereafter, led by Cossacks and fur trappers, the Russians progressed steadily across Siberia, easily vanquishing the many indigenous tribes, which could not withstand invaders armed with guns. By the mid-seventeenth century the Russians had reached the Pacific; they were soon to cross the Bering Strait and repeat the process in Alaska. There were no significant powers to block them in the east. By contrast, the Russian government saw the conquest of territory in the west and southwest as necessary to protect against the threats posed by the Ottoman Empire, Poland, and Sweden.

As for integrating the many non-Russian and non-Slavic ethnic groups into this already heterogeneous empire, the tactic that would adhere for much of Russian history was introduced: the Kremlin co-opted ethnic elites, making them servitors of the state and in some cases entering them in the ranks of the Russian nobility. At the same time, local ways and religions were by and large tolerated for the pragmatic purpose of reducing frictions that could slow the assertion of tsarist rule (Kappeler 2001). This approach, as well as the size of the territory and its multiethnicity, further set Russia apart from the nations of Western Europe, which were relatively more compact and homogeneous despite their internal divisions and recently created overseas empires. Closer analogies to the Muscovite tsardom can be found in the ethnically diverse agrarian empires of Habsburg Austria, Ottoman Turkey, Mughal India, and Qing China (Bayly 2004, Chap. 1).

■ Peter the Great and the Birth of Imperial Russia, 1682–1725

Imperial Russia is so named to signify the new era initiated by Peter the Great (reigned 1682–1725), who adopted the title "emperor." Even more than before, this was a time when Russia was forced to come to terms with the power and culture of the West. In its efforts to transform itself through selective adaptation of European innovations, Russia experienced great triumphs, among them rising military importance on the world arena, vigorous territorial expansion, remarkable literary and artistic achievements, and eventual industrial development. But many of these successes only widened the gap between the privileged elite and subordinate masses and multiplied the challenges faced by the government in maintaining control of this society.

Contemporaries viewed Peter's reign as a sudden break with the past, hence historians' reference to a "Petrine Revolution." Even if, as some scholars argue, Peter was following in the footsteps of his centralizing Romanov forebears, he was doing so at a dramatically faster pace. His urge to transform the nation had two main wellsprings. As a child he had developed an intense dislike for the Muscovite *boyar* clans, whose bloody rivalries destroyed members of his family. Secondly, he had been enamored of the military since boyhood, and he would involve his country in warfare nearly every year of his reign.

Peter's famous tour of England and Holland in 1697–1698 gave him first-hand knowledge of European society, technology, and military affairs. In order for Russia to achieve military advantage against Sweden and Turkey, and thereby obtain new territories that would convey European great-power status, Peter was determined to adopt the administrative, military, and economic model of the advanced nations to the west. He sent Russian noblemen abroad to learn about Europe and hired thousands of foreigners to enter Russian service and teach Russians their expertise. Of a piece with tsarist centralizing traditions as well as the practices of European absolutism, he imposed on the nobility tighter, life-long state-service obligations in place of the irregularity that had become the norm. He founded the Russian navy and reorganized the army by introducing a more regularized draft than previous ad hoc conscription drives (now one male peasant from a certain number of households would be taken away to serve for life) and by modernizing command, control, and training through the introduction of European military innovations. After much trial and error, it all paid off with the defeat of Sweden in the Great Northern War, the conquest of the eastern Baltic (roughly corresponding to today's Estonia and Latvia), and the founding of a new capital at St. Petersburg in 1703, his "window on the West."

Raising government revenues for military purposes was the key to the success of all absolutist regimes. Peter, accordingly, increased direct and indirect taxes and attempted to systematize the state administration through the creation of various new political institutions. Ultimately he replaced the tangled *prikazy* (bureaucratic departments) with functionally coherent colleges, each running a branch of government and overseen by the recently established Senate. This reorganization of government, however, was hampered by rampant corruption, which frustrated Peter to no end, and by the failure to carry out substantive reforms of local administration, which still largely involved the exploitation of peasants by noblemen and government officials.

A more successful administrative reform was the introduction of the Table of Ranks. This replaced aristocratic bloodline with merit as the main criterion for advancement within the civil service and military hierarchies. Peter had hoped that it would eliminate the squabbling inherent in the Muscovite system and weaken the power of the *boyars*. Inevitably, given their advantages, the old elites continued to dominate in the service structure, but the Table of Ranks did introduce a more modern and efficient way of determining who stood where on the ladder of officialdom. With modifications, it remained in place until 1917.

Driven by his desire to break with Muscovy and remold the nation along more European lines, Peter also initiated a cultural revolution. Relying on the power of decree, he ordered the upper class to adopt Western dress and rules of etiquette, forced noblemen to shave their beards and send their children to school, ended the seclusion of elite women, and commanded the aristocracy to relocate to the new, foreign-designed capital. Inevitably, these reforms provoked a backlash among traditionalists who not only opposed these changes but also resented the role of upstarts at the court such as Peter's crony, the former pie peddler, now prince, Alexander Menshikov, and Peter's second wife, the illiterate Baltic maidservant Marfa Skavronskaia, later Empress Catherine I. In response, Peter cracked down on growing opposition to his policies by turning the Orthodox Church into a department of state and expanding police surveillance of the populace. In the final years of his reign, the number of trials for capital crimes reached an average of one a

Michael L. Bressler

Contrasting architectural styles:
Moscow's Red Square, with St. Basil's Cathedral and the
Kremlin's Savior Tower (top); and St. Petersburg's Palace Square,
featuring the Alexander Column and the
General Staff Building (bottom).

Elizabeth A. Smith

day (Cracraft 1988, 28). Evidence was gathered routinely through denunciations and torture.

Torture was also a component of Western judicial procedure at the time. Even so, the more Peter tried to Europeanize Russia, the more he moved the country away from the general course of Western development. Although his personal tastes were simple and nonaristocratic, and his admiration of Holland was second only to that which he felt for his own country, the culture he introduced to Russia was the baroque of the European courts, not the bourgeois culture of Holland's urban middle class, the social basis for which Russia, in any case, still lacked. As for Holland's parliamentary institutions, Peter was certainly curious about them but had no interest in establishing such a form of government in Russia.

This last point reveals a key difference between Russia and its neighbors to the west: the powers of the state were far greater in Russia at the top, but far weaker at the bottom. Even in those parts of Germany and Scandinavia where the "well-ordered police state" (Raeff 1983) prevailed, for instance, elites were committed to an ideal of selfless, incorruptible, and efficient service, enjoyed corporate rights within the political system, and in some instances accepted a measure of popular self-rule at the local level. These aspects of the systems Peter borrowed from were not imported into Russia. The best Peter could do was to rail constantly against corruption and red tape (L. Hughes 1998, Chap. 4). The extension of political rights was not on the table.

In Russia, the central state remained the driving force in society. Although it is now apparent that the economy had a large segment engaged in private-market exchange, which Peter tried to encourage, the government dominated the major sectors of land, labor, and capital (Hellie 1999). Nothing here compared to the dynamic, early-modern commercial economies of Holland, England, or France with their highly developed financial techniques and contract rights. Peter's quasimercantilist spur to industrial development had limited results because of the immobility of serfs, the only potential source of labor, and for the most part entrepreneurs remained dependent on state subsidies.

Intellectual life provides another example. Printing flourished for the first time in Russia under Peter, but the presses were controlled by the government, and compared to other parts of Europe the reading public remained extremely small: by the end of the eighteenth century, whereas 80 percent of males were literate in Prussia, 68 percent in Britain, and 47 percent in France, at most 7 percent were literate in Russia (Dixon 1999, 157).

The fact is that for the purposes of revenue extraction, military recruitment, and cultural transformation, Peter opted for more rather than less centralization, coercion, and social stratification, and the greater the state extended its reach the greater were the opportunities for corruption and abuse by officials and *pomeshchiki* who were its agents on the ground. Furthermore, as this elite began to look and act more European, they seemed more foreign to the peasant masses, and the divide between the upper and lower classes widened.

Nonetheless, Peter's reforms achieved his goals of breaking from the legacy of Muscovy and turning Russia into a great military power. Unlike Poland and Turkey in this period, Petrine Russia became stronger rather than weaker, and it was inevitable that any reforms adapted from European models would have to be applied differently in this Eurasian empire. Additionally, Peter introduced the Western notion of a well-ordered government, but one which acted on behalf of the common good, rather than the good of the individual (L. Hughes 1998, 387). He also laid the foundation for Russian science. And by beginning the practice of sending Russian students abroad for their education, he opened the door to the future penetration of European political ideas.

■ The Age of Women Rulers, 1725–1796

After Peter's death, the aristocratic factionalism he had tried to undermine was back in full force. This was the "Age of Women Rulers," which included a few short-lived male emperors. Under Catherine I (reigned 1725–1727), Anna (reigned 1730–1740), Elizabeth (reigned 1741–1761), Peter III (reigned 1761–1762), and Catherine the Great (reigned 1762–1796), the nobility gradually reestablished its independence, often in accord with Enlightenment rhetoric that stressed the political liberties of the gentry vis-à-vis the monarchy.

But this did not mean the aristocracy weakened the power of the autocracy or gained representation in a parliament; quite the opposite. The one attempt to curtail the powers of the crown was in 1730 upon the accession of Anna, who tore up the constitutional conditions a small coterie attempted to force upon her. She did this after seeing that a majority of noblemen were suspicious of the intentions of this group and would throw their support to her. In return for their loyalty to the monarchy, she and her successors rewarded the nobility handsomely. In 1762 Peter III finally freed the *dvorianstvo* (the courtier class) from obligatory service: this reform was intended not only to help the treasury by cutting the number of salaries it paid out but also to enhance the professionalism of the officers and officials who remained at their posts.

Later that year, Peter was overthrown by Catherine II (eventually known as Catherine the Great), whose humiliation as his unloved spouse spurred her personal ambitiousness. She conspired with important factions within the elite that held grave suspicions of Peter for his political goals and erratic personality, but as a German-born usurper of the throne, she was in no position to challenge the aristocracy. In 1785 she granted it corporate status (that is, certain guaranteed legal rights specific to a social group) with the Charter of the Nobility. Previously she had confirmed her husband's decree that noble-held land and serfs constituted private property, contrary to the original understanding that they were given by the government conditionally, in return for service to the state. Only about 15 percent of noblemen owned more than one hundred serfs, the bare minimum for an independent existence, so the rest continued to seek employment in the civil service or military out of economic necessity. Many mortgaged their serfs and estates and fell hopelessly into debt.

Interestingly, noble women had far greater landownership rights than elsewhere in Europe. Their fathers were now free to dispose of their property as they pleased and often gave it to their daughters in the form of dowries, and many of their husbands were too preoccupied with state service to involve themselves in matters of real estate (Marrese 2002).

If on the surface the Charter of the Nobility appeared to be a Europeanizing reform, of a piece with Catherine's well-publicized attachment to enlightened absolutism, in truth it signified once again how far removed her nation was from those in the West. Catherine understood that most Western political models were inapplicable to the empire she ruled, that the powers of the Russian state were both far greater and more limited. According to David Moon (1999a), her incorporation of the nobility, as well as her creation of a merchant estate, should be seen not so much as an attempt to mimic European society as the continuation of the long-standing tsarist tactic of co-opting elites to support the status quo. It was at that same time, moreover, that estate privileges were starting to vanish in Western Europe.

The crown had little choice but to give nobles absolute rights over the enserfed half of the population, as it had inadequate means with which to govern the countryside. This was brought home by the Pugachev Rebellion in the Volga region (1773–1775), an uprising of Cossacks, serfs, Old Believers, and ethnic minorities with a host of grievances against the Europeanized elite and the Russian government. In its wake Catherine made moves, inspired by British and Baltic examples, to introduce a greater police presence and some welfare institutions at the local level. But the results were minimal because of the size of the territory and constraints on the number of officials available in this rigidly structured society.

Also in contrast to Western Europe at this time, with limited peasant mobility the proportion of the Russian empire's population living in urban centers of more than ten thousand stagnated at around 4 percent in the 1790s (Hamerow 1983, 94). Russia continued to lag behind the West in this regard for the next half century. The same was true with respect to the density of its urban network. In France, for instance, the average distance between cities in this period was a little less than 9 miles, whereas in European Russia it was just over 53 miles and in Siberia 315 miles. Furthermore, the majority of Russian towns were predominantly agrarian or administrative rather than commercial in nature (Mironov 1991, 706, 709–710, 715). These figures speak to the relatively minor role played by a middle class in Russia before the late nineteenth century.

In high politics and culture the monarchy retained its primacy. With its extensive patronage of art and architecture, the crown set the cultural tone for the aristocracy, whose male members were socialized in the Cadet Corps and other educational institutions founded by the regime. Through Catherine's literary sponsorship, contemporary intellectual currents of Enlightenment rationalism and the mystical reformism of Freemasonry penetrated elite circles. She encouraged the nobility to sojourn abroad and allowed for the appearance of private publishing houses and a relatively free press. Then, startled by the French Revolution, she jailed freethinkers such as Alexander Radishchev and Nikolai Novikov, whose writings had pointed out the defects of Russian as compared to European society. The monarchy's Westernizing cultural impulses had called forth these challenges. By the end of Catherine's reign, the crown was just beginning to perceive the potentially subversive effects of its own policies.

In foreign and imperial policy, too, the very successes of the state bore within themselves the seeds of potential future troubles. Catherine won for the empire a total of approximately two hundred thousand square miles of territory: in the south at the expense of Turkey and the Crimean Tatars, and in the west at the expense of Poland, which, divided with Prussia and Austria, disappeared from the map. This land grab gave Russia strategic and economic advantages and ensured Catherine's reputation at home, but it also initiated a perpetual fear of Russian aggression in the rest of Europe, and it engulfed large numbers of Poles and Jews, both ethnic groups that proved exceptionally difficult to assimilate into the empire.

■ Absolutism and Its Discontents, 1801–1855

In the early nineteenth century, Catherine's grandsons, Tsars Alexander I (reigned 1801–1825) and Nicholas I (reigned 1825–1855), contended with the multiple shockwaves of the French Revolution and the Napoleonic Wars. Alexander I was brought up to admire Enlightenment ideals, and he was attracted to the egalitarian and meritocratic features of the Napoleonic state. But the attempts of his chief adviser, Mikhail Speransky, to introduce the rule of law and separation of powers were thwarted by Alexander's unshakeable if contradictory attachment to Russian autocratic principles, a legacy that was perhaps too powerful and instinctive for any Russian ruler to overcome, least of all someone as fickle as Alexander. For the time being, therefore,

Speransky succeeded only in streamlining the bureaucratic structure by replacing the collegial system of central administration with ministries headed by individuals.

After the defeat of Napoleon in the 1812 invasion, Alexander's prestige at home and abroad soared, but he now took a turn toward mysticism, which inspired many of his subsequent political projects. His paradoxical quest for both enlightened reform and government-controlled orderliness was evidenced by his unpopular and utopian venture into social engineering, supervised by Count Alexei Arakcheev, which attempted to settle peasants in colonies run on excessively rationalistic and military lines.

In the early nineteenth century, educated society was developing ideas of its own. Freed from obligations of state service, the nobility's attachments to the monarchy's ideological influence loosened. The Russian elite was infected, as was all of Europe during the Napoleonic conquests, by a heightened sense of nationalism, and the postwar military occupation of Paris gave many Russians familiarity with the relatively more fluid social hierarchy in the relatively more prosperous France. Questions of Russian identity vis-à-vis Europe were hotly debated, and many Russian noblemen for the first time began to reexamine critically their own archly inegalitarian social structure and the very lives they led on their family estates, whose prosperity was contingent on the bondage of peasant laborers. One of the consequences of this awakening social consciousness was the rise of both constitutional and Jacobin factions within the noble officer corps. They came to be known as the Decembrists after their badly planned revolt of December 14, 1825, following the death of Alexander I.

The mutiny was easily put down by the army, but the new emperor, Nicholas I, would be haunted by what he saw as the treason of the nobility. Uprisings in Poland (1830–1831) and the 1848 revolutions across Europe would confirm his inclination to stamp out the slightest sign of dissent. Accordingly, Nicholas strengthened both censorship and the powers of the political police with the newly created Third Department. As an alternative to the European republicanism that was in the air, he articulated a set of guiding principles for the empire summarized by the exclusivist slogan "Orthodoxy, Autocracy, and Nationality." Fearful of the instability that could result from social mobility, he discouraged extensive railroad construction in Russia.

At the same time, Nicholas saw merit in many of the criticisms of the Decembrists. But he was mistrustful of the nobility and determined to introduce controlled, quiet, limited reforms from above. He gave Speransky the charge of codifying Russian laws for the first time in nearly two centuries, and he oversaw the creation of the Imperial School of Jurisprudence, which trained an entire cadre of lawyers and judges. Nicholas thus laid the groundwork for significant improvement in the quality and sophistication of the Russian courts. The number of technical institutions and learned societies was expanded during his reign, to the benefit of economic and scientific development. He also experimented in a few locales with the elimination of serfdom, whose evils he recognized, but the immediate abolition of which he considered to be too radical.

Still, these were reforms carried out by a repressive ruler who stifled the free development of society and thereby prevented the nation from keeping pace with rapidly changing, industrializing Europe. This lag heightened the critique of the Russian intelligentsia, which emerged during Nicholas's reign.

Members of the intelligentsia were largely, though not exclusively, young, educated noblemen discontented with Russia's fate and guilt-ridden over the enserfment of fellow Russians. Eager for a reconciliation of their divided nation and troubled by their consciences, they took to a variety of messianic solutions derived from Hegelianism, utopian socialism, or Romantic nationalism. Overt opposition was out of the question in Nicholas's police state, but they formed discussion circles and journals in which to cautiously debate their ideas. They split largely along two lines, with Slavophiles idealizing the pre-Petrine past and Westernizers seeking the formation of a new social order. Despite the name of the latter, both groups idealized the communal peasantry, were skeptical of the bourgeois-dominated West, and rejected the status quo.

The intelligentsia's critique was kept in check by the regime's security apparatus until Nicholas's conservatism was discredited by Russia's defeat by England and France in the Crimean War (1853–1856). A manifestation of European balance-of-power rivalries in the mid-nineteenth century, the war showed that Russia, with its lack of strategic railroads and modern weaponry, had fallen behind Western military advances made possible by the rise of industry, free markets, and a capitalist middle class. The eighteenth-century system that continued to reign in Russia was no longer adequate to the task of maintaining its great-power stature, and this in turn raised the question of the competence of the tsarist form of government.

■ Reform and Reaction, 1855–1904

It fell to Nicholas's son, Tsar Alexander II (reigned 1855–1881), to save the autocracy. The era of Great Reforms was another transformation from above, carried out by the central government in order to catch up with the military strength of its rivals and to let off a controlled amount of steam so as to prevent spontaneous mass upheaval and challenges to the monarchy's authority.

The Great Reforms made remarkable advances, as intended, in "modernizing" the nation by introducing many of the essential socioeconomic and administrative elements of European nation-states of the time. First, and most important, the serfs were emancipated by tsarist decree in 1861, whereby the twenty million serfs and thirty million state peasants (roughly 80 percent of the empire's population) were granted personal freedom (Moon 2001). Second, institutions of municipal and rural local government were introduced in the central Russian parts of the empire (the urban *duma* and the rural *zemstvo*), to which all citizens were eligible to be elected, regardless of class, and which provided vital public health and other services. Third, by 1864, legal reforms were in place that created an independent judiciary, successfully introduced jury trials, and gave all segments of the population access to the courts—although separate district courts were instituted for peasants where rural customary law remained in force. Fourth, censorship was greatly relaxed as a spirit of *glasnost* (openness) was announced, resulting in intense public debate of political and social issues through a burgeoning periodical press. Fifth, universities became self-governing and opened their doors more widely to the lower classes and nationalities. Sixth, the military was reformed with the introduction of mass conscription, which encouraged male literacy with the requirement that all soldiers be able to read. Seventh, the government stimulated industrialization with new banking laws and the promotion of private and state railroad construction.

Instead of strengthening the autocracy, the Great Reforms tended to undermine it by making its absolute authority untenable when elements of a modern society began to emerge. The *zemstvos* formed seedbeds of constitutionalism. Expanded schooling and literacy helped spawn a small but growing middle class with expectations of being granted the right of political participation. A consumer lifestyle was coming into existence in the cities, which also encouraged the notion of political as well as economic choice. Professional organizations and civic groups were formed, all with a sense of social commitment. Industry required the existence of a proletariat, or working class, which lived in squalid urban slums and soon sought an improvement in the conditions of labor and life. The tsarist regime was unwilling to accommodate any demands on the part of these social groups that might diminish its political authority. This stubborn rigidity only encouraged the growth of radicalism.

Especially problematic was the condition of the majority of the population that lived off of agriculture. A majority of nobles were incapable of functioning as farmers without free labor, were already heavily indebted, and experienced a steady hemorrhaging of land. As for the peasantry, it was now juridically free but still bound to rural communes to prevent uncontrollable mobility on the part of the lower class, something feared by security-conscious bureaucrats who wanted to avoid the social crisis apparent in urban centers across Europe.

But it was happening anyway. The emancipated serfs were saddled with the costs of redeeming the value of the land taken from the nobility and distributed to the communes, in addition to a high tax burden. Although the communes provided a decent existence for many peasants, with their periodic redistributions of land and other forms of mutual aid, they were not conducive to efficient farming. Peasants, therefore, supplemented their incomes with seasonal work in factories located in the growing cities of the empire. They themselves believed that the solution to their poverty lay in being given all of the land outside of the communes, including that retained by the nobility. This would have amounted to radical subversion of property rights, however, and there simply was not much land left.

The problem was that rural Russia was undergoing the same demographic explosion as the rest of Europe at this time. What had once been a thinly peopled territory was now becoming more densely populated as the number of inhabitants of the Russian empire tripled to 170 million between 1860 and 1914. Even when the government built the Trans-Siberian Railroad in the 1890s and made a heroic effort to resettle peasants with grants of land in the fertile Siberian Black Earth Zone, the most it could benefit was five million individuals (Marks 1991). Remarkable as the colonization project was, it was not enough.

Reform was also applied to tsarist nationality policy in this era, with equally destabilizing results. The whole thrust of the Great Reforms was to bring Russia more in line with Western society and administrative practices. Among the features of the European nation-state admired by the later imperial

Peasant migrants in Siberia.

Russian monarchs was its relative homogeneity. The governments of Alexander II, Alexander III (reigned 1881–1894), and Nicholas II (reigned 1894–1917) all sought to impose a similar kind of uniformity on their empires through a policy of Russification and the assertion of Russian nationalism as the unifying element of the regime. Although the policy was applied unevenly, attempts to impose Russian language use, preferential treatment for ethnic Russians, and more aggressive support for conversion to Orthodoxy all represented a departure from the accommodating nationalities policies of the past. Perhaps it is understandable considering the spirit of the age and the frustrations involved in ruling an empire that had continued to grow by leaps and bounds in the age of imperialism: in half a century Russia had acquired Finland and central Poland during the Napoleonic Wars and absorbed or conquered the ethnic hothouse of the Caucasus regions, the Muslim emirates of Central Asia, and, at the expense of China, the immense Russian Far East.

However, not only did many of the minority peoples come to resent Russian policy, it was also costly to maintain this empire. Thousands of miles of borders had to be defended, and in some regions armies of occupation were kept in place for years, most visibly in Poland and the Jewish Pale where the government suspected the highest levels of resentment. Even had there been no such issues, the costs of building infrastructure in one of the largest polities on earth were enormous and, along with military expenditures, ate up much of state investment. After the railroad construction boom of the late nineteenth century, which gave Russia one of the most extensive rail networks in the world, per square mile it was at the level of the poorest nations of Europe. In 1913 defense spending required 5.67 rubles per capita; 90 kopecks per capita went toward health and education (Gregory 1994, Table A-1).

Underneath the Great Reforms lay a desire to preserve the autocracy. For that reason, although efforts were made to systematize the government, the powers of the emperor were not diminished. In this fundamental way, therefore, no matter how hard the tsars tried to gain on the West, they were not going to succeed unless they introduced some measure of popular participation in the political system and accepted the notion that laws could come into existence without reference to the ruler. But they never did.

That obstinate refusal was in part a reaction to the rise of the revolutionary intelligentsia, which, after the expansion of higher education, now saw an influx of commoners, ethnic minorities, and women into its ranks. Increasingly it was radicalized, its rejectionism, apocalypticism, and penchant for violence growing as it became disillusioned with the unfulfilled promises of the Great Reforms, unsettled by rapid industrialization and urbanization, and angered by the glaciated political structure. Not all the intelligentsia advocated revolution. Moderate liberals sought a constitution and some form of parliament. But in Russia even this was considered an unacceptably radical platform. In any case, the number of those who did advocate extremist solutions was growing in the 1870s. Ever more effective terrorist organizations were formed that attempted to inspire mass uprisings through political assassinations. One such group, the People's Will, succeeded in killing Alexander II in 1881.

That put an end to the age of reforms. Alexander III and Nicholas II, son and grandson of the martyred tsar, were political reactionaries who refused to budge on the issue of the autocracy, imposed martial law on parts of the country, revived and augmented the secret political police (now called the Okhrana), and frequently suspended civil liberties and judicial procedure in the fight against what was broadly defined as subversion. Official ideology under the last two Romanov rulers was a return to the slogan of "Orthodoxy, Autocracy, and Nationality," but now it was even more out of tune with the complex society that was coming into being. Many within governing circles of the nation, including the tsars themselves, turned to anti-Semitism for a warped understanding of Russia's troubles. For them, Jewish capitalists and revolutionaries figured as the source of all evils.

Not all the branches of government were so reactionary. The Ministry of Finance, led by Sergei Witte from 1892 to 1903, adopted the gold standard and opened the country to foreign investment in order to spur further industrial growth. In large part due to his efforts, by 1914 Russia had the fifth largest industrial sector in the world, although again per capita figures were less impressive, with the United States ten times stronger than Russia in this respect (Falkus 1972, 12–13). The wealth of entrepreneurs and the size of the middle class and proletariat continued to grow as a result. By 1914 there were a hundred towns of over fifty thousand compared to just fifteen in 1870. The proportion of the urban population, at just over 13 percent, was small compared to England's 72 percent, Germany's 47 percent, and the United States' 38 percent, but the number of urban residents had tripled since Emancipation, with some cities increasing in size by 700 to 1,000 percent (Rogger 1983, 125–126).

Witte himself was less concerned about foreign influences in Russia than were others. He advocated loosening restrictions on Jews and was closely linked to Westernizer circles. Yet he was no classical liberal. He stated that Russia was different than the West and that it required more state intervention in political and economic life. For much of his career he opposed any restrictions on the power of the autocracy. Even under his administration Russian entrepreneurs remained hemmed in with far more restrictive regulations than Indian industrialists under the English Raj (Owen 1991, 180 and throughout).

If Witte as the most liberal of Russian bureaucrats retained a strong suspicion of capitalism and the new ways of political life, one can imagine what most of the others felt. The last two monarchs, along with many of their courtiers and top officials, were incapable of understanding that the autocracy itself had undermined the old social hierarchy and created a modern, autonomous, urban society that would seek participation in the political process, a concession the tsars were not prepared to make.

The ultimate test of the autocracy's ability to retain its authority at home and status abroad was warfare. The government faced this test twice in the early twentieth century, first in the Russo-Japanese War of 1904–1905, then in World War I. In both it was humiliated, and the revolutions that followed were expressions of society's dissatisfactions.

▮ The Revolutionary Era, 1905–1923

Japan went to war with Russia to block tsarist penetration of Manchuria and Korea, which threatened to derail Japanese imperialist ambitions in Northeast Asia. On land and at sea the Russian military was no match for its foe, and defeat at the hands of a nonwhite enemy surprised the world and undermined the aura of tsarist authority at home. The military's ability to maintain order in the center was diminished by having so many soldiers in China. Already, moderate intelligentsia and professional groups had been campaigning for political reforms, striking workers had been agitating for their rights, and radical terrorism was on the upswing. As news of the Russian military's humiliation spread, protest movements picked up steam, and violence escalated in the towns and countryside. In the latter, acts of vandalism against manor houses suggested a desire to purge the villages of the alien "European" presence. Widespread opposition to the regime was countered by the formation of radical-right vigilante movements, the so-called Black Hundreds, who launched bloody attacks against Jews in numerous pogroms.

The 1905 Revolution ended when Nicholas II, at the urging of Sergei Witte, issued the October Manifesto, promising that Russia would become a constitutional monarchy with an elective parliament, or State Duma, and the issuance of full civil liberties. But Nicholas believed the promises he had made were invalid as they had been issued under duress, and he never fully accepted the notion of sharing political power. Large portions of the country still lived under martial law, revolutionary activism was brutally suppressed, and the electoral laws were changed to give preferential voting rights to Russians, noblemen, and the rich at the expense of minorities, workers, and peasants.

Because of World War I and the 1917 Revolution the "constitutional experiment" (Hosking 1973) did not last long enough for us to know whether the Duma and tsar would have reached a compromise. There were some signs that this was taking place as the government became accustomed to working with parliamentarians on a wide array of legislative projects. Prime

Minister Peter Stolypin, furthermore, introduced a promising agrarian reform in 1906 that would allow peasants to take their land out of the communes and become individual farmers. Inspired by the political conservatism of the Western European peasantry, the dual purpose was to boost productivity and lessen the anarchic tendencies of Russian peasants by instilling a respect for private-property rights that had remained weak in the communal setting.

On the negative side, Stolypin often acted in a high-handed manner, proroguing the Duma when he was frustrated with its opposition and legislating by decree. Although this embarrassed the tsar, who showed little signs of regret when Stolypin was assassinated in 1912, Nicholas himself remained largely out of touch with the new political realities of the nation, as he and his wife, Alexandra, were not only kept insulated by their courtiers, but also preoccupied with their hemophiliac son Alexei, the heir to the throne. The demands of the masses were not being met as workers' collective-bargaining rights and labor conditions were still inadequate, and peasants continued to (incorrectly) view large private estates as the source of their land hunger. The nationalities resented Russification policies and, in the case of Central Asia, Russian settlement of nomadic lands. Exclusion rather than inclusion remained the hallmark of tsarist Russian politics. The potential existed for either further stabilization and growth or further upheaval. World War I ensured that it was the latter rather than the former.

World War I was fatal for the Romanov dynasty, as it was for the German, Austrian, and Turkish empires. It began in 1914 with conflict between Serbia and Austria, followed by the preemptive German invasion of Belgium and France and declaration of war against Russia. But the deeper cause was German kaiser Wilhelm II's aggressive push for global power, which ended up bringing former rivals France, Russia, and England together into a coalition against Germany and its ally Austria. Few had anticipated that this would be a long war, and when it turned into one it broke the back of the tsardom. Hard-won fiscal reform of the preceding decades was undone by inflationary war finance. Already delicate relations with the nationalities were upset by the Russian army's expulsion of an estimated one million Jews, Poles, Balts, and Ukrainians from their homes in the broad area of the front lines and by the suppression of a Kazakh revolt protesting wartime forced labor and Russian intrusion onto nomadic lands. Total Russian military deaths from 1914 to 1917 reached from 1.3 to 2 million, a sacrifice equaling that of France or Germany (Merridale 2001, 97; Pipes 1990, 418).

Accommodation between tsar and society was also called into question by Nicholas's wartime leadership. Modern total war required a high level of coordination between government, industry, labor, and parliament. Nicholas II opposed sharing responsibilities for the war effort for fear that it would be followed by the Duma's insistence that he share power. But without it Russian industry was not going to be able to produce efficiently for the needs of either the military or the civilian populace.

As Nicholas moved to the front and took over command of the army, he bore the brunt of the blame for Russian losses to the Germans. In the capital (renamed Petrograd), government paralysis set in as the Empress Alexandra was left in charge. Her closest confidant was the corrupt pseudo–holy man Grigory Rasputin, whose ability to somehow stop Tsarevich Alexei's hemophiliac bleeding gave him enormous psychological power over the royal family. Ministers who opposed his growing political influence were removed from office. The quality of the highest government officials at this time of grave crisis declined rapidly, and to save the country a group of monarchists assassinated Rasputin in December 1916. Increasingly, however, the call was no longer for limiting the tsar's power but for eliminating it, and by early 1917 the officer corps and the bureaucracy joined the liberals of the Duma in the ranks of Nicholas's opponents.

In February 1917 riots over bread shortages spread into a general strike in the capital, followed quickly by the breakdown of order and the mutiny of troops stationed there. Persuaded by his generals that he had no options, the tsar abdicated on March 2, and the monarchy was replaced by a Provisional Government led by former Duma deputies (the royal family was murdered by the Bolsheviks the following year). At the same time, reflecting the broader cultural divide in the nation, workers and soldiers across the nation formed democratic councils, or soviets, to protect their own interests from the Westernized elite whom they mistrusted. Peasants formed equivalent institutions in the countryside. Whereas the intellectuals who led the soviets, especially its national organization in Petrograd, were radical socialists, those in the Provisional Government were a mix of liberals and moderate socialists. The soviets often negated the undertakings of the government. This dual authority paralyzed the nation at a time when the front was collapsing, soldiers were streaming homeward, and Germany was conquering the south and west of the former empire. The Provisional Government made serious mistakes, among them delaying finalization of a constitution and naively believing that democracy would be strengthened by abolition of the despised Russian bureaucracy and police. This only pushed the nation further into anarchy, and as workers began taking control of factories and peasants seized private lands, the economy deteriorated. By the fall, when Prime Minister Alexander Kerensky saw that the government needed to flex its muscles to resist its revolutionary opponents, it was too late.

The beneficiary of the disarray was the Bolshevik (later Communist) Party, led by Vladimir Lenin (1870–1924). The son of a provincial school inspector whose civil-service rank conferred hereditary noble status, Lenin became a revolutionary after being expelled from university for participating in a student demonstration. The Bolshevik Party was the extremist wing of the Marxist-Socialist movement in Russia. With its conspiratorial proclivities it drew on the legacy of previous generations of Russian revolutionaries, but added a Marxist emphasis on the growing urban-industrial working class rather than the rural peasantry, whom Lenin considered market-oriented capitalists. Lenin, though, had come to distrust the instincts of the working class, which he felt were insufficiently radical, and he saw other socialists as ineffective intellectuals. For that reason he founded the Bolshevik Party in 1903 to constitute a revolutionary elite that would lead the masses to communism.

The leaders of the party were in exile during the war and returned in the spring of 1917 with the connivance of the German general staff, which hoped they would disrupt and weaken the Russian political system. Few Russians had heard of Lenin at that point, and even fewer were familiar with his platform. Lenin was certain that his views represented Marxist revolutionary truth, but however much he was an ideologue, he was also a hard-nosed realist who did what was necessary to win mass support, seize power, and hold onto power. He had the advantage over his opponents in his fanatical willingness to use any means, however ruthless, to bring about the victory of communism in Russia.

One of those means would be the Marxist-inspired dictatorship of the proletariat, but that was not well publicized in the summer of 1917 when the party was seeking popular support in the soviets. In Russia and abroad, the Bolshevik talk of the withering away of the state was such that Lenin was often mistaken for an anarchist individualist when his immediate priority was to establish a centrally organized state, in line with his understanding of Marxism in which individuals were, to use a common term in Bolshevik circles, "cogs" in the machine of communist society (Figes 1997, 742–743). But with a militant stance that appealed to the increasingly desperate masses, and slogans of "peace, bread, land," "industry for the workers," and "all power to the soviets" that promised the world when the Provisional Government seemed incapable of anything, the Bolshevik Party won a majority of votes in the factories and big-city soviets by the fall.

This electoral success made it possible for the Bolsheviks to seize power. The main architect of the coup was Lenin's right-hand man Leon Trotsky, whose Military Revolutionary Committee commanded the pro-Bolshevik soldiers of the Petrograd garrison and, in tandem with radical workers' militias known as Red Guards, overthrew the shell of the Provisional Government in the name of the soviets on October 25–26, 1917. In the year to come, the democratic nature of the soviets was undermined and they became a set of phony legislative institutions rubber-stamping the decrees issued by the Communist Party dictatorship in Moscow, where Lenin moved the capital when the German army came perilously close to Petrograd.

Thus was born the model of a one-party state with a façade of representative government concealing a top-down, centrally controlled system run by the Communist Party hierarchy. Lenin's government outlawed all other political organizations, abolished the imperial legal system, launched an all-out assault on established religion, introduced strict censorship, disseminated propaganda through the party-controlled media, and attempted between 1917 and 1921 to abolish private property and the market economy. The power of the new regime was backed up by a vastly expanded secret-police service, which acted with unprecedented violence (originally called the Cheka, and later, in turn, the GPU, OGPU, NKVD, MGB, and KGB), and the creation of a network of corrective-labor concentration camps, the Gulag, where opponents of the regime were isolated and in many cases exterminated.

The appearance of a new autocracy in Russia is explained to varying degrees by the antidemocratic nature of Bolshevism, the dogmatic Marxist-Leninist fixation on the proletarian dictatorship and class warfare, and the utopian desire of radical intellectuals to create a perfect society and to sweep aside anyone who stood in their way. But many of its characteristics also took shape in the midst of the warfare precipitated by the Bolshevik takeover, what Peter Holquist (2002, 5) calls "a series of overlapping civil wars and national conflicts."

Outlawed political parties, from socialist to monarchist, took up arms, forming a disconnected series of "White" army fronts fighting against the communist "Reds." Ethnic regions declared independence. In cities under Bolshevik control, workers resented being forced by the party to accept the return of factory managers whom they had booted out a few months earlier and whose government-directed task was to reverse the economic collapse by reimposing workplace discipline. Soldiers protested the return of military discipline in the new Red Army, which brought many ex-tsarist officers back into positions of command. The Communist Party's forcible seizure of grain from the countryside, to feed the cities, enraged the peasants, provoked widespread rural rebellions, and helped bring about a famine in 1921–1922 that killed millions in the Volga region.

The Bolsheviks had the upper hand due to their opponents' inability to unite or win the trust of the masses: the unappealing political programs of the White movements called for restoration of the Provisional Government and Russian rule over a reconstituted empire. Both sides committed atrocities, but the Red Army, inspired by its founder Trotsky, was more effective at crushing resistance through the use of mass killing of civilian populations, in some instances with aerial bombardment and chemical weapons (Figes 1997, 768). By 1922, all regions of the old empire had been reconquered, with the exception of Finland, the Baltic states of Estonia, Latvia, and Lithuania, Poland, and

Bessarabia. Between five and seven million people died as a result of the civil war and accompanying epidemics (Merridale 2001, 102).

A pragmatic strategist, Lenin recognized that the resolution of the civil war required more than outright conquest of the land and suppression of dissent. In both economic policy and relations with the nationalities he offered carrots as well as the stick to encourage the population to accept his dictatorship. In 1922–1923 the Union of Soviet Socialist Republics (USSR) was created by Lenin and his nationalities commissar Joseph Stalin, as a compromise between the highly centralized ideal of the Bolshevik Party and the desire of the national minorities for autonomy. Major ethnic groups were given their own republics while lesser ones were granted so-called autonomous regions. In this "affirmative-action empire" (Martin 2001), ethnic culture was encouraged and ethnic elites were co-opted through leadership positions in regional soviets or in the local Communist Party branches. This was a pseudofederal structure where power rested with the Russian Communist Party in Moscow. It suited Lenin's purposes, but in the long run nationalist aspirations in the ethnic enclaves did not disappear as he had hoped. On the contrary, over the subsequent decades they grew and became frustrated by the prerogatives of the Russians in their Soviet empire. As Hosking states, "non-Russians were being endowed with identity but denied sovereignty—an explosive mixture" (Hosking 2001, 433).

Likewise Lenin showed ideological flexibility with the New Economic Policy, which he introduced in 1921. The NEP was an abandonment of the nationalized "war communist" economy and a reinstatement of retail business and the free market in agricultural goods. The "commanding heights of industry," that is, banking, utilities, big business, and foreign trade, remained state monopolies, and prices were controlled by the government, but the NEP made enough of a concession to capitalism to jump-start the economy after years in utter collapse, and it took the wind out of urban and rural unrest. Relaxation on economics was not accompanied by political concessions, however, and with the quiescence of the masses, the secret police were able to uproot the remaining political opposition. In the meantime, the privileged position of the party brought an influx of newcomers into its ranks, people who were more opportunistically inclined than the Old Bolshevik veterans of the revolutionary underground.

In the first years of the revolution, the Kremlin resorted to maximum military force and police coercion to retain power and maintain Russian territorial integrity. In part this assertion of strong central authority was the traditional reflex of Russia's statist political culture when the unity of the realm was under threat. In part it was a product of the Bolshevik command structure, formed in its days as an underground revolutionary-combat organization. In part it stemmed from the amorality of the party, which redefined as ethical whatever served the needs of the revolution and its vanguard party.

The sanctioning of political violence also followed from the new dictatorship's disparagement of civil rights and its experimentation with radical social engineering. And to a large extent the militaristic and hierarchical ethos inherent in Bolshevism was deepened during the civil war: thereafter, the political system seemed incapable of functioning without military-style mobilization and the notion that enemies were ever-present.

Perhaps, as many scholars contend, the Bolshevik Party never achieved full totalitarian control of this vast nation, but there can be no doubt that this is what it strove for and that it asserted far greater authority over the lives of its citizens than any other state in prior history. Guided by an extremist ideology with secularized messianic overtones, the communist project in Russia was a conscious effort to both reject European bourgeois society and best it. Ultimately, the revolution would end up inheriting the "uncultured" and "non-European" features of the Russian state and make a cynical mockery of the humanitarian impulses that inspired the Russian intelligentsia (Lenin 1965, 481, 487, 501; Service 1995, 299).

In their violence and dictatorship the Russian revolution and Bolshevik regime anticipated the trajectory of many of the traditional societies of the non-Western world in the twentieth century as they too were torn apart by urbanization, industrialization, and the influx of Western ideas. But one can argue as well that Communist Russia was in line with tendencies in Europe. There, too, both empire-building and the devastation of World War I had wrecked the old economic, political, and moral certainties and accustomed Europeans to bloodshed and ideological extremism. Aside from Mussolini's Italy and Hitler's Germany, both of which learned many tricks of the totalitarian trade from the Soviet Union, plenty of others in Europe were glad to see dictatorships of the right or left come to power at home to destroy their imagined enemies and impose order and stability. There were certainly few democracies left on the continent by 1939. On the other hand, with Nazi Germany excepted, no other country went to the extremes that Russia did under Lenin or his successor, Stalin. The system they created, even more than that of its tsarist predecessors, can only be seen as standing outside (or at least on the far fringes) of the general European pattern.

■ Stalinism, 1924–1953

Born Iosif Djugashvili to a poor cobbler's family in Russian Georgia, Stalin (1879–1953) had been a long-time member of the Bolshevik Party and became commissar for nationalities after the revolution. Even so, he preferred to stay in the shadows of more prominent leaders like Trotsky, Lev Kamenev, Grigori Zinoviev, and Nikolai Bukharin. He began to throw his weight around once Lenin became ill, and he outmaneuvered and later liquidated these rivals in the struggle to replace Lenin as party leader after 1923. He succeeded by skillfully playing one rival off against the other and taking control of the party personnel rolls, which allowed him to shift his supporters into positions of influence and undermine those in competing camps. He demanded personal loyalty of the functionaries (*apparatchiki*) whom he promoted in the *nomenklatura,* the painstakingly calibrated pecking order within the party and government that gave its name to the new Soviet elite. Tellingly, Stalin viewed it as a lord-vassal system (Heller and Nekrich 1986, 129–130, 183, 609), which reveals not only consciousness of a new social hierarchy but also the central importance personal patronage relationships would play in Soviet politics. At the pinnacle of the pyramidal structure were the Central Committee and Politburo, the latter functioning as the dictator's cabinet.

Stalin was a former Orthodox seminary student whose theocratic cast of mind produced some of the distinctive features of Soviet Communism. He referred to the Bolsheviks as "a sort of military-religious order" (Montefiore 2004, 85). Ubiquitous posters, statuary, and banners glorified the founder of Bolshevism in a quasireligious Lenin cult that was the centerpiece of Stalinist propaganda. Stalin's status as a lesser deity in the official ideology altered over time until he equaled or surpassed Lenin. The writings of Marx-Lenin-Stalin had a catechistic function, legitimizing the party's supremacy, replacing independent thought with indoctrination, and enabling the government to identify nonadherents as political heretics. The ideological and propaganda emphases shifted frequently in response to events and in so doing provided subtle policy guidelines for party *apparatchiki*—who could pay a high price for missing their cues.

Unlike Lenin, who abhorred Russian chauvinism, Stalin increasingly relied on Russian nationalism as a unifying ideological force alongside Marxism. This partly reflected his frustration with the consolidation of ethnic identities in the republics, a direct result of Soviet nationalities policies. Stalin's *nomenklatura* system had also brought about the entrenchment of local ethnic elites, especially in Muslim Central Asia. Concerned with these potential threats to Moscow's control of its empire, he reversed Lenin's approach and opted for Russification and repression of so-called bourgeois nationalism. However much this was couched in terms of a supranational Soviet culture, the reverence paid to powerful tsars and Russian culture is indicative of its thrust. During World War II, Marxist ideology was downplayed even further in favor of the more effective rallying cries of the Russian motherland and even the Orthodox Church, which was allowed to reestablish the patriarchate, albeit under the strict supervision of the state.

The purpose of Stalinist official culture was to create a "new Soviet man" and "new Soviet woman." Party radicals may have once dreamed of an egalitarian social order and experimented with the destruction of the bourgeois family by allowing divorce and abortion, but after 1936 much of this was jettisoned out of fear that these policies were encouraging social disarray. Now the ideal citizen was to be obedient to the party and state, mouth the Kremlin's formulaic ideology, and labor for the higher good of the USSR. Women performed domestic duties in addition to working outside the home, but their pay was substantially lower than that of men. Not only was all this an emanation of the authoritarian nature of the political system, it also reflected the cultural conservatism of the party rank and file, who from the mid-1920s on were drawn from the lower classes rather than the intelligentsia, lacked familiarity with the wider world, and were unsympathetic to the emancipation of women. When the Stalinist purges of the 1930s killed off their superiors, these were the people who replaced them. They became the leaders of the country in the 1950s to 1970s, and their values would shape Soviet domestic and foreign policies of that period.

Cultural production in the Stalin era was controlled by the state. Although there was remarkable ferment in all branches of the arts in the first decade and a half after the revolution, by the late 1930s artists and writers were intimidated (or bought off with pay and privileges) into following the guidelines laid down by the party: most of those who tried or even seemed likely to buck the system wound up in the hands of the secret police. The officially mandated artistic canon was known as "Socialist Realism," which required art and literature to glorify "party-mindedness," Soviet/Russian patriotism, "the people," and a golden future under communism.

That future was to come about by means of Stalin's drive to build "socialism in one country," which entailed the termination of the NEP and the introduction of a centrally planned economy, rapid industrialization, and the collectivization of agriculture. All these initiatives were designed to fulfill the predictions of Marxism, enhance Stalin's stature, extend the authority of the ruling party to the distant reaches of the territory, and defend the USSR from capitalist nations that were its potential military adversaries.

The first step toward this vision of the future was taken in 1928–1930 with the conquest of the countryside. The Soviet Union was still a largely rural nation, inhabited by a majority of peasants whom Bolshevik ideologues perceived as a petty-capitalist class enemy, despite the persistence of the prerevolutionary communes. Stalin feared that the peasants, as for-profit producers, would always be hostile to communism and could hold the regime hostage by refusing to bring their crops to market. Government price controls that disadvantaged farmers in order to benefit urban workers had, naturally, led to a decline in the availability of food, but that only confirmed Stalin's suspicions of the peasantry. The answer was for the state to shut down the old communes, confiscate the peasants' private possessions, and force them into government-run collective farms (*kolkhozy* and *sovkhozy*) that would ensure delivery of agricultural goods to the cities.

Stalin spoke of class warfare in the countryside and gathering "tribute" from its vanquished inhabitants (J. Hughes 1996, 14–15, 71). Peasants fought what they rightly saw as the imposition of a new serfdom. Resisters were labeled *kulaks* (rich peasants), and the ensuing *dekulakization* amounted to a frontal assault on the peasants' world. Brainwashed members of the Soviet youth movement, the Komsomol, joined police detachments and occasionally military units in demonizing opponents of the collective farms and laying waste to their homes, accompanied by widespread physical and sexual violence. In 1930–1933, over four million men, women, and children were rounded up and either shot or shipped off in cattle cars to concentration camps or remote unsettled regions of the Russian north. Hundreds of thousands died (Moon 1999b, 363).

In the chaos of *dekulakization* and collectivization, farm production collapsed and most cattle were slaughtered rather than given up to the state. Between five and seven million people starved to death in the famine of 1932–1933, whose epicenters were in Ukraine and Kazakhstan (Moon 1999b, 363). Thereafter, Soviet collectivized agriculture was crippled by the abysmally low pay given to peasants and the constant intervention of party officials. It was a political victory for Stalin, however, as it ensured that the minimal food needs of the cities would be met and the state never again need worry itself about the independence of the peasantry.

Forced collectivization also sped up rural migration to the cities, a process that had begun in the previous century, although it would not be until the late 1950s that the majority of the population lived in urban centers. With the establishment of the Five-Year Plans and the introduction of forced industrialization in 1928, demand for workers skyrocketed and peasants poured by the millions into the cities, including old ones like Moscow, but also new ones like Magnitogorsk in the southern Urals that were built virtually overnight. Conditions were hazardous in rapidly erected smoke-stack industries modeled after those of Detroit, Michigan, and Gary, Indiana, and often using blueprints purchased from US corporations such as Ford and Westinghouse. Collective bargaining rights for workers were nonexistent, but technical education was available for the masses, upward mobility was promised (although how many actually benefited is debatable), and the sense of building a new society was palpable. The Five-Year Plans also bedazzled leftists the world over. While capitalist countries were mired in the Great Depression, the supposedly backward Russians had full employment and were industrializing under the auspices of Gosplan, the state's central planning agency in Moscow.

The results were indeed impressive in industrial production, but the Soviet command economy also imposed an enormously high price. The emphasis of Stalinist planners was on heavy, especially military-related, industry. Light, consumer-goods manufacturing and housing, the mainstays of capitalist economies, received relatively little investment. Members of the party elite in the *nomenklatura* received access to consumer goods, provisions, and apartments, but the common citizen was forced to spend hours in lines waiting to purchase the most elemental foodstuffs and shabby products. The basic wants of the populace were thus sacrificed in the interests of the party-state.

Even in the favored sectors of the economy, shortcomings were severe. Bureaucratic disarray was the norm in state planning agencies. For the sake of boosting output, pollution controls were disregarded, to the detriment of public health. Many of the most visible prestige projects of the Stalinist Five-Year Plans, including the construction of the Belomor Canal and the Moscow and Leningrad subway systems, were dependent on slave labor provided by the Gulag administration. Slaves also staffed the vital lumber and mining industries in remote regions, where a free workforce was nonexistent. Perhaps the greatest defect, at least in terms of economics, was that the planning system sapped entrepreneurial drive and efficiency: what paid a factory manager was not technological or organizational innovation, but fulfillment of centrally imposed production figures. Falsifying the books was a common technique in this circumstance and so was resorting to the black market, which filled the gaps for both consumers and producers. The persistence of this underground economy belied the much-touted successes of Soviet planning and the utopian dream of transforming humanity.

Despite the party's tight grip on the society via its far-reaching control over political and economic life, Stalin was well aware of the internal criticism of his personal dictatorship and economic policies. Relying on the secret police apparatus he inherited from Lenin, Stalin's inclination was to resort to terror to keep potential opposition at bay and to guarantee that functionaries carried out the party's demands rather than go their own way, as was their tendency. His ruthless personality was given free rein in a system that had destroyed legal and moral standards. His policies also reflected the traditional urge of Russian rulers to maximize state power in order to counterbalance what they perceived as ever-reviving centrifugal forces.

Stalin's terror was partly inspired by Adolf Hitler's 1934 Night of the Long Knives, a surgical strike against the Fuehrer's Nazi Party rivals. This was a two-way street, however, as the Germans had already borrowed techniques from the Soviets in setting up their version of a one-party dictatorship (Marks 2003, 299–310). But whereas Nazi violence was limited to specific opposition figures, Jews, and homosexuals, an exceptionally wide net was cast during Stalin's Great Terror. No one could feel secure, whether scientists and poets, high-ranking party officials, members of Stalin's inner circle, or even the secret police chiefs, Genrikh Yagoda and Nikolai Ezhov, who fell victim when it was convenient for Stalin to dispose of them. The arbitrary nature of the Stalinist terror kept people on guard against each other, ready to denounce their closest colleagues to prevent suspicion being cast on themselves. It could also catch them off guard while at the heights of their power and influence, unaware that someone was plotting their imminent doom. Either way, this capriciousness was a crucial attribute of Stalin's absolutism.

The height of the terror was 1936–1938, an era when all citizens feared the midnight arrival of the police and the disappearance of their loved ones. The number of victims multiplied as quotas of arrests were assigned to police officers, and the government issued instructions to incarcerate associates and relatives of arrestees, the better to quell the festering of resentment according to one of Stalin's henchmen, Vyacheslav Molotov (Chuev 1993, 277–278). Show trials were staged for the most prominent of the Old Bolshevik rivals of Stalin, who were tortured before confessing to trumped-up charges (Trotsky was assassinated later in Mexico). Mass shootings were common.

Those who were spared from execution were sent into squalid and remote exile communities or to the concentration camps of the Gulag, whose inmate ranks in some years swelled beyond two million. Anne Applebaum (2003, 579–584) calculates that between 1929 and 1953 a total of eighteen million Soviet citizens spent time in the camps; including exiles in special settlements, the figure rises to more than twenty-eight million. The Soviets did not set up death camps like the Nazis: in Stalin's USSR forced labor as a form of punishment and exploitation, rather than extermination, was the rule. But conditions in the Gulag were harsh, and many died of disease, starvation, and the cold, as well as from maltreatment by guards or gangs of criminals. How many people perished at the hands of the secret police or in the camps may never be known for sure, but for the entire Stalin era the most reliable estimate thus far is more than 3.5 million untimely deaths. The trauma inflicted by Stalin and his regime on the nation's psyche is immeasurable.

Among the hardest hit segments of the society was the Soviet officer corps, which lost 90 percent of its highest ranks in the purges. Those targeted included the experts on German blitzkrieg tactics. Hitler took this weakness into account in making his decision to launch Operation Barbarossa and invade the USSR on June 22, 1941. The Stalinist Great Terror was thus followed by an even greater bloodletting. In the Great Fatherland War, as World War II is known in Russia, the Soviet Union suffered higher numerical losses than any other belligerent nation, with a death toll of around twenty-five million (Overy 1998, 287–289).

Hitler's longstanding ambition was to acquire German *Lebensraum* (living space) by conquering Russia, annihilating its Jews, and enslaving the rest of the population. Initially, however, to avoid a two-front war, Hitler saw the necessity of making an agreement with the USSR, and in August 1939 the two dictatorships signed the Nazi-Soviet Non-Aggression Pact. This was an alliance bought by the promise that Germany would partition

Poland with the Soviets and tolerate Moscow's reabsorption of Estonia, Latvia, Lithuania, and Bessarabia, all of which the Soviets conquered along with a slice of Finland in the next year and a half. Stalin then furnished the Nazi war machine with supplies as it overran the rest of Europe. But when it became expedient, Hitler launched a surprise attack on the Soviet Union that resulted in the devastation of the country and the death or capture of millions as the Wehrmacht moved relentlessly toward the Volga River and the Caucasus Mountains. Stalin had refused to believe intelligence that preparations for Barbarossa were under way and made few preparations, lest Hitler take them as a provocation and be handed an excuse to invade.

Stalin's delaying tactic was disastrous for both the military and the civilian population, which were caught unawares and trapped behind enemy lines. The Nazis occupied Ukraine and the rich southern Russian steppe, and Leningrad starved for three years under a blockade. Long-term advantages, however, were on the side of the Soviets. Stalin worked round the clock and acquiesced to the advice of his general staff, led by Marshal Georgi Zhukov. Patriotism ultimately rallied most Soviets, who were promised nothing but enslavement or extermination by the Nazis. The command nature of the society was well suited to evacuating central Russia's industries to Siberia, where at breakneck speed they were rebuilt and reconfigured for military production, which eventually surpassed that of the Third Reich. And the German army, overstretched after conquering the rest of Europe, was ill-equipped for the often boggy and, in winter, frozen Russian interior. With the German defeat at Stalingrad during the winter of 1942–1943, the Nazi onslaught was reversed and Soviet troops began the long slog to Berlin.

Following the May 1945 victory over Nazi Germany, the prestige of the military in Soviet political life was higher than ever and the martial spirit became even more ingrained in the mindset of Communist Party officials. In the Cold War that followed and lasted for the next four decades, representatives of the defense establishment and the military-industrial complex became intertwined with the party elite and formed a powerful interest group within the nation.

The Cold War hostility of the United States and its allies, which was a response to Stalin's forcible imposition of communist dictatorship on Eastern Europe, contributed to the deep freeze in postwar Soviet politics. The period was marked by a xenophobic "anticosmopolitan" terror campaign targeting intellectuals and Jews. After Stalin's death the campaign was ended, but Jews continued to face discrimination until the fall of the USSR because of the strong undercurrent of anti-Semitism that existed among communist officials, who had brought their lower-class prejudices with them into high office. The post-Holocaust revival of Jewish nationalism and the founding of the state of Israel also made it appear that Jews were guilty of dual loyalties, which this monolithic system could not abide.

"The Motherland Calls!," the centerpiece of the Soviet war memorial to the Battle of Stalingrad. Overlooking the site of the battle, this free-standing statue is nearly 280 feet high.

This was not the only instance of maltreatment of ethnic minorities by the Russian-dominated state. During the war Stalin had "ethnically cleansed" peoples suspected of welcoming the Nazi invaders. Among them were the Crimean Tatars and Greeks, Volga Germans, and Chechens, all of whom were deported from their homelands to Siberia or Central Asia. The Korean population of the Russian Far East and others suffered the same fate. Ethnic Russians were then encouraged to move into these regions as well as into the newly annexed Baltic states, western Belorussia, western Ukraine, and Bessarabia. The Soviets conquered these regions first between 1939 and 1941 in agreement with the Nazis, then again en route to Germany in 1944–1945, with cleanup operations against resisters continuing for another two years. Brutal repressions ensured Moscow's success. Those who were not shot on location were arrested and permanently exiled to Siberia, with many hundreds of thousands in each region dying in the process—between 5 and 10 percent of their respective populations (Applebaum 2003, 423; Gross 1988). The resentments of the affected peoples simmered for decades.

Popular discontent had other sources as well, unconnected to nationalities policies or the wave of repressions that accompanied the Cold War. Above all, Stalin intended to reassert the grip of the party by reversing the looser restrictions on private-market farming he had allowed during the war to boost the food supply. The peasant population was disheartened after imagining that he might dismantle the collective farms. A famine brought on by drought, but exacerbated by the *kolkhoz* (collective farm) system and state expropriations, killed two million in 1946 (Zubkova 1998, 47). In addition, well over a million surviving Soviet prisoners of war who had been held by the Germans were transferred directly from Nazi camps to the Gulag on suspicion of colluding with the enemy (Service 1997, 300–301). Hardened by years of fighting they staged strikes and revolts that rocked the camps and disrupted their economic functions. Party leaders were aware of these and other social tensions, but as long as the elderly and increasingly paranoid Stalin was alive, no one dared propose any major changes.

▓ Hope, Apathy, and Decline: The Soviet Union, 1953–1991

Stalin died of a stroke in March 1953, even as he was planning yet another party purge. Before the year was out the surviving members of the Politburo, wishing to put an end to the use of terror as a means of control and to save their own necks in the process, had Stalin's secret police chief, the much feared Lavrenti Beria, arrested, tried, and executed. In turn, they subordinated the secret police (reorganized and renamed the KGB) to what was now a collectively run party-state, instead of a one-man dictatorship. In the succession struggle that followed Beria's demise, Nikita Khrushchev (1894–1971) won out against Georgi Malenkov (1902–1988), the prime minister. Malenkov's reform proposals (later adopted by Khrushchev) were opposed by party hardliners, whose support Khrushchev cultivated. Khrushchev was a barely educated former miner who had joined the party in 1918 and benefited from the purges to become party boss of Ukraine and then Moscow in the 1930s and 1940s. Although he had worked his way into Stalin's inner circle, he was underestimated by his colleagues. Once Stalin was dead, however, he revealed himself to be a master of Kremlin intrigue, betraying allies and manipulating party personnel appointments to his benefit. Signifying a departure in Soviet politics, however, Khrushchev demoted Malenkov and other defeated rivals rather than having them executed.

Repelled by the harshness of Stalin's policies and aware of the economic weaknesses of a system based on enserfed peasants and enslaved prisoners, Khrushchev sought to take the edge off the communist dictatorship by adopting a program of de-Stalinization, which he formally announced at the Twentieth Party Congress in February 1956 in his "Secret Speech," so called because, in deference to his colleagues who feared the public's reaction, the text was not published in the official press. The Secret Speech initiated a process in which Stalin's "cult of personality" and other excesses were officially denounced, the Gulag was downsized, and innocent arrestees were rehabilitated, many posthumously.

But as Khrushchev had plenty of blood on his own hands as one of Stalin's henchmen, his condemnation of his predecessor could only go so far. The Secret Speech was limited mainly to the injustices committed against the *nomenklatura,* which yearned for personal security and the discontinuation of the purges. Khrushchev neither questioned the collectivization of agriculture nor the party's dictatorship, to which he as a Leninist was committed. He was intolerant of cultural experimentation and criticism that crossed certain boundaries, hence the Soviet government's persecution of Boris Pasternak after the publication in Italy of his novel *Dr. Zhivago,* with its damning portrayal of the revolution. Those who were perceived as calling into question the political monopoly of the Communist Party were arrested and sentenced to prison camps.

For good reason, though, this also was known as the era of the "Thaw," after a novel by Ilya Ehrenburg. People could breathe more freely without the threat of the terror hanging over them. Within certain parameters, writers, journalists, and filmmakers were given greater latitude in exposing social problems. Among them was Alexander Solzhenitsyn, whose novels probed the experience of Gulag inmates. Furthermore, at Khrushchev's direction, the government increased investment in the needs of the common citizenry, from prefabricated apartments and consumer goods production to medical care and schools. The Soviet space program was a source of great pride, with the launch of the first satellite, *Sputnik 1,* in 1957, and the first manned space flight in 1961. Despite their continuing frustrations with a deficient economy, never had the Soviet population been as optimistic as it was now.

Yet in 1964 Khrushchev was overthrown by his colleagues and forced into retirement after being discredited at home and abroad. Although he had made significant gains for Soviet foreign policy in the recently decolonized third world, he deepened the rift between his own country and Maoist China, antagonized the West by allowing construction of the Berlin Wall, and engineered the Cuban Missile Crisis, which was, in the words of a Soviet admiral, "a crackpot scheme" that brought the world close to nuclear war (Taubman 2003, 551). De-Stalinization in the Soviet Union inspired rebellion in Hungary, which Khrushchev crushed using military force. His personal appearances at the United Nations and summits with world leaders were often characterized by uncontrollable and vulgar outbursts that embarrassed Soviet diplomats and eroded his support in the Presidium, as the Politburo was then called. Overall his conduct of foreign policy was highly erratic, based on bluffs and brinksmanship, and did little to improve the international standing of the USSR vis-à-vis either the communist or capitalist nations of the world.

Nikita Khrushchev's
grave, Novodevichii
Cemetery, Moscow.

Michael L. Bressler

In the domestic arena his ill-conceived initiative to cultivate the "virgin lands" of the arid Kazakh steppe and his irrational demand that collective farms raise corn regardless of soil or climatic conditions (an idea reinforced by a trip to Iowa) undercut Soviet agricultural production. To alleviate shortages he increased prices and lowered wages in 1962, sparking food riots and workers' strikes in the city of Novocherkassk and elsewhere that turned into violent confrontations with police. Later, when the Soviet government began purchasing grain on the world market, the party leadership was in effect forced to admit that the much-vaunted *kolkhozy* system could not feed the nation. Of course, this too makes clear the difference between the Khrushchev and Stalin eras. Stalin did not care if people starved to death. Even as Khrushchev boasted that Soviet Communism was about to overtake the capitalist West, everything he did seemed to prove the opposite.

Most damaging to Khrushchev politically was his loss of support within the *nomenklatura,* which resented his attempts to bring fresh blood into the system by imposing term limits and to fix attention on rural Russia by splitting, or "bifurcating," the party so that half of the party apparatus would concentrate on agriculture and the other half on industry. This amounted to harassment by a capricious leader in the eyes of the party elite, who wanted nothing more than to enjoy their perks and pass them on to the next generation, the defining feature of a true ruling class. His populist style, furthermore, suggested a political role for the public that was anathema to his colleagues in the leadership who were uncomfortable with anything but a bureaucratic manner of decisionmaking. For them, negotiation and compromise between *nomenklatura* interest groups precluded consultation with the public (Breslauer 1982). Khrushchev's populism was compromised further by his boorishness and impetuosity, and a growing arrogance that caused him to ignore, if not publicly disdain, the opinions of his colleagues.

He had survived one attempt by party hardliners to remove him in 1957 because of the support of his patronage network in the Central Committee, the ruling body of *apparatchiki* from which Politburo members were chosen, but that support had vanished in the interval. He was retired in 1964 and replaced as party leader by his erstwhile protégé, the more conservative and consensus-building Leonid Brezhnev (1906–1982), a career party functionary whose program for the nation was to defend the privileges of the *nomenklatura.* As he put it, in a rebuke to Czech Communist reformer Alexander Dubcek, "[D]on't talk to me about 'socialism.' What we have we hold" (Tucker 1981–1982, 429).

With preservation of the system as the governing principle of Brezhnev's Soviet Union, stagnation set in. The Soviet command economy was incapable of improving popular living standards and maintaining the country's superpower status at the same time, and the more the latter became the priority the more the former suffered. Continuing priority in the planned economy was given to heavy industry over social or consumer investment because of the lobbying power of the defense establishment and the ultraexpensive program of military expansion that pursued parity with US and North Atlantic Treaty Organization (NATO) forces, including construction of a navy with a global reach. Aid commitments in the form of subsidies and weaponry to third-world allies such as Cuba were costly. After the 1979 Soviet invasion of Afghanistan and the ensuing collapse of East-West arms-control negotiations, defense spending rose in the United States and increased the financial pressures on the Soviet government exponentially. By that time, between 15 and 25 percent of the USSR's gross national product (GNP) was taken up by military expenditures (Goldman 1991, 130).

Administering, defending, and developing the immense territorial expanse of the USSR also drained potential resources from social welfare and the central Russian regions of the country. Investment in Siberia and Central Asia yielded income through exploitation of rich natural gas, oil, and diamond deposits, although the environmental impact was catastrophic. Furthermore, as Stephen Kotkin (2001, 10–19) has pointed out, the windfall profits earned from the sale of petroleum on the global market during the oil crunch of the 1970s allowed the state to subsidize inefficient industries instead of forcing the Soviet economy to become more competitive, as in the West.

Labor and infrastructure costs in these and other extractive industries were inordinately high due to geographical remoteness and construction on permafrost. In Central Asia, overfertilization and irrigation of cotton farms in semidesert conditions polluted the soil and drained the Aral Sea. The federal government's expenditures on the region, meanwhile, benefited the ethnic party elite, who ran the local republics as their own fiefdoms, with little oversight from Moscow, and often discriminated against ethnic Russians resident there. Such was the price of maintaining the Soviet empire, which in the post-Stalin era resorted to the traditional imperial tactic of co-optation.

One wonders whether even without military and imperial priorities the command economy would have functioned much better. The absence of profit incentives provided little motivation to emphasize quality of production or respond to consumer demand. Mass apartment housing, to give one prominent example, was shoddily built and still scarce, with a bare eight to nine square meters available per person in the 1970s (Desai 1987, 36). Toilet paper was a rarity in the country with the largest forest reserves on earth. Much of the problem had to do with the implicit deal made between the government and the citizenry to buy social peace for the party dictatorship: consumer prices were kept low, health care was free, employment and old-age pensions were guaranteed, and enforcement of rules at the workplace was minimal.

That sounds wonderful, but it ignored the laws of economics and human nature. Price controls resulted in shortages that required the average citizen to spend hours every day in long lines to buy the most basic items. To meet their needs, people resorted to bribery and the black market, the latter supplied by would-be entrepreneurs stealing public property and an organized crime network with links to corrupt factory managers and party officials. Out of necessity and the moral confusion created by the notion of "people's property," the USSR had become a political system and a society that could not function without thievery.

Inefficiency was also rampant in a socioeconomic system where, as a worker in a Soviet anecdote explained, "they pretend to pay us, and we pretend to work." Factories did often provide their employees with social services, grocery items, housing, and childcare, but at great cost in revenue. Their "make-work" function and laws prohibiting lay-offs sapped productivity, which was among the lowest in the industrial world. By the 1980s Soviet growth rates were negative, and whatever technological innovations appeared were imported from Western firms. For similar reasons agriculture was in an even more perilous state. The collective farms ate up more than 25 percent of total economic investment in the USSR, as opposed to less than 5 percent in Western nations, whose private farmers were at least ten times more productive than Soviet state-farm workers (Buck and Cole 1987, 72, 74–75).

Social problems mounted in Brezhnev's Soviet Union. The birth rate and life expectancy were declining along with the free but poor-quality health care. Abortion, legalized again in 1955, was the most common method of birth control as contraceptive devices were not manufactured. Alcoholism, divorce, prostitution, teenage "hooliganism," and violent crime are common in all urban societies, but were not supposed to grow under socialism. That they did is a reflection of the Soviet populace's apathy and frustrations, which grew deeper by the day while standing in long lines at barren shops and living in crowded flats in bleak apartment blocks.

This was an educated, predominantly urban society that caught glimpses of Western culture through music and movies and the occasional contact with foreigners. Despite, or because of, the efforts of censors and party propagandists, who harped on the ills of capitalist nations, many Soviet citizens regarded the West with a mixture of admiration and envy. They saw the hypocrisy of a hierarchical system that spoke of equality and classlessness while denying them political and civil rights. They dreamed of consumerism and resented the special privileges of the oligarchy. The official Brezhnev cult was laughable and Lenin was irrelevant. The old men in the Politburo, who came of age under Stalin and were still running the country, guided by their stale anticapitalist, anti-Western ideology, were as out of touch with the nation they had helped create as the tsars had once been.

In addition, the USSR was still a police state. The threat of repression and the existence of even a scaled-down Gulag system kept most people cowed and publicly compliant no matter what they thought in private. Even so, it was no longer the Stalin era. A flourishing underground press known as *samizdat* (meaning "self-publishing") produced illegal literature, despite its cat-and-mouse relationship with the KGB. *Samizdat* was the forum in which the dissident movement, dating from the mid-1960s, publicized its views and protest activities. The political orientations of dissidents ran the gamut from reformist-socialist to liberal to Russian nationalist, with heavy representation by ethnic minorities like Jews, Tatars, and Ukrainians pressing for their rights. Others sought a revival of Russian Orthodoxy or campaigned for environmental causes. Increasing numbers of citizens ended up under arrest and they had little overt support from the population at large. Their existence, however, was another indicator of the system's ill health, and their well-publicized mistreatment at the hands of the regime brought the country negative international exposure for its human-rights violations.

The ruling elite knew by the mid-1970s that the country was in a mess. After trying and failing to put a man on the moon, they began to perceive that the Soviet economy was not technologically capable of competing with the United States, and the KGB kept them informed of the pervasive corruption and social malaise. After Brezhnev's death in 1982, Politburo wrangling led to the appointment of two geriatric leaders, Yuri Andropov and Konstantin Chernenko, who died in short order. Andropov had been the KGB chief and moved to root out corruption in the party and improve worker productivity by railing against drunkenness and the extremely lax on-the-job behavior. Chernenko, who succeeded him, was a Brezhnev clone whose appointment signaled a reversion to the ways of his patron. Even so, Chernenko, over the objections of his old-guard backers and perhaps in a deal with his opponents in the Politburo, demanded that Mikhail Gorbachev, a relatively young (born in 1931), reform-minded leader, be appointed as the number two person in the party. The implications of such a move were great, as it gave Gorbachev an inside track to succeed Chernenko as party leader. Gorbachev, an Andropov protégé, did just that after Chernenko's death in March 1985.

Gorbachev had been raised on a collective farm and knew well the hardships and tribulations of Soviet peasant life. As a former law student, he had looked favorably on the Czech reform movement of 1968, which was quashed by Soviet tanks. He kept quiet, however, and became a party apparatchik, adroitly promoting himself and rising rapidly through the ranks of the *nomenklatura*. By the early 1980s, already a member of the ruling Politburo, he was acknowledging privately that "everything's rotten"; "we can't go on living in this way" (Brown 1996, 81). He saw "Brezhnevism [as] nothing but a conservative reaction against Khrushchev's attempt at reforming," which he felt it was "obligatory" to revive (Taubman 2003, 648). As leader of the country, he announced that dramatic changes were needed for the Soviet Union to catch up with the West and "enter the new millennium . . . as a great and prosperous power" (Kaiser 1991, 76). He was an idealistic communist, one of the last ones left, who believed that it was possible to create a Leninism with a human face. As it turned out, he could not square the circle: the one-party dictatorship was incompatible with a free society.

Gorbachev's policies reflected these contradictory impulses. In his first year, he followed Andropov's example in favoring disciplinary measures, such as raising the price of alcohol to combat widespread drunkenness, which was a cause of economic and social problems and a symptom of the system's malfunctioning. In the years that followed he intended to give Soviet society a shot in the arm with a dose of free-market economic incentives boosted by reining in the KGB and cutting the military budget. These reforms became urgent in his mind after the April 1986 explosion at the Chernobyl nuclear power plant in Ukraine discredited party officialdom (Brown 1996, 163, 355n30; Kaiser 1991, 125–132).

Gorbachev's economic policies, known as *perestroika* or restructuring, looked toward reviving the 1920s NEP with its compromise between national- ized and private enterprise. Being largely ignorant and ever suspicious of mar- ket economics, however, he was unsure how to achieve this. As a result, *pere- stroika* amounted to a haphazard series of stop-gap measures that dismantled the planned economy without providing proper support for the private sector in the way of laws, infrastructure, or consistent policy. Bureaucratic opponents of the free market strangled the growth of nonstate enterprises through a com- bination of taxes and regulations. At the same time, the powers of the state economic agencies were curtailed. Factories were now able to set their own prices and wages, a situation which wreaked havoc with the planning system and yet was unrelated to any market signals. Bankrupt or uncompetitive firms were not allowed to fail or shed redundant employees. In agriculture, nothing was done to fix the collective farms.

As price controls lapsed so did the social compact with the population. Government revenues fell due to Gorbachev's antialcohol campaign (which is discussed in Chapter 8 by Timothy Heleniak), the decline in world oil prices, and the loosening of the state's grip on the economy. Inflation rose steadily in the late 1980s and early 1990s as the government expanded the money supply to meet its social-welfare obligations and allowed workers to elect factory managers, who, perhaps not surprisingly, raised wages dramat- ically. This occurred at the same time that the chaos in the industrial sector was producing shortages of many goods, putting upward pressure on prices. Chernobyl and the war in Afghanistan drained the budget further. Food short- ages and lines at state-owned shops were worse than ever; prices at the few newly founded private cooperative kiosks selling consumer goods climbed ever higher.

The *nomenklatura* read the writing on the wall. Many within it aban- doned the party and positioned themselves for the future by using their con- nections to strip the state of industrial assets or joining with organized crime to extort wealth from the embryonic private sector. Regional and republican authorities asserted control over local industries without regard to Moscow. Bribery and corruption were rife. The unified, command economy was in a tailspin. Workers went on strike, criminals worked overtime, and the popu- lace was frustrated, angry, and stunned at the sudden collapse in living stan- dards. Increasingly they held Gorbachev responsible.

Culture and politics followed suit as Gorbachev unwittingly unleashed forces that brought down the Soviet state. His policy of *glasnost* (openness) was a gamble that the relaxation of the dictatorship would stimulate the ren- ovation of society without undermining the preeminence of the Communist Party. Gorbachev released political prisoners such as Andrei Sakharov and was responsible for a cultural and religious reawakening and the stirrings of a civic society. All manner of associations were formed by the likes of anti-Stalinists and Stalinists, environmentalists and historic preservationists, social workers and neo-Nazi skinheads. Allowing the unimpeded circulation of ideas was a dangerous move for the regime as taboo after taboo fell in the now-free press. The myths that sustained the Soviet system were exposed as lies, resentments came out into the open, and protests were directed against the Communist Party.

The ethnic republics, where nationalism had filled the void left by the failure of communism, also fell into turmoil in the late 1980s. Communal riots shook Central Asia, the Baltics agitated for independence, and war broke out between Armenia and Azerbaijan. Ethnic Russians, a minority in each of the fourteen non-Russian republics, watched anxiously as anti-Soviet nationalist movements launched street demonstrations in Georgia, Latvia, and Lithuania. In January 1991 Soviet special forces shot and killed twenty protesters in Vilnius and Riga in an attempt to stamp out separatism there. This inflamed local feeling and raised fears everywhere of a revived dictatorship, despite Gorbachev's claims not to have given the orders. By then ethnic leaders in many of the other republics were already contemplating independence from Moscow as a means of protecting their privileges and elite status. As the internal empire unraveled so too did the external one as Gorbachev withdrew troops from Afghanistan and the East European satellite states, where communist regimes, unable to rely on Soviet military backing, collapsed in 1989.

Gorbachev also lost control of the political structure of the nation. Only a few months after coming to power he had begun to remove Brezhnevite stalwarts from office and replace them with supporters of reform such as Boris Yeltsin, the party leader of the industrial city of Sverdlovsk, whom Gorbachev appointed as Moscow party chief, and Eduard Shevardnadze, the Georgian Communist Party boss who became Soviet foreign minister. To further undermine conservatives in the party apparatus who were systematically blocking reform, between 1987 and 1989 Gorbachev revitalized the soviets as truly representative, elective institutions. This further convinced the *nomenklatura* that their days were numbered, and, indeed, in 1990 Gorbachev annulled the political monopoly of the Communist Party, paving the way for multiparty elections. Still convinced that socialism had merit, however, he was reluctant to adopt even more decisive economic and political reforms. He also failed to recognize that in dissolving the *nomenklatura*'s exclusive hold on power he was dissolving the main institutional prop of the centralized regime established by Lenin and Stalin, not to mention his own patronage base within it.

The communist leadership was divided, with some dead set against further change and others pushing hard for faster, more radical measures. Gorbachev found himself isolated, playing each side against the other or oscillating between one tendency and the next with what appeared to be a split political personality. As events seemed to spin out of control in 1990–1991, and he came under heavy criticism for the turmoil in the economy and the republics, he leaned more and more toward the conservatives, then switched course, moving yet again in the direction of reformers. Both soon abandoned him.

The most outspoken of the reformers and eventually Gorbachev's main rival was the impulsive, impatient, and ambitious Boris Yeltsin (Breslauer 2002). By late 1987 he had become such an irritant in pressing for radical change that he was forced out of office, at which point he dedicated himself to undermining both Gorbachev and the Soviet system. That he was able to do so by appealing to the public rather than operating within the party was a measure of how much the system had changed in the preceding two years. He was soon the most popular politician in the capital, where Muscovites applauded his electoral-campaign attacks on the *nomenklatura*. In 1990 he became chairman of the Supreme Soviet of the RSFSR (Russian Soviet Federated Socialist Republic), and in June 1991 he won the first free presidential elections in the Russian Republic.

Yeltsin, in June 1990, had led the Russian Republic to declare its sovereignty from the USSR, at that point a mostly symbolic gesture but with the implication that the survival of the Union was at risk. Increasingly, Yeltsin and the other republican leaders pushed Gorbachev, as the Soviet president, to the sidelines. Through much of the spring and summer of 1991, Gorbachev attempted to negotiate a new, looser federal relationship to win the republics back to the Soviet fold, but on August 19, hardliners in the party, the KGB, and the military staged a coup and arrested Gorbachev to prevent the new Union Treaty from being signed. Three days later, the incompetent coup plotters capitulated in the face of mass protests led by Yeltsin and the soldiers' refusal to shoot civilians.

Gorbachev returned to Moscow, but in the wake of Yeltsin's victory over the coup plotters was now politically irrelevant. In the days that followed, Yeltsin outlawed the CPSU (Communist Party of the Soviet Union) in the territory of the Russian Republic and a few weeks later announced measures for the introduction of a full-fledged market economy. The Baltic states seceded from the Soviet Union with the support of the international community, and Ukraine declared its independence in December. In the end, Gorbachev had no choice but to sign an understanding that recognized the fifteen republics of the USSR as sovereign nation-states. With this act, not only was Gorbachev out of power, but the Soviet Union was no more.

■ Conclusion

In seeking an explanation for the downfall of the USSR we can adduce an array of factors, from the crippling moral legacy and economic policies of communism to the personal shortcomings (or human decency) of Gorbachev. It is important to recognize, however, that many longer-term forces were also at play in bringing about the collapse. These forces have been the basic themes of modern Russian history.

The Challenge of the West

From the seventeenth century onward, Russia was forced to contend with Western technology, culture, and military power, all of which advanced while Russia stagnated under the weight of an autocratic system that stifled social and economic dynamism. Periodically, the autocracy sought to create the conditions for that dynamism by introducing reforms based on the adaptation of Western political or economic models. But the resulting transformations produced hostile resistance to change, often from within the regime itself, resistance born either of nationalist pride or fear of the instability that would result from a disrupted mode of day-to-day existence. Attempts to slow the process, however, led to political strife as Westernization was also readily accepted by influential segments of the population that did not want to see the clock stopped.

This was the situation that resulted from the modernizing Great Reforms of Alexander II, which gave birth to a society that could not happily coexist with the tsarist autocracy. It would not be correct to argue that the subsequent Russian Revolution was inevitable, but it is fair to say that the need to borrow from the West created as much potential for weakening the state's position as for strengthening it. The pattern was repeated in Gorbachev's USSR: the successes of the Soviets' capitalist competitors forced the adoption of reforms that brought about the rapid downfall of the regime, whose authoritarianism, party oligarchy, and command economy were short-circuited by the introduction of Western-style electoral politics and civil freedoms.

An Overdeveloped Central State

The gradual evolution of an overdeveloped central state whose leader introduces sudden, sweeping, lurching reform from above also played a part in the eventual collapse of the USSR. This trait stemmed from the ruler's monopoly of political power and the converse weakness of civil society: it was the tsar or Communist Party leader who made the decision to reform or not to reform. Society was not often able to take the initiative on its own or allowed to have input into the deliberation process. Mainly out of concern for the domestic and international standing of the autocracy, the central government would whip up a whirlwind of reform legislation that would then blow disruptively across the land.

In this regard the Gorbachev era was similar to those of Peter the Great, Alexander II, and Khrushchev. Whereas Peter the Great and Alexander II by and large accomplished what they set out to do in their own times, their initiatives disquieted the nation and set in motion changes that in the long run helped to bring down the monarchy. For his part, Khrushchev gave a good shaking to the Soviet system. His removal from office was followed by the termination of his populist approach to leadership, but even his conservative successors could not put a lid on society's discontentment by restoring the full-strength Stalinism he had succeeded in diluting. Gorbachev was more successful than Khrushchev at ramming his agenda through the party. *Perestroika* and *glasnost* entailed a greater break with Leninism than Gorbachev seemed to realize, however, the unintended consequence of which was the dismantling of the Soviet Union.

The Centrifugal Tendencies of the Periphery

Heightened ethnic-nationalist tensions weakened both the tsarist and Soviet empires. In each of these historical epochs we see a desire for regional autonomy or independence that the central government fights against or appeases but cannot fully suppress. The flexible tactic of co-optation of ethnic elites held the empire together along with periodic displays of repressive violence, but when the threat of force was removed, as in 1917 with the discrediting of the tsardom and again under Gorbachev in the late 1980s, separatism grew apace and the empire unraveled.

A Privileged and Often Corrupt Administrative Elite

The powers granted to tsarist *pomeshchiki,* imperial bureaucrats, or Soviet *apparatchiki* in their respective historical eras were essential to the governance of a geographically immense realm where state finances, means of communication, and local political institutions were all lacking. Acting as the arm of the autocratic state, their power was absolute and they often considered themselves above the law. Graft and a proclivity to exploit the populace were conspicuous among them (in all periods one could find upstanding and well-meaning officials, but their labors were negated by the heavy-handed and self-serving actions of their colleagues). For these reasons, local affairs were often badly administered, which provoked popular resentment against the government. Complicating matters further, officials did not always carry out the orders of the central authorities, who were, after all, far away, but dragged their feet or acted on behalf of a variety of regional, local, or personal interests. For all their defects, however, the nation could not do without them. When they withdrew their allegiance to the central government or their powers were curtailed, as in early 1917 and in the late 1980s, the institutional fragility of the political system became strikingly clear.

The Resentments and
Unfulfilled Longings of the Masses

Overburdened, oppressed, exploited, or simply disregarded, the masses were often deeply unsatisfied with their lot and with the existing order. Denied a legitimate means of seeking redress for their grievances within the existing political system, some became apathetic and others gave vent to their frustrations through subtle forms of resistance. Periodically, they engaged in violent revolt. Although censorship often kept them ill-informed of the real causes of their condition, it did not keep them from turning on the government. In late Soviet as in late imperial times the urbanized and educated masses were becoming aware of conditions in the rest of the world and unfavorable comparisons to life in Russia. The government's failure to provide adequate mechanisms for political participation, social mobility, and consumerism, all essential features of successful modern societies, lay at the heart of the erosion and eventual withdrawal of popular support for both the tsarist and communist regimes.

Geography

Russia is one of many resource-rich but poverty-stricken nations in the world. At least until recent times, the cost of extraction has been high, as many of its mineral resources are located in forbidding conditions on the territory's periphery. Awareness of that wealth also served as an excuse for a lack of fiscal and economic discipline, as for instance under Brezhnev. In the Stalin era, the temptation was to utilize slave labor as a cost-saving measure and as a shortcut compensating for an inadequate labor force in the Soviet far north and east. Under Witte's economic management, the late imperial government resorted to massive deficit financing to build a transcontinental, Siberian railroad network to facilitate the center's exploitation of Russia's distant Asian territories. In all three cases, despite the political differences between the regimes, the state's immediate interests prevailed over those of the populace. Under Alexander III and Nicholas II, as well as under Stalin, Khrushchev, and Brezhnev, investment in remote and underpopulated regions often meant lost opportunities for the vast majority of citizens resident in central Russia (with regard to energy resources, Soviet-era subsidies kept the price artificially low for consumers, but the inflow of petrodollars in the 1970s did not improve the overall standard of living; it remains to be seen whether the post-Soviet oil and gas boom will bring long-term benefits). Add to that the cost of defending a nation that covered one-seventh of the globe's landmass, and one begins to comprehend the burden that geography placed on Russian history. Modern technology and integration into the global economy may lessen that burden, but all in all, geography has made it difficult for the government to satisfy the basic needs of its people and ensured that Russia, if for fiscal reasons alone, would often lag behind its Western competitors, forcing the kinds of massive catch-up efforts that brought calamity to the political system.

Defects in the Procedures for Political Succession and Idiosyncratic Personalities of the Rulers

In the history of Russian politics, succession to the leadership was based on one of the following: familial relationship to the tsar, seizure of power, under-the-table manipulation of the bureaucracy, or undemocratic selection by an oligarchic elite. None of these methods are conducive to building stable and successful nation-states. The impact of the leader's personality was magnified by the often arbitrary exercise of absolute power, which was uncontrolled in a system lacking a historically autonomous society or institutional checks and balances, among them a fully independent judiciary. To the detriment of the nation, policy decisions by the rulers were rarely subjected to publicly aired national debate and criticism. Even deliberation by higher ranking officials was not always tolerated.

Thus, ruthless, indecisive, incompetent, or utopian rulers have been common in Russian history, unhindered from adopting policies that impoverished or oppressed or simply did not accord with the wishes of the country at large. In different ways this was true of the reactionaries Nicholas II and Brezhnev, the martinet Nicholas I, the transformer-tyrants Peter the Great, Lenin, and Stalin, and the mercurial Khrushchev, but even relatively benign figures like Catherine the Great, Alexander I, Alexander II, and Gorbachev. Democratic elections do not guarantee the selection of an ideal leader, but there is no doubt that without constitutionally agreed-upon procedures for replacing the ruler, the likelihood of winding up with someone who would help run the country and the political system into the ground is rather high.

To what degree these seven major determinants of Russia's past will remain relevant in the future is the vital question.

*   *   *

Check Out Receipt

Westminster Branch Library (WEC)
410-386-4490
http://library.carr.org
Friday, March 18, 2011 11:06:47 AM

TERVALA, DEBRA J

Item: 00000009660556
Title: Understanding contemporary Russi
a
Due: 4/8/2011

Total Items: 1

Thank You!

Figure 3.1 Chronology, 750–1991

Kievan Rus, 750–1240

ca. 860–880 Founding of Riurikid dynasty by Swedish Varangians
ca. 988 Conversion of Prince Vladimir to Orthodox Christianity
1237–1240 Mongol conquest of Rus

Mongol Rule, 1237–1400

ca. 1242 Formation of Qipchak Khanate (Tatar Golden Horde)
1325–1341 Reign of Muscovite Prince Ivan I "Kalita" (Moneybag)
1326 Moscow becomes residence of Orthodox Metropolitan
1367–1368 Construction of Moscow Kremlin

Muscovy, 1400–1700

1450s Russian Orthodox Church independent of Constantinople
1462–1505 Reign of Ivan III
1477 Muscovite conquest of Novgorod
1480s–1490s Breakup of Golden Horde
1505–1533 Reign of Vasili III
1510 Muscovite conquest of Pskov
1533–1584 Reign of Ivan IV, the Terrible
1552 Muscovite conquest of Kazan
1581 Muscovite government imposes first restrictions on peasant mobility
1581–1639 Muscovite conquest of Siberia
1589 Moscow becomes an Orthodox Patriarchate
1598–1613 Time of Troubles
1613 Founding of Romanov dynasty
1613–1645 Reign of Mikhail Romanov
1645–1676 Reign of Alexei
1650s–1660s Muscovy acquires Kiev
1670–1671 Stenka Razin Rebellion

Peter the Great and the Birth of Imperial Russia, 1682–1725

1682–1725 Reign of Peter I, the Great
1697–1698 Peter the Great visits Europe
1700–1721 Great Northern War
1703 Peter founds St. Petersburg
1716–1717 Peter's second trip to Europe
1725 Peter founds the Academy of Sciences

The Age of Women Rulers, 1725–1796

1725–1727 Reign of Catherine I
1730–1740 Reign of Anna
1741–1761 Reign of Elizabeth

Figure 3.1 continued

1755 University of Moscow founded
1757 Academy of Arts founded
1761–1762 Reign of Peter III
1762 Peter III frees *dvorianstvo* from obligatory state service
1762–1796 Reign of Catherine II, the Great
1768–1774, 1787–1792 Wars with Ottoman empire
1772, 1793, 1795 Partitions of Poland
1773–1775 Pugachev Rebellion
1785 Charter of Nobility
1796–1801 Reign of Paul

Absolutism and Its Discontents, 1801–1855

1801–1825 Reign of Alexander I
1802 Beginning of Russian conquest of the Caucasus
1809 Russia acquires Finland
1812 Napoleonic invasion of Russia
1815 Russia acquires central Poland
1825 Decembrist revolt
1825–1855 Reign of Nicholas I
1826 Establishment of Third Department
1830 Codification of laws
1830–1831 Polish uprising
1835 Founding of Imperial School of Jurisprudence
1853–1856 Crimean War

Reform and Reaction, 1855–1904

1855–1881 Reign of Alexander II
1858–1860 Acquisition of Russian Far East
February 19, 1861 Emancipation of serfs
1863 Polish uprising
1864 Legal reforms
1864 Introduction of *zemstvos*
1864–1880 Conquest of Turkestan
1874 Military reforms
1877–1878 Russo-Turkish War
1881 People's Will assassinates Alexander II
1881–1894 Reign of Alexander III
1891 Construction of Trans-Siberian Railroad begins
1892 Franco-Russian alliance
1892–1903 Ministry of Finance under Sergei Witte
1894–1917 Reign of Nicholas II
1903 Lenin founds Bolshevik Party
1904–1905 Russo-Japanese War

The Revolutionary Era, 1905–1923

1905–1906 1905 Revolution
1905 October Manifesto
1906–1915 Duma era
1906 Stolypin's agrarian reforms
1907 Anglo-Russian entente
1914–1918 World War I
1916 Assassination of Rasputin
February 1917 February Revolution, abdication of tsar, formation of
  Provisional Government
October 1917 Bolshevik seizure of power
1917–1922 Civil war
1917 Creation of Soviet secret police
1918 Moscow becomes Soviet capital
1918 Murder of royal family
1921–1922 Famine
1921 New Economic Policy
1922 Formation of the Union of Soviet Socialist Republics (USSR)

Stalinism, 1924–1953

1924 Death of Lenin
1924–1953 Stalin era
1928 End of NEP and introduction of first Five-Year Plan
1929 Introduction of collectivization and *dekulakization*
1932–1934 Famine
1936–1938 Great Terror
1939 Nazi-Soviet Non-Aggression Pact
1940 Assassination of Trotsky
June 22, 1941 Nazi invasion of the USSR
1941–1944 Siege of Leningrad
1942–1943 Battle of Stalingrad
May 9, 1945 Surrender of Nazi Germany
1946 Famine
1948–1949 Berlin blockade
1949 USSR tests atomic bomb
1953 Death of Stalin

Hope, Apathy, and Decline, 1953–1991

1953–1964 Khrushchev era
1954 Introduction of Virgin Lands campaign
1956 Secret Speech and beginning of de-Stalinization
1956 Hungarian uprising
1957 *Sputnik 1*
1959–1960 Sino-Soviet split
1961 Berlin Wall

Figure 3.1 continued

1962 Cuban Missile Crisis
1962 Novocherkassk riots
1964–1982 Brezhnev era
1968 Prague spring
1979 Soviet invasion of Afghanistan
1982–1984 Andropov
1984–1985 Chernenko
1985–1991 Gorbachev era
1986 Chernobyl nuclear explosion
1989 Soviet withdrawal from Afghanistan
1989 Fall of Berlin Wall
1990 End of political monopoly of Soviet Communist Party
June 1991 Boris Yeltsin elected president of Russian Republic
August 1991 Failed hard-line coup attempt
December 1991 Dissolution of the USSR

▪ Note

The author would like to thank David Goldfrank, Valerie Kivelson, and Aviel Roshwald for their comments on segments of this chapter.

▪ Bibliography

Alexander, John T. 1989. *Catherine the Great: Life and Legend.* New York: Oxford University Press.
Applebaum, Anne. 2003. *Gulag: A History.* New York: Doubleday.
Bayly, C. A. 2004. *The Birth of the Modern World, 1780–1914.* Malden, MA: Blackwell.
Brandenburger, David. 2002. *National Bolshevism: Stalinist Mass Culture and the Formation of Modern Russian National Identity, 1931–1956.* Cambridge, MA: Harvard University Press.
Breslauer, George. 1982. *Khrushchev and Brezhnev as Leaders.* London: Allen and Unwin.
———. 2002. *Gorbachev and Yeltsin as Leaders.* Cambridge, UK: Cambridge University Press.
Brooks, Jeffrey. 1985. *When Russia Learned to Read: Literacy and Popular Literature, 1861–1917.* Princeton, NJ: Princeton University Press.
———. 2000. *Thank You Comrade Stalin! Soviet Public Culture from Revolution to Cold War.* Princeton, NJ: Princeton University Press.
Brown, Archie. 1996. *The Gorbachev Factor.* Oxford, UK: Oxford University Press.
Buck, Trevor, and John Cole. 1987. *Modern Soviet Economic Performance.* Oxford, UK: Basil Blackwell.

Bushkovitch, Paul. 2001a. *Peter the Great.* Cambridge, UK: Cambridge University Press.

———. 2001b. *Peter the Great.* Lanham, MD: Rowman and Littlefield.

Chuev, Feliks. 1993. *Molotov Remembers.* Chicago: Ivan Dee.

Clowes, Edith W., Samuel D. Kassow, and James L. West, eds. 1991. *Between Tsar and People: Educated Society and the Quest for Public Identity in Late Imperial Russia.* Princeton, NJ: Princeton University Press.

Conquest, Robert. 1990. *The Great Terror: A Reassessment.* New York: Oxford University Press.

Cracraft, James. 1988. "Opposition to Peter the Great." In *Imperial Russia, 1700–1917: State, Society, Opposition.* Ed. Ezra Mendelsohn and Marshall S. Shatz. DeKalb: Northern Illinois University Press.

———. 2003. *The Revolution of Peter the Great.* Cambridge, MA: Harvard University Press.

Daly, Jonathan. 1995. "On the Significance of Emergency Legislation in Late Imperial Russia." *Slavic Review* 54(3): 602–629.

Desai, Padma. 1987. *The Soviet Economy.* Oxford, UK: Basil Blackwell.

Dixon, Simon. 1999. *The Modernisation of Russia, 1676–1825.* Cambridge, UK: Cambridge University Press.

———. 2001. *Catherine the Great.* Harlow, UK: Longman.

Engel, Barbara Alpern. 2004. *Women in Russia, 1700–2000.* Cambridge, UK: Cambridge University Press.

Evtuhov, Catherine, David Goldfrank, Lindsey Hughes, and Richard Stites. 2004. *A History of Russia: Peoples, Legends, Events, Forces.* Boston: Houghton Mifflin.

Falkus, M. E. 1972. *The Industrialisation of Russia, 1700–1914.* London: Macmillan.

Figes, Orlando. 1997. *A People's Tragedy: A History of the Russian Revolution.* New York: Viking.

Fitzpatrick, Sheila. 1994. *Stalin's Peasants: Resistance and Survival in the Russian Village After Collectivization.* New York: Oxford University Press.

———. 1999. *Everyday Stalinism: Ordinary life in Extraordinary Times: Soviet Russia in the 1930s.* New York: Oxford University Press.

———. 2005. *Tear Off the Masks! Identity and Imposture in Twentieth-Century Russia.* Princeton, NJ: Princeton University Press.

Fitzpatrick, Sheila, Alexander Rabinowitch, and Richard Stites, eds. 1991. *Russia in the Era of NEP: Explorations in Soviet Society and Culture.* Bloomington: Indiana University Press.

Forsyth, James. 1992. *A History of the Peoples of Siberia: Russia's North Asian Colony, 1581–1990.* Cambridge, UK: Cambridge University Press.

Franklin, Simon. 2001. "Pre-Mongol Rus': New Sources, New Perspectives?" *Russian Review* 60(4): 465–473.

Franklin, Simon, and Jonathan Shepard. 1996. *The Emergence of Rus, 750–1200.* London: Longman.

Gleason, Abbott, Peter Kenez, and Richard Stites, eds. 1985. *Bolshevik Culture: Experiment and Order in the Russian Revolution.* Bloomington: Indiana University Press.

Goldman, Marshall I. 1991. *What Went Wrong with Perestroika.* New York: Norton.

Gorodetsky, Gabriel. 1999. *Grand Delusion: Stalin and the German Invasion of Russia.* New Haven, CT: Yale University Press.

Gregory, Paul. 1994. *Before Command: An Economic History of Russia from Emancipation to the First Five-Year Plan.* Princeton, NJ: Princeton University Press.

———. 2004. *The Political Economy of Stalinism: Evidence from the Soviet Secret Archives.* Cambridge, UK: Cambridge University Press.

Gross, Jan T. 1988. *Revolution from Abroad: The Soviet Conquest of Poland's Western Ukraine and Western Belorussia.* Princeton, NJ: Princeton University Press.

Halperin, Charles J. 2002. "Muscovy as a Hypertrophic State: A Critique." *Kritika* 3(3): 501–507.

Hamerow, Theodore S. 1983. *The Birth of a New Europe: State and Society in the Nineteenth Century.* Chapel Hill: University of North Carolina Press.

Heller, Mikhail, and Aleksandr M. Nekrich. 1986. *Utopia in Power: The History of the Soviet Union from 1917 to the Present.* Trans. Phyllis B. Carlos. New York: Summit Books.

Hellie, Richard. 1999. *The Economy and Material Culture of Russia, 1600–1725.* Chicago: University of Chicago Press.

Hoffmann, David L. 2003. *Stalinist Values: The Cultural Norms of Soviet Modernity, 1917–1941.* Ithaca, NY: Cornell University Press.

Holquist, Peter. 2002. *Making War, Forging Revolution: Russia's Continuum of Crisis, 1914–1921.* Cambridge, MA: Harvard University Press.

———. 2003. "Violent Russia, Deadly Marxism?" *Kritika* 4(3): 627–652.

Hosking, Geoffrey. 1973. *The Russian Constitutional Experiment: Government and Duma, 1907–1914.* Cambridge, UK: Cambridge University Press.

———. 2001. *Russia and the Russians: A History.* Cambridge, MA: Harvard University Press.

Hughes, James. 1996. *Stalinism in a Russian Province: A Study of Collectivization and Dekulakization in Siberia.* New York: St. Martin's.

Hughes, Lindsey. 1998. *Russia in the Age of Peter the Great.* New Haven, CT: Yale University Press.

Kaiser, Robert G. 1991. *Why Gorbachev Happened.* New York: Simon and Schuster.

Kappeler, Andreas. 2001. *The Russian Empire: A Multiethnic History.* Trans. Alfred Clayton. Harlow, UK: Pearson Education.

Keep, John. 1995. *A History of the Soviet Union, 1945–1991: Last of the Empires.* Oxford, UK: Oxford University Press.

Kershaw, Ian, and Moshe Lewin, eds. 1997. *Stalinism and Nazism: Dictatorships in Comparison.* Cambridge, UK: Cambridge University Press.

Khlevniuk, Oleg V. 2004. *The History of the Gulag: From Collectivization to the Great Terror.* New Haven, CT: Yale University Press.

Kivelson, Valerie A. 1996. *Autocracy in the Provinces: The Muscovite Gentry and Political Culture in the Seventeenth Century.* Stanford, CA: Stanford University Press.

———. 2002. "On Words, Sources, and Historical Method: Which Truth About Muscovy?" *Kritika* 3(3): 487–500.

Koenker, Diane, William G. Rosenberg, and Ronald Grigor Suny, eds. 1989. *Party, State, and Society in the Russian Civil War: Explorations in Social History.* Bloomington: Indiana University Press.

Kolchin, Peter. 1987. *Unfree Labor: American Slavery and Russian Serfdom.* Cambridge, MA: Harvard University Press.

Kollmann, Nancy Shields. 1987. *Kinship and Politics: The Making of the Muscovite Political System, 1345–1547.* Stanford, CA: Stanford University Press.

———. 1997. "Muscovite Russia, 1450–1598." In *Russia: A History,* ed. Gregory L. Freeze. Oxford, UK: Oxford University Press.

Kotkin, Stephen. 1991. *Steeltown, USSR: Soviet Society in the Gorbachev Era.* Berkeley: University of California Press.

———. 1995. *Magnetic Mountain: Stalinism as a Civilization.* Berkeley: University of California Press.

———. 2001. *Armageddon Averted: The Soviet Collapse, 1970–2000*. Oxford, UK: Oxford University Press.

Kuromiya, Hiroaki. 2005. *Stalin*. Harlow, UK: Pearson.

Lenin, V. I. 1965. *Collected Works*. Vol. 33. Moscow: Progress.

Lieven, Dominic. 1994. *Nicholas II: Twilight of the Empire*. New York: St. Martin's Press.

Malia, Martin. 1994. *The Soviet Tragedy: A History of Socialism in Russia, 1917–1991*. New York: Free Press.

Marks, Steven G. 1991. *Road to Power: The Trans-Siberian Railroad and the Colonization of Asian Russia, 1850–1917*. Ithaca, NY: Cornell University Press.

———. 2003. *How Russia Shaped the Modern World: From Art to Anti-Semitism, Ballet to Bolshevism*. Princeton, NJ: Princeton University Press.

Marrese, Michelle Lamarche. 2002. *A Woman's Kingdom: Noblewomen and the Control of Property in Russia, 1700–1861*. Ithaca, NY: Cornell University Press.

Martin, Janet. 1995. *Medieval Russia, 980–1584*. Cambridge, UK: Cambridge University Press.

Martin, Terry. 2001. *The Affirmative Action Empire: Nations and Nationalism in the Soviet Union, 1923–1939*. Ithaca, NY: Cornell University Press.

Matthews, Mervyn. 1986. *Poverty in the Soviet Union*. Cambridge, UK: Cambridge University Press.

Medvedev, Zhores A. 1988. *Gorbachev*. Oxford, UK: Blackwell.

Merridale, Catherine. 2001. *Night of Stone: Death and Memory in Twentieth-Century Russia*. New York: Viking.

———. 2006. *Ivan's War: Life and Death in the Red Army, 1939–1945*. New York: Metropolitan Books.

Mironov, Boris N. 1991. "Les villes de Russie entre l'Occident et l'Orient (1750–1850)" [The cities of Russia between the West and the East (1750–1850)]. *Annales* 46(3): 705–733.

———. 2000. *The Social History of Imperial Russia, 1700–1917*. 2 vols. Boulder, CO: Westview Press.

Montefiore, Simon Sebag. 2004. *Stalin: The Court of the Red Tsar.* New York: Knopf.

Moon, David. 1999a. "The Problem of Social Stability in Russia, 1598–1998." In *Reinterpreting Russia*, ed. Geoffrey Hosking and Robert Service. London: Arnold.

———. 1999b. *The Russian Peasantry, 1600–1930: The World the Peasants Made*. London: Longman.

———. 2001. *The Abolition of Serfdom in Russia*. Harlow, UK: Longman.

Ostrowski, Donald G. 1998. *Muscovy and the Mongols: Cross-Cultural Influences on the Steppe Frontier, 1304–1589*. Cambridge, UK: Cambridge University Press.

Overy, R. J. 1998. *Russia's War.* New York: Penguin Books.

Owen, Thomas C. 1991. *The Corporation Under Russian Law, 1800–1917*. Cambridge, UK: Cambridge University Press.

Pipes, Richard. 1974. *Russia Under the Old Regime*. London: Weidenfeld and Nicolson.

———. 1990. *The Russian Revolution*. New York: Knopf.

———. 1993. *Russia Under the Bolshevik Regime*. New York: Knopf.

———. 2005. *Russian Conservatism and Its Critics: A Study in Political Culture*. New Haven, CT: Yale University Press.

Poe, Marshall. 2002. "The Truth About Muscovy." *Kritika* 3(3): 473–486.

———. 2003. *The Russian Moment in World History.* Princeton, NJ: Princeton University Press.

Raeff, Marc. 1983. *The Well-Ordered Police State: Social and Institutional Change Through Law in the Germanies and Russia, 1600–1800*. New Haven, CT: Yale

University Press.

Raleigh, Donald J. 2002. *Experiencing Russia's Civil War: Politics, Society, and Revolutionary Culture in Saratov, 1917–1922.* Princeton, NJ: Princeton University Press.

Rieber, Alfred. 2001. "Stalin, Man of the Borderlands." *American Historical Review* 106(5): 1651–1692.

Rogger, Hans. 1983. *Russia in the Age of Modernisation and Revolution, 1881–1917.* London: Longman.

Saunders, David. 1992. *Russia in the Age of Reaction and Reform.* London: Longman.

Scott, John. 1942. *Behind the Urals: An American Worker in Russia's City of Steel.* Boston: Houghton Mifflin.

Service, Robert. 1995. *Lenin: A Political Life.* Vol. 3. Bloomington: Indiana University Press.

———. 1997. *A History of Twentieth-Century Russia.* Cambridge, MA: Harvard University Press.

———. 2000. *Lenin: A Biography.* Cambridge, MA: Harvard University Press.

Slezkine, Yuri. 1994. *Arctic Mirrors: Russia and the Small Peoples of the North.* Ithaca, NY: Cornell University Press.

Solzhenitsyn, Aleksandr I. 1974–1978. *The Gulag Archipelago, 1918–1956.* 3 vols. Trans. Thomas P. Whitney. New York: Harper and Row.

Stites, Richard. 1989. *Revolutionary Dreams: Utopian Vision and Experimental Life in the Russian Revolution.* New York: Oxford University Press.

———. 1992. *Russian Popular Culture: Entertainment and Society Since 1900.* Cambridge, UK: Cambridge University Press.

———. 2005. *Serfdom, Society, and the Arts in Imperial Russia: The Pleasure and the Power.* New Haven, CT: Yale University Press.

Swain, Geoffrey. 2006. *Trotsky.* Harlow, UK: Pearson.

Taubman, William. 2003. *Khrushchev: The Man and His Era.* New York: Norton.

Tucker, Robert C. 1981–1982. "Swollen State, Spent Society: Stalin's Legacy to Brezhnev's Russia." *Foreign Affairs* 60(2): 414–435.

Viola, Lynne. 2007. *The Unknown Gulag: The Lost World of Stalin's Special Settlements.* Oxford, UK: Oxford University Press.

Volkogonov, Dmitrii. 1991. *Stalin: Triumph and Tragedy.* New York: Grove Weidenfeld.

———. 1994. *Lenin: A New Biography.* New York: Free Press.

Werth, Nicolas. 2007. *Cannibal Island: Death in a Siberian Gulag.* Princeton, NJ: Princeton University Press.

Wortman, Richard S. 1995 and 2000. *Scenarios of Power: Myth and Ceremony in Russian Monarchy.* 2 vols. Princeton, NJ: Princeton University Press.

Zubkova, Elena. 1998. *Russia After the War: Hopes, Illusions, and Disappointments, 1945–1957.* Trans. Hugh Ragsdale. Armonk, NY: M. E. Sharpe.

4

Politics

Michael L. Bressler

Contemporary Russia is caught between two worlds. One, oppressive and autocratic, is anchored in the country's tsarist and Soviet pasts. The other, liberal and democratic, provides an alternative vision of Russia's future that is based on radically different conceptions of leadership, legitimacy, and accountability. This conflict between old and new lies at the very heart of contemporary Russian politics. As we know from Steven Marks in Chapter 3, this is not the first time that Russia has wrestled with the question of political change. For the country's leaders, political transformation brings with it not only great hopes of a vibrant, modernized Russia but also great fears of a society falling into chaos if the process of change is not carefully controlled.

After the Soviet Union's collapse in 1991, many who studied that country were hopeful that Russia would break free from its autocratic moorings and chart a democratic course. Such hopes were disappointed, however, by the inept and erratic leadership of Russia's first democratically elected president, Boris Yeltsin, and by the centralizing policies of his successor, Vladimir Putin. If Yeltsin's actions were often a source of frustration for those who followed events in Russia, Putin's were frequently a cause for alarm. Even as Putin declared in his 2005 annual address to the Federal Assembly that he "consider[ed] the development of Russia as a free and democratic state to be our main political and ideological goal," his policies seemed to suggest otherwise.

Indeed, in a Freedom House report issued a few months before Putin's speech, Russia was the only country in the world that was downgraded from "partly free" to "not free" status (Puddington and Piano 2005). On almost every Freedom House measure (electoral process, civil society, independent media, governance, judicial framework, and independence), Russia's 2005 ratings were markedly lower than those of 1999, the year before Putin came to power. On only one measure, corruption, was the decline not so dramatic (Orttung 2006). To some observers, Putin's policies smacked of a Soviet-style revival. Although some aspects of today's Russia do resemble the Soviet past, a complete return to Soviet-era practices is unlikely. At the same time, the prospects for the eventual consolidation of democracy in Russia are distant at best.

This chapter examines some of the reasons why Russia has struggled in the development of democracy in the years since the end of Soviet rule. Of special interest is how post-Soviet Russia's first two leaders, Boris Yeltsin and Vladimir Putin, understood the nature of change, and how the institutional and policy choices they made have influenced the course of Russia's political development. As a counterpoint to this discussion, the chapter also reviews recent findings on Russian mass attitudes toward democracy. Because the question of democracy looms so large in any discussion of contemporary Russian politics, the chapter begins with a brief discussion of what democracy is and an explanation of some of the factors that are critical to its development.

◾ Concepts: Democracy, the State, and Institutions

Simply defined, democracy is a form of government in which public office holders have gained the right to govern through regular, competitive elections. Although elections are a necessary element of democracy, many scholars argue that elections alone do not mean that a political system is in fact democratic. Larry Diamond, for one, draws a sharp distinction between "electoral" and "liberal" democracies (1999, 8–12). In electoral democracies, the simple definition applies. In liberal systems, however, the definition of democracy is much more complex. In liberal polities the rule of law is supreme, the judiciary is independent, and civil society is vibrant. The legal system defends the civil rights and civil liberties of the people, and the constitution contains sturdy and effective checks on executive power. In liberal democracies, too, "no group that adheres to constitutional principles is denied the right to form a party and contest elections" (Diamond 1999, 11).

One of the paradoxes of liberal democracy is that although the rule of law places strict limits on the power of the state, liberal democracy cannot survive without a strong state. Or, as Juan Linz (1997, 118) succinctly declares: "no state, no *Rechtsstaat* [a rule-of-law-based state], no democracy." The state is preeminent among all other actors in the political system in that it alone has the authority to use force to defend the country's constitution and to enforce its laws. Without such enforcement on the part of the state the rule of law will be weakly and inconsistently defended, ensuring that any attempt at democratic development will be feeble at best and futile at worst. Thus, even if a country holds regular elections, absent *Rechtsstaat,* democracy is "incomplete" (Rose and Shin 2001). The problem is that creating a rule-of-law-based state out of dictatorship is not easy. It requires the crafting of institutions that will support the establishment of such a state and through this encourage the development of liberal democratic government.

In liberal polities institutional checks and balances play a vital role in the creation of a more level playing field in the political system. Placing strict limits on the powers of the executive branch is especially important as it is the best placed among the three branches of government to abuse its authority. The most effective checks on executive power are a strong legislature and an independent judiciary. Absent these checks the executive branch can exercise power unhindered by the rule of law. With this can come the violation of civil rights and civil liberties, the intimidation of legitimate political opposition, and interference in the work and development of civil society.

If checks on executive power are important in the development and maintenance of liberal democracy, so too is elite trust. Support for democratic government on the part of the masses alone is not enough to sustain democracy. If opposing elites cannot trust each other with political power the stability of the regime is undermined. This is not so much a question of elites trusting their opponents, as it is one of elites trusting their country's institutions to regulate and moderate politics. If opposing elites are in agreement on these basic rules of the game, and thus are willing to exercise mutual restraint, they will have little reason to fear one another (Higley and Burton 1989, 19). In terms of democratic development, if the new rules of the game prove their worth over time in managing and containing conflict, trust in the system will grow (Rustow 1970, 360).

In short, the institutional choices elites make play a critical role in a country's political development. In Russia's case, the country's first democratically elected leader, Boris Yeltsin, promised to transform Russia both politically and economically. Although Yeltsin had benefited a great deal from the support of Russia's prodemocracy movement in his rise to power in 1990 and 1991, the institutional choices he made during that period and in the years that followed have impeded, not promoted, Russia's democratic development.

◼ High Hopes and Harsh Realities: Post-Soviet Russia, 1991–1993

In the fall of 1991 Yeltsin had his work cut out for him. The good news for Yeltsin was that with the collapse of the August coup the Communist Party of the Soviet Union (CPSU) lost what legitimacy it had left. What might have been an orderly retreat for the party had Gorbachev been allowed to sign the Union Treaty, turned into a route when party reactionaries made their half-hearted grab for power. With Gorbachev also discredited in the process, Yeltsin found the opportunity he had been looking for to finish off the Soviet system once and for all and with this achieve Russia's full independence.

The Russian economy, however, was on the verge of collapse. Public euphoria in the cities over Yeltsin's victory and the party's defeat soon gave way to concerns over how people were going to survive the coming winter. Some even feared the possibility of famine (Gaidar 1999, 65–66; Aron 2000, 481–483). Yeltsin had other concerns, too. Now that he had an opportunity to transform Russia, he was troubled by the country's long history of partial reforms and unfinished revolutions. In Yeltsin's view, every previous attempt to transform the country had fallen far short of the mark. "In a certain sense," he wrote, "Peter the Great's reforms have not been achieved to this day." Not even seven decades of Soviet rule, he believed, had "changed anything fundamental in Russia" (Yeltsin 1994, 145). Although overstating his case, Yeltsin was correct on one important point: every attempt to transform the country from above had been met with stiff resistance from below.

In part out of fear that his own attempt to transform Russia would suffer a similar fate, Yeltsin believed he had no alternative but to take "determined action" before the most reactionary elements of the old system, in disarray following the August coup's defeat, could rally and respond. In this way he hoped to achieve what no Russian tsar or Soviet leader had accomplished: "to make reform irreversible" (Yeltsin 1994, 146). This would require, he believed, the adoption of a radical plan of economic transformation. It would also require breaking away from the Soviet Union.

Yeltsin's approach to policy during the fall of 1991 reveals much about how he and his advisers understood the nature of the challenges they faced. For his part, Yeltsin had no idea how to bring about the sweeping changes he sought. At the suggestion of an adviser, Yeltsin turned to a young, Russian free-market economist named Yegor Gaidar. Like Yeltsin, Gaidar believed that only decisive action could save Russia. As Gaidar wrote later (1999, 72), "At the end of 1991 there was no time to measure once, let alone twice—we had to cut, and we had to cut to the quick." Gaidar's plan, known as "shock therapy" (described in detail by James Millar in Chapter 5), called for the rapid transformation of Russia's economy. Although this radical turn toward free markets at first would be painful for the Russian people, Gaidar was convinced that his plan would begin to show positive results within a year. For Yeltsin, shock therapy's promise of relatively quick results through decisive action appealed to his own desire to chart a radical, irreversible course. Its appeal also lay in its demand that Russia strike out on its own economically, independent of the other Soviet republics. Doing so would mean the Soviet Union's certain demise.

In late October of 1991, two months after the failed August coup, Yeltsin put Gaidar's plan before the Russian Republic Congress of People's Deputies. Yeltsin also asked the congress to grant him emergency powers for one year, the time Gaidar thought it would take for his policies to establish firm roots. The congress approved both Gaidar's plan for economic transformation and Yeltsin's call for additional presidential powers. Yeltsin's interest in acquiring more power was political, not constitutional. Not trusting the congress to remain supportive of economic policies that promised to be both painful and unpopular, Yeltsin sought to marginalize the legislative branch through an expansion of presidential powers.

Although he had gained the free hand he wanted from the congress, Yeltsin and his advisers misjudged the meaning of the moment. The fundamental problem was that Russia's heavily amended constitution was rife with contradictions, especially concerning the division of powers between the executive and legislative branches. The original document, approved in 1978 during the Brezhnev era, was parliamentary in form. In 1990, following the example set at the all-union level, amendments to the constitution allowed for the creation of a new legislative body, the Russian Republic Congress of People's Deputies, whose members were chosen through relatively competitive elections. The congress, in turn, elected a smaller, more active legislative body, the Supreme Soviet. Although the basic framework of this reformed legislature differed greatly from that of its predecessor, the overall structure of the political system remained parliamentary in form. When, through a public referendum, the Russian Republic created an executive presidency in 1991, this new position, won by Yeltsin, was grafted onto the existing constitution. The purpose of this move was purely political: to strengthen Yeltsin and Russia in the struggle for power with Gorbachev and the Soviet system.

Neither Yeltsin nor the Congress of People's Deputies considered the constitutional implications of having created a system of dual power (*dvoevlastie*) based on a popularly elected executive president and a legislature that retained significant executive authority. Instead of being a parliamentary system (with the legislative and executive branches fused) or a presidential one (with the two branches separate), the Russian Republic was both. By not clearly delineating the lines of authority between the president and the parliament, conflict between the two was bound to occur.

In asking the congress for an expansion of his presidential powers, Yeltsin seemed not to recognize the ramifications of such a move. Instead, he and his closest advisers were reaffirming a long-held belief in Russian politics: to get anything done, an all-powerful executive would have to lead the way. If congress could rewrite the rules of the game at Yeltsin's urging, however, what was to prevent it from rewriting the rules again as it saw fit?

The lack of attention Yeltsin and his staff gave to such fundamental constitutional questions (and thus fundamental questions of power), combined with policies that, although approved by the congress, would be unpopular both in the country and in the legislature, set the stage for a bitter and ultimately debilitating conflict between Yeltsin's presidential administration and the parliament. In a system in which the boundaries of executive power were difficult to discern, Yeltsin unwittingly had placed himself on shaky constitutional ground. The institutional weaknesses of the system also reinforced the dominant elite view that politics was a zero-sum, winner-take-all game. Seemingly unaware of the potential consequences of what they had done, Yeltsin and his administration had made a compelling case for constitutional reform.

That Yeltsin and others had missed this, however, is not surprising. Up to that moment most of the political elite had defined the question of political transformation almost exclusively in terms of Russia's relationship with the Soviet state. Viewed in this way, constitutional reform meant the radical restructuring of the balance of power between the Russian and Soviet governments and had little to do with power relations within the Russian Republic. Attaining Russian sovereignty, not crafting a new constitution, had been the focus. Once Russia's sovereignty seemed assured with the collapse of the August 1991 coup, many of Russia's political elites, among them Yeltsin, his advisers, and a number of Russia's democrats, believed that the political revolution was over and that the most important constitutional question had been answered. To the extent that Yeltsin and his team thought at all about constitutional reform during the fall of 1991, the dominant view was that, given the state of the economy, creating a new political system would take time Russia did not have. Anything that delayed the launching of radical economic transformation would result in Russia's ruin (see Gaidar 1999, 114).

Yeltsin had always been a polarizing figure within Russia's political elite. Before his election as president, the Russian Congress of People's Deputies split along ideological lines between those who supported liberal political and economic transformation and those who did not. However, as long as the two sides had common foes in Gorbachev and the all-union government, they could get along. Absent such enemies following the defeat of the August 1991 coup, the left-right ideological rift that had characterized the first four congresses took on a new form as deputies turned their attention to the question of how much power Russia's president should have. The effect was to transform the legislature's left-right divide into a pro-Yeltsin, anti-Yeltsin one (Remington et al. 1994). The ensuing struggle for power between the executive and legislative branches, combined with the lack of elite consensus over the direction of economic policy, worked against any attempt to craft a new constitution.

To the extent that Yeltsin was concerned about constitutional questions, his interest was primarily instrumental. Only as relations with the legislature grew increasingly tense over the course of 1992 did he and his team give serious consideration to the question of political reform. Even then, Yeltsin's motivation had little to do with the country's long-term institutional health. Rather, constitutional reform would be yet another way for him to amass political power and outmaneuver the parliament. Such an approach reflected his understanding of the nature of Russian politics. In March 1993, as the two sides fought to limit each other's powers, Yeltsin explained his position:

> I am a proponent of strong presidential power in Russia. But not because I am the President. Rather, because I am convinced that without this Russia cannot survive and get on its feet. Above all, because the President is elected by the citizens of the entire state. He personifies its integrity, its unity. I emphasize: not the Congress, not the Supreme Soviet, not any other institution of government, but the President. I am speaking to you in the utmost candor. (Yeltsin 1993a)

In short, Yeltsin's conception of authority and accountability drew a direct line between the president and the people, bypassing the legislature.

The parliament would have none of Yeltsin's logic as each side continued to seek supremacy over the other. Finally, on September 21, 1993, Yeltsin moved to break the constitutional impasse by issuing a decree disbanding the Congress of People's Deputies and the Supreme Soviet. The decree, number 1400, also set a deadline for the submission of a draft constitution and a date for elections to a new legislative body. Yeltsin had no legal authority to issue such a decree but felt he had no other choice in the face of what he saw as the parliament's "irreconcilable opposition" (Yeltsin 1993b).

Predictably, the legislature and its leaders reacted negatively to Yeltsin's move, rejecting it out of hand. Within hours the Supreme Soviet impeached Yeltsin and swore in Vice President Alexander Rutskoi (an ardent opponent of Yeltsin's) as acting president. Less than two days later the Congress of People's Deputies convened at the Russian White House, the site of the congress's and the Supreme Soviet's sessions (Aron 2000, 522–523). At the same time, the legislature armed civilians and established a guard around the White House in preparation for a showdown with Yeltsin. In an ironic twist, this had been the scene of Yeltsin's stand against the August 1991 coup two years earlier. Confident they would win, the parliament rejected any efforts to bring the conflict to a peaceful end. Yeltsin, too, was in no mood to compromise. As the tension between the two sides mounted, violence broke out between rioting demonstrators and the police on October 2. The next day, armed opposition civilians and government forces fought a bloody pitched battle over control of Moscow's Ostankino television center. Finally, on the morning of October 4, the army, hesitant to get involved, fearing that it would be held responsible for any bloodshed, responded to

Now the seat of the Russian government,
the White House was the home of the Russian legislature
during the dramatic events of August 1991 and October 1993.

Yeltsin's call to send in tanks and open fire on the White House. By late afternoon, unable to defend itself in the face of such force, the parliament surrendered. Yeltsin had won (Shevtsova 1999, 84–86).

With the Congress of People's Deputies and the Supreme Soviet defeated, Yeltsin turned his attention to the completion and passage of a new constitution. This new document, written expressly for him, was designed to give Yeltsin a virtual free reign over politics. When put before the voters that December, a "weak majority" (58.4 percent) gave their assent (White, Rose, and McAllister 1997, 99).

■ The 1993 Constitution

The framers of the 1993 Constitution sought the creation of a political system that would heavily favor the presidency over the legislature. Forgoing the creation of a presidential system based on separation of powers or a parliamentary system in which the executive branch would be dependent on a legislative majority, the authors of this document opted for a mixed presidential-parliamentary (or semipresidential) structure.

The distinguishing features of a semipresidential system are a powerful, popularly elected president and a prime minister who serves at the pleasure of the parliament. At first glance, such a system seems to establish a strong legislature that can hold its own against the president. As it turns out, however, not all semipresidential systems are the same when it comes to the balance of power between the executive and legislative branches. Of the nine postcommunist countries that adopted semipresidential systems some have very strong legislatures (such as Lithuania), while others have quite weak ones (for example, Kazakhstan). Comparing the experiences of the postcommunist countries of the world, Fish (2005) finds that those with stronger legislatures are more democratic. Conversely, the stronger the president is in relation to the legislature, the less democratic the country will be. Such is the case with Russia.

The 1993 Constitution created a bicameral legislature, the Federal Assembly. The lower house, the State Duma, has 450 members, half of whom, according to federal law, were elected from single-member districts. The other half were elected by means of party lists through proportional representation (PR). To qualify for seats on the PR side of the ballot, a party or bloc had to receive at least 5 percent of the party list vote. The upper house, the Federation Council, had 178 members, with two representatives from each of the country's original 89 "subjects," or regions.[1]

For the most part, the 1993 Constitution favors the executive over the legislative branch. With respect to the selection of the prime minister, for instance, while the Duma may have the sole authority to accept or reject the president's nominee, the president has the power to dissolve the Duma and call for new legislative elections if it rebuffs his choice of candidates three times. Furthermore, although the Duma has the right to a vote of no confidence in the prime minister and the cabinet, the president has the privilege of ignoring the Duma's opinion, thus keeping the government in office. This is in stark contrast to parliamentary systems where a vote of no confidence almost always results in the government's resignation. If the Duma votes no confidence in the government for a second time within three months, the president has two options: announce the government's resignation or dissolve the Duma.

Although the formal rules of the game allow the president to disband the Duma with relative ease, the complex process through which the president may be impeached ensures the near impossibility of such an outcome. Not only must the legislature's upper house, the Federation Council, vote by a two-thirds majority to impeach the president on the basis of charges put forward by a two-thirds majority of the Duma, the validity of the charges must be confirmed by the highest court of appeal, the Supreme Court, and the validity of the process of leveling these charges must be confirmed by yet another body, the Constitutional Court. As if these requirements were not enough, the entire process must take place within three months. Otherwise, the accusations brought forth by the Duma against the president will be dropped.

The seat of Russian presidential power, the Moscow Kremlin.

The constitution also gives the president broad powers to legislate by decree, which gives him the legal authority to encroach on the prerogatives of the legislature. Although no decree may be at odds with the federal constitution or federal law, two factors during the 1990s enhanced Yeltsin's powers to rule by decree: first, federal laws of this period were frequently silent on pressing issues of the day (on property rights, for instance), and second, many of these laws were of questionable legitimacy as holdovers of the Soviet era. This expanded authority boded ill for the advancement of democracy in Russia as it gave Yeltsin "little incentive to nurture the development of parties or parliament" (Huskey 1999, 164, 177). Instead, he sought to free himself as much as possible from the constraining influences of both.

As much as the constitution favors the president, it does not make him omnipotent. Indeed, a number of its provisions grant powers to the Federal Assembly that at times have made the Duma and the Federation Council forces to be reckoned with, limiting what the president may accomplish on his own. For instance, even though the prime minister and the cabinet are responsible for preparing the federal budget, it may not enter into law without the approval of both houses of the Federal Assembly. Furthermore, even though provisions in the constitution for the nomination and approval of candidates for prime minister generally support the president, circumstances may not always work to the president's advantage. On one notable occasion, in the midst of a deep economic crisis during the late summer of 1998,

Yeltsin was forced to back down in a dispute with the Duma over his choice of prime minister.

Despite these limits, the overall balance of power benefits the president. By placing so much power in the president's hands the 1993 Constitution essentially negates an essential element of semipresidentialism, the legislature's ability to check the power of the executive branch (Fish 2005).[2] Semipresidential in name, the Russian political system is "superpresidential" in reality.

The implications of such a constitutional choice are great. In the absence of strong legislative and judicial checks on executive authority, there is little to prevent members of the presidential administration or the federal bureaucracy from using their positions of power to enrich themselves personally or to launch politically inspired attacks against their opponents. Paradoxically, formal rules that invest great powers in the presidency are sources of institutional weakness. Facing an executive branch riddled with corruption, even a well-meaning, reform-minded president will find that there are limits to what he or she can accomplish. Corrupt officials and bureaucrats look out for their own interests not those of the state or the public. The result is a weak, incompetent state that is hard pressed to carry out policies designed to promote the country's political, social, and economic development.

Ultimately, the only way to reform such a system is to mobilize the public. Huskey and Obolonsky (2003, 32) observe that "in open societies, vigorous public debate and pressure from below, exercised by parties, groups, and citizens, combine with leadership from above to ensure the remaking of the state." The only reliable way for parties, groups, and citizens to have an impact, however, is through a powerful, freely elected legislature. Fish (2005) finds that among postcommunist countries, the stronger the legislature the lower the level of corruption. A strong legislature ensures accountability within the executive branch and through this the enforcement of the rule of law.

There is another problem too. Rather than creating a system based on strong checks and balances that might serve as a stable foundation for Russia's democratic development, the 1993 Constitution perpetuates a style of politics in which few formal limits are placed on the personal authority of the president and in which loyalty to the leader trumps loyalty to institutions and ideals. Instead of promoting Russia's democratic development, the 1993 Constitution has hindered it.

■ Russian Politics Under Yeltsin

During the last years of Soviet rule, Yeltsin convincingly played the part of a valiant, embattled democrat as he rose up in opposition to Gorbachev and the CPSU conservatives. Once in power, however, and with the Soviet system no more, Yeltsin, who placed little faith in institutions, preferred the role of dealmaker and power broker to that of leader of the democratic movement. Instead of understanding politics and Russia's political development in terms of the creation of formal institutions that would set limits on the exercise of political power, Yeltsin viewed politics as a game in which he not only wrote the rules but was above the rules. Essentially viewing himself as an elected tsar of the Russian people, Yeltsin sought to free himself from as many institutional checks as possible. This included distancing himself from "pro-Yeltsin" political parties. For Yeltsin, becoming a party leader would mean curbing his freedom of action. Instead of working through institutions, he preferred to rely on the counsel of a small group of close advisers and associates. Unhindered by many of the institutional constraints normally felt by the leaders of democratic countries, Yeltsin would try to build a modern Russia through traditional means.

Despite Yeltsin's commanding position of political authority in the system, his plans to remake Russia went awry from the start. Even though a majority of voters cast ballots in favor of his constitution in December 1993, they also elected a State Duma that would be hostile to him. Politically isolated and in poor health, Yeltsin began to withdraw from politics as he missed important meetings and spent more time out of the public eye. His ill-conceived war in the breakaway republic of Chechnya (which Katherine Graney discusses at some length in Chapter 7), increased doubts about Yeltsin's leadership. Over time, Yeltsin became increasingly stubborn, irritable, and suspicious, making it more difficult for even his closest advisers to work with him. His public-opinion poll numbers also dropped sharply. In a February 1995 survey, nearly half of all respondents reported that they had completely lost faith in Yeltsin. An August poll from the same year showed that in Moscow, long a Yeltsin stronghold, his approval rating had fallen to 16 percent (Shevtsova 1999, 120–121, 139). The Communist Party's first-place finish in the December 1995 Duma elections underscored his lack of popular support.

In early 1996, Yeltsin's flagging poll numbers and poor health prompted some in his camp to advise the "postponement" of that June's presidential election (Aron 2000, 580–584). Yeltsin gave serious thought to such a maneuver, which would have included dissolving the Duma and outlawing the Communist Party. As Yeltsin considered his options, his minister of internal affairs, Anatoly Kulikov, warned that with the Communist Party in control of half of the country's local legislatures, he could not be certain how his subordinates in the field would react to a constitutional face-off between the president and the Communists. "What would we do," Kulikov asked, "if some units of the police sided with the president and others against? Fight? That is civil war" (Yeltsin 2000, 32). Yeltsin, by his own account, was talked out of taking such drastic measures by his daughter and adviser, Tatyana Dyachenko, and by the man who would end up running the Yeltsin campaign, Anatoly Chubais. The "young reformer" who a few years earlier had directed Russia's privatization effort, Chubais predicted that unlike the results of Yeltsin's showdown with the Congress of People's Deputies in 1993, this time Russia's president would not prevail (Yeltsin 2000, 33). Not wanting to risk such an outcome, and reportedly concerned about his place in history, Yeltsin resisted the temptation to cancel the election (Remnick 1998, 331–333).

Once Yeltsin committed to the elections, his campaign got into full swing. With little positive to run on, Chubais and his team avoided discussion of Yeltsin's record and instead reminded people of the political repression and economic hardships of the country's Soviet past. The implication was that if the Communist Party's candidate won, the country would return to the bad old days of the Soviet dictatorship. The strategy worked. Although the vast majority of voters were displeased with Yeltsin's performance as Russia's president, the majority were also hesitant to see the Communist Party in power in the Kremlin. Slowly, Yeltsin's numbers began to rebound. Although he could not run on his record, he did enjoy important advantages of incumbency. He issued decrees promising the payment of pensions and back wages and while on the stump promised transfers from the federal treasury to pay for local projects. In all, these pledges totaled as much as ten billion dollars (see White, Rose, and McAllister 1997, 257).

Yeltsin also benefited from slanted coverage provided by the country's three television networks, ORT, RTR, and NTV, which were either state owned or controlled by economic oligarchs who feared a return to Soviet-era politics (White, Rose, and McAllister 1997, Chapter 12). Conflicts of interest were common. For instance, Igor Malashenko, the man who directed the day-to-day operations of privately owned NTV, was the person in charge of Yeltsin's ad campaign. Although such practices are frowned upon in consolidated democracies, the choice was simple for Yeltsin and his supporters: either manipulate the electorate and the election to get the results they wanted, or be prepared to use force to prevent the Communists and their candidate, Gennady Zyuganov, from taking the presidency. Wishing to avoid violence, Yeltsin had to win the election at all costs (Remnick 1998, 336). In the end, Yeltsin did win, in two rounds, not because he was popular, but because of fears on the part of the majority of voters of what a Communist victory might bring.

Often weak and in poor health during his second term, Yeltsin relied even more on his closest advisers and associates. This inner circle, nicknamed "the Family" by the Russian media, was led by Yeltsin's daughter Tatyana Dyachenko. Other "Family" members included, among others, Anatoly Chubais, top Yeltsin aides Alexander Voloshin and Valentin Yumashev, and business magnates Boris Berezovsky and Roman Abramovich. Although it was "impossible to make any decisions against Yeltsin's will," the Family's influence was so great that some viewed it as a "parallel, alternative government" (Dikun 1999). Even as the Family reportedly reigned in the impetuous Yeltsin (preventing him from making any number of rash decisions), many believed that its chief interest was "to amass as much wealth as it [could] while it still [had] the chance" (Paddock 1999).

Yeltsin's second term also facilitated the rise to power of a small group of businessmen who had already managed to accrue great wealth through their government connections. In addition to financing Yeltsin's reelection bid, they provided loans to the Russian government in return for claims on shares of lucrative state holdings (the so-called loans for shares scheme, which Millar explains in some detail in Chapter 5). The fortunes they amassed through this deal left them in control of much of the Russian economy, further enhancing their clout. Such was the extent of their influence over policy that many observers believed that these economic oligarchs, not Yeltsin, ran the country.

The dual rise to power of the Family and of the oligarchs revealed the inherent weaknesses of superpresidentialism. In a system that lacked effective legislative and judicial checks on executive power, there was little to stop the Family or the oligarchs (or the state bureaucracy, for that matter) from manipulating the political system to their advantage. Short of running afoul of Yeltsin (or each other), they were essentially unaccountable for their actions.

With Russia's dysfunctional political institutions as the backdrop, Yeltsin's second term was dominated by power struggles among the oligarchs over which of them, along with their allies in the government and the presidential administration, would expand their control over state-owned property. At stake, too, was the direction of economic policy. Interestingly, these battles were fought out in the national print and broadcast media, which were either owned or controlled by competing oligarchs and thus wielded as weapons by the warring factions (Shevtsova 1999, 218–220). Yeltsin's second term was also marred by political scandals, stalled economic reforms, deepening corruption, and a financial crisis in the late summer of 1998 that wiped out the savings of Russia's emerging middle class. By early 1999, with the 2000 presidential election looming, the Family began a desperate search for a successor who would ensure that neither they nor Yeltsin would have anything to fear once Yeltsin left office. They had reason to be concerned. With corruption rife within Yeltsin's inner circle the possibility of prosecution was real should an "unfriendly" candidate win the presidency. They needed to find someone who would be willing to grant Yeltsin legal immunity. After a search spanning several months that included the use of focus groups to discover what Russian voters wanted in a presidential candidate, "a non-ideological 'strongman' who could restore law and order and a sense of national pride" (Thornhill 2000), the Family settled on a relative unknown in Russian politics named Vladimir Putin.

■ Putin's Road to Power

Putin's path to the presidency was an unlikely one. In contrast to Yeltsin, Putin was neither a career politician nor someone who was used to being in charge. Before winning the presidency in March 2000, he had never held elective office. With the exception of a few months in 1999, when he served as Yeltsin's last prime minister, and before that from July 1998 to August 1999 when he was director of the KGB's successor, the Federal Security Service (more commonly known by its Russian initials, FSB), Putin had never been in charge of a large organization, public or private. Instead, he had normally played the role of a loyal functionary.

A review of his life suggests that he was born to serve in subordinate roles. As a working-class youth in Leningrad (now St. Petersburg), he dreamed of entering state service as an officer of the KGB, an aspiration that was fulfilled upon his graduation from university in 1975. By all accounts, Putin had an undistinguished career. Indicative of this was his posting in 1985 to the KGB's field office in Dresden, East Germany, then considered a backwater in the Cold War conflict between the United States and the Soviet Union (Jack 2004, 63–65). Putin was still serving in Dresden in November 1989 when the Berlin Wall came down bringing an end to four decades of communist rule in East Germany. In early 1990 he was recalled to the USSR where he became an assistant to the vice rector for international affairs at Leningrad State University, his alma mater.

The Soviet Union he returned to in 1990 was much different from the one he had left five years earlier. Indeed, the political and economic reforms of this period had changed the country dramatically. For Putin, still a KGB officer, a change in career seemed prudent. At the urging of a friend he interviewed for a position on the staff of Anatoly Sobchak, a well-known reformer and former Leningrad State University law professor. At the time, Sobchak was chair of the Leningrad city council (Putin 2000b, 87–89). In his job interview with Sobchak, Putin told his future boss about his KGB background. Putin recalls, "He was silent for a moment. I must have really surprised him. He thought and thought, and then suddenly he said, 'Well, screw it!'" (Putin 2000b, 88). Putin got the job. Over the next few years Putin's life revolved around Russia's new democratic politics. Although some suspected that Putin was a KGB plant in Sobchak's administration, Sobchak saw in Putin a person he could trust amidst the graft and corruption of Leningrad city politics. As Sobchak later recalled in a television interview, Putin's "inability to betray, his loyalty, reliability and honesty are the main traits of his character, which really make him a rare person in our times" (as quoted in Paddock 2000).

As a trusted assistant, Putin made a point of looking after Sobchak's interests. During the August 1991 coup attempt, when a vacationing Sobchak quickly returned to Leningrad to throw his support behind the coup's opponents, Putin met his boss at the airport with bodyguards to ensure his safety. At the same time, Putin built a reputation as a competent, reliable, and gifted administrator. When Sobchak was elected mayor of Leningrad in 1991, Putin remained on his staff, eventually rising to the rank of first deputy mayor. As a leader, Sobchak had much in common with Putin's future boss, Boris Yeltsin. A charismatic and effective speaker, Sobchak, like Yeltsin, was a democrat in rhetoric but an autocrat at heart. With a disdain for the day-to-day affairs of government, he relied heavily on the ever reliable and efficient Putin to keep the mayor's office running. Like Yeltsin, Sobchak also had a habit of ruffling people's feathers, which his loyal lieutenant Putin would smooth over (Jack 2004, 68–71).

Loyalty, in fact, is a defining feature of Putin's personality. When another of Sobchak's deputies, Vladimir Yakovlev, defeated him in his bid for reelection in 1996, Putin refused to work with the new chief, viewing him as a traitor. Not long after, when Sobchak was under investigation for corruption, Putin helped him leave the country under the pretext of needing medical treatment abroad. Later, when Putin was the head of the FSB, all charges against Sobchak were dropped, allowing him to return to Russia (Jack 2004, 74).

Following Sobchak's defeat in 1996, Putin was again seeking employment. Through personal connections he soon found work inside Yeltsin's presidential administration. There, true to form, he served loyally and competently. Recognizing these qualities, Yeltsin named Putin director of the FSB in July 1998.

A little more than a year later, on August 9, 1999, Yeltsin nominated him for the post of prime minister. Following the Duma's approval of his nomination a few days later, and with the next presidential election less than a year away, Putin moved into position as Yeltsin's heir apparent.

A central factor in Yeltsin's selection of Putin as prime minister was his record of steadfast and enduring loyalty to Sobchak. In the rough-and-tumble world of Russian politics, where losing political power may also mean losing one's personal wealth and freedom, such qualities are to be prized in successors and subordinates. When asked if Putin could be trusted, one influential Family member, Valentin Yumashev, replied, "He didn't give up Sobchak. He won't give us up" (Baker and Glasser 2005, 52).

On August 2, 1999, just a week before Yeltsin's nomination of Putin as prime minister, rebels from the breakaway Chechen Republic invaded the neighboring Republic of Dagestan to begin post–Soviet Russia's second

Chechen war. Within weeks, four apartment bombings (including two in Moscow) killed around three hundred people, putting the entire country on edge. Although the exact nature of the war's origins and of the apartment bombings is still uncertain (some have speculated, for instance, that the apartment bombings in Moscow were actually the work of the FSB), the war's most important effect was clear: Putin, a virtual unknown at the time of his appointment as prime minister, quickly became the country's most popular and trusted politician through his aggressive prosecution of the war.

If the war in Chechnya helped give Putin's electoral fortunes a boost, so too did the machinations of Yeltsin's Family in outmaneuvering his potential competitors. In contrast to the 1995–1996 election cycle, the Kremlin's most formidable opponent this time was not the Communist Party of the Russian Federation (CPRF), but rather the newly formed electoral bloc Fatherland-All Russia (OVR). Comprised of establishment elites from the regions and Moscow, Fatherland-All Russia sought to wrest control of the federal executive away from Yeltsin and the Family. Led by Moscow's popular mayor Yuri Luzhkov and the much respected former prime minister Yevgeny Primakov, OVR presented a formidable challenge. In mid-September, just three months before the Duma election, a public opinion poll conducted by VTsIOM (the All-Russia Center for the Study of Public Opinion) placed OVR second behind the CPRF. The same poll showed Primakov running a strong second in the presidential race behind CPRF leader Gennady Zyuganov. Putin, meanwhile, still stuck in single digits, ran a distant sixth (SDI Project 1999).

Even though the CPRF led the field early on, the Family knew that its real opponent in the upcoming elections was the OVR. As a would-be "party of power," Fatherland-All Russia was in a position to become Russia's primary alternative to the Communist Party. And unlike the inept Zyuganov, the popular Primakov might actually win the presidential race. No friend of the Family, as he proved during his short tenure as Russia's prime minister from September 1998 to May 1999, Primakov posed a grave threat to Yeltsin and his inner circle's interests. At the same time, the Family knew that a weaker than expected showing by Fatherland-All Russia in the Duma elections that December would lessen Primakov's credibility as a candidate in the ensuing presidential contest. Faced with this challenge from the OVR and Primakov, the Family responded by creating a political movement of its own named Unity.

The brainchild of economic oligarch and Family member Boris Berezovsky, Unity's primary goal was to stop Fatherland-All Russia in the upcoming Duma elections and through this derail Primakov's presidential aspirations. Its full name was the Interregional Movement Unity (in Russian, Mezhregionalnoe dvizhnenie Edinstvo). Out of this unwieldy name Berezovsky could take the first two letters of each word to create the catchy acronym Medved, or "bear" in Russian (Baker and Glasser 2005, 56). This was a clever move as the bear is an ancient and enduring symbol in Russian culture. Indeed, bears represent many things for Russians. Awesome creatures, they are the guardians and masters of the forest. They are also symbols of honesty, simplicity, and dignity (on this see Billington 1970, 21–22, and Gerhart 1995, 297). In choosing the bear as an emblem, the message of Unity's founders was clear: of all those vying for seats in the Duma, Unity's candidates were the ones who were strong, the ones who could be trusted, and the ones who could be counted on to protect Russia and its people.

Formed just a few weeks before the official opening of the 1999 Duma campaign, Unity's approach was two-fold. First, it embraced the decisive and increasingly popular Putin and kept the much-disliked Yeltsin at arm's length. Second, Unity styled itself as an electoral bloc of young rebels from the regions (the *real* Russia in their view) who, unlike the Duma's self-interested Moscow-based politicians, were concerned about solving the real problems of real people. Electing OVR candidates, Unity argued, would simply mean continuing with business as usual in the Duma. If Fatherland-All Russia represented the face of a corrupt, self-interested establishment, Unity presented itself as set to overturn that establishment to get the country moving again. In reality, Unity was itself a product of the establishment, that which had control over the federal executive and was controlled by Yeltsin and the Family.

The most well-funded party in the campaign, Unity gained favorable and often biased media coverage from the state-owned television networks RTR and ORT, and from the privately owned network TV-6. Although ORT was 51 percent state-owned, in reality it was controlled by Boris Berezovsky, who not only held private shares in the company but also owned TV-6. Fatherland-All Russia benefited from biased coverage from TV-Center, owned by the Moscow city government, and NTV, owned by Kremlin critic and economic oligarch Vladimir Gusinsky. Unity had the advantage, however, in that ORT and RTR were the only networks that could reach nearly every corner of the country (Colton and McFaul 2003, 55–56; Oates 2000, 11–12).

Playing to the broadest electoral base possible, Unity refused to associate itself with a particular ideology. Indistinct in its platform, Unity "conveyed an attitude more than a solid program" (Colton and McFaul 2003, 57). Speaking in vague terms about the importance of patriotism and national unity, the party took a hard line on Chechnya. Economically, its positions were essentially free-market oriented. Its main message, however, was that it was Putin's party and that by voting for Unity the people would be electing a legislature he could work with. Initially reluctant to reveal his preferences, the increasingly popular Putin eventually declared his support for Unity. Now with Putin's backing, Unity pulled ahead of Fatherland-All Russia in public opinion polls even as it continued to lag behind the front-running CPRF. On election day, however, Unity drew almost even with the Communists in the party list vote. OVR came in a distant third. Although Fatherland-All Russia won a number of single-member district races (bringing it close to Unity in total number of seats), its humiliating defeat in the party list vote effectively neutralized it as a political force. This, combined with Putin's skyrocketing poll numbers, forced Primakov out of the presidential race. In the end, the Family had gotten what it wanted: a hobbled OVR, a Duma that Putin could work with, and a presidential contest that would pit Putin against CPRF leader Zyuganov.

Hedging his bets, Yeltsin gave Putin additional help by resigning from the presidency. According to Article 92 of Russia's constitution, Putin, as prime minister, automatically became acting president following Yeltsin's resignation. In his first act as the country's new leader Putin signed a decree granting Yeltsin immunity from prosecution. Putin benefited from Yeltsin's resignation in two ways. First, its timing, on New Year's Eve, meant that the presidential election scheduled for June 2000 would now take place in March as stipulated by Article 92. This earlier date not only gave the opposition much less time to organize for the presidential race, it also ensured that the election would be held before Putin's popularity had a chance to fall. Second, as the country's acting president, Putin would enjoy the administrative advantages of incumbency. Appealing to a broad cross-section of voters, Putin easily defeated Zyuganov in the election's first round by a 52.9 to 29.2 percent margin (Colton and McFaul 2003, 185–187; White and McAllister 2003, 384–386; Levada Center and CSPP 2007c).

Unlike in 1996 when the Yeltsin campaign played on public fears of what might happen if a Communist were to win the presidency, in 2000 a return to the Communist era seemed a remote possibility. Instead, most Russian voters wanted an end to the upheavals and conflict that had marked Yeltsin's tenure in office. The desire for a "strong state" and a "strong leader" was the order of the day (Shevtsova 2005, 73). Despite the vagueness of his proposed plans, Putin was an attractive candidate because he seemed to be everything Yeltsin was not—reliable, steady, sober, and strong. In a public opinion survey conducted shortly after the election, 54 percent of those who said they had voted for Putin cast ballots for him because they thought he was trustworthy. Another 14 percent voted for him because they viewed him as a "man of power." Although some observers have suggested that many voters believed they had no other choice than to vote for Putin, only 12 percent in this survey indicated that they had voted for the "lesser evil." This stands in stark contrast to the 36 percent of voters who said the same in 1996 (Rose and Munro 2002, 181–182). If Yeltsin won in 1996 because his campaign had convinced enough of the electorate that they could not trust the Communist Party, Putin won in 2000 because he had gained the confidence of most voters.

■ Putin's Understanding of the Problem

The day Yeltsin resigned from the presidency the Russian government issued a document under Putin's name titled "Russia at the Turn of the Millennium." Part diagnosis and part prescription, this essay soberly reviewed the legacy left to Russia not only by the events and decisions of the Yeltsin years but also of many of those of the Soviet era. The document also provided a broad plan of action that essentially served as a critique of Yeltsin's policies. To a people weary of grand schemes, Putin vowed a return to normalcy. Instead of "political and socio-economic upheavals, cataclysms, and radical reforms," Putin offered "a strategy of revival and prosperity" that would draw on the "positive elements" of the political and economic reforms of the 1990s. In stark contrast to Yeltsin's approach, this strategy would be implemented through "gradual, prudent methods" in an environment of "political stability." To do this, Russia would chart its own course by "combining the universal principles of the market economy and democracy with Russian realities" (Putin 1999).

In doing so, Russia would reclaim its "traditional values," the most important of which was reliance on a strong state. This would not mean a return to dictatorship, however. Democracy, Putin claimed, was still the goal:

> Russia needs a strong state power. I am not calling for totalitarianism. History proves all dictatorships, all authoritarian forms of government are transient. Only democratic systems are lasting. Whatever our shortcomings, humankind has not devised anything superior. A strong state power in Russia is a democratic, law-based, workable federal state.

On the face of things, Putin's understanding of the situation appeared to echo Juan Linz's view that a weak state means weak rule of law, which in turn means weak democracy. Putin also seemed to recognize the vital role played by the federal executive in enforcing the constitution and federal laws at lower levels. Without enforcement, the federal constitution and federal laws would be meaningless. For all his interest in the creation of a strong state, Putin also acknowledged that "the main threat to human rights and freedoms" was the executive branch, which must be kept in check by civil society (Putin 1999).

As sophisticated as some of Putin's ideas were, a significant gap remained in his thinking. For Putin, the problem of the weak state was not one of weak institutions (and therefore weak checks and balances on executive authority) but of weak executive control over the polity, economy, and society. Out of this greater control, he assumed, would emerge the well-ordered society he and most Russians wanted. To this end, Putin sought to make Russia's superpresidential system work. He did not seem to understand that the system itself was a big part of the problem.

■ Taking Control of the System

Early in his presidency Putin set about the construction of a "power vertical" that would allow him to exert control over the political system. Even
before the March 2000 election, some Russian commentators began referring to Putin's regime as a "managed democracy" (*upravliaemaia demokratiia*). Sergei Markov, a self-described "Kremlin-connected political analyst"
and one of the architects of managed democracy, defines Putin's system as
"a combination of democratic institutions and authoritarian institutions." In
Markov's view, Russia is in transition from the "anarchy and chaos" of the
Yeltsin era to a time when the country will have "functioning democratic
institutions." Markov argues that to ensure that this process does not spin
out of control, the "Kremlin has to use both democratic and not democratic
methods" (Markov 2004). Another Russian observer, scholar Nikolai Petrov
(2005, 182), understands managed democracy much more critically, seeing
it as little more than a method of controlling society through the guise of
democratic institutions. If for Markov (2004) managed democracy is "a natural stage in the development of Russia from Soviet dictatorship to normal
democracy," for Petrov (2004) it is "a transitional stage between the chaotic
democratic model of the Yeltsin years and a more authoritarian model."

Reining in the Regions

One of Putin's early targets in his effort to develop managed democracy
was the Russian legislature's upper house, the Federation Council. Under
Yeltsin it had become a haven for regional governors who, according to
federal law, were allowed to fill half of its seats. Direct representation in
the council gave the governors a powerful institutional platform from which
to promote their interests and, if necessary, to oppose the president. For
Putin, this was an intolerable situation. His solution, with the support of the
Duma, was the passage of legislation that prohibited the governors from
taking seats in the council. The result was a much more reliable and pliable
upper house.

Putin also sought direct control over the regions through the creation of
seven federal super districts under the supervision of plenipotentiaries who
answered only to him. Their primary responsibility was to report regional
noncompliance with the federal constitution, federal laws, and presidential
decrees. In another blow to the regions, these presidential representatives
would be responsible for the coordination of the work of the regional offices
of federal agencies, including the appointment of personnel. As long as the
governors had control over federal appointments in their regions (as had
been the case under Yeltsin) they could effectively derail the implementation
of practically any federal policy that conflicted with their interests (Ross
2004, 157). Through his policies, Putin hoped to make it more difficult for

regional leaders and legislatures to ignore or resist the will of the federal authorities in Moscow.

The ongoing war in Chechnya provided the backdrop for other significant federal reforms. The search for a military solution to the conflict ensured that conditions in Chechnya would remain unstable, sometimes with catastrophic results. Notable was the October 2002 Palace of Culture theater incident in which several hundred people were taken hostage in the heart of Moscow by a group of well-armed and well-equipped Chechen rebels. In the ill-conceived rescue that followed, 130 theatergoers were killed. Even worse was the September 2004 Beslan tragedy in which rebels took an entire school hostage in North Ossetia. The incident, which included yet another ill-fated rescue attempt, led to the deaths of more than 330 people, over half of whom were children (for a detailed discussion of these events, see Baker and Glasser 2005, Chapters 1 and 8).

Putin took advantage of the climate created by the Beslan crisis to push through legislation eliminating the direct election of governors, claiming that such a move would strengthen the Russian state. Governors would now be nominated by the president. It would be up to the regional assemblies to accept or reject the president's nominees. If a particular regional legislature rejected the president's choice for governor three times, however, the president would have the authority under the new law to dissolve the assembly. How such an expansion of presidential powers would prevent a future Beslan was unclear. One thing was certain, however: under this law regional executives and legislatures would have much less room to maneuver in their relations with the federal executive in Moscow.

Taming the Media

In addition to reining in the regions, Putin sought control over the national media. According to a leading Russian broadcast journalist, Aleksei Venediktov of radio station Echo Moskvy, Putin "sees the media as someone's instrument. He looks at them as an industry, not a societal institution" (as quoted in Jack 2004, 169). In a system in which politics is viewed as a "winner-take-all" proposition, there is little room for influential independent media. The most important of these is television, the primary source of information for nearly 90 percent of Russia's population (Hale, McFaul, and Colton 2004, 311). Both a beneficiary and a target of slanted television coverage during the 1999–2000 election season, Putin recognized the role the media could play in shaping and manipulating public opinion.

As the Yeltsin era drew to a close, only one national television network, RTR, was fully under state control. The other leading broadcasters, ORT and NTV, were under the control of economic oligarchs Boris Berezovsky and Vladimir Gusinsky respectively. NTV, which had opposed both

Unity and Putin in the 1999–2000 elections, was Putin's first target. Since its creation in 1993, NTV had done some good things. As the country's main independent television network, NTV provided hard-hitting, honest coverage of the first Chechen war, greatly influencing Russian public opinion in the process. NTV also produced some of the best political commentary of any of the national broadcasters. Although NTV was independent of the state, it was not always independent of its owner, Vladimir Gusinsky, who at times influenced the tenor of its reporting. Such was the case when NTV joined forces with Yeltsin in support of his 1996 reelection bid. Concluding later that he had not been sufficiently rewarded for his support, Gusinsky turned NTV against Yeltsin and the government (Lipman and McFaul 2003, 69).

Although Yeltsin generally tolerated media criticism during his presidency (even as his popularity plummeted), the same cannot be said of Putin. In the fall of 1999, still serving as prime minister, Putin was "offended" by NTV's critical coverage of the second Chechen war (Lipman and McFaul 2003, 70). For Putin, criticism of his leadership was at best a sign of disloyalty and at worst a mark of treason. His response to media coverage of the August 2000 sinking of the Russian nuclear submarine *Kursk* is indicative of such an understanding of the world. The disaster, in which all hands were lost, was the result of an on-board explosion. Although most of the crew were killed in the explosion, some survived only to be left to their fates in the face of a half-hearted and incompetent Russian rescue effort. When Russian media, led by Gusinsky's NTV and Berezovsky's ORT, revealed that the government and the navy not only had bungled the rescue attempt but also had lied about what was really going on, Putin was furious. By the time of the *Kursk* incident Gusinsky had already left the country and gone into exile after having been arrested earlier in the summer on charges of embezzlement. Following the tragedy, under the legal pretext of collecting Gusinsky's unpaid debts to the state (about 1.5 billion dollars), NTV would eventually fall under government control (Jack 2004, 152–166). ORT's coverage of the *Kursk* incident would cost Berezovsky control over the network's operations. Soon, he too would flee the country under the threat of arrest (Baker and Glasser 2005, 87–91).

In time, print media would also come under fire. In September 2004, Raf Shakirov, the editor in chief of *Izvestia,* lost his job as a result of his newspaper's extensive and vivid coverage of the Beslan crisis. *Izvestia*'s reporting stood in stark contrast to the subdued coverage provided by state-controlled television. Reports at the time suggested that Shakirov's dismissal was the result of Kremlin pressure (Coalson 2004). Less than a year later, in June 2005, state-owned Gazprom-Media acquired the newspaper, reportedly at the Kremlin's behest (Corwin 2005).

Despite such incidents, the Russian people for the most part have remained silent. Some interpret this silence as a lack of interest or concern.

According to Viktor Shenderovich, creator of NTV's *Kukly* (a puppet show of political satire that was constantly critical of Putin and eventually forced off the air), "The majority of people didn't feel freedom of speech to be necessary. The majority thinks this is a privilege of the intelligentsia [that is, the country's intellectual elite]. . . . That's why the authorities were able to win" (Baker and Glasser 2005, 98). Shenderovich may be overstating his case. Surveys taken not long before the state's opening salvos against Gusinsky and NTV showed that a large majority of Russians (around 80 percent) believed that media freedoms were important (Colton and McFaul 2002, 104). At the same time, surveys also revealed that few Russians understood the state's actions against NTV as an attack on these freedoms. In a VTsIOM survey only 15 percent of respondents thought that the conflict with Gusinsky and NTV was over freedom of the press. A solid majority (57 percent) believed the government's story that the primary issue was financial (Levada Center and CSPP 2007b; see also Lipman and McFaul 2003, 78).

That the much-hated oligarchs were either the owners or chief operators of NTV and ORT helped Putin's case. To be sure, Gusinsky and Berezovsky had at times employed their media empires for personal or political gain. Putin was not far from the mark in suggesting in his July 2000 address to the Federal Assembly that "[j]ournalistic freedom has become a coveted item for politicians and major financial groups, and a convenient tool for war between [oligarchic] clans." Furthermore, he observed,

> The economic ineffectiveness of a significant part of the media makes it dependent on the commercial and political interests of its owners and sponsors. It makes it possible to use the media as a way to score points off rivals, and sometimes even to turn it into a means of mass disinformation, *a means of fighting the state.* (Putin 2000a, emphasis added)

In 2005, with the national television networks now under state control, Putin spoke of the importance of the public having "objective information," declaring that "state television and radio broadcasting are as objective as possible, free from the influence of any particular groups, and . . . they reflect the whole spectrum of public and political forces in the country" (Putin 2005). Bias and objectivity only seemed to be issues for Putin, however, when media reporting undercut his administration. As much as he spoke of the value of a free press, Putin's interest in defending it was conditional.

In fact, government attacks on the media, often through the enforcement of restrictive media laws, have led to self-censorship on the part of most broadcasters and many journalists. Indicative of the direct control the Kremlin exercises over television, the head of the presidential administration under Putin held weekly meetings with network executives to provide instructions on how to cover certain news items, as well as directions on what not to cover (Baker and Glasser 2005, 294; Jack 2004, 170–172). With this level of control, television networks that once provided hard-hitting commentary on the most pressing issues of the day are now, for the most part, obedient servants of the state.

Neutralizing the Oligarchs

Gaining control of the country's major television networks was part of a larger effort by Putin to neutralize Russia's powerful economic oligarchs. Some argue that the political power of the oligarchs was exaggerated (Jack 2004, 185). Without doubt, in the aftermath of the August 1998 financial crisis their influence seemed diminished. Even so, the apparent ability of certain oligarchs to make or break presidential candidates meant that their power was still great. Boris Yeltsin may have been willing to live with such arrangements, but Vladimir Putin was not.

Putin did not wait long after his inauguration as president in May 2000 to begin putting the oligarchs in their place. In a mid-summer Kremlin meeting, with most of the oligarchs present, Putin delivered a simple message: "You stay out of politics and I will not revise the results of privatization" (Baker and Glasser 2005, 87). According to one of the businessmen present, Putin also had another message:

> The situation in the country is difficult, power practically doesn't exist, and you claim that your business is under threat. Do your business and you will get support if your money is working for the country. The president is restoring order and don't make this difficult task more difficult or I will not forgive you, because you are partly responsible. (Jack 2004, 193)

In short, it was time for the oligarchs to start behaving themselves by staying out of politics, investing more in Russia, and contributing more to the greater good. Those who broke the new rules would suffer the consequences. Putin's declaration did not mean an end to the oligarchs but rather an end to the way they had operated under Yeltsin. Whereas Yeltsin had allowed the oligarchs to behave as free agents, Putin demanded their loyalty.

The actions taken against Gusinsky and Berezovsky during his first year in office demonstrated that Putin was serious. One oligarch who did not get the point, even after Gusinsky and Berezovsky were forced into exile, was banker and oil baron Mikhail Khodorkovsky. As a beneficiary of the "loans for shares" scheme (explained by Millar in Chapter 5), Khodorkovsky acquired Russia's second largest oil company, Yukos, setting him on a course to become the richest person in Russia. Initially making a reputation as a shrewd, ruthless businessman, Khodorkovsky later recast his image as a reliable partner who carefully followed accepted international business practices. Eventually, he turned his attention to politics with the dream of helping to transform Russia into a "normal country."

As the 2003 Duma elections approached, it became clear how Khodorkovsky hoped to achieve this end as he spoke openly about his desire to buy enough influence in the Duma to amend the constitution and thus rewrite the formal rules of the game. Russia's semipresidential system would be scrapped in favor of a parliamentary one in which the prime minister, not the president, would be the central and most powerful figure. In this new system the once-powerful president would be reduced to the status of figurehead. The new, powerful prime minister would be Khodorkovsky. To devise such a plan virtually guaranteed a response from Putin. Khodorkovsky demonstrated another lapse in judgment in a February 2003 Kremlin meeting between Putin and the oligarchs during which he openly confronted Putin about corruption in the presidential administration (Baker and Glasser 2005, 280–282).

By getting involved in politics at all, let alone brazenly challenging Putin's authority, Khodorkovsky was violating one of the key terms of the contract set forth by Putin in his mid-summer 2000 meeting with the oligarchs. Unlike Gusinsky and Berezovsky, Khodorkovsky refused to leave the country even when it became clear that he would soon be arrested. When he was finally taken into custody in late October 2003, few doubted that the authorities would make an example of him.

The other oligarchs got the point. The influential Russian Union of Industrialists and Entrepreneurs (essentially an association of oligarchs) quickly caved in to the Kremlin's pressure. Igor Yurgens, vice president of the organization, explained why it could not support Khodorkovsky: "Of course the press, especially the liberal [that is, democratic] press, painted it as complete capitulation of the union, which it probably was. But it was hell. If we would have acted otherwise, in two or three hours we would be arrested. I would say that's worse than capitulation." Added oligarch Mikhail Fridman: "Putin has . . . decided he must show who is boss. And the country has this tradition—it's very bloody about that" (Baker and Glasser 2005, 292). After a lengthy legal process in which he was charged with tax evasion and fraud, Khodorkovsky was found guilty in May 2005 and sentenced to nine years in prison. On appeal the sentence was reduced to eight. In defeating Khodorkovsky, Putin and his men sent a loud and clear message to the remaining oligarchs that they were not to participate in politics except at the Kremlin's invitation and only then under the Kremlin's control.

Khodorkovsky's arrest and prosecution served another purpose by allowing the state to expand its control over the country's vast natural resource wealth. In going to prison, Khodorkovsky not only lost his freedom, he also lost his oil company. Following Khodorkovsky's arrest, the state froze Yukos's assets and eventually sold them off to various state-controlled enterprises. This was part of a much larger plan to redistribute property from the remnants of the old ruling elite under Yeltsin (to which Khodorkovsky had belonged) to the new ruling elite under Putin (Shevtsova 2005, 366). In the process, several high-ranking officials close to Putin (including members of his presidential administration) were appointed chairmen of a number of the country's leading state-owned enterprises. Among these are the natural gas monopoly Gazprom, the oil company Rosneft, and the defense contractor Almaz-Antei. Added up, state enterprises controlled or influenced by members of Putin's inner circle accounted for 40 percent of the country's gross domestic product (Mazneva 2008; Yasmann 2005).

Relations with the Duma

Unlike Yeltsin, Putin had support in the Duma from the start of his first term. The first steps toward the creation of this legislative base came with the formation of Unity and its strong showing in the 1999 Duma elections. In outmaneuvering and defeating Fatherland-All Russia, Unity legitimately laid claim to being the only viable party of power. Indicative of Unity's clout was the deal it cut with the now weakened CPRF (which had lost forty-four seats) over the division of Duma leadership and committee chair positions. Bowing to reality, Fatherland-All Russia's legislative leaders entered into an informal coalition with Unity in April 2001. By the end of that year, it would join Unity to form a new party of power named "United Russia." Even before the creation of a Unity-led coalition and the subsequent formation of United Russia, the results of the 1999 elections meant that Putin would have a Duma he could work with. Whereas Yeltsin had relied on the power of decree to achieve his goals (a limited strategy in that presidential decrees may not overturn existing legislation), Putin viewed the legislative process as a more effective means of promoting his policy aims.

After the 1999 elections, Putin and his team cobbled together a legislative coalition of four Duma factions: Unity, Fatherland-All Russia, People's Deputy, and Regions of Russia. If they remained united, their 234 votes (226 are required for a simple majority) would ensure the passage of any piece of legislation. A split within the Duma between deputies elected through single-member districts and those chosen through party lists influenced the management of this coalition. Among the coalition's four factions, People's Deputy and Regions of Russia were dominated by representatives elected through single-member district mandates. As a result, these deputies sometimes fell under the sway of the local interests they served. Because Putin could not always count on these votes, he sometimes had to make concessions or negotiate side deals to keep individual deputies on board. As a last resort, he and his administration could look to factions outside the coalition to secure a legislative majority (Remington 2006, 14–15).

President Vladimir Putin, left, in a 2007 meeting
with US secretary of defense Robert Gates.

Although Putin and his administration were effective in passing legislation, the necessity of compromise at times limited what they could achieve. Wishing to extend his control over the system and to minimize the need for compromise or side deals, Putin threw his full support behind United Russia in the 2003 Duma elections. Such backing included bringing to bear "the government machine and its financial resources at all levels to gain advantage over the opposition in formally free elections" (Menshikov 2003). The Kremlin employed these "administrative resources" to great effect, prompting David Atkinson, head of the Council of Europe monitoring team, to declare the elections "free," but "certainly not fair" (Fak 2003; see also OSCE/ODIHR 2004). United Russia won 223 out of 450 seats in the election. The Communists came in a distant second with 52. In the end, United Russia wound up with 306 seats as the vast majority of independent deputies and a few others declared their allegiance to the party. With this supermajority, United Russia enacted rules changes in the Duma that "cut the president's bargaining costs for building voting majorities to almost zero" (Remington 2006, 25).

One of the more important rules changes came in 2005 with revisions to the federal Duma election law. In line with Putin's wishes, United Russia passed legislation that eliminated single-member district mandates in favor of a system based entirely on proportional representation. The new rules—

the final element in Putin's strategy to gain control over the Duma—went into effect with the 2007 elections. Putin used the Beslan tragedy as the pretext for change. As was true of the legislation that abolished the direct election of governors, it was unclear how rewriting the election law would prevent another Beslan. With the elimination of single-member district seats, however, Putin and United Russia removed the last source of legislative independence (Remington 2006, 25–26).

Parties and the Party System

The health of a democracy is in large measure a function of the health of its parties. By bringing together those who hold similar worldviews, parties provide order and cohesion to a political system. Parties also help organize public opinion, shape policy agendas, and provide channels for political action. In performing these functions, parties help people make sense of politics. Distinct from interest groups, parties also supply candidates for public office. In the competition for votes, parties in consolidated democracies have an incentive to present clear choices to the electorate through the formation of distinct party platforms. This enhances accountability: if the party in power does not follow through with its promises, it runs the risk of losing the next election. In this way parties serve as an important check on state power.

To date, Russian parties have yet to play a constructive role in Russia's democratic development. Internal divisions mean that few Russian parties present the public with clear and consistent platforms, thus making it difficult for voters to distinguish one party from another (Smyth 2006). Partly as a result, partisan identification is low in Russia. In a 2004 survey, 49 percent of those questioned indicated no party preference at all. Of the remaining 51 percent, nearly half expressed support for United Russia. Much of this support, however, seemed to be based on United Russia's close association with Putin. In general, Russians have a low opinion of their parties. Viewed as being primarily out for their own interests and having little regard for the public good, parties are the least trusted of all of Russia's political and social institutions (White 2006, 9–10, 16).

A big part of the problem is that Russia's party system is "supply driven" not "demand driven." In more demand-driven systems, parties form in response to voter demands for certain policies and try to satisfy those demands by winning seats in public office. In systems that are more supply driven, parties are created to serve specific elite interests and goals: from wanting to secure the perks and privileges associated with public office to achieving certain, relatively narrow, political ends. Unity's creation, just months before the 1999 Duma elections, is a case in point. The primary aim of its founders was not to win a plurality of seats in the Duma in the pursuit of specific programmatic goals. Their purpose was to prevent a strong showing by Fatherland-All Russia so as to undercut the presidential aspirations of its leaders, Yevgeny Primakov and Yuri Luzhkov (Hale 2004).

The result of a supply-side approach is a "floating" party system in which the parties "supplied" to voters changes from one election to the next (Rose 2000). Among the more prominent examples to date, three parties not in the field for the 1995 Duma elections (Unity, Fatherland-All Russia, and the Union of Rightist Forces) won 45 percent of the proportional representation vote in 1999. All told, more than 60 percent of the PR vote in 1999 went to parties that had not existed four years earlier (Rose 2000, 55). By the 2003 Duma elections, Unity and Fatherland-All Russia had merged to form United Russia and a new party, Motherland, had been created with the support of the Kremlin to draw away votes from the Communists. In the year leading up to the 2007 Duma elections, the creation of A Just Russia (through the merging of three left-wing parties: Motherland, the Pensioners Party, and the Party of Life) and the promotion of Civil Force (a right-of-center party seeking middle-class votes), represented yet another effort to ensure that parties friendly to the Kremlin remained in control of the Duma. The problem with Russia's floating party system is that as parties are formed, dissolved, and merged, voters miss the opportunity to hold accountable those whom they have previously elected. With accountability low, the Russian party system is "disconnected from society" (Riggs and Schraeder 2004, 282)

Indicative of this disconnect is that Russia's parties fail to reach much of the population. According to one survey, although two-thirds of respondents reported having received mail from one party or another in the 2003 Duma campaign, only one party, United Russia, managed to make contact with at least a third of the electorate. Just 10 percent reported having spoken with a party or electoral bloc representative. Only slightly more than half said they had seen campaign posters or literature in their communities, with United Russia being the only party to have reached at least a fourth of the population (Hale, McFaul, and Colton 2004, 311).

Two new laws may have an effect on party development. The first, mentioned earlier in the chapter, is an election law that eliminates all single-member district seats in the Duma. The same law also increases the minimum share of the total vote required for a party to receive seats in the lower house from 5 to 7 percent (Levada Center and CSPP 2007a). The second is the recently amended law on parties. It requires that parties have at least fifty thousand members nationwide (as opposed to ten thousand according to the original law), branches of at least five hundred members (instead of one hundred) in half of the Federation's subjects (administrative regions), and at least two hundred and fifty members (instead of fifty) in each of the country's remaining regions (*O vnesenii* 2004; see also *On Political Parties* 2001). Taken at face value the potential effects of these changes on the party system are not necessarily negative. Indeed, they might actually encourage the growth of stronger, nationwide parties and at the same time reduce the number of marginal contenders. In a climate in which the Kremlin seeks to expand its control over the polity, however, few believe that these laws are intended to promote Russia's democratic development.

The character of Russia's party system is both a cause and an effect of the weakness of the country's political institutions. Because the Duma is relatively weak, political elites are inclined to view parties as vehicles to serve their own narrow self-interests. Unlike in parliamentary systems where the executive branch is directly responsible to the legislature, or in a US-style presidential system where the Congress possesses formidable checks on executive power, the Duma by comparison has much less leverage over the president and his administration. Although self-interest will always be a part of politics no matter how strong a country's institutions, a powerful legislature in Russia would surely change the way national office holders regard politics and the public. In a legislative body that had the authority to check the power of the executive branch, the rewards of service as a Duma deputy would extend far beyond the perks of office. The result would be a more demand-driven party system and with it greater accountability between politicians and the electorate. A stronger Duma and a demand-driven party system would also help encourage the development of civil society, further empowering the electorate.

■ Mass Attitudes Toward Democracy

Putin's popularity and the absence of mass opposition to his reforms are viewed by some as proof that Russians are culturally inclined to accept and support authoritarian rule. Richard Pipes (2004, 15), for instance, believes that Putin "is popular precisely because he has re-instated Russia's traditional model of government: an autocratic state in which citizens are relieved of responsibility for politics."

Recent research suggests a more complex reality, however. Analyzing the results of public opinion surveys taken before and after the 1999 Duma elections, Colton and McFaul (2002) find that most Russians are in fact supportive of many basic democratic ideals. In a pre-election survey 64 percent of respondents indicated support for the "idea of democracy." Only 18 percent were opposed. In another poll, taken after the elections, 60 percent responded that they thought democracy would be a "good way" to govern Russia. Twenty-four percent said it would be a "bad way," while 16 percent said they did not know. Another question asked respondents to weigh the pros and cons of democratic government. Forty-seven percent agreed with the statement that even though democracy has its problems it is still the best form of government. Seventeen percent disagreed with the statement, 20 percent were indifferent, while 17 percent indicated that they did not know. Although some might argue that such results are hardly a ringing endorsement of democracy (Colton and McFaul acknowledge that "democracy is not yet a consensus value in Russia"), these findings nevertheless challenge the view that Russians are culturally predisposed toward dictatorship (Colton and McFaul 2002, 101, 111).

Indeed, when asked specific questions about how government should operate, many Russians are uncomfortable with the notion that political power should be concentrated in the hands of the few. For instance, when respondents were asked to consider power relations between the executive and legislative branches, a large plurality (45 percent) favored an equal balance of power between the president and the parliament. Only 25 percent indicated that the president should be stronger, while 23 percent favored the legislature. On the question of relations between the federal government in Moscow and Russia's regions, 53 percent of respondents supported an even balance of power. Only 15 percent said that power relations should favor the federal government, while 29 percent said it should favor the regions (Colton and McFaul 2002, 106).

Concerning civil rights and civil liberties, Colton and McFaul find overwhelming support among Russians for such democratic notions as the freedom to elect one's leaders (87 percent), freedom of expression (87 percent), freedom of the media (81 percent), and freedom of religion (70 percent). Although the results are more mixed on questions relating to the balance between democracy and order, pluralities of those polled expressed confidence in democracy (Colton and McFaul 2002, 104, 110).

Interesting, too, is that among Putin's supporters in the 2000 election, a sizable majority, 68 percent, favored the "idea of democracy." Only 15 percent rejected it. When asked what kind of political system they favored, only 12 percent of Putin voters indicated a preference for the pre-*perestroika* USSR. Thirty-eight percent favored a reformed Soviet system, 31 percent the existing polity, and 9 percent Western democracy. These responses stand in stark contrast to those of Communist Party leader Zyuganov's supporters, half of whom said they desired a return to the pre-*perestroika* Soviet Union, while 41 preferred a return to a reformed USSR. Only 3 percent of Zyuganov voters favored the existing system. Two percent preferred Western democracy (Colton and McFaul 2002, 116).

At the same time that most Russians expressed support for the "idea of democracy," few held illusions about the nature of their own system. When asked in 1999 if they thought their country was a democracy, only 19 percent of respondents said yes (down from 34 percent in 1996), while 52 percent said no (up from 29 percent three years earlier). The level of public satisfaction in Russia's democratic development also declined. Whereas 26 percent of all respondents were pleased with how well democracy was developing in Russia in 1996, only 12 percent said the same in 1999. At the same time, 80 percent expressed dissatisfaction in 1999 compared with 57 percent in 1996. Russians were also discouraged about the extent to which they had a say in politics. In a survey taken just after the 1999 Duma election, 84 percent of those interviewed agreed with the statement, "It seems to me government officials do not especially care what people like me think." Only 6 percent disagreed. In response to the statement, "People like me have no say in what the government does," 56 percent agreed, whereas 29 percent disagreed (Colton and McFaul 2002, 96, 98). Viewed as a whole, Colton and McFaul's findings suggest that dissatisfaction on the part of Russians with their political system reflects not so much uneasiness with the idea of democracy as it does a clear-eyed realism and understanding of how their political system actually works.

In light of these findings, what is the likelihood that a majority of Russians would support the imposition of total dictatorship? Colton and McFaul think it improbable. In more recent research, Rose, Munro, and Mishler (2004) also see this as a remote possibility. Eighty percent of respondents in their 2004 survey rejected the notion that "a tough dictatorship is the only way out of the current situation." When asked to consider other possible autocratic alternatives to the current system (a return to communist rule, the imposition of military government, or the suspension of the legislature and the elimination of elections), large majorities responded negatively to each option. Although only 55 percent rejected every possible autocratic alternative, no single option garnered more than 30 percent support (Rose, Munro, and Mishler 2004, 203).

In fact, most Russians are willing to live with the current system despite its many shortcomings. This support, Rose, Munro, and Mishler (2004) argue, is not based on a deep-seated approval of the regime but rather on a "resigned acceptance" of the status quo. Believing that a change in the system is unlikely, most Russians are willing to settle for what they have, however flawed and ineffective. Interestingly, Rose and his coauthors also find that Putin's popularity has little effect on the public's acceptance of the current system. The most important variable is the public's expectation of regime change. Without viable alternatives to the present system, anticipation of such a change on the part of most Russians will remain low. This in turn serves as a source of stability for the current regime.

◼ Conclusion

In the fall of 2007, Russia entered a new political season with Duma elections scheduled for that December and a presidential election set for the following

March. Even though Putin was constitutionally barred from serving a third consecutive term, public opinion polls showed that most Russians wanted him to stay on as president. Some of Putin's closer associates, among them the so-called *siloviki* ("men of power" who in their professional lives had direct ties to either the military or the security services), also wanted him to remain as the country's president. Throughout his second term, Putin declared that he would abide by the terms of the constitution. With elections approaching, however, few believed that he was ready to trade public life for a quiet retirement.

In early October, as speculation about his future grew, Putin began to reveal his intentions by announcing that he would head United Russia's federal party list in the upcoming Duma elections (Abdullaev et al. 2007). At the same time, he said he would consider becoming prime minister under two conditions: "First, United Russia would have to win the State Duma election on December 2, and second, our voters would have to elect a decent, effective and modern-thinking President with whom it would be possible to work" (Putin 2007a). By heading the party list, a vote for United Russia would now be a vote for Putin. Under the campaign slogan "Putin's Plan Is Russia's Victory!" (Plan Putina—Pobeda Rossii!), United Russia turned the election into a referendum on Putin's eight years in office.

In elections that the Organization for Security and Cooperation in Europe (OSCE) and the Council of Europe observers declared were "not fair," United Russia won 64.3 percent of the vote (Council of Europe 2007; TsIK Rossiia 2007). Because 8.25 percent of the vote went to parties that failed to cross the 7 percent threshold, 37 "unclaimed" seats were distributed roughly proportionally among the four parties that did meet the minimum vote requirement (see Table 4.1). This left United Russia with 315 seats (70 percent of the total), more than enough to maintain its control over the Duma and to approve amendments to the constitution.

A week after the Duma elections, Putin announced that he was supporting Dmitri Medvedev, the first deputy prime minister, in March's presidential

Table 4.1 2007 Duma Election Results

Party	Percent Vote	Seats	Percent Seats
United Russia	64.30	315	70.00
CPRF	11.57	57	12.67
LDPR	8.14	40	8.89
A Just Russia	7.74	38	8.44
All others	8.25	—	—
Total	100	450	100

Sources: Gosudarstvennaia Duma 2008; TsIK Rossiia 2007.

race. The next day, Medvedev offered to appoint Putin as prime minister, should he be elected president. A week later, Putin (2007b) accepted Medvedev's offer, pledging that in a Medvedev administration he would not seek to alter the existing balance of power between the presidency and the government, which he as prime minister would lead.

True to form, Putin chose a successor he could trust. In proposing that United Russia nominate Medvedev as its candidate for the presidency, Putin (2007b) called him "an absolutely decent man of great integrity." A St. Petersburg lawyer by training, Medvedev has known Putin since the early 1990s when they served together on Sobchak's staff, first in the Leningrad city council and later in the mayor's office. According to Putin (2007b), the two men had "an excellent working and personal relationship." By one account, Medvedev "worships Putin like a father figure, or at least like an older brother" (Abdullaev 2007). Given the close nature of their relationship, and the fact that Medvedev lacks a power base independent of Putin's, it seemed unlikely that as president he would try to push Putin aside or dramatically change the course of policy. On the question of policy, Medvedev, in his only campaign appearance, declared, "I, of course, will simply be bound to continue the course that has proven its effectiveness over the last eight years, the course of President Putin" (White and Cullison 2008).

Under the slogan "Together we will win!" (Vmeste pobedim!), Medvedev and Putin were cast as a "team" by the Medvedev campaign. A series of video spots on the Medvedev campaign website (http://www.medvedev 2008.ru/avm.htm) could not have communicated this message more clearly. In one advertisement, former Soviet hockey star and current president of the Russian Hockey Federation, Vladislav Tretiak, explained, "I understand why Putin and Medvedev must work together, because that team is a team that will lead our country to victory." In another spot, the director of an ambulance manufacturer told viewers how important it was to have "strong, competent people like Medvedev and Putin" running the country. In a third ad, a thirty-something entrepreneur, a member of the "lost generation" of the 1990s, spoke of his cohort's success during the Putin years. For him it was important that Putin was running "together" with Medvedev; Russia's future was at stake. "We must," he said, "live in a country of successful people."

As the March election approached, the only question was not whether Medvedev would win, but by what margin. Against a weak field and with Putin as his "running mate," Medvedev won easily with just over 70 percent of the vote. With this victory, the Putin era would continue.

Despite Putin's success in gaining and maintaining control over Russia's political system, his is ultimately a losing proposition. The paradox of the country's superpresidential system is that the more power the executive branch has the less effective the state will be in carrying out policy. For all the power Russia's president has to act independently of the legislature and the judiciary, without their help he is hard-pressed to bend the state bureaucracy to his will.

US president George W. Bush with then Russian president-elect Dmitri Medvedev during Bush's April 2008 visit to Russia.

The fundamental problem of contemporary Russian politics is accountability. When accountability is low among the three branches of government, the federal bureaucracy, lightly constrained by parliament and the courts, has the freedom to pursue its own narrow aims and interests at the expense of the public good. Conversely, when accountability is high, starting with a legislature that has the power to keep the president and the executive branch in line, so too is the willingness of federal agencies to execute policy and uphold the rule of law.

If Russia is to have any chance of creating a strong, modern state a necessary step will be the crafting of political institutions that allow the legislative and judicial branches to check executive power. This will require a significant restructuring of the system that Yeltsin created and Putin perfected. If the basic framework of semipresidentialism is to be preserved, restructuring, at a minimum, will require granting the Duma sole authority over the prime minister and the cabinet (greatly increasing the government's accountability to the lower house) and denying the president the right to dissolve the legislature.

The likely benefits of such a redistribution of power between the executive and legislative branches are many. First, with a powerful Duma in place political elites will have a reason to form demand-driven parties because winning a legislative majority will have real meaning. Instead of simply dabbling in politics, deputies will be in a position to exert a level of influence over the content and direction of policy unknown under the current constitution. With the development of a healthy, demand-driven party system, the level of accountability between voters and their elected representatives will increase, thus enhancing the legitimacy of the political system. The quality of those serving in the legislature will also rise as more talented people are drawn into careers in politics. Weak legislatures attract political amateurs. Strong legislatures attract genuine leaders (Fish 2005, 230–237). With the strengthening of legislative checks on executive power one could expect to see Russians becoming less reliant on personalities, in the form of an "all-powerful" executive, and more confident in institutions to solve their country's problems. With the ruling elite's continued distrust of institutions, however, the possibility of such a transformation seems remote. One potential source of optimism, however, is that most of Russian society seems ready to accept the logic of liberal democracy, even if those who run the country are not. Yet without viable alternatives to the current ruling elite, there will be little pressure for change from below. Short of a fundamental restructuring of the political system, however, Russia will continue to be limited in what it can achieve politically, economically, and socially.

■ Notes

1. Because of recent and planned mergers of some of Russia's regions, these figures are in the process of changing. For a brief explanation, see Table 7.2.
2. One other advantage the president has is his ability to gain legislative support through his office's control over the dispersal of legislative perks, among these the provision of living accommodations in Moscow.

■ Bibliography

Abdullaev, Nabi. 2007. "A Soft-Spoken, 'Smart Kid' Lawyer." *Moscow Times,* November 2.
Abdullaev, Nabi, et al. 2007. "Putin Will Run on United Russia Ticket." *Moscow Times,* October 2.
Aron, Leon. 2000. *Yeltsin: A Revolutionary Life.* New York: St. Martin's Press.
Baev, Pavel K. 2004. "The Evolution of Putin's Regime: Inner Circles and Outer Walls." *Problems of Post-Communism* 51(6): 5–13.
Baker, Peter, and Susan Glasser. 2005. *Kremlin Rising: Vladimir Putin's Russia and the End of Revolution.* New York: Scribner.
Balzer, Harley. 2003. "Managed Pluralism: Vladimir Putin's Emerging Regime." *Post-Soviet Affairs* 19(3): 189–227.
Billington, James H. 1970. *The Icon and the Axe: An Interpretive History of Russian Culture.* New York: Vintage Books.
CEIP (Carnegie Endowment for International Peace). 2004. "What Has Putin's Russia Become?" Discussion Meeting with Carnegie Senior Associates Lilia Shevtsova, Michael McFaul, Anatol Lieven, and Anders Åslund, September 23. http://www.carnegieendowment.org/files/PutinsRussia09-23-04.pdf.
Coalson, Robert. 2004. "End Note: A War on Terrorists or a War on Journalists?" *Radio Free Europe/Radio Liberty (RFE/RL) Newsline* 8(170), September 7. http://www.rferl.org/newsline/.

Colton, Timothy J., and Michael McFaul. 2002. "Are Russians Undemocratic?" *Post-Soviet Affairs* 18(2): 91–121.

———. 2003. *Popular Choice and Managed Democracy: The Russian Elections of 1999 and 2000.* Washington, D.C.: Brookings Institution Press.

Corwin, Julie A. 2005. "Gazprom Confirms Purchase of Izvestiya . . . As Observers See Launch of New Kremlin Media Offensive." *RFE/RL Newsline* 9(106), June 6. http://www.rferl.org/newsline/.

Council of Europe. 2007. "Russian Duma Elections 'Not Held on a Level Playing Field,' Say Parliamentary Observers." Press release 867 (December 3). https://wcd.coe.int/ViewDoc.jsp?id=1221469&Site=DC&BackColorInternet=F5CA75&BackColorIntranet=F5CA75&BackColorLogged=A9BACE.

Diamond, Larry. 1999. *Developing Democracy: Toward Consolidation.* Baltimore: Johns Hopkins University Press.

Dikun, Yelena. 1999. "The Big Kremlin Family: Anatomy and Physiology of the Yeltsin Family." *Obshchaya Gazeta,* July 22-28. In *Johnson's Russia List,* no. 3420, August 4. http://www.cdi.org/russia/johnson/3420.html##7.

Fak, Alex. 2003. "OSCE: Vote Fundamentally Distorted." *Moscow Times,* December 9.

Fish, M. Steven. 2005. *Democracy Derailed in Russia: The Failure of Open Politics.* New York: Cambridge University Press.

Gaidar, Yegor. 1999. *Days of Defeat and Victory.* Trans. Jane Ann Miller. Seattle: University of Washington Press.

Gerhart, Genevra. 1995. *The Russian's World: Life and Language.* 2nd ed. Fort Worth, TX: Holt, Rinehart and Winston; Harcourt Brace College Publishers.

Gosudarstvennaia Duma. 2008. "Sostav i struktura Gosudarstvennoi Dumy: Fraktsii v Gosudarstvennoi Dume po sostoianiiu na 7 fevralia 2008 goda" [Composition and structure of the State Duma: Fractions in the State Duma as of 7 February 2008]. http://www.duma.gov.

Hale, Henry E. 2004. "The Origins of United Russia and the Putin Presidency: The Role of Contingency in Party-System Development." *Demokratizatsiya* 12(2): 169–194.

Hale, Henry E., Michael McFaul, and Timothy J. Colton. 2004. "Putin and the 'Delegative Democracy' Trap: Evidence from Russia's 2003–04 Elections." *Post-Soviet Affairs* 20(4): 285–319.

Higley, John, and Michael G. Burton. 1989. "The Elite Variable in Democratic Transitions and Breakdowns." *American Sociological Review* 54(1): 17–32.

Huskey, Eugene. 1999. *Presidential Power in Russia.* Armonk, NY: M. E. Sharpe.

Huskey, Eugene, and Alexander Obolonsky. 2003. "The Struggle to Reform Russia's Bureaucracy." *Problems of Post-Communism* 50(4): 22–33.

Jack, Andrew. 2004. *Inside Putin's Russia.* New York: Oxford University Press.

Kahn, Jeffrey. 2002. *Federalism, Democratization, and the Rule of Law in Russia.* New York: Oxford University Press.

Kotkin, Stephen. 2001. *Armageddon Averted: The Soviet Collapse, 1970–2000.* Oxford, UK: Oxford University Press.

Levada Center and Centre for the Study of Public Policy (CSPP). 2007a. *Duma Election Law: Details.* http://www.russiavotes.org/duma/duma_election_law.php.

———. 2007b. *Public Opinion of the Media.* http://www.russiavotes.org/national_issues/media.php.

———. 2007c. *Results of Previous Presidential Elections.* http://www.russiavotes.org/president/presidency_previous.php.

Lieven, Anatol. 2005. "The Essential Vladimir Putin." *Foreign Policy* 146: 72–73.

Linz, Juan J. 1997. "Democracy Today: An Agenda for Students of Democracy." *Scandinavian Political Studies* 20(2): 115–134.

Lipman, Masha, and Michael McFaul. 2003. "Putin and the Media." In *Putin's Russia: Past Imperfect, Future Uncertain,* ed. Dale R. Herspring. Lanham, MD: Rowman & Littlefield.

Markov, Sergei. 2004. "The Future of Managed Democracy." *Moscow Times,* January 27.

Marks, Simon. 2003. "Managing Democracy." *The NewsHour with Jim Lehrer,* December 5. http://www.pbs.org/newshour/bb/europe/july-dec03/russia_12-05.html.

Mazneva, Elena. 2008. "The Successor's Team: State Officials on the Boards of State Corporations." *Vedomosti,* February 6.

McFaul, Michael. 2001. *Russia's Unfinished Revolution: Political Change from Gorbachev to Putin.* Ithaca, NY: Cornell University Press.

Menshikov, Stanislav. 2003. "Funny Elections: Kremlin Uses 'Administrative Resource.'" *Moscow Tribune,* November 21. http://www.fastcenter.ru/smenshikov/MT/MTRIB161.html.

O vnesenii izmenenii v Federalnyi zakon "O politicheskikh partiiakh" [On the insertion of changes into the Federal law *On Political Parties*]. 2004. Rossiiskaia Federatsiia Federalnyi zakon N 168-FZ [Russian Federation Federal law No. 168-FZ], December 20. http://www.akdi.ru/GD/proekt/095698GD.SHTM.

Oates, Sarah. 2000. "The 1999 Russian Duma Election." *Problems of Post-Communism* 47(3): 3–14.

On Political Parties. 2001. Russian Federation Federal Law No. 95-FZ, July 11. http://www.democracy.ru/english/library/laws/parties_fz95_eng/.

Orttung, Robert W. 2006. "Russia." In *Nations in Transit 2006: Democratization from Central Europe to Eurasia.* Freedom House. http://www.freedomhouse .org.

OSCE/ODIHR (Organization for Security and Cooperation in Europe/Office for Democratic Institutions and Human Rights). 2004. "Russian Federation: Elections to the State Duma, 7 December 2003. OSCE/ODIHR Election Observation Mission Final Report." January 27. http://www.osce.org/documents/odihr/2004/01/1947_en.pdf.

Paddock, Richard C. 1999. "Yeltsin's Daughter Viewed as Power Behind Throne." *Los Angeles Times,* October 10.

———. 2000. "Putin's Rise Chalked Up to Close 'Family' Ties." *Los Angeles Times,* January 4.

Petrov, Nikolai. 2004. "Managed Democracy on Auto-Pilot." *Moscow Times,* March 10.

———. 2005. "From Managed Democracy to Sovereign Democracy: Putin's Regime Evolution in 2005." PONARS Policy Memo No. 396 (December). http://www.csis.org/component/option,com _csis_pubs/task,view/id,2198/.

Pipes, Richard. 2004. "Flight from Freedom: What Russians Think and Want." *Foreign Affairs* 83(3): 9–15.

Puddington, Arch, and Aili Piano. 2005. "Worrisome Signs, Modest Shifts." *Journal of Democracy* 16(1): 103–108.

Putin, Vladimir. 1999. "Russia at the Turn of the Millennium," December 31. http://www.publicaffairsbooks.com/publicaffairsbooks-cgi-bin/display?book=1586480189&view=excerpt.

———. 2000a. Annual Address to the Federal Assembly of the Russian Federation, July 8. http://www.kremlin.ru/eng/speeches/2000/07/08/0000_type70029type82912_70658.shtml.

————. 2000b. *First Person: An Astonishingly Frank Self-Portrait by Russia's President.* Trans. Catherine A. Fitzpatrick. New York: Public Affairs.

————. 2005. Annual Address to the Federal Assembly of the Russian Federation, April 25. http://www.kremlin.ru/eng/speeches/2005/04/25/2031_type70029type 82912_87086.shtml.

————. 2007a. Concluding Remarks at the United Russia Party Congress, October 1. http://www.kremlin.ru/eng/speeches/2007/10/01/2210_type82912type82913 type84779_146510.shtml.

————. 2007b. Excerpts from the Transcript of the Closing Session of United Russia's VIII Party Congress, December 17. http://www.kremlin.ru/eng/text/speeches/ 2007/12/17/1541_type82912type82917type84779_154600.shtml.

Remington, Thomas F. 2006. "Presidential Support in the Russian State Duma." *Legislative Studies Quarterly* 31(1): 5–32.

Remington, Thomas F., et al. 1994. "Transitional Institutions and Parliamentary Alignments in Russia, 1990–1993." In *Parliaments in Transition: The New Legislative Politics in the Former USSR and Eastern Europe,* ed. Thomas F. Remington. Boulder, CO: Westview Press.

Remnick, David. 1998. *Resurrection: The Struggle for a New Russia.* New York: Vintage.

Riggs, Jonathan W., and Peter J. Schraeder. 2004. "Russia's Political Party System as an Impediment to Democratization." *Demokratizatsiya* 12(2): 265–293.

Rose, Richard. 2000. "A Supply-Side View of Russia's Elections." *East European Constitutional Review* 9(1/2): 53–59.

Rose, Richard, and Neil Munro. 2002. *Elections Without Order: Russia's Challenge to Vladimir Putin.* Cambridge, UK: Cambridge University Press.

Rose, Richard, Neil Munro, and William Mishler. 2004. "Resigned Acceptance of an Incomplete Democracy: Russia's Political Equilibrium." *Post-Soviet Affairs* 20(3): 195–218.

Rose, Richard, and Doh Chull Shin. 2001. "Democratization Backwards: The Problem of Third-Wave Democracies." *British Journal of Political Science* 31(2): 331–354.

Ross, Cameron. 2004. "Putin's Federal Reforms." In *Russian Politics Under Putin,* ed. Cameron Ross. Manchester, UK: Manchester University Press.

Rustow, Dankwart A. 1970. "Transitions to Democracy: Toward a Dynamic Model." *Comparative Politics* 2(3): 337–363.

Sakwa, Richard. 2005. "The 2003–2004 Russian Elections and Prospects for Democracy." *Europe-Asia Studies* 57(3): 369–398.

SDI (Strengthening Democratic Institutions) Project. 1999. *Russian Election Watch,* no. 3. Cambridge, MA: BCSIA. http://bcsia.ksg.harvard.edu/publication.cfm? program=CORE&ctype=paper&item_id=327.

Shevtsova, Lilia. 1999. *Yeltsin's Russia: Myths and Reality.* Washington, D.C.: Carnegie Endowment for International Peace.

————. 2005. *Putin's Russia.* Rev. and expanded ed. Trans. Antonina W. Bouis. Washington, D.C.: Carnegie Endowment for International Peace.

Smyth, Regina. 2006. "Strong Parties, Weak Parties? Party Organizations and the Development of Mass Partisanship in Russia." *Comparative Politics* 38(2): 209–228.

Surkov, Vladislav. 2005. "Vladislav Surkov's Secret Speech: How Russia Should Fight International Conspiracies." *Mosnews.com,* July 12.

Thornhill, John. 2000. "Hard-pressed Family Finds a Way Out." *Financial Times,* January 3.

Trenin, Dmitri. 2005. *Reading Russia Right.* Policy Brief No. 42, Special Edition (October). Washington, D.C.: Carnegie Endowment for International Peace.

http://www.carnegieendowment.org/publications/index.cfm?fa=view&id=17619 &prog=zru.

TsIK Rossiia (Central Election Commission of the Russian Federation). 2007. "Re-zul'taty vyborov: Vybory deputatov Gosudarstvennoi Dumy Federal'nogo So-braniia Rossiiskoi Federatsii, piatogo sozyva" [Election results: Elections of deputies to the fifth State Duma of the Federal Assembly of the Russian Feder-ation]. http://www.vybory.izbirkom.ru/region/izbirkom?action=show&global= 1&vrn=100100021960181&region=0&prver=0&pronetvd=null.

White, Gregory L., and Alan Cullison. 2008. "Medvedev Reveals Little, Save Loy-alty." *Wall Street Journal,* February 28.

White, Stephen. 2006. "Russians and Their Political System." *Demokratizatsiya* 14(1): 7–22.

White, Stephen, and Ian McAllister. 2003. "Putin and His Supporters." *Europe-Asia Studies* 55(3): 383–399.

White, Stephen, Richard Rose, and Ian McAllister. 1997. *How Russia Votes.* Cha-tham, NJ: Chatham House.

Yasmann, Victor. 2005. "Putin's Advisors Control over $200 Billion in Key Indus-tries." *RFE/RL Newsline* 9(140), July 27. http://www.rferl.org/newsline/.

Yeltsin, Boris. 1993a. "Speech by B. N. Yeltsin, President of Russia." *Rossiiskiye vesti,* March 12. In *Current Digest of the Post-Soviet Press* 45(10), April 7.

———. 1993b. "Yeltsin's Address on National Television." Official Kremlin Inter-national News Broadcast, September 21.

———. 1994. *The Struggle for Russia.* Trans. Catherine A. Fitzpatrick. New York: Times Books.

———. 2000. *Prezidentskii marafon* [Presidential marathon]. Moscow: AST.

5

The Economy

James R. Millar

As much as Russia has changed politically since the collapse of the Soviet Union in 1991, so too has it undergone a great economic transformation. This chapter chronicles that transformation from the launching of "shock therapy" by Boris Yeltsin in 1992 to the economic crisis of 1998. It continues with an examination of the subsequent recovery, followed by an assessment of the economic boom of the Putin years. Throughout, the chapter will evaluate the strengths and weaknesses of post-Soviet Russian economic policy. Before doing so, however, the chapter will devote considerable space to the economic policies of the Soviet era. One needs a firm grounding in the Soviet experience, especially an understanding of the nature of the Soviet planned economy, to appreciate the challenges facing those who seek to transform Russia's economy.

■ The Institutions and Workings of the Planned Economy

In Chapter 3 of this volume Steven Marks examines in some detail the historical origins of the Soviet planned economy. With his discussion as our backdrop, we begin this chapter with an overview of the ideas and institutions that informed and influenced Soviet economic planning and development. A commitment to Marxism on the part of the Bolshevik regime meant that Soviet economists agreed on certain general principles of economic organization. Following Karl Marx's critique of capitalism and his theory of economic development, they viewed socialism as the negation of capitalism. As such, the creation of a socialist economy would mean the abolition of private property, free markets, and the private hiring of labor for profit. Ultimately, a socialist economy would also dispense with prices, debt instruments, money, wages, and taxes. The price system would disappear because it would not be needed to serve as a guide to allocation decisions for enterprises and individuals. The "anarchy" of the free market would be replaced by conscious state planning.

This was a tall order, and Soviet economists did not agree on how to achieve it. In particular, how was the planning apparatus to function? Two schools of thought emerged during the 1920s. Economists of one school, called the *geneticists,* argued that there were certain limits on rates of growth that were inherent in an economy and that these constraints limited economic planning to the forecasting and setting of guidelines. Economists of the other school, known as the *teleologists,* argued that planning should consist of denying natural limits and setting high goals that would serve as incentives for workers and enterprise managers. Ultimately, the teleologists won the debate and Soviet planning became an exercise in setting comprehensive targets for outputs, inputs, productivity increases, the wage bill, and every other aspect of the economy. Targets were set high to ensure that no output would be lost through lack of incentive or effort, and incentives and disincentives were designed to focus attention on attainment of planning goals. Thus, Soviet planning was ambitious, comprehensive, and mandatory (Gregory and Stuart 2001, 67–82; Millar 1981, 16–33).

Enterprises participated annually in the development of "tekhpromfin plans," or technical-industrial-financial plans. An initial plan was drawn up for current operations by the enterprise that specified the planned output, including specification of the assortment and quality of outputs, the inputs required to produce output, with delivery dates corresponding to production cycles, changes in productivity and other indicators of efficiency, and the finance required to pay for inputs and labor. The most basic operational plans were quarterly. An overriding Five-Year Plan was created as a framework for annual plans. Final annual and quarterly plans were negotiated between the higher planning agencies, most important of which was Gosplan (the State Planning Committee) and the economic ministries. This process has been described as a form of economic "guerrilla warfare," as enterprises and central planners sought, respectively, to achieve a realistic central plan and one that stretched the enterprises' capacities.

The superstructure of planning consisted of a Council of Ministers led by high-ranking members of the Communist Party. Reporting to the Council of Ministers were two types of plan agencies. There were line ministries, which oversaw particular industries and services such as steel, mining, railroads, and consumer goods. These were divided into all-union ministries and republic ministries. The fifteen republic ministries were responsible for local industries and services. All-union ministries had nationwide application. The second type of planning agency was functional in character. These included Gosplan, Gosbank (the State Bank), and other agencies that set goals, supervised performance, and evaluated results (Gregory and Stuart 2001, 89–117; Millar 2004).

In short, Soviet economic planning was based on a massive bureaucracy. Monetary policy, fiscal policy, and the regulatory agencies that are common in capitalist systems played no determining role. All were governed by the central plan. This included investment planning and allocation, and the volume and composition of consumer goods.

The Soviet planning system was created by Stalin, with the support of the Communist Party, in the late 1920s and the 1930s under the banners of rapid industrialization and mass collectivization. Despite a commitment to ideological purity as Marxists, peasant resistance and economic reality forced Stalin and his regime to make certain compromises in the socialist economic structure. It proved impossible to eliminate all markets, all private enterprise, and money wage payments. Thus money and prices continued to play a role in the Soviet planned economy. First, peasants were allowed to keep small garden plots surrounding their homes for private productive use and to raise a limited number of farm animals. Thus, a private market, the collective farm market, existed through which peasants could sell a portion of their private output to townspeople and each other.

The direct distribution of consumer goods and services to workers was also beyond the capacity of the Soviet system, at least for the foreseeable future. Instead, state enterprise workers were paid money wages, which they were free to spend in the state retail system or the collective farm market, or to deposit in the state savings bank (which, incidentally, paid interest). Collective farms also were an anomaly. Even though they were seen as an intermediate step on the way to full-fledged factory farms, they continued a fitful and unproductive existence to the very end of the Soviet era, never having recovered from the adverse effects of their involuntary formation and compulsory deliveries to the state (Millar 1981, 61–81; Millar 2004). Even so, the system of direct allocation by state planning prevailed in several key areas of the economy, resulting in the elimination of certain markets. Among these were financial markets, investment goods markets, international trade, and markets for existing enterprises.

World War II was the planned economy's first true test. Nazi Germany invaded the Soviet Union on June 22, 1941, with devastating results as the German army quickly overran Belorussia (now known as Belarus), Ukraine, and vast expanses of European Russia. Unprepared for war, Soviet economic losses in potential industrial and agricultural production in these regions were enormous. Even so, Germany was unable to defeat the USSR. Much of the credit for the eventual Soviet victory over the Nazis belonged to the planned economy. Ideally suited for the wartime mobilization of the USSR's vast resources, the military and economic weight it brought to bear against the Nazis was decisive in bringing about their destruction and defeat. For the Soviets, the war not only demonstrated the viability of their economic institutions and planning in time of war, but also served to reinforce their confidence in the system (Harrison 1996; Millar 1981, 35–52).

Little time was spent celebrating the successful conclusion of the war, however. The economy was smaller than it had been at the outset of the war. Mines, factories, schools, hospitals, homes, and farms had been destroyed first with the German advance and then again with the German retreat from Soviet territory. Reconstruction was relatively rapid thanks to central planning and to the extraction of war reparations from the territories in East-Central Europe. The Soviets would not match their prewar production levels, however, until 1950. Thus the USSR lost about two Five-Year Plans' worth of capacity and output as a result of the war (Millar 1981, 50–55).

■ The Planned Economy After Stalin, 1953–1964

As well as the planned economy had performed during World War II, gaps existed, most notably with respect to the provision of consumer goods and services. Having geared the planned economy toward rapid industrialization and military production, Stalin paid little attention to the population's standard of living. However, after Nikita Khrushchev won the lengthy power struggle that ensued within the Communist Party leadership following Stalin's death in March 1953, he began to introduce changes in the Stalinist system. One of his first moves was to make an effort to increase the availability of consumer goods and services. The population's standard of living was not much higher than that of the late 1920s, just before the imposition of the planned economy. Because of Khrushchev's policies consumer goods production increased, more housing was built, and more attention was paid to agriculture. From 1956 to 1960, gross domestic product (GDP) and per capita consumption increased at rates that were unmatched during the remainder of the Soviet era. Khrushchev appeared to be riding a wave of success (Millar 1981, 52–53; Taubman 2003, Chapter 18).

These early policy triumphs, however, led him to expect results from the Soviet economy that could not be achieved. In 1961, in the drafting of a new party program (the first since Lenin was in power), Khrushchev instructed its authors to include as one of its goals the achievement of economic parity with the United States by 1970. If this were not ambitious enough, when Khrushchev presented the draft of the new program to the Central Committee at its June 1961 plenum, he avowed that by the early 1980s "communism in our country will be just about built" (Taubman 2003, 508–511).

Aside from the utopian character of these aims, several fault lines underlay Khrushchev's economic policies. Some were rightly called "harebrained schemes." Others had lasting positive significance. His Virgin Lands program, for instance, greatly expanded grain production in Kazakhstan and Siberia. This in turn allowed for increases in the number of livestock, which positively affected dairy and meat production. Much of the land put under cultivation under the program, however, was not suitable for the sustained production of grain. Although Khrushchev benefited politically in the short run from the program, by 1964 the Soviet Union was obliged to import grain from the West. This made little sense economically as it would have been more rational to import meat directly from the West because Soviet livestock herds were of low quality and therefore inefficient in converting grain into meat.

Several other agricultural policies also had dubious outcomes. After his trip to the United States in 1959, during which he was impressed by the high corn (maize) yields obtained by US farmers, he instituted a corn program that greatly expanded the area devoted to this crop's production. The basic idea was not entirely unsound. Corn is excellent as fodder for livestock, and indeed the program enjoyed some success. However, overly enthusiastic regional party leaders, seeking Khrushchev's favor, expanded production into areas that were ill-suited for corn with disastrous results. In yet another policy failure, Khrushchev encouraged the "plow up" of grasslands and fallow, which eventually backfired by depleting soil fertility.

Khrushchev had more success in raising the living standards of people in rural areas, but even these policies failed to create a vital and productive agricultural sector. Prices were increased for obligatory deliveries to the state, the pension system was extended to collective farm workers, and the Machine Tractor Stations (MTS) that had served to provide mechanical and motorized support for the farms were sold to the farms to eliminate conflicts of interest between the MTS and the collectives. Unfortunately, prices were not raised enough to serve as strong incentives to work, the cost of the MTS offset the benefits of better organization, and investment in the sector continued to lag.

Some of Khrushchev's economic policies also created potentially powerful enemies in the party and state apparatuses. His splitting of the regional party apparatus into separate rural and urban hierarchies, for instance, was so strongly opposed by regional party elites that it was quickly abandoned after his removal from power in 1964, and in fact was one of the reasons for his dismissal. Khrushchev also experimented with radical changes in the structure of central planning. In 1957 he introduced the Sovnarkhoz reform that was designed to change the fundamental unit of planning from the Moscow-based all-union ministries, which focused on functional and product divisions, into

105 regional organizations. The idea was to break down monopolistic barriers and inefficient layers of command and replace them with a system that Khrushchev hoped would encourage regional coordination and specialization. The fundamental weakness of the scheme, however, was that abolishing the all-union ministries could not solve the underlying problems of the system. With the all-union ministries gone, "localism" simply took over, in which regional leaders focused on their own narrow interests at the expense of the whole. This, combined with geographical barriers, ensured the economy's continued inefficiency (Millar 2003, 110–113; Taubman 2003, Chapters 18 and 20).

■ The Brezhnev Era, 1964–1982: From Stability to Stagnation

Khrushchev's ouster in October 1964 brought the end of an era of instability and ill-advised economic schemes and the beginning of a period of stability that brought with it the promise of economic prosperity. The new men in charge, Communist Party leader Leonid Brezhnev and chairman of the Council of Ministers Aleksei Kosygin, stood in stark contrast to the sometimes erratic Khrushchev. Initially, too, it appeared that the Soviet Union would continue efforts to reform the planned economy, but this time led by a steady hand. Kosygin was most identified with this reform effort, so much so that his 1964 reforms are still known as the "Kosygin reforms" even though they represented the culmination of his predecessor's reform efforts. These reforms, as the previous ones under Khrushchev, failed to bring about any fundamental improvements in economic performance. The main problem, as in the past, was how to bring about a harmony of interests, instead of bureaucratic guerrilla warfare, between the principals, that is, the central planners, and their agents, enterprise managers, and other lower ranking officials in the state bureaucracy. The Kosygin reforms failed to solve this problem, one that some argue could not be solved (Gregory 2004). Kosygin's opponents in the bureaucracy found a willing supporter in Communist Party of the Soviet Union (CPSU) leader Leonid Brezhnev who relied on the party and state apparatuses to stay in power. For all his efforts to strengthen the Soviet economy, Kosygin was gradually isolated politically by Brezhnev. All subsequent reform attempts under Brezhnev suffered a similar fate (Gregory and Stuart 2001, 224–238).

For his part, Brezhnev not only was a skilled politician in his ability to outmaneuver Kosygin, but was also the beneficiary of global economic forces that he did not control that allowed him to avoid having to confront the inherent weaknesses of the Soviet planned economy. For starters, in August 1971, the United States, responding to changes in the international economy, ended its long-standing policy of maintaining the price of gold at thirty-five dollars an ounce. With the price of gold now determined by free markets, the dollar value of the Soviet Union's vast gold stock rose substantially during the 1970s. Three years later, in 1974, the Organization of Petroleum Exporting Countries (OPEC) cut back production, driving up the price of oil on world markets. As a major producer and exporter of oil, the Soviet Union benefited greatly from OPEC's actions. Finally, the Soviet Union's postwar baby boom allowed the USSR to continue to rely upon extensive economic growth, as opposed to increases in efficiency. These windfalls in gold, oil, and labor allowed Brezhnev to ignore the country's economic problems, to continue placating an entrenched economic bureaucracy that he relied upon for support, and to engage in an expensive arms race that would allow the Soviets to achieve a rough parity with the United States. By the time of Brezhnev's death in November 1982, the USSR had essentially attained that objective while at the same time maintaining stability at home, all at the expense of the long-term health of the economy.

In fact, economic indices reveal that in the mid-1970s, even with the windfalls provided by gold, oil, and labor, the Soviet economy had begun to slow down. Unlike years past, the Soviets could no longer rely on increasing inputs to maintain high rates of growth. In the emerging hi-tech world, such growth could only come through greater efficiency. Thus, even though the Brezhnev era represented a time of relative prosperity and stability for the Soviet people, and one in which the Soviet military had achieved strategic parity with the United States, Brezhnev's successors inherited an economy in drastic need of an overhaul (Hanson 1992, 7–32; Millar 1981, 175–187; Millar 1985). In fact, economic reform was essential. Even before the Brezhnev era had ended, a number of Soviet economists worked out reform proposals that were then set aside until political conditions were right for them to be given a public hearing.

Following Brezhnev's death in November 1982, however, events intervened to delay the launching of significant reform. His immediate successor, Yuri Andropov, did set out to shake up the party and state apparatuses. A Communist Party puritan who disdained corruption, he headed the KGB (Soviet secret police) from 1967 to 1982. During the 1970s he directed the repression of a growing and increasingly active dissident movement. Thus, he was no democrat. However, because of his knowledge of economic reforms in Hungary, and his intolerance for corruption, some believed he might be amenable to similar reforms in the Soviet Union. His promise in this respect was undermined, however, by serious health problems that surfaced soon after he became CPSU general secretary. Although he initiated efforts to deal with corruption, the ailing Andropov was limited in what he could accomplish. However, before declining health confined him to a hospital bed, he had managed to remove a number of Brezhnev's CPSU cronies and to promote a number of younger, idealistic followers into the upper ranks of the Communist Party leadership, among them, Mikhail Gorbachev.

Andropov also initiated strict reforms that aimed to restore discipline and commitment among the workers, relying on mild KGB methods of enforcement, including the stopping of people on the streets to find out if they were supposed to be at work. Before much progress could be made in his efforts to instill discipline in Soviet society and the party, Andropov died in February 1984, just fifteen months after having taken power.

In an effort to stop the momentum of reform, the old guard in the Politburo maneuvered Brezhnev loyalist Konstantin Chernenko into power. The seventy-two-year-old Chernenko, however, was also in poor health and would not last long. Although economic reform was put on hold under Chernenko, the younger leaders Andropov had promoted, outmaneuvered by the old guard once, would not be denied again. Thus, after Chernenko's death in March 1985, one of their own, Mikhail Gorbachev, would become the Communist Party's leader. Committed to rejuvenating the Soviet economy, his reform efforts instead would help bring about the USSR's destruction (Millar 2004).

■ The Gorbachev Era and the End of the Soviet System

Gorbachev's six years as CPSU general secretary, from the spring of 1985 through the fall of 1991, changed not only the Soviet Union but the world. Gorbachev considered himself a "child of the Twentieth Party Congress," at which Nikita Khrushchev, in 1956, denounced Stalin's cult of personality and his crimes against the Communist Party and the Soviet people. Gorbachev surrounded himself with several other young communists who remained loyal Marxists but who sought to cleanse Soviet socialism and restore it to its rightful place in Soviet society. Unlike his patron Andropov, Gorbachev was not a product of the KGB. Trained as a lawyer and fascinated with ideas, he relied on the legal system and intellectual concepts to change society. The main impetus to reform was the gradual but steady decline in the rate of economic growth since 1975. As growth stagnated, so did increases in personal consumption. Thus, although the Soviet Union had reached essential parity with the United States militarily under Brezhnev, it was falling behind economically. Gorbachev faced a stark choice. He could preserve the current system, without substantial economic reforms, and accept second-class economic standing to capitalism indefinitely, as the nuclear weapons standoff with the United States assured the Soviet Union's security. Or he could risk deep reforms designed to get the socialist economy moving again to compete with capitalism. As a committed Marxist, Gorbachev was not prepared to give up the dream of proving the superiority of socialism. This is the sense in which economics figured into the ultimate collapse of the Soviet system. It was the attempt to stimulate economic performance with real reforms, both economic and political, that led to political instability, which, in turn, further undermined the Soviet economy (Brown 1996; Millar 1988; Millar 2004, 577–583).

Initially, Gorbachev's economic reforms, collectively known as *perestroika,* or restructuring, encountered the bureaucratic resistance all previous efforts to reform the Soviet economy had, and as a result, little changed. Several of his early reforms actually proved counterproductive. An anti-alcohol campaign, conducted with the usual heavy-handed administrative measures of the Soviet system, deprived the state budget of an important source of revenue and encouraged the illegal distillation of liquor in private homes. As the production of *samogon* (a Russian form of "home brew") boomed, sugar and fruit disappeared from retail stores. Gorbachev also sought under *perestroika* to decrease the degree of centralization of state economic planning. One piece of legislation that backfired was the Law on State Enterprises, which increased the discretion of state enterprises and reduced the authority and power of the central economic ministries. Instead of boosting the economy, the new law, by weakening the authority of state planners, led to shortages, inflation, a decrease in tax collections, and an increase in inter-enterprise debt. At the same time, product quality remained poor and productivity stagnant. Another important change was legislation that permitted private cooperative small-scale enterprises to operate in competition with state enterprises. Private restaurants and one-person enterprises, such as hairdressing, and radio and TV repair, quickly came into being. While a welcome change, these enterprises competed for scarce retail goods, increasing the length of queues and causing ordinary citizens to become disgruntled. As central control of the economy loosened and some private enterprise was encouraged, the system began to unravel (Gregory and Stuart 2001, 233–250; Hanson 1992, 128–173).

Perestroika unintentionally threatened the viability of the Soviet system in other ways too. For Gorbachev, change not only meant restructuring at home, but also a transformation in the country's relations abroad, including those with its Central and East European neighbors. Unlike his predecessors, who uniformly had resisted, sometimes with force, any attempts by these Soviet satellite states to loosen their bonds with the USSR through radical political change at home, Gorbachev encouraged the leaders of these countries to engage in their own forms of *perestroika,* and for their societies to chart their own courses, which they did, one by one, in the late 1980s.

Because the Soviet empire, as an economic unit, had been designed to be as self-sufficient as possible, and as a deliberate attempt had been made during the post–World War II years to integrate Central and East European

Michael L. Bressler

One sign of the times during the late Soviet era: the opening of
Western shops in Moscow on Gorky Street (now Tverskaia Ulitsa).

industries and agriculture into the Soviet economy and central planning as
a whole, the disintegration of these relationships undermined production
and distribution in the system. As the Central and East European economies
strenuously sought to shift trade to Western Europe, the Soviet Union was
left with a disrupted trade network.

Moreover, the various republics that comprised the USSR also became
increasingly restless, seeking greater autonomy and even independence.
These developments undermined the central plan and destabilized the system
of production and distribution. By 1989, the Soviet economy was beginning
to break down. Shortages of goods were pandemic. Inflation became a bigger
problem and the population found it increasingly necessary to buy goods illegally outside the controlled retail market at what were essentially market
prices. The central government was increasingly losing control as the system
fractured into its component national and regional parts (Millar 1993).

Meanwhile, in the summer of 1990, Gorbachev, with the cooperation of
Russian Republic leader Boris Yeltsin, organized a team of the country's top
market-oriented economists to develop a strategy to reverse the country's economic decline and to rescue his reforms. Known as the Shatalin-Yavlinsky
group (after its lead economists, Stansilav Shatalin and Grigory Yavlinsky),
the team authored a daring plan that called for a radical transformation of
the Soviet planned economy into a full-fledged market economy in just five

hundred days. An alternative approach, promoted by the director of the Economic Institute of the Soviet Academy of Sciences, Leonid Abalkin, and the chairman of the USSR Council of Ministers, Nikolai Ryzhkov, represented a modest revision of central planning, with some support for limited open markets.

Initially enthusiastic about the radical "Five Hundred Days Plan," Gorbachev soon had second thoughts. Part of his change of heart came from legitimate concerns over the economic workability of the Shatalin-Yavlinsky program. Although setting precise timetables for change, the plan was often vague on particulars. Gorbachev was also concerned about the social welfare of the Soviet population in the process. Political considerations also loomed large in Gorbachev's thinking. First, he feared that the Shatalin-Yavlinsky plan, by giving the republics primary authority over economic policy and taxation, could mean an end to the Union. Second, he was under immense pressure from powerful party and government conservatives to oppose the plan. In an effort to bring the two opposing camps together, Gorbachev pushed for a compromise program. The result was a reform plan of half-measures that had no chance of success and only deepened the rifts within the system (Brown 1996).

From then on, political developments would overshadow any efforts at economic reform. As the Soviet system continued to fragment politically, Gorbachev felt compelled during the summer of 1991 to negotiate a Union Treaty that would have increased the autonomy of the republics. Conservatives in the CPSU, however, opposed any loosening of the bonds between the central government in Moscow and the republics. Fearing a complete collapse of the system, they attempted a coup in August 1991. The poorly planned coup and the clear incompetence of its supporters played into the hands of Gorbachev's one-time protégé and now bitter rival Boris Yeltsin. Yeltsin foiled the coup and seized the opportunity to take the Russian Republic out of the Soviet Union, along with Belarus, Ukraine, and Kazakhstan. As Russia was the USSR's keystone, all of the other republics became independent whether their leaders wanted them to or not. In the end, Gorbachev found that he could not reconcile the many contradictory political and economic currents in the Soviet system. Radical market reform along the lines of the Five Hundred Days Plan threatened to undermine the political viability of the Union. Without action, however, the Soviet economy would continue its descent, further increasing the pressure on Gorbachev from radicals to do something. At the same time, his efforts to establish a new set of relations with some of these same radicals through the negotiation of a Union Treaty alienated hard-line elements within the party that refused any compromise.

True to his personal convictions, Gorbachev was unwilling to resort to the widespread use of force and repression to keep the Soviet polity and its economy intact. Even if he had been willing to play the part of a heavy-handed dictator, the time for such an approach, at least in the Soviet context, had passed. Ultimately, Gorbachev would be incapable of action. In the aftermath of the failed August coup, it would be Boris Yeltsin who would take the next decisive steps of dismantling the USSR and its system of economic planning.

▨ Boris Yeltsin and the Transition to Capitalism

Boris Yeltsin was brought into the political limelight by Gorbachev, whose sponsorship led to Yeltsin's appointment as first secretary of the Moscow City Communist Party Committee. The position was essentially that of mayor of Moscow. His forthright effort to promote reform and limit the privileges of party elites (such as their access to special schools, medical facilities, and retail stores) made him very popular with the people. Indicative of his growing status in the party, he was also a candidate, or nonvoting, member of the Politburo. The brash populism that Muscovites responded to so well, however, irritated many of his party colleagues and staff. His personal attacks on Gorbachev and other party leaders in an October 1987 meeting of the CPSU Central Committee, in which he criticized the party and Gorbachev for not moving quickly enough on reform, overstepped the bounds of acceptable behavior by a senior party leader. Having embarrassed Gorbachev and called into question the validity of the reform effort, Yeltsin was removed from office as Moscow party leader and stripped of his membership in the Politburo. Later appointed to the post of first deputy chair of the USSR State Construction Committee (Gosstroy), Yeltsin's political career seemed to be at an end.

Not long after, however, reforms passed in July 1988 at the Nineteenth Party Conference that called for the creation of the Soviet Union's first ever freely elected legislature offered Yeltsin an opportunity to resurrect his political career. Against the wishes of the party leadership, Yeltsin was elected to that body, the USSR Congress of People's Deputies, in March 1989 as a representative from Moscow. Subsequently, he took a seat in the congress's permanent legislative body, the USSR Supreme Soviet, also against the wishes of the party leadership. His upward mobility was one measure of the loss of the CPSU's control over the composition of the country's political leadership. As the fifteen republics that comprised the USSR gained increased autonomy, Yeltsin was also elected to the Russian Republic (RSFSR) Congress of People's Deputies in March 1990, and then as chairperson of the RSFSR Supreme Soviet in May 1990. In mid-June, the Russian Congress declared the Russian Republic sovereign. Thus began a long, bitter struggle between Yeltsin and Gorbachev over control of Russia's economy.

Unlike the other republics of the USSR, the Russian Republic did not have an economic bureaucracy separate from the all-union Soviet bureaucracy, with the result that Yeltsin and Gorbachev fought head-to-head over control of the various agencies as well as the central budget. For example, the State Bank of the USSR (Gosbank) was a Soviet institution. Yeltsin sought to convert it into a bank of the Russian Republic so that he would be able to influence credit creation and monetary policy. The stakes were high in this struggle: if Yeltsin won and the Russian Republic became truly sovereign, meaning that it and not the USSR had control over the Soviet bureaucracy, there would be no need for all-union Soviet political and economic institutions.

Yeltsin had the advantage over Gorbachev in that he not only had become alienated from the CPSU, but had also freed himself from Marxist ideology. Yeltsin also joined the leadership of the opposition "Inter-Regional Group of Deputies," which called for a new constitution and the end of the CPSU's political dominance. The feud between Gorbachev and the party on the one hand, and Yeltsin and the Supreme Soviet of the Russian Republic on the other, was carried out largely in economic terms, and the economy of the USSR suffered as a result. Having been directly elected president of the Russian Republic by the people in June 1991, Yeltsin was in perfect position to take advantage of the failed coup of August 1991 and of Gorbachev's resulting political weakness. The end result was the breakup of the Soviet Union into its fifteen constituent republics in December 1991, and the termination of Gorbachev's political career. Yeltsin had won the political battle, clearing the way for radical market reform (Shevtsova 1999, 5–30).

The Russian economy that Yeltsin and his team faced at the end of 1991 was in dire straits. Under Soviet central planning, of course, prices and quantities of consumer goods and services available in the state retail network were set centrally by state committees without regard to whether these markets cleared. Undesirable products lingered on the shelves. Desirable ones disappeared within hours of their arrival at state stores. No attempt was made to adjust prices to bring supply and demand into equilibrium. Although few dared to challenge such arrangements under Stalin, as the fear of punishment diminished and oversight declined under his successors, private purchases of state retail goods for resale at a profit increased, as did sales "out the backdoor" at market prices. Thus, at the same time that central planning inadvertently created shortages and long lines for goods desired by Soviet consumers, it also fueled the development of black markets through which these goods could be sold at a premium.

The breaking away of the former communist countries of Central and Eastern Europe from direct Soviet control in 1989 and 1990 disrupted the system further, as these economies had been integrated into a single system by the Soviet State Planning Committee, Gosplan. Not only did Soviet factories depend on supplies from these former clients of the USSR, they also depended on them as markets for goods that could be sold in few other places in the world. Soviet consumers were also dependent on imports from these countries. Thus, as the system of state planning and supervision began to break down, the Soviet people faced even more uncertainty with respect to the supply of consumer goods. The normal response under such circumstances is for individuals to stockpile scarce goods, and, as the population and enterprises did so, scarcity became even more of a problem. Such was the challenge that Yeltsin and his entourage faced upon assuming full power for the newly independent Russian Federation in the fall of 1991 (Lavigne 1999, 108–112; Millar 1993).

With the collapse of the August 1991 coup attempt by Communist Party hardliners, Yeltsin was determined to destroy the Soviet political and economic systems. By declaring Russia independent of the USSR, banning the CPSU, and seizing the party's assets, the political system was changed irrevocably. As to the economy, Yeltsin's goal, unlike Gorbachev's, was its complete transformation. The question was how to do it. Many Russian economists, including the director of the Russian Academy of Sciences' Institute of Economics, Leonid Abalkin, and a handful of Western economists, made a case for the gradual transformation of the system. It had taken over sixty years to create the Soviet-style command economy. To dismantle the system in one fell swoop, they feared, would cripple what was left of Russia's economy.

Others disagreed, among them several younger Russian economists. They, along with a number of more market-oriented economists from the West, supported radical economic reforms that were designed to transform Russia's economy as quickly as possible. The economic system was collapsing. The stores were empty. Inflation was raging. It would be impossible to make gradual changes, they argued, because the system would implode before reforms could take effect. Something had to be done quickly and drastically. Moreover, they added, the population would not stand for gradual, painful reform. Pain was inevitable in any thoroughgoing reform, but it would be better to impose it in the shortest possible time.

For his part, Boris Yeltsin was not trained in economics, much less in free-market economics. Furthermore, his agenda was not simply economic, but political. Once having dismantled the Soviet system, he wanted to be sure that it would be gone for good. With this as his goal, he was especially attracted to those who called for a radical approach to the economy. Rapidly transforming Russia's economy would bury the Soviet system once and for all. The key was finding an economist who would lead the country's economic transformation. Given the enormity of the task, few were willing to take it on. One of those few was the young economist Yegor Gaidar. Long on convictions, but short in experience, Gaidar was convinced that radical market reform was necessary and could be implemented in less than a year. Although radical reform would be painful for the population, he was certain that the reforms would begin to bear fruit within nine months. In retrospect it is clear that Gaidar and others who gave similar advice to Yeltsin were naïve in believing that the old institutions could be dismissed easily and that a market economy could arise spontaneously. The weight of the past was simply too great, not only in terms of the traditional attitudes and practices of workers and management but also in terms of the country's broader economic and political realities.

Radical economic reform had two immediate aims: (1) to end price controls in most markets and allow prices to rise to equilibrium levels where demand matched supply; and (2) to convert most state enterprises into privately owned firms as rapidly as possible. These reforms would render the various ministries that had controlled the economy during the Soviet era unnecessary, and would undermine the need for such central agencies as Gosplan and Goskomtsen, the State Committee on Prices.

These policies, commonly known as "shock therapy," were derived from the so-called Washington Consensus formulated by Western development economists on the basis of their experience with macroeconomic reform in Latin America. Basically, the Washington Consensus focused on policies that were: (1) designed to reduce government ownership and intervention in the economy, and (2) aimed to eliminate price controls and other obstacles to the achievement of freely formed market prices. Thus, governments were encouraged to divest themselves of total or partial ownership of industry and resources, such as steel, coal, ship building, and oil. They were also told to eliminate price controls on real estate, food, and utilities, for example, and to phase out subsidies supporting enterprises and exports. Proponents of shock therapy argued that this package of policies would halt unwanted inflation, stimulate growth, promote exports, and invite direct foreign investment.

The Washington Consensus represented a shift in policy toward developing countries on the part of the International Monetary Fund (IMF) and the World Bank. Early development strategies encouraged governments of less developed countries to create and protect "infant industries." Governments were also encouraged to encourage and invest in industries that had export potential. Over time, this approach to development failed, however, as special interests prevented infant industries from reaching maturity and facing world-class competition. The Washington Consensus was designed to reverse these negative developments, and indeed the process appeared to work in a number of Latin American countries.

Shock therapy represented a similar package of policies modified to apply to the centrally planned economies of the former Soviet Union and Central and Eastern Europe, each of which had featured widespread state ownership of productive resources and government-set wages and prices.

The objective in Russia's case, as was true everywhere shock therapy was applied, was not to reform the planned economy but to replace it. An abrupt cessation of state intervention, combined with the privatization of formerly state enterprises, was intended to "shock" the economy, end high rates of inflation, and lay the foundation for a free-market economy. Because of shock therapy's apparent success elsewhere, first in Latin America and then in Poland, its proponents believed it would also work in Russia.

Introduced in January 1992 under the guidance of Yegor Gaidar, shock therapy involved the following steps:

1. The release of all, or at least most, retail prices on consumer goods and services, with the expectation that market forces would: (a) achieve rational relative prices at market-clearing levels; (b) curtail aggregate consumer demand, making the hoarding of goods unprofitable; (c) reduce the population's financial assets; and (d) undercut privileged access to special markets, with the result that prices would generally move upward as they adjusted to reflect actual scarcities in the economy.

2. The freeze of all money wages, incomes, and pensions, which, combined with the freeing of prices, would cause real wages and incomes to fall. Such a freeze, it was believed, however, would prevent a wage and price spiral that would aggravate the high rate of inflation and would reduce the costs of production in the economy as a whole, thus making it more competitive internationally.

3. The reduction of government expenditures by cutting entitlements, subsidies, and defense spending.

4. The restriction of deficit spending through spending cuts (see number 3 above), more effective tax collection, and the elimination of tax loopholes.

5. The creation of a true central bank to control credit and supervise the creation of commercial banks.

6. The opening of the economy to the world market with the aim of floating the exchange rate and establishing complete convertibility of the ruble.

In addition to these steps, the privatization of the economy through the sale of state enterprises was to begin as soon as possible. This process was to take place equitably by means of vouchers distributed to every member of Russian society as their share in ownership of the public assets they had created during the Soviet era. These vouchers were to be applied to the purchase of shares in individual enterprises or sold for cash (Millar 1993).

Thus, the state-run and state-owned economy of the Soviet era was to be transformed into a free-market economy as soon as possible. Although the going would be rough at first for the Russian people, the proponents of shock therapy promised that the hardest days of the transformation would be behind them by September 1992, nine months after the policy's launch. However, things did not go entirely as planned.

With the initiation of shock therapy, retail prices rose substantially and goods reappeared in markets. As expected, the freeing of prices reduced demand as many could not afford the much higher market prices, and it no longer paid for individual consumers to hoard commodities. In fact, the fall in real personal income caused by the jump in retail prices made the selling of goods that individuals had previously hoarded necessary and profitable. This was the easy part, however.

Even as prices rose, it was not politically feasible for the Russian government to freeze money wages and income completely. Instead, wages and income crept upward in response to demands from workers, pensioners, and welfare recipients, causing a wage-price spiral that fed upon itself. Thus, price stabilization failed and the rate of inflation rose to more than 1,500 percent in the first year of shock therapy. Furthermore, the reduction in redundant employment that was supposed to occur as inefficient enterprises were sorted out by market forces did not occur, at least not at first, and then only gradually over many years. Enterprise managers were reluctant to fire or downgrade employees even when sales of their low-quality or unwanted output declined precipitously. In the worst case, employers retained employees on the payroll but deferred paying their wages. In the best case, employers tried to develop new or higher quality products to keep the workforce occupied. However, these efforts were rewarded, if at all, only gradually. In the meantime most workers were in fact unemployed or underemployed.

As expected, real wages (that is, the retail purchasing power of money wages) did decline, and with it domestic consumer demand. However, the anticipated boost that lower production costs would give Russian exports did not occur. The problem was that most manufactured Russian goods, either because of their type or quality, were not saleable on world markets at any price.

Furthermore, the Russian Central Bank, Gosbank, was not a true central bank and therefore did not have the means to control credit or set interest rates. Some private commercial banks did spring up, but they were neither in a position financially nor had the experience to serve new business interests.

Finally, the government budget had little choice but to continue paying subsidies and a wide variety of welfare payments to the population. Cutting subsidies and welfare payments, with nothing to fill the gap for most people, threatened to create a revolutionary situation for the country. Thus, it proved politically impossible to prevent the state's budget deficit from growing, with the result that Russia's leaders resorted to printing money and selling government bonds to finance it. In short, by the summer of 1992, at a time when the worst should have been nearing an end, shock therapy, as originally conceived, had failed. Russia's macroeconomic policy, thereafter, drifted aimlessly and ineffectually (Lavigne 1999, 113–161; Millar 1997).

The privatization effort also was slow and disappointing. Initially, in early 1992, many local shops and small-scale service industries were quickly privatized. These included restaurants, local transportation, construction, trade, and housing. The most serious drawbacks at the local level were crime, racketeering, and protection scams.

Large-scale privatization posed a more serious problem for reformers, as they faced a great dilemma when it came to achieving rational reform. Logically, one needs a rationally operating price system that reflects true supply and demand in order to evaluate the worth of state enterprises. If prices are not rational, with some outputs overpriced and others underpriced, then the enterprises producing them will similarly be overvalued or undervalued. However, in order to have rational prices one needs competition among privately owned enterprises seeking to maximize profits. The architects of Russia's economic transformation could not come to terms with this logic. Instead, enterprises were privatized in a helter-skelter manner. Many were acquired at bargain-basement prices. Others were sold and continued to operate despite continuing losses and being without hope of ever making a profit.

The Red October candy factory in Moscow. Founded in 1851, the Einem company produced candy of such high quality that it became a supplier to Tsar Nicholas II and the imperial court. After the Bolshevik Revolution in 1917, the factory was taken over by the state and renamed "Red October." During the Soviet era, the factory continued to thrive, and, in the early 1990s, it was privatized as part of the massive privatization effort.

As part of the privatization of large-scale enterprises, all Russian citizens received vouchers worth ten thousand rubles, about fifty dollars at the time. The management and employees of enterprises slated for privatization were allowed to band together and acquire 51 percent of the enterprise at a discounted price. This variant accounted for 70 percent of all enterprises privatized by the end of June 1994, when all unused vouchers expired. Out of political necessity, not by choice, most of these enterprises fell under the control of the old management and thus continued to operate as before. For citizens who were not employees of such enterprises the situation was confusing at best. The population at large did not know how to make optimal use of their vouchers. In the face of rapid inflation many sold their vouchers for a song. Others were bamboozled by the clever, dishonest few. Voucher privatization primarily benefited Russia's political and economic elite: enterprise managers and managerial personnel, former higher ranking members of the CPSU, and members of the state *nomenklatura* (that is, the government bureaucracy). Some were scoundrels and others were just well positioned to take advantage of the situation (Gregory and Stuart 2001, 283–289; Lavigne 1999, 162–202).

A second round of privatization took place in conjunction with President Boris Yeltsin's 1996 reelection bid. It was known as the "loans for shares" program, under which a small number of well-placed businessmen, with good connections to the Kremlin and the *nomenklatura,* were allowed to loan money to the cash-strapped Russian government in exchange for claims on valuable enterprises in the event that the loans could not be repaid. In addition, these businessmen generously funded Yeltsin's 1996 reelection bid. The loans were set at levels nowhere near the true market value of these enterprises. Thus, the "loans for shares" program was yet another opportunity for a few powerful people to obtain ownership of valuable enterprises on the cheap, this time including major oil concerns and other natural resources production. The privatization of these large-scale enterprises through the "loans for shares" scheme created a group of very wealthy economic elites who became known as the "oligarchs" (Freeland 2000; Millar 2002).

The oligarchs created conglomerates known as financial industrial groups (FIGs). Most FIGs combined industrial enterprises, major media outlets, and insurance companies with a bank at the core of the conglomerate. The banking core was important because it allowed FIGs to depend upon their own banks for financing their operations and investments. FIGs were not formed on the basis of economic logic, but by what could be grabbed by the oligarchs when the grabbing was good. Because of cross subsidies between enterprises within each of these conglomerates, and the easy credit that could be obtained from their in-house banks, FIGs, not surprisingly, proved to be economically inefficient. They did, however, provide a basis for acquiring great individual wealth by the oligarchs, in large part through the skimming of profits and financial reserves (Millar 2002).

The effects of privatization and shock therapy on Russia's economy were disastrous. Gross domestic product fell from $1,063 billion (at purchasing power parity, PPP) in 1991 to $672 billion in 1996. Per capita GDP fell from $7,200 in 1991 to $4,500 during the same period. Fixed investment declined by more than 60 percent over these years also. Extremely high inflation, one effect of shock therapy as it was implemented in Russia, wiped out the savings of the population and greatly diminished the value of fixed-ruble pensions. In fact, Russia experienced a more devastating decline in the 1990s than did the United States, Britain, or Germany during the Great Depression of the 1930s (see Table 5.1, 1992–1998). A third or more of the population fell below the poverty level, while a tiny clique surrounding Yeltsin, including the new economic oligarchs, became fabulously wealthy.

Meanwhile, a reckless macroeconomic policy was creating a financial bubble. Unable to eliminate the government's large budget deficit (see Table 5.2, 1992–1998) and despite large IMF loans, the government began issuing short-term securities (known as GKOs) at a furious rate in 1995 to bridge the gap. Economic performance, for the first time since 1990, actually improved in 1997, with a modest increase in GDP. Even so, it would be too little, too late. By the summer of 1998, the outstanding stock of GKOs was more than 100 percent of total anticipated, central government budget revenues and was still growing. At this rate, it was only a matter of time before the Russian government could no longer pay its bills. With a crisis looming, the IMF in July, at the urging of the United States, granted Russia a new loan to give Russia's leaders the time they needed to get the country's financial house in order. The hope was that the new loan would convince foreign investors that their money would be safe in Russia. Instead, the bailout plan provided an opportunity for investors to pull out their money, with the result that in early August the economy was again on the verge of financial collapse. The Russian government again turned to the IMF for help. This time, contrary to its earlier behavior, the IMF took a much firmer line and refused to extend additional funding. Russia's financial bubble finally burst on August 17, 1998, when the Russian government devalued the ruble and defaulted on its outstanding debt. In essence, the country was bankrupt (Millar 2002; OECD 2000, 33–81). As a result of the default and devaluation, the population lost most of its savings, and the purchasing power of their incomes fell precipitously.

Unlike shock therapy, the shock that came with the bursting of the 1998 financial bubble was a healthy one. After years of avoiding hard choices, Russian policymakers, with their country on the brink of national economic disaster, changed some of their ways. For starters, budgetary policy has been more conservative and debt has been better managed (see Table 5.2, 1999–2007). Since the 1998 crisis, they have also avoided depending on IMF financing and advice. The IMF for its part admitted that it allowed political

Table 5.1 Basic Economic Indicators (percent change)

	1992	1993	1994	1995	1996	1997	1998	1999	2000	2001	2002	2003	2004	2005	2006	2007
Gross domestic product	-14.5	-8.7	-12.7	-4.2	-3.6	1.4	-5.3	6.4	10.0	5.1	4.7	7.3	7.2	6.4	7.4	8.1
Industrial production	-18.8	-14.6	-20.6	-3.0	-3.5	1.9	-6.6	11.0	11.9	2.9	3.1	8.9	8.3	4.0	3.9	6.3
Agricultural production	-9.0	-4.0	-12.0	-8.0	-5.1	0.1	-12.3	2.4	3.0	11.0	2.0	1.5	1.6	1.1	1.7	—
Consumer prices	2,650	940	320	131	22	11	85	37	21	19	15	12	12	11	9	11.9
Real disposable income	-41.0	14.0	-8.0	-13.0	5.0	2.5	-13.8	-15.1	9.0	8.5	8.8	14.5	10.4	9.3	10.2	11.5

Source: Bush 2008, 8.

Table 5.2 Federal Budget as Percentage of GDP

	1992	1993	1994	1995	1996	1997	1998	1999	2000	2001	2002	2003	2004	2005	2006	2007
Revenues	16.6	14.5	14.1	13.7	12.5	13.3	11.4	12.6	15.4	17.8	20.3	19.5	20.1	23.7	23.6	23.9
Expenditures	27.7	15.9	18.1	16.6	20.9	20.9	17.4	16.8	14.6	14.8	19.0	17.8	15.8	16.3	16.1	18.4
Balance	-11.1	-1.4	-4.0	-2.9	-8.4	-7.7	-6.0	-4.2	0.8	3.0	1.4	1.7	4.4	7.5	7.5	5.5

Source: Bush 2008, 8.

aims to override good economic policy. Russia's economy began to recover quickly, so much so that in 1999 it managed to return to the positive trajectory established in 1997 (see Table 5.1, 1998–1999). The year 1999 was significant, too, in that Yeltsin's surprise resignation as president finally brought to a close what had been a period of sometimes frantic and often erratic leadership.

■ Vladimir Putin and the Quest for Stability

Few leaders have risen to power as quickly as Vladimir Putin. Chosen as Yeltsin's heir apparent in August 1999, Putin became Russia's acting president before the year was out. From the outset he stressed the achievement of economic and political stability as his goals. A year into his presidency, Putin declared to the country that the old cycle of revolution and counterrevolution, and the search for the "guilty" that comes with each stage, would not be repeated (Putin 2001). In his Federal Assembly address two years later (Putin·2003), he said:

> Russia must become and will become a country with a flourishing civil society and stable democracy, a country that fully guarantees human rights and civil and political freedoms. Russia must become and will become a country with a competitive market economy, a country that gives reliable protection to property rights and provides the economic freedoms that allow its people to work honestly and make money without fear and limitations.

On the face of things, Putin's support for such goals is beyond reproach. The question is how these goals are playing out in reality.

Putin, like Brezhnev, was lucky with the economy. Shortly before his first term as president the price of oil began to rise on global markets at a time when Russian petroleum producers were modernizing their operations and increasing their export capacity. The result has been a windfall for the Russian economy. Since then, the price of oil has continued to increase, reaching record levels after adjusting for inflation. Reasons for the price rises include burgeoning Chinese and Indian demand to fuel their fastgrowing economies, delays in restoring and maintaining oil output in Iraq, political unrest in other petrostates, concerns about the security of Western investments in oil production in Russia, and, until recently, uncertainty over the fate of Russian oil giant Yukos.

The devaluation of the ruble during Russia's 1998 financial crisis, which gave an enormous boost to Russian domestic manufacturing (see Table 5.1, Industrial production), also worked in Putin's favor. With the ruble no longer worth as much, imports became very expensive, giving Russian producers an opportunity to exploit domestic demand. Thus, Russia's economy was boosted in three ways: the value of oil exports more than doubled and then tripled, imports of consumer goods declined, and sales of Russian manufactured goods increased. With the rapid growth of GDP, tax receipts also increased, producing a surplus in the state budget, making it possible to begin to restore Russia's credit abroad. These economic gains gave Putin an opportunity unique in Russia's post-Soviet experience to introduce much-needed economic reforms at a time of economic growth and stability.

Although a proponent of market reforms, Putin moved more slowly than outside observers such as the World Bank and the IMF would have liked. The initiation of a flat income tax of 13 percent has proven successful in encouraging individuals to pay, rather than avoid, their taxes. Individuals and firms are now allowed to own and sell urban land, but with a number of restrictions. Rural land sales are now permitted, too, but with even greater restrictions. Such restrictions, in general, are born out of fears of absentee and foreign ownership of land. Nonetheless, some progress has been made toward creating a market in land, something that was unthinkable until relatively recently. Putin also attempted to encourage the development of small business, a sector of the economy in which Russia lags behind not only the United States and Western Europe, but also the former communist states of Central and Eastern Europe (Millar 2002).

Yet despite gains in some areas, the results of Putin's actions in other ways have been less certain. At the outset of his tenure as Russia's leader, Putin informed the country's oligarchs that he would not support a renewed nationalization of their questionably acquired economic empires if they stayed out of politics. Three oligarchs became targets of his ire, all, to varying degrees, for having crossed the political line he had drawn. Two, Boris Berezovsky and Vladimir Gusinsky, are in external exile, and a third, Mikhail Khodorkovsky, the owner of Yukos Oil, was arrested in October 2003 on charges of tax evasion and fraud, among other things. In May 2005, he was found guilty and sentenced to nine years in prison.

The state's attacks on the oligarchs have been quite popular with the public, as it is well known in Russia that these entrepreneurs achieved their great wealth through personal connections and clever manipulation of the policymaking process, acquiring their most important holdings at prices far below market rates. Public opinion and high oil prices provided Putin with all the leverage and freedom he needed to call the oligarchs to account, allowing him to further consolidate his power by neutralizing potentially formidable political opponents. Although Putin has a strong hand politically, his ability to strike out against the oligarchs at will creates a great deal of uncertainty concerning the status of private property in Russia. Such uncertainty not only hinders the efficient management of the nation's economy but also discourages potential direct foreign investment.

The problem is that Russia historically has been organized as a service state, not a state based on the rule of law (Millar 2004, 1371–1373). In a service state individuals are allowed to hold positions of power, wealth, and productive resources, but only at the pleasure of the tsar, general secretary, or president, and only as long as they are seen to be using these positions, wealth, and resources prudently and wisely, as defined by the leader. Consequently, today, even after privatization, private ownership of the nation's resources, land, capital stock, and so forth depends very much on the quality of the "service" being rendered to the leadership.

A less disruptive and more legally sound approach to the challenge presented by the oligarchs would rely on economic, not political, levers to level out the individual income and wealth of the oligarchs. A wealth tax, a tax on dividend income, forcing oligarchs to issue new shares for the benefit of schools, orphanages, and so forth would go a long way toward correcting the country's disparities in wealth and income. Instead, as has long been Soviet and Russian practice, what Russians refer to euphemistically as "administrative measures" have been preferred over economic ones. Thus, instead of a policy that applies to all oligarchs and solves the problem in general, legal and police methods are applied to individual oligarchs who have displeased or challenged the president. Recently, the state has employed such measures against certain foreign investors, notably oil companies.

Relying on economic levers, equity could be served and the Russian population would benefit without disrupting production and markets. Putin's reliance on administrative measures, however, has benefited only a small coterie of his closest supporters, who in essence have become, or are in the process of becoming, oligarchs in their own right. Simply put, as the old oligarchs are destroyed, new ones are created. Thus, the great danger of an administrative approach to the economy is that such reallocations of national economic wealth occur at the expense of economic rationality and productivity. Although popular with the public, such attacks on the oligarchs and on foreign investors come at the expense of the Russian people.

■ Conclusion

Even though Russia has developed a market economy and achieved a degree of stability under Putin, it is a unique kind of market system. What has emerged in Russia since Gorbachev's initiation of economic reforms in the mid-1980s is essentially a variant of the New Economic Policy (NEP) that Lenin launched in the 1920s. Small and medium-sized enterprises are private and compete in free markets. Large-scale industries and enterprises, such as oil, gas, transportation, and electricity generation and distribution—that is, the so-called commanding heights of the economy—are shared by the state and the oligarchs. In some cases the oligarchs own the properties outright. In other cases the state is the sole owner. This is particularly true of any industry considered strategic, such as defense. However, in more cases than not, private individuals and the state share ownership. Given this mixture of public and private, the Russian economy today may be described as "neo-NEP." Whether this structure is stable in the long run is open to question, but for the immediate future it appears to be stable, in part because such an arrangement appears to be not only what Putin wants, but also what much of elite and mass opinion seems to want (Millar 2003; Shevstova 2003, 261–276).

The biggest economic danger the Kremlin faces is a possible decline in the price of oil to the low levels of the late 1980s and early 1990s. This does not appear to present an immediate danger, but history suggests that eventually the price will come down again. For this reason Russia would be well-advised to take advantage of the current windfall in revenue by investing in industries and services that can replace the petroleum industry when it is exhausted. Dramatic increases in energy revenues, however, tend to weaken the impulse for economic and political reform, an outcome that is increasingly obvious today in Russia.

A second, related, challenge facing Russia is the rising value of the ruble against the dollar. As the ruble increases in value, in part as a result of higher earnings from oil and gas, the competitiveness of Russian industry, both domestically and internationally, will decline as imports become cheaper. A third problem is the need to encourage the development of domestic industries to supplement oil and gas exports and to serve domestic demand. Along these lines, domestic industries need to be modernized. Russia does not suffer a shortage of investment funds internally, but it also needs foreign investment, which offers access to technology, management practices, and marketing skills that Russian enterprises need to become competitive.

Foreign direct investment (FDI) pertains to investment in plant and equipment in Russia, not to financial investment in government securities or private stocks. FDI is, therefore, more risky than merely advancing funds because it is not liquid and requires a long-term commitment to the enterprise or venture. Foreign investors are very sensitive, therefore, to the degree to which their investments will be protected against nationalization and against adverse legal judgments. Russia is deficient in these kinds of assurances, which is a major reason why, until recently, FDI in the country has been so small in comparison with FDI in Poland, Estonia, and other former communist states that have successfully transitioned from planned economies to free markets. The state's rough treatment not only of Yukos but also of foreign oil companies underlines the uncertainty of foreign investors about investing in Russia. In addition, Russia's leaders and the Russian public are reluctant to encourage foreign ownership of Russian land and industries out of an age-old fear of foreign domination. Both of these obstacles will have to be resolved before FDI in Russia becomes a major source of investment.

Another issue is the Kremlin's decision to continue the Soviet practice of urging its economic advisers to set sufficiently "ambitious" growth targets for GDP. No leadership of a Western capitalist country would think of ordering a higher rate of economic growth than legitimate forecasts can provide. Of course, political leaders in the West often urge their economic advisers to set monetary and fiscal policies so as to encourage growth and to minimize inflation and unemployment. This is standard macroeconomic policy. In making the demands he did on his cabinet, Putin was still thinking like a Soviet bureaucrat, but such an approach is not conducive to Russia's economic progress.

Finally, Russia still seems to be drawn to the idea of autarky, the creation of a market system that minimizes a country's dependence on the rest of the world economy. The Soviet Union traveled down this road at great cost. Not only did the USSR fall behind technologically, its devotion of vast resources to production for which it held no competitive advantage prevented it from reaping the benefits of participation in the international division of labor and trade. As the Putin era continues, with the March 2008 election of Dmitri Medvedev as president, how committed Russia's leaders will be to following a path to freer and more open markets, instead of heeding the historic longing of many among the country's elites and masses to chart a separate, distinctively *Russian* course, is unclear.

For now, a continuation of the present economic course is most likely, especially as it seems that Putin will continue to play a dominant role in Russian politics well past his second term in office. Stability in Russia today depends primarily upon two factors: the price of oil, which is out of Russia's control, and Putin's popularity, which cannot be willed to his successor. Eventually, the price of oil will fall. When it does, the country's current economic policies will be severely tested (Shevtsova 2007).

■ Bibliography

Arvedlund, Erin E. 2004. "Russian Growth Accelerates, Stoked by Oil." *New York Times,* January 7.
Brown, Archie. 1996. *The Gorbachev Factor.* Oxford, UK: Oxford University Press.
Bush, Keith. 2008. *Russian Economic Survey,* February. https://www.usrbc.org/resources/russiaeconomicsurvey/.
Eberstadt, Nicholas. 2004. "The Emptying of Russia." *Washington Post,* February 13.
EBRD (European Bank for Reconstruction and Development). 1999. *Transition Report 1999: Ten Years of Transition.* London: EBRD.
Fainsod, Merle. 1963. *How Russia Is Ruled.* Rev. ed. Cambridge, MA: Harvard University Press.
Freeland, Chrystia. 2000. *Sale of the Century: Russia's Wild Ride from Communism to Capitalism.* New York: Crown Business.

Gregory, Paul R. 2004. *The Political Economy of Stalinism: Evidence from the Soviet Secret Archives.* Cambridge, UK: Cambridge University Press.

Gregory, Paul R., and Robert C. Stuart. 2001. *Russian and Soviet Economic Performance and Structure.* 7th ed. Boston: Addison-Wesley.

Hanson, Philip. 1992. *From Stagnation to Catastroika: Commentaries on the Soviet Economy, 1983–1991.* New York: Praeger.

Harrison, Mark. 1996. *Accounting for War: Soviet Production, Employment, and the Defense Burden, 1940–45.* New York: Cambridge University Press.

Hedlund, Stefan. 1999. *Russia's "Market" Economy: A Bad Case of Predatory Capitalism.* London: UCL Press.

Hewett, Ed A. 1988. *Reforming the Soviet Economy: Equality vs. Efficiency.* Washington, D.C.: Brookings Institution Press.

Hough, Jerry F., and Merle Fainsod. 1979. *How the Soviet Union Is Governed.* Cambridge, MA: Harvard University Press.

Lavigne, Marie. 1999. *The Economics of Transition: From Socialist Economy to Market Economy.* 2nd ed. New York: St. Martin's Press.

Millar, James R. 1981. *The ABCs of Soviet Socialism.* Urbana: University of Illinois Press.

———. 1985. "The Little Deal: Brezhnev's Contribution to Acquisitive Socialism." *Slavic Review* 44(4): 694–706.

———, ed. 1987. *Politics, Work, and Daily Life in the USSR: A Survey of Former Soviet Citizens.* New York: Cambridge University Press.

———. [1988] 1990a. "'*Perestroika* and *Glasnost*': Gorbachev's Gamble on Youth and Truth." In Millar, *The Soviet Economic Experiment,* ed. Susan J. Linz. Urbana: University of Illinois Press.

———. 1990b. *The Soviet Economic Experiment.* Edited and with an introduction by Susan J. Linz. Urbana: University of Illinois Press.

———. 1991. "Prospects for Economic Reform: Is (Was) Gorbachev Really Necessary?" In *Europe in Transition: Political, Economic, and Security Prospects for the 1990s,* ed. J. J. Lee and Walter Korter. Austin, TX: Lyndon B. Johnson School of Public Affairs.

———. 1993. "The Economies of the CIS: Reformation, Revolution, or Restoration? In *The Former Soviet Union in Transition.* Study Papers, Joint Economic Committee, Congress of the United States, 103rd Cong., 1st sess. Vol. 1. Washington, D.C.: US Government Printing Office.

———. 1997. "The Importance of Initial Conditions in Economic Transitions: Evaluation of Economic Reform Progress in Russia." *Journal of Socio-Economics* 26(4): 359–382.

———. 2002. "Normalization of the Russian Economy: Obstacles and Opportunities for Reform and Sustainable Growth," *NBR Analysis* 13(2): 5–43.

———. 2003. "Putin and the Economy." In *Putin's Russia: Past Imperfect, Future Uncertain,* ed. Dale R. Herspring. Lanham, MD: Rowman & Littlefield.

———, ed. in chief. 2004. *Encyclopedia of Russian History.* 4 vols. New York: Macmillan Reference USA.

Millar, James R., and Elizabeth Clayton. 1987. "Quality of Life: Subjective Measures of Relative Satisfaction." In *Politics, Work, and Daily Life in the USSR: A Survey of Former Soviet Citizens,* ed. James R. Millar. New York: Cambridge University Press.

OECD (Organization for Economic Cooperation and Development). 1997. *OECD Economic Surveys: Russian Federation 1996/1997.* Vol. 1997, supplement 5 (December).

————. 2000. *OECD Economic Surveys: Russian Federation 1999/2000*. Vol. 2000, issue 7 (March).

Pereira, Luiz Carlos Bresser, José María Maravall, and Adam Przeworski. 1993. *Economic Reforms in New Democracies: A Social-Democratic Approach*. New York: Cambridge University Press.

Putin, Vladimir. 2001. Annual Address to the Federal Assembly of the Russian Federation, April 3. http://www.kremlin.ru/eng/speeches/2001/04/03/0000_type 70029type82912_70660.shtml.

————. 2003. Annual Address to the Federal Assembly of the Russian Federation, May 16. http://www.kremlin.ru/eng/speeches/2003/05/16/0000_type70029type 82912_44692.shtml.

Rutland, Peter. 2003. "Putin and the Oligarchs." In *Putin's Russia: Past Imperfect, Future Uncertain*, ed. Dale R. Herspring. Lanham, MD: Rowman & Littlefield.

Schroeder, Gertrude E. 1993. "Post-Soviet Reforms in Perspective." In *The Former Soviet Union in Transition*. Study Papers. Joint Economic Committee, Congress of the United States, 103rd Cong., 1st sess. Vol. 1. Washington, D.C.: US Government Printing Office.

Shevtsova, Lilia. 1999. *Yeltsin's Russia: Myths and Reality*. Washington, D.C.: Carnegie Endowment for International Peace.

————. 2003. *Putin's Russia*. Washington, D.C.: Carnegie Endowment for International Peace.

————. 2007. *Russia: Lost in Transition*. Washington, D.C.: Carnegie Endowment for International Peace.

Taubman, William. 2003. *Khrushchev: The Man and His Era*. New York: W. W. Norton.

United Nations. 2004. Economic Commission for Europe. *Economic Survey of Europe 2003*, No. 2. Geneva: United Nations.

Weafer, Christopher. 2004. "The Chilean or Indonesian Model?" *Moscow Times*, August 18.

6

International Relations

Allen C. Lynch

The Soviet Union's dissolution in 1991 witnessed the disintegration of a centuries-old political order in Russia that was characterized by a state that was: (1) patrimonial, in which economics was largely subordinated to politics; (2) autocratic, in which one man or one party ruled; and (3) imperial, in which Russian or Russified elites were predominant over non-Russians. This distinctive fusion of wealth, despotism, and colonial rule (as true for the communists as it was for the tsars), permitted Russia's rulers to defend and extend their territorial and political jurisdiction in the hostile Eurocentric international order that persisted throughout modern Russian history and continued in a different form in the Cold War confrontation between the Soviet Union and the United States (Pipes 1974; Poe 2003). Interestingly, the reduction in international tensions at the end of the 1980s reflected internal Soviet reforms designed to modernize this archaic system, efforts that in the process unintentionally helped bring about the disintegration of this distinctive Russian regime.

Since the collapse of the Soviet Union in December 1991, the Russian Federation that emerged to succeed the USSR has faced an international environment without precedent in recent centuries. Compared with the USSR, Russia today is practically without alliances of significance. The security vacuum in Eastern Europe created by the demise of the Cold War–era, Soviet-led Warsaw Pact has been filled by the US-led North Atlantic Treaty Organization (NATO), which now includes virtually all of Soviet Russia's East European satellites as well as the three Baltic states of Estonia, Latvia, and Lithuania, which were annexed by Stalin in 1940 and remained part of the USSR until late 1991 (Black 2000). Moreover, in the spring of 2004 these same states joined the European Union (EU), underscoring that their primary foreign trade and investment orientation now lies with Western Europe rather than Russia. Soviet disintegration also represented the collapse of a multi-national state as the USSR fragmented into fifteen separate nation-states. In the key western borderlands, the newly established independence of the Baltic states, Belarus, and Ukraine finds the borders of the Russian state removed to those of the mid-seventeenth century, before the union of the Russian and Ukrainian crowns by the Treaty of Pereyaslav of 1654 (LeDonne 1997). As a consequence, more than twenty-five million ethnic Russians, equal to one-sixth the population of contemporary Russia (and a fifth of the ethnic Russians living there), reside outside Russia's borders.

Moreover, a decade-long economic depression (1989–1998), combined with frequent administrative chaos following the implosion of the USSR, saw the sinews of Russian power, including military power, wither away. For instance, Russia remains mired in war in the rebellious province of Chechnya (1994–present), where the Russian army can destroy at will but lacks the capacity to provide adequate security for the restoration of genuine Russian sovereignty (Lieven 1998).

In spite of its much-reduced international presence, Russia still matters in world politics for three reasons: "the atom, the veto, and the location" (Legvold 2001). First, Russia remains the world's second great nuclear weapons power, and for this reason the United States must treat Russia with a gravity that its economic weight alone would not warrant. This is not simply a question of Russia as a potential nuclear threat to the United States but as an enormous stockpiler of nuclear, chemical, and biological materials, civilian as well as military, that could fuel terrorist catastrophes should political order in Russia break down.

Second, as the main Soviet successor state, Russia occupies the former Soviet seat on the United Nations Security Council. Any efforts to forge UN-sanctioned international security coalitions have to take Russian interests into account, as Russia is one of five veto-wielding permanent members of the council (together with the United States, United Kingdom, China, and France).

Third, inasmuch as Russia occupies three-fourths of the territory of the former USSR, it remains a transcontinental power, spanning Europe and Asia and bordering sixteen countries. These include China, North Korea, Mongolia, and Finland, as well as NATO members Norway, Poland, Lithuania, Latvia, and Estonia (the last three being former Soviet republics), in addition to five other former republics of the USSR (Kazakhstan, Azerbaijan, Georgia, Ukraine, and Belarus). Russia also shares maritime borders with the United States (at the Bering Strait dividing Alaska from Russia's Chukotka Peninsula) and Japan (with which Russia has a territorial dispute over islands acquired by the USSR at the end of World War II).

In addition, Russia claims as its security frontier (as distinct from its legal territorial boundaries) the external borders of the former Soviet Union, including the Commonwealth of Independent States (CIS), formed in December 1991 as a divorce mechanism from the USSR (Mandelbaum 1998). The significance of this more extensive Russian security claim, akin to the US Monroe Doctrine in Latin America, became apparent after the terror attacks of September 11, 2001: in close cooperation with the United States, Russia engineered a massive delivery of weapons to the Afghan-based Northern Alliance from bordering Tajikistan, where Russia's 201st Motorized Rifle Division was based. Those deliveries played a pivotal role in rapidly overthrowing the Taliban government that had harbored Osama bin Laden and Al-Qaida, in November 2001. If we thus add the former Soviet boundaries to those of the Russian Federation itself, we see that contemporary Russia is involved directly in the affairs of no fewer than two dozen states.

Even more interesting, and hopeful, is the fact that for the first time in its history, Russia faces no state-based threats to its vital interests and recognizes this fact. How, then, are we to understand the forces shaping contemporary Russian foreign policy?

■ Historical Patterns in Russian Foreign Policy

Russian foreign policy in the imperial period (for our purposes 1682–1917) proved on the whole remarkably successful in managing an external context that allowed both for the state's impressive expansion and the preservation of a distinct internal political order. Throughout this period, the Russian state, initially driven by the reforming tsar Peter the Great (reigned 1682–1725), was able to assimilate sufficient economic, technological, administrative, and military techniques from Europe without in the process transforming Russian society or the political system itself according to European standards. This policy of selective borrowing proved highly effective until the onset of the industrial revolution, which favored efficiency of production and organization over the mobilization of sheer mass. Between the Crimean War (1854–1856) and World War I (1914–1918) Russia progressively lost its ability to match its internal order to its external environment (Fuller 1992; Vernadsky 1936). Despite otherwise impressive absolute gains in industrialization after 1880, Russia fell further behind its chief foreign rivals in relative terms, especially Germany and Japan. In addition, Russian industrialization generated new internal forces (i.e., professional and working classes) that the old regime was unwilling or unable to accommodate politically. This combination of growing external vulnerability and latent social instability at home created a fatal mixture under the pressure of World War I as tsarist Russia collapsed under the pressure of waging modern industrialized warfare (Von Laue 1993).

Having said that, several qualifications are necessary. First, Russia was not the only state to collapse as a result of World War I, merely the first. One should not, therefore, exaggerate the distinctiveness of imperial Russia's failed modernization. Most of Europe failed the challenge of integrating the mass economic and political forces unleashed by industrialization and the influence of democratic and revolutionary nationalism. A stable settlement in Western Europe would only arise after World War II. Second, the bulk of the Russian empire, and to a lesser extent its international standing, was rapidly reconstituted after a decade of devastating war and civil upheaval. By the end of 1922, the USSR was formally established; in the same year, the Soviet-German Treaty of Rapallo announced Soviet Russia's emergence as one of the great powers. By 1925, all major European states had recognized the USSR without previous conditions having been met regarding the settlement of foreign debt repudiated by the Bolsheviks, restitution for the confiscation of private property by the Soviet government, and the halting of the activities of the Soviet-backed Communist International, or Comintern, which sought the overthrow of capitalist governments (Jacobson 1994). This was an impressive accomplishment, suggesting that tsarist Russia had bequeathed important legacies both in terms of state-building and diplomacy.

These diplomatic legacies included: first, the absence on the part of imperial Russia of concerted schemes of aggression directed against the most powerful states in the international system. Unlike Germany between 1890 and 1945, tsarist Russia expanded incrementally and usually in conjunction with significant international alliances. By contrast, enduring suspicions about the global ambitions of "international communism" magnified threat perceptions of the USSR.

Second, tsarist Russia, for all of the distinctiveness of its autocratic order at home, proved able not only to play by the rules of the European balance of power, but also to achieve Russia's acceptance as a legitimate actor in the "Christian republic" of European monarchies. This meant that Russia's territorial gains were seen as legitimate, less threatening, and more permanent than was true of the Muslim Ottoman Empire's European holdings in the Balkans. Imperial Russia was part of the international community of its time (Malia 1999). By contrast, the USSR's assertion of its international identity as a communist power dedicated to the overthrow of capitalist governments was incompatible with the existing international system and left it always partially outside the predominant global order, thereby increasing the burdens on Soviet diplomacy. Contrast the failure of Stalin's USSR to conclude an anti-Nazi alliance with Britain and France in the 1930s with the ability of tsarist Russia and republican France (and later Great Britain) to ally against imperial Germany in the two decades before 1914 (Carley 1999).

Third, tsarist Russia's relationship with Germany proved central to its welfare and security. When that tie was sound, Russia was secure both internationally and domestically. When ties between the two countries broke down, usually at Germany's initiative, the emergent threats to Russia's security could not be compensated for by distant alliances with great powers

France and Britain. Because of their relative geographic isolation from Eastern Europe, neither country could easily assist their Russian ally. So important was Germany to Russia's position in the international system, however, that even after the Bolsheviks seized power, it remained a focal point of Russian foreign policy, but for different reasons. On ideological grounds, the new Soviet leaders saw the potential for a socialist revolution in Germany as central to the fulfillment of their own revolutionary aspirations. On security grounds, the Bolsheviks believed that without a German ally, "international capitalism" would be unable to organize a successful military campaign against the fledgling Soviet state.

■ The Early Soviet Period

Vladimir Lenin's Bolshevik Party seized power in the fall of 1917 with the clear expectation that a communist victory in Russia would be the trigger for a broader socialist revolution in Europe. Indeed, Lenin at first believed that communism could not survive in Russia without that broader revolution, above all in Germany. Lenin's hope was that a communist Germany would immediately stop fighting and thus end World War I and the tremendous pressure of German troops on Russian soil. In the longer run, a socialist Germany was to provide Soviet Russia with the capital and technology needed to industrialize rapidly, thereby establishing socialism on a firm economic footing. Lenin's early hopes for world revolution were soon dashed by the menacing progress of German armies toward the Russian capital, Petrograd, compelling Russia to sign the Treaty of Brest-Litovsk with the Germans in March 1918. This treaty, insisted upon by Lenin against the protests of a majority of his comrades, deprived Russia of vast stretches of territory in the west and south and, had Germany won the war, would have reduced Russia to the status of a tributary state of the German empire. The treaty symbolizes the tension between the global revolutionary aspirations of the Russian communists and the frequent need to accommodate the realities of international power politics. Still, with Germany defeated after the US intervention in France in 1917–1918, the Bolsheviks' revolutionary aspirations soared again, and to the best of their abilities they encouraged communist revolutions in Germany, Hungary, Poland, Estonia, and elsewhere in the early years of Soviet rule. Indeed, revolutionary objectives were institutionalized in the form of the Comintern, an alliance of communist parties worldwide that rapidly became an instrument of Soviet state power (Ulam 1974).

By the early 1920s it became clear that there would be no general European socialist revolution. In response, Soviet Russia, now exhausted by years of war, began to adopt the formal institutions of diplomacy with the Western powers and others. By then, the basic template for Soviet foreign policy was set in place: both revolutionary and great-power objectives were part of Soviet diplomacy. The Comintern and the Soviet Ministry of Foreign Affairs were the institutional embodiments of these twin, often contradictory directions of Soviet external relations. Consequently, Soviet efforts to conduct ambitious diplomatic undertakings with Western states were usually laborious, fragile, and fleeting accomplishments. Not until the Gorbachev era (1985–1991), when the USSR renounced the ideological objectives in its foreign policy, did Western states fully rid themselves of the suspicion that Soviet objectives included the destruction of their respective social, economic, and political orders (Lynch 1987).

The major exception to this earlier pattern, however, and one that in fact proves the rule, is the Soviet anti-Nazi alliance with Great Britain and the United States during World War II (1941–1945). Having concluded a neutrality pact with its ideological arch-nemesis Nazi Germany in August 1939, in order to avoid being dragged into war and expand its territorial reach at the expense of Poland, the USSR was caught by surprise by a massive Nazi invasion on June 22, 1941, and nearly defeated that year. For the moment it was saved by the transfer of some forty Siberian divisions to Moscow made possible by a Soviet-Japanese neutrality pact of April 1941 and the knowledge, revealed by Soviet espionage, that the Japanese would attack US and British interests in the Pacific instead of Soviet interests in Siberia. In the longer run, the Soviet victory over Nazi Germany was assured by the division of German forces required by the coordination of Soviet with British and above all US military and aid efforts. In spite of growing political differences as the war drew to a close, there was a real military alliance between the USSR, Britain, and the United States so long as the war lasted. Indeed, at the Yalta conference of February 1945, the United States was desperate to get the USSR involved in the war against Japan. As a result, the USSR invaded Japanese-occupied Manchuria on August 8, 1945, three months after the Nazi surrender.

■ The Cold War

Victory saw the USSR in control of much of Eastern and Central Europe, as well as northeast China, while much of the Soviet Union lay in ruins. Twenty-seven million Soviet citizens, one-seventh of the population, the majority of them civilians, had been killed. More than seventeen hundred cities and towns, seventy thousand villages and settlements, and thirty-two thousand industrial establishments had been seriously damaged or leveled. An area as large as that of the United States east of the Mississippi River had been essentially razed to the ground. Yet victory in war did not lead to a peaceable pattern of international relations among the victorious powers.

Disputes over the future of Germany, the evident communist domination of the Polish government, and more generally the fear in the United States and Britain that the chaotic economic, social, and political conditions in postwar Europe could lead to an orientation of the continent as a whole toward a Soviet orbit, generated a US commitment to the rapid economic reconstruction of Western Europe through the Marshall Plan, announced in June 1947 (Leffler 1992). Stalin, who beforehand seemed unconcerned with the consequences of continued European stagnation, which appeared likely to benefit the powerful mass-based communist parties in France and Italy and perhaps even turn Germany as a whole away from the West and toward the USSR, was now alarmed at the prospect that US economic weight in Western Europe might undermine Soviet influence in Eastern Europe, where the USSR was still consolidating its influence. To paraphrase the ancient Greek Thucydides' explanation for the outbreak of the Peloponnesian War, it could be said that the Cold War was caused by the rise of Soviet power and the fear this caused in the United States; and conversely by the rise of US power and the fear this caused in the USSR. Stalin's refusal to participate in the Marshall Plan, and his rejection of East European participation in it, signaled the collapse of negotiations between the USSR and the West and the beginning of the Cold War that would define international relations for the next four decades. It had become clear that the wartime alliance was cemented by a negative coincidence of interest, that is, the defeat of the Nazis, rather than any common interest in the structure of the global order, or in a shared sense of values and political community.

Very rapidly, a series of dramatic events signaled that an "iron curtain" (as Winston Churchill foresaw in March 1946) had descended across Europe and would soon be closing off parts of Asia. Early incidents included a successful communist coup in Czechoslovakia in February 1948 and a Soviet land blockade of Berlin from June 1947 through May 1948. Although it could do nothing to reverse the course of events in Czechoslovakia, the United States, with British assistance, organized a sustained and successful airlift of vital supplies to Berlin that eventually broke the blockade. Tensions between the United States and the Soviet Union mounted after the Soviets conducted their first atomic bomb test in late August 1949, and communists led by Mao Zedong took power in China about a month later. At about this same time, Germany was formally divided between the communist German Democratic Republic (East Germany) and the democratic Federal Republic (West Germany).

In June 1950, communist North Korea, with the Soviet Union's blessing, invaded South Korea. The Korean War (1950–1953), in which the United States suffered thirty-eight thousand combat deaths (in addition to perhaps five million deaths on all sides, civilian and military), would see the United States at war against Soviet satellite North Korea and Soviet ally communist

China, with the USSR providing indirect military and diplomatic assistance to the warring communist states. The Cold War had now become global, it had a military focus, and it was fueled by mutual ideological suspicion that the ultimate objective of the United States and the USSR, respectively, was the destruction of the other.

Stalin, it is clear, did not desire a Cold War along the lines formed after 1947. Stalin's interests as they emerged from World War II included, first, an understanding with the United States that would allow for the disarmament of Germany, reparations from the US and British zones of western Germany, and a major US postwar loan to the USSR; second, consolidation of Soviet influence throughout Eastern Europe and eastern Germany, if need be through communist political control; and third, keeping the door open to the eventual expansion of pro-Soviet influence in Western Europe, including France, Italy, and West Germany itself. What Stalin seems not to have realized until it was too late was that he would have to choose among these goals. A continuing commitment to the extension of the communist system as the best guarantor of Soviet state interests proved incompatible with a stable understanding with the United States (Gaddis 1997).

This intermixture of ideological and great-power definitions of interest helped create Soviet and US commitments in such far-flung regions of the world as Cuba, where in October 1962 a secret Soviet attempt to install medium-range nuclear missiles aimed at the United States brought the world to the brink of nuclear war, and Vietnam, where the United States would lose fifty-eight thousand soldiers between 1961 and 1973 (in addition to more than a million Vietnamese deaths on all sides) in an effort to prevent the victory of the North Vietnamese communists in South Vietnam. Efforts to regulate the Soviet-US competition, such as were accomplished in the early 1970s through a policy of *détente,* or relaxation of tensions, were rapidly undermined by continued Soviet-US competition throughout the third world (Gaddis 1982; Garthoff 1985). By the late 1970s, a series of Soviet interventions in Africa and elsewhere, including the transport of twenty thousand Cuban troops to decide the Angolan civil war of 1975–1976 and the invasion of Afghanistan in December 1979, combined with North Vietnam's victory over the South in spring 1975, seemed to herald a high point of Soviet global influence in a post-Vietnam world.

In reality, the USSR was seriously overextended in its external relations and the Afghan invasion only reinforced this. Aging Soviet leaders, themselves socialized in the Stalin era, had mortgaged what we now know to have been an ailing, hypercentralized, overly militarized economy, to a global competition with the United States and its allies in which the weight of economic and technological potential of the anti-Soviet coalition (the United States, NATO Europe, Canada, Japan, and communist China, which had split from Moscow in the late 1950s) was on the order of eight to one against Moscow. In effect, each step that Moscow now took in the Cold War competition saw the USSR fall further behind its adversaries. Moreover, Soviet satellite states in Eastern Europe, above all Poland, were becoming increasingly and openly restive under Moscow's tutelage (Ouimet 2003). Perceptive Soviet observers, still in the wings until Mikhail Gorbachev came to power in March 1985, had come to the conclusion that the cost of pursuing ideological objectives in foreign policy, in however attenuated form, was too great to the material interests of the Soviet state itself.

◼ Gorbachev's Foreign Policy Revolution

Mikhail Gorbachev assumed the office of general secretary of the Communist Party of the Soviet Union (CPSU), in March 1985, determined to revitalize the Soviet economy. Central to this aim was a relaxation of international tensions that would allow for a redirection of resources away from military to civilian uses as well as for a fundamentally new level of Soviet-Western economic relations. Within eight months of taking office, Gorbachev, in November 1985, met with US president Ronald Reagan in Geneva, Switzerland, and while the summit had few substantive achievements, both leaders emphatically declared that a nuclear war could not be won and must not be fought, thereby shifting the trajectory of the Soviet-US relationship. By October 1986, at a hastily arranged summit meeting in Iceland, the two leaders, much to the initial alarm of their staffs, had come close to agreeing on a framework for eliminating nuclear weapons altogether. The pact fell through due to Reagan's refusal to compromise on US plans for building a defensive, antiballistic missile (ABM) system. Undaunted, and unable to affect Reagan's basic stance, in 1987 Gorbachev accepted an original US negotiating position to eliminate all intermediate-range nuclear missiles, even though the USSR retained a significant superiority in numbers of such missiles and failed to obtain US concessions on ABM systems, namely SDI, the Strategic Defense Initiative, more popularly known as "Star Wars." The INF Treaty (Intermediate-Range Nuclear Forces Treaty), signed in December 1987, was not only the first nuclear disarmament treaty but also included for the first time provisions for the on-site inspection of compliance with the agreement, a major break with Soviet precedent and altogether a major confidence-building measure with the United States. Reagan's visit to Moscow, in summer 1988, signaled that the Cold War was now over. In December 1988, in a major address to the United Nations, Gorbachev made a series of specific policy commitments that underscored the waning of the Cold War, including major reductions in Soviet conventional armed forces and implicit pledges not to interfere in social, economic, and political change in Eastern Europe (Garthoff 1994).

Just as the bilateral framework for a post–Cold War Soviet-US relation-ship had been settled, the broader foundation of Soviet foreign policy, itself a consequence of the victory in 1945 and the ensuing Cold War, was coming apart. Central to Gorbachev's political vision in both domestic and foreign affairs was a determination to overcome the Stalinist legacy, especially on the use of force but also in terms of ideological influences on foreign policy. By 1987–1988, Gorbachev and his advisers had made it plain that they wanted to see economic and political reforms throughout Soviet-dominated Eastern Europe, but at the same time they made it clear that East European communist leaders could no longer count on military support from the USSR if faced with defiance from their own populations. This was in stark contrast to Soviet decisions to invade Hungary in November 1956 to crush an anticommunist uprising, and Czechoslovakia in August 1968 to suppress a peaceful communist-led, but anti-Stalinist, reform movement. At the same time, Gorbachev publicly declared that the "class struggle," central to Soviet ideology since the establishment of the Soviet state itself, was to be subordi-nate to the idea of "common human values" that bound nations to each other rather than divided them. In a startling and indicative contrast, in early June 1989, while the Chinese communist government ordered the massacre of thousands of peaceful demonstrators on Tiananmen Square in Beijing, the first free elections in postwar Poland saw the communists routed in favor of the previously banned labor movement Solidarity (Gati 1990).

A series of rapidly moving developments signaled the end of commu-nism in Eastern Europe and with it the end of Soviet political, economic, and military influence. Thus, the opening of the Hungarian border with neu-tral Austria in summer 1989 meant that East German tourists in Hungary could escape to West Germany through Hungary. In effect, the Berlin Wall had been breached even before it came down physically on the night of No-vember 9, 1989. A peaceful transition to a coalition government already had been negotiated in Hungary in the spring of 1989, followed by the peaceful exit of Czechoslovakian communists in November 1989 in the face of or-ganized mass opposition. The fall of the Berlin Wall signaled the end of communist East Germany; within the year, a united Germany would be es-tablished within NATO while Soviet troops began to vacate German soil. Only in Romania was significant violence involved, as the brutal and resist-ant dictator Nicolae Ceausescu was executed in what amounted to a palace coup in front of a mass audience.

By early 1991, the Warsaw Pact military alliance lay in tatters as the USSR itself was in its final death throes. Much as the United States sought to preserve Gorbachev in power and indeed to keep the USSR intact, if only to prevent the splintering of a nuclear superpower into a number of nuclear weapons mini-states, it could not stop the tide of the powerful nationalist movements chipping away at the foundations of the Soviet state. Ironically,

Gorbachev had managed to place Soviet-Western relations on a sound footing just as the USSR itself was becoming undone, in large part due to the unintended consequences of Gorbachev's efforts to reform it. For instance, once Gorbachev formally shed the ideological component of Soviet foreign policy, the USSR was embraced as a member of the Western community of states. To give one example, during 1989–1991, the G-7 states (referring to the group of seven leading industrialized democracies, that is, Canada, France, Germany, Italy, Japan, the United Kingdom, and the United States) extended eighty billion dollars of capital resources in loans, credits, and grants, a sum comparable to that extended by the United States in grants to Western Europe under the Marshall Plan between 1948 and 1951 (twelve billion in 1950 dollars). The United States made every effort to prevent the disintegration of the USSR, cutting a deal with Gorbachev at Malta in December 1989 to restrain Baltic aspirations for independence, ignoring rising Russian president Boris Yeltsin in favor of Gorbachev, and warning the Ukrainians at the beginning of August 1991 in their capital Kiev against what President George H. W. Bush termed "suicidal nationalism" (Beschloss and Talbott 1993).

This honeymoon period in Soviet-Western relations, culminating in the unification of Germany on German and US terms, was deeply resented and belatedly resisted by post-Soviet Russia's foreign policy and national security establishment (Zelikow and Rice 1995). At the same time, the prospects of Russia's genuine integration into the North Atlantic economic, political, and security community seemed to offer a major inducement to Russia's political elites to accommodate themselves to this new, post-Soviet community of democratic industrial states. Promises of international community seemed to prevail over contests of state interest defined through the prism of material power.

■ Patterns of Russian Foreign Policy in the Yeltsin Period

Throughout much of the 1990s the framework for partnership between Russia and the Western community of states established by Gorbachev continued to inform the priorities and direction of Russian foreign policy, although with diminishing influence over time. The primary question in the Russian-Western relationship soon after the Soviet collapse in 1991 concerned the breadth and depth of cooperation, not the centrality of cooperation itself. Russian policy elites tended to welcome the prospect of Russia's integration into the West, led by the G-7. By the late 1990s, however, the integrationist logic of Russian foreign policy had come under fire as a result of NATO expansion, the failure of economic reform at home, and NATO's spring 1999 war against Russia's client, Serbia. At the same time, Russian foreign policy

The Ministry of Foreign Affairs, built in Stalinist Gothic style, is one of seven "wedding cake" skyscrapers constructed in Moscow during the late 1940s and early 1950s.

BigStockPhoto.com; © Igor Zhorov

was careful not to jeopardize its key relationships with the leading powers of the West, including the United States. What happened, how are we to explain it, and what were the implications for Russian foreign policy under Boris Yeltsin's successor, Vladimir Putin?

The initial premises of post-Soviet Russia's foreign policy toward the West were rooted in the liberal internationalism of Foreign Minister Andrei Kozyrev. For Kozyrev, Russia's international interests paralleled those of the democratic world and were to a large extent a reflection of Russia's own democratic aspirations. Russia could not therefore afford to alienate the West, lest exclusion from the international democratic community jeopardize Russia's own democratic prospects. Yet it soon became clear that Russia's real chances for early integration into the Western world were much smaller than had first been imagined. Moreover, there were far more urgent issues arising out of the disintegration of the USSR for which Russia was not prepared and to which the G-7 states had little to contribute.

These problems, concentrated in the newly independent and highly fragile former Soviet republics along Russia's new interstate periphery, found Russia's Western-oriented diplomats with few concepts or tools to deal with them. An enormous policy vacuum thus existed, and even before 1992 was out, a nationalist reaction against Kozyrev's ideologically inspired liberal internationalism had become a part of Russian politics.

Even though Russian foreign policy did move away from Kozyrev's liberal line, it never approached the nationalist mania advanced by politicians like Vladimir Zhirinovsky (who claimed Alaska for Russia!) or the more representative communist leader Gennady Zyuganov. Importantly, the Russian political system evolved into a highly centralized one of presidential rule in which the presidency and the executive branch under both Boris Yeltsin and Vladimir Putin proved highly resistant to claims for accountability on the part of the parliament. Given the limited public interest in foreign affairs in general, as well as the institutional constraints on parliamentary influence, the Russian president has been free to conduct a foreign policy that has sought to balance a complex set of foreign and domestic interests rather than simply giving expression to one vocal stream of nationalist sentiment. Moreover, the visibility of extremist sentiment should not obscure the fact that, at least with respect to elites with access to the decisionmaking process, a fairly stable consensus seems to have emerged in favor of what British scholar Margot Light has termed "pragmatic nationalism," a position that has few illusions either about the West's willingness or capability to integrate Russia or about the extent of Russia's current dependence on access to Western trade and financial markets (Malcolm et al. 1996).

As a consequence, Russian diplomacy since the defeat of the pure liberal line in foreign policy has been far from the unilateralist, anti-Western, and generally ineffective statecraft suggested by some of the scholarly literature, much of the journalistic analysis, and the Russian government's domestic opponents. Rather, two Russian presidents have presided over a diplomacy that has attempted, with a fair degree of success, to balance two objectives that are in potential contradiction: establishing Russian predominance in the CIS region and Russia's status as a great international power, and avoiding a rupture with the G-7 states, whose cooperation remains essential to Russia's internal and external prospects.

In the Yeltsin period a series of key diplomatic episodes illustrate this proposition. Note, for instance, that Russia consistently and successfully separated the issues of its relations with NATO from its relations with the European Union, as well as its attitude toward NATO expansion from its bilateral relations with the states constituting NATO. Thus, even as Russia vocally opposed the enlargement of NATO membership to include former Soviet-bloc allies in Eastern Europe, it accepted with equanimity these same states joining the EU. At the same time, Russia continued to maintain

US Defense Department; Linwood Moore

President Boris Yeltsin and his wife, Naina,
during a 1994 visit to the United States.

profitable relations with individual NATO states, including the United States, right through Boris Yeltsin's two terms as Russian president (1991–1999). Indeed, US support for Yeltsin proved critical at several junctures during his presidency. Such backing was often economic, including billions of dollars in International Monetary Fund loans, but also political, in its support of Yeltsin during his confrontation with the Russian parliament in 1993 and during his reelection bid three years later (Talbott 2002). In the end, Moscow accepted what it could not change and in the process negotiated a symbolic compensation with NATO in the form of a joint Russia-NATO consultative council, established in May 1997.

In another example of Russian statecraft, in the spring of 1994, despite its stance as a patron of Serbia in the wars following the breakup of Yugoslavia, Russia agreed to the formation of the five-power Contact Group with the United States, Britain, France, and Germany so as to ensure that its specific differences with the Western powers on the Balkans did not undermine its overall relations with those states. As NATO's war against Serbia over ethnic Albanian rights in Kosovo would show, Russia would not allow its relations with the West to become a hostage to the whims of its alleged client, Serbian dictator Slobodan Milosevic, even at the point of Serbian defeat by NATO forces in June 1999. Such was its concern for good relations with the West that even though it was genuinely outraged by NATO's actions, in the end, Russia cooperated with the alliance to bring the war to an end on NATO's terms.

Interestingly, when Russia has opposed the United States, it has been careful to do so in coordination with key US allies. This was true under Yeltsin, in opposing, for example, the lifting of an arms embargo on Bosnian Muslims during the summer of 1993 (this time acting in support of Serbian interests), but also more recently under Putin when Russia sided with France and Germany against President George W. Bush's plan to invade Iraq in 2003. In this way, Moscow has avoided a Soviet-type diplomatic isolation.

Within the CIS zone, Russia realized early on that it would be left by the West to fend for itself. Targeted military interventions, direct and indirect—supporting Slavic minorities in independent Moldova (wedged between Ukraine and Romania) and aggrieved ethnic minorities in the Abkhazian and South Ossetian regions of Georgia in the Caucasus, sending a motorized rifle division to police the border between Tajikistan and Afghanistan, or providing a billion dollars worth of arms to Armenia in support of Armenian territorial claims against neighboring Azerbaijan— would not trigger significant Western opposition. Where resistance was understood to be likely, however, as over the withdrawal of Russian forces from the Baltic states of Estonia, Lithuania, and Latvia in 1994, the Kremlin behaved in much more circumspect ways. In this case, Moscow was unwilling to run the risk of congressionally mandated economic sanctions from the United States or criticism from EU member states (Russia's main trading partners) by delaying a previously agreed upon withdrawal date. In the end, the Russian forces withdrew ahead of schedule.

At the same time, if there were limits to Western influence in post-Soviet conflicts, the same was true of Russia's attempt to establish itself as the regional policeman in the CIS region, in the fashion of the United States' Monroe Doctrine (see Torbakov 2006a). The penetration of Western energy concerns such as British Petroleum and Exxon into energy-rich regions of Central Asia and the Caucasus illustrates this point, as does the curious minuet in the fall of 2002 among Russia, Georgia, and the United States, culminating in an apparent defusing of Russian-Georgian tensions on October 6, 2002, with an agreement between Moscow and Tbilisi on joint patrols along the Georgian border with Chechnya, where Russia has been attempting to suppress a secessionist movement since 1994. Since then, a small group of US troops has been in Georgia training Georgian troops, with the agreement of Moscow, to police that frontier. US scholar Stephen Sestanovich (2002) described the situation as follows:

> The United States may not mind Russian pressure if it focuses [then Georgian leader Eduard] Shevardnadze on what he has to do. The Russians may not mind American influence if it yields a change in Georgian policy. And the Georgians may not mind being told they have to make decisions they find it hard to make themselves.

The response of Russia's foreign minister at the time, Igor Ivanov, to the question of "whether Russia didn't in fact need a larger American presence in Georgia" perhaps summed up the situation best: "'Maybe,' he shrugged" (Sestanovich 2002, 30).

A number of patterns formed during the Yeltsin years continue to influence the character of Russian foreign policy. First, for the first extended period since the nineteenth century there is no ideological animus driving the Russian-Western relationship. Unlike during the communist era, post-Soviet Russia can expect to be received as a legitimate member of the international community of sovereign states.

Second, key groups in the Russian economic elite, especially in the energy and metals sectors, which together accounted for three-quarters of Russia's exports in 2006 (Bank of Finland 2007b), require reliable access to Western commercial and financial markets. Receipts from energy exports now make up close to 60 percent of the Russian government's annual budget (Lipman 2007). These receipts, in turn, support Russia's natural gas monopoly, Gazprom, which is constrained to sell gas to Russian consumers at a fraction of the price that it fetches from European consumers, as well as keeping vast stretches of Russia itself alive and warm during the seven-month heating season. Seen in this light, Russian energy relations with the European Union are a truly vital element sustaining Russia's economic and political prospects. Consider the following facts: The EU is Russia's largest trading partner, accounting for 44.8 percent of Russia's imports and 56.2 percent of its export trade. Russia, in turn, is the EU's third largest trading partner, accounting for 9.1 percent of EU imports and 5.3 percent of EU exports (European Commission 2006).

As such, Russia is disproportionately dependent upon EU trade, all the more so as it runs a large trade surplus with the Union. At the same time, Russia's importance as an energy supplier to the EU inserts some balance into the relationship: Russia provides 27.5 percent of the Union's imported fuel and 39 percent of Germany's natural gas requirements (European Commission 2006; Gelb 2007). Trade between Russia and the EU is, for the most part, liberalized. Russian oil and gas exports to the EU are free of tariffs, and a 1998 revision of the EU's antidumping rules has resulted in a dramatic drop in the percentage of Russian goods that are subject to EU antidumping regulations (European Commission n.d.).

The logic of dependency in foreign trade and finance thus sustains Russia's Western orientation, as was also true of late imperial Russia. Unlike the late nineteenth and early twentieth centuries, however, there are no state-based threats to Russia's territorial or political integrity. Even Russian foreign policy elites who brandish threats against the West openly admit (as did presidential adviser Andranik Migranyan) that the purpose in doing so is to bluff, to be traded "in exchange for Russia's integration into the Western world" (*Washington Post* 2002).

Third, Russia's top leaders, proceeding from these facts and from the general recognition that few if any of Russia's national interests (or those of its key elites) could be served through genuine confrontation with the United States and its allies, have continuously sought to preserve lines of communication with the West, even as they tack to the increasingly nationalist wind of Russian domestic politics.

Fourth, given the absence of irreconcilable interests, territorial disputes, or ideological conflict, there is no reason to expect that intelligent diplomacy cannot maintain a normal Russian-Western relationship. Diplomacy, however, presupposes negotiation. A pattern whereby Russian-Western interactions are simply defined by the projection of superior Western power upon a weak Russia will continue to erode political support for Russia's Western option. Paradoxically, a more representative political system in such a climate could produce a radical turn against collaboration with the West (Zimmerman 2002)

Finally, the danger of a fraying Russian-Western relationship does not lie in the recreation of a putative Russian threat. The decomposition of Russian military power, as well as the transformation of Russia's elites, is too far gone for that. Rather it lies in the greater difficulty and higher costs of obtaining Russian cooperation where such is essential to maintaining international security, for example, in the fields of nuclear weapons arms control, the policing of Central Asia, and the use and misuse of energy resources.

▓ Patterns of Russian Foreign Policy Under Putin

From the start of his presidency, Vladimir Putin continued the pattern of Russian foreign policy observed under Boris Yeltsin, although with a more determined and interventionist leadership style. Putin appeared to have an almost entirely unsentimental, nonideological, pragmatic understanding of Russia's internal situation and of Russia's relationship to its external environment. Two fundamental premises seemed to inform Putin's initial outlook on Russia and the world: (1) Russia was weak and would remain so for the foreseeable future; and (2) Russia's chief danger was the threat of isolation from the international system economically, politically, and militarily. As such, Russia would need to avoid direct conflicts with the most powerful states and regional actors in the system, and where conflicts were unavoidable it would have to find allies to prevent its isolation from the rest of the world.

Other elements also came into play that would have a great influence on the content and conduct of Russian foreign policy under Putin. One is Russia's continued dependence on North Atlantic trade. As noted earlier, the EU accounts for upward of 50 percent of Russia's foreign trade, far surpassing the amount with any other region or country in the world. Together, Russia's trade with Western Europe, North America, and Japan exceeds its trade with China by a ratio of ten to one. The same is true of China's bilateral trade with Russia. As often as the Kremlin has spoken in recent years of the desirability of forming an alliance with China against the West, the reality is that as long as both countries are governed by leaders who value the gains that can be obtained from global economic integration, the possibility of such a pact is remote.

Another economic element working in the same direction is the political influence of the country's export-oriented lobbies. This, combined with the fiscal dependence of the Russian government on export receipts, has kept Russian diplomacy focused on its relations with the West despite the nationalist and protectionist voices that can be heard from across the Russian political spectrum.

As was true under Yeltsin, the "superpresidential" nature of Russia's political system, which Putin reinforced, has continued to facilitate a Westward orientation, even though such an approach was far from being unanimously accepted among Russian political parties and the national security establishment. Putin's remarkable orientation of Russian diplomacy toward the United States after September 11, 2001, serves as an important case in point.

After the terror attacks of September 11, Putin placed his country foursquare behind US policy in the war against international terror. Disregarding the views of his senior generals, eighteen of whom published an open letter in the Russian press protesting the alignment of Russia's foreign policy with that of the United States and the stationing of US forces in the former Soviet republics of Uzbekistan and Tajikistan, Putin proved to be one of the United States' most important allies. In the US invasion of Afghanistan in the fall of 2001, Putin provided the United States with basing and overflight rights, and accelerated arms deliveries to the Northern Alliance. This remarkable shift in the tenor of the bilateral Russian-US relationship was reflected in the relative calmness with which the Russian president reacted to the US announcement in December 2001 that it would abandon the 1972 ABM Treaty, which banned significant antimissile defenses, thereby underscoring mutual Russian and US vulnerability, a macabre sort of equality. Putin appeared to be committed to shaping a truly substantial bilateral relationship with Washington, one in which no particular issue could be deemed worthy of undermining that relationship and in the process jeopardize Russia's standing in the West, where Putin had clearly placed his bets (Goldgeier and McFaul 2003).

Most dramatically, Putin's alignment of Russia with the United States in the war on terror reflected a programmatic commitment, one possibly as profound as that undergirding Mikhail Gorbachev's "new political thinking," that a fragile Russia should not advance its most pressing and vital state interests against determined US opposition, and that it would be far preferable to advance them with positive US support. To be sure, Russia had its own specific interests at stake in the war against the Taliban in Afghanistan and the Al-Qaida terror network. As early as September 2000, Russian foreign policy elites spoke in private of an eventual Russian-US military campaign against the Taliban, reflecting an understanding that Russia alone did not have the power to neutralize the threat that the Taliban posed to Russian interests in Central Asia. Putin accepted this prospect with apparent equanimity. US forces thus accomplished for Putin what he was unable to accomplish for himself. As noted, however, Russia played a vital role in providing massive arms deliveries to the Northern Alliance during the US campaign. Moreover, Putin's intervention to allow US forces to be based in several Central Asian states underscores the fact that the United States operates in the region with Russian permission, thus reinforcing Russia's assertion of a privileged sphere of influence in this sensitive, energy-rich part of the world.

As a flurry of Russian-US diplomacy in the fall of 2001 showed, however, Putin had greater aims in mind. He seems to have calculated that full support for the United States in its hour of need could help transform the Russian-US and, more broadly, the Russian-Western relationship, thereby insulating those relations from any particular conflict of interest within them. In the best-case scenario, mutual commitment to a new relationship would advance Russian interests on three vital issues:

1. A new framework for nuclear arms control. Putin sought to engage the United States in a framework for relating defensive to offensive weaponry in a way that corresponded to Russia's reduced financial circumstances (by triggering further reductions in offensive arms), avoided a break with Washington over US withdrawal from the 1972 ABM Treaty, and preserved Russia's unique status as the second nuclear weapons power by ensuring that any US antimissile deployment will be a limited and not a comprehensive one.

2. NATO enlargement. Putin, aware that Russia could not influence the dynamic of further NATO expansion eastward, sought to dissociate the question of enlargement from the nature of Russia's bilateral relations with the states constituting NATO. Ultimately, Russia desired a true Russia-NATO partnership. Would NATO desire one likewise, if such a partnership meant it must refrain from taking action that Moscow deemed contrary to Russia's vital interests? Would NATO desire a substantive rather than a symbolic consultative relationship with Moscow, one that would go far beyond the failed experiment of the first Russia-NATO Council established in spring 1997? Was NATO prepared to negotiate with Russia, as distinct from presenting its terms to Russia, however neatly packaged?

3. Economics. Putin also sought to enlist the support of Western governments, especially the United States, for two major projects: (a) a further rescheduling, if not outright liquidation, of the bulk of Russia's Soviet-era debt; and (b) sustained support for direct foreign investment in the Russian economy. Although Putin made little progress in gaining Western assistance in debt liquidation, in the end, soaring energy prices solved the problem for him. In 2006, Russia paid off its Paris Club debt and reduced its debt over-all (including Soviet-era debt) to $46 billion. To put this figure in perspective, Russia's foreign debt in 2000, Putin's first year in office, was just under $150 billion (Bank of Finland 2007a).

In terms of his core strategy, however, Putin could find little encouraging in US behavior. In response to Russia's unprecedented support for US military operations on both sides of the old Soviet border, the United States announced its withdrawal from the ABM Treaty, offered Russia a relationship with NATO that did not appear to go beyond the symbolic connection that collapsed during NATO's war against Russia's client state Serbia in the spring of 1999, and dragged its feet on taking measures that would have recast the nature of the Russia-Western economic relationship. For instance, the 1974 Jackson-Vanik Amendment, prohibiting the extension of normal trading relations status to the USSR, remained on the US legislative books, even as there was (and still is) talk in Washington of repealing it. Progress on Russia's possible entry into the World Trade Organization (WTO) was also slowed by the United States. Thus, Putin's calculated gamble that a pro-US stance after September 11 could trigger a deeper Russian-US relationship had not borne fruit. At the same time, Putin remained committed to a steady relationship with Washington, on the pragmatic grounds that power realities allow no real alternative. All the while, as Putin's first term came to an end, broader Russian political support for a pro-US orientation virtually disappeared.

As Putin began his second term in office, the general framework that has channeled Russian foreign policy since 1993–1994 remained intact. Russia's foreign policy leadership continued to reject ideological considerations (democratic or otherwise) and, ever conscious of Russia's profound vulnerabilities within the broader global system, sought to preserve maximally harmonious relations with the leading countries of the West. The task of Russian economic recovery and development was understood to be a matter of decades, not years. As such, Putin continued to develop Russian relations with the Western powers so as to maximize Russia's economic growth potential and minimize the obstacles to dealing with pressing issues within and along the borders of the Russian Federation. At the same time, conscious of NATO and the EU enlargement, which now included the Baltic states, and of the greater vulnerabilities of Russia's neighbors in the CIS, Russia persisted in trying to consolidate a position of predominance within the CIS region. The main task of Russian diplomacy was to avoid having to

US Air Force

In a scene reminiscent of the Cold War, a US Air Force F-15 Eagle escorts a Russian Tu-95 Bear bomber that had approached Alaska's western coast during a Russian military exercise in September 2006.

choose between these two vital areas of interest. All of this reflects the "pragmatic nationalist" approach to foreign policy that has prevailed in Russia since the mid-1990s.

On the general political level, this meant avoiding isolation. Unlike the USSR, postcommunist Russia has taken great pains not to oppose the United States on its own. Putin, for instance, would not allow US differences with Russia over North Korea's and Iran's nuclear programs to be differences with Russia alone. Nor would Putin see relations with Europe as a substitute for healthy ties with Washington. Europe is simply not a security factor beyond the confines of the continent. Only the United States can work with Russia at the level of the broader international security system.

On the economic level, Putin worked hard to conclude a workable rapprochement with the WTO, which will necessarily entail numerous exceptions for Russia's largely uncompetitive industrial base. But in the end, Russian membership in the WTO, and economic ties with the EU, cannot compensate for the consolidation in Russia of a political economy dependent on the export of raw materials, especially energy.

In considering the future course of its foreign policy, Russia will most likely continue to maintain the fabric of its relations with Western Europe and the United States at the same time that it seeks to consolidate a preeminent economic, political, and security position within the CIS region. Europe and the United States are in fact forcing the pace of the Russian agenda here as both the eventual consolidation of an expanded EU and NATO economic and security realm along Russia's western border and a US security presence in Central Asia are pushing Russian leaders to consolidate what they can while they can. US plans announced in 2007 to establish the foundations of an antiballistic missile system in the Czech Republic and Poland are emblematic of this tendency. Within the CIS context, however, superior Russian resources (energy, troops, bases, clients) combined with a high intensity of interest suggest that Russia can succeed in this task at least in part if not in whole. Key areas include:

1. Central Asia. Although pragmatically welcoming a US presence to defeat the Taliban in neighboring Afghanistan, from the start Moscow has been determined to maintain a Russian basing structure in Central Asia that sends the message that while the United States may be in the region for now, Russia is there to stay. To support this aim, Russia maintains military bases in Tajikistan, Kyrgyzstan, and Kazakhstan and has recently signed agreements with these governments extending Russian basing rights. The US withdrawal of military forces from Uzbekistan's Karshi-Khanabad Air Base in early 2006, following a prolonged diplomatic dispute between Washington and Tashkent (the base had been made available to the United States by the Uzbeks following Al-Qaida's September 11 attacks), lends credence to Russia's claim that it is the preeminent and permanent foreign power in the region.

2. The South Caucasus. Russia aspires to the role in the South Caucasus (encompassing the former Soviet republics of Georgia, Armenia, and Azerbaijan) that the United States has long played in the Middle East, namely, one in which no regional solutions are possible except through Moscow, whatever the part played by others. Russia's interest in the region derives in part from security concerns within its own borders in the North Caucasus (see Torbakov 2005). In Georgia, for instance, this has meant direct involvement in that country's internal affairs, chiefly in its conflict with breakaway regions Abkhazia and South Ossetia. Russia has also applied economic pressure in an attempt to bend Georgia to its will, including cutting off energy supplies and embargoing Georgian goods. In response, Georgia, which now sees its future in the West, has been at work with neighboring Azerbaijan in an effort to reduce its energy dependence on Russia (Socor 2007). As Russia's military incursion into Georgia proper (in response to Georgia's introduction of combat troops into South Ossetia) in August 2008 has shown, however, Russia remains determined that Georgia stay within a Russian sphere of foreign policy influence. Russia is above all determined that Georgia (and by implication Ukraine) not join NATO. The confused and passive reaction to Russia's military action on the part of the

NATO powers, many of whom are dependent on Russian deliveries of natural gas, suggests that Russia may have its way on Georgia's future security orientation.

3. Ukraine. Ukraine represents the most important but also most difficult and complex foreign policy challenge facing Russia. Russian foreign policy makers continue to believe that, at a minimum, Ukraine must not be allowed a viable Western option, that is, to substitute NATO and the EU for Russia as the focal point of Ukraine's external relations. At the same time, the inclusion of bordering states Poland, Slovakia, Hungary, and Romania into both NATO and the EU means that Ukraine cannot avoid being part of Europe's business. Yet Ukrainian energy dependency on Russia seems destined to ensure that Ukraine cannot afford to antagonize Russia in fundamental ways (see Torbakov 2006b). For example, the electoral triumph of pro-Western presidential candidate Viktor Yushchenko in Ukraine's fall 2004 elections angered and alarmed the Russian government, which had invested a great deal of time, energy and money to foil his candidacy. While Putin's entourage feared a gravitation of Yushchenko's Ukraine away from Russia and toward the West, Ukraine's energy dependence on Moscow, reinforced by the acquisition of key Ukrainian natural gas companies by Russian firms with ties to the Russian government, seems destined to limit Ukraine's ability to adopt an openly anti-Russian stance in its foreign relations. The political comeback of Yushchenko's opponent in the spring 2006 elections, pro-Russian Viktor Yanukovych, also served Moscow's interests. Likewise, enduring and deeply rooted problems of political corruption, which led Yushchenko to fire his entire government in September 2005, remain a major obstacle to Ukraine's acceptance into European and trans-Atlantic economic and security institutions.

4. Belarus. Belarus is likely to assume increasing importance and urgency for Russia, as the Baltic states have now been admitted into NATO. We may expect continued Russian economic pressure on Belarus, to bring the government of the despotic Aleksandr Lukashenka to heel to stop energy siphoning and nonpayment as well as political initiatives to convert such pressures into a closer Russian-Belarus relationship. Such a bond could constitute a symbolic reply to Baltic incorporation into NATO, possibly involving the deployment or preparation to deploy tactical nuclear weapons, and the renunciation of the constraints of the 1990 Conventional Forces in Europe Treaty governing the deployment of land armed forces.

5. Moldova. Russian support for the breakaway, Slavic-majority, Moldovan province of Transnistria will persist so long as Ukraine, which borders Moldova on its east, does not formally recognize Russian preeminence in that state's foreign relations. Yet the complications of EU expansion for Russia's ties with its historical western borderlands were shown in November 2002 when Russia brokered a peace deal that would have allowed Russian troops to remain in Transnistria until 2020. Moldovan leaders, encouraged by European resistance to the arrangement, renounced the accord at the last minute, much to the fury of the Russian leadership. At the same time, Russian military units, which have sustained the secession of the province since 1992, remain in place for the foreseeable future. As has been true in Russia's dealings with several other of the former Soviet republics, Moscow has also leveraged its economic power (especially as a supplier of energy) to put pressure on Chisinau.

Russia can likely succeed in the balancing act of preserving relations with Europe and the United States while striving for a more reliable preeminence within the CIS. Factors working in Russia's favor include the fact that Russian policy is reactive rather than proactive in its motivations (that is, it is motivated not by hostility to the West per se but by attempts to define its boundary with the West); that Russia has a far greater intensity of interest throughout the CIS region than does either Europe or the United States; and that Russia retains a superiority of diverse power resources vis-à-vis the CIS states comparable to that which the West wields with respect to Russia in the wider world system. The combination of a Russian military presence, local energy dependency on Russia, and increasing Russian penetration of oil, gas, and electricity concerns in these states tends to underwrite Russia's claim to primacy within the Commonwealth of Independent States (Trenin 2001).

At the same time, Russia's ability to maintain this balance depends on three important variables. First, that the Russian presidency remains essentially unaccountable to the formal institutions and vested interests in Russia's national security bureaucracy, which are increasingly anti-Western and especially anti-US in outlook. Second, that US domestic political pressures to react to aggressive Russian behavior close to home are kept to a minimum. Third, and perhaps most critically, that world oil prices remain relatively high given the dependency of Russia's economy and the solvency of the state budget on revenues from energy exports.

Indeed, if world oil prices should fall for an extended period of time, the central premise of the above analysis could well be called into question. Close to half of Russia's economic growth derives from the natural resources sector (Tikhomirov 2004). Even a decline of just a few dollars per barrel can mean slower economic growth, which in turn can eventually put pressure on the state budget. The collapse of world oil prices in 1986 and 1998 had dramatic consequences for Gorbachev and Yeltsin. For the former, it meant reform without resources, and for the latter, default. Should oil prices collapse once again, the grip of Russia's president and the pragmatic nationalist consensus that has so far prevailed would likely be loosened, while xenophobic and chauvinist nationalist groups would be strengthened, propelling a backlash that would tend to undermine Russia's delicate balancing act (from a position of weakness) between harmony with the West, on the one hand, and primacy within the CIS on the other. For the time being, with oil fetching record prices, the Russian government seems able to finance its various internal and external commitments without serious institutional strain.

Outside of the CIS, a number of thorny issues will continue to influence Russia's relations with the G-7 states. These include:

1. Human rights. Despite Putin's repeated declarations of support for the development of democracy in Russia, his political machine has stifled virtually all significant opposition to Kremlin rule. In response, a number of influential nongovernmental organizations and legislative institutions in the European Union and the United States have raised the alarm, putting pressure on their own governments to respond negatively and critically to such abuses. Of late, the United States has been more critical of Russia's internal affairs even at the risk of straining relations between the two countries.

2. Global security issues. The decision by the United States to deploy elements of an ABM system in the Czech Republic and Poland underscores US determination, despite Russian objections, to pursue its security interests in countries that were once a part of the Soviet bloc. Likewise, Washington's refusal to date to consider detailed, legally binding constraints on deployments of its offensive nuclear forces has given rise to fears in Moscow that one day US strategic deployments, in conjunction with a fully developed US ABM system, will neutralize Russia's remaining nuclear deterrent.

3. Regional security issues. Although Russia may safely oppose the United States on the question of Kosovo's independence from Serbia because the issue is of decidedly secondary importance to Washington, such is not the case with respect to Iran, where the United States has been careful to preserve the option to use force to prevent Tehran from acquiring nuclear weapons. Russia's attempts to play the role of honest broker between Iran and the West (as reflected in Putin's visit to Iran in October 2007) will work only so long as the United States and its European allies continue to see noncoercive diplomacy as a viable means to resolving the crisis. If the West were to abandon noncoercive diplomacy, however, Russia would have to choose between maintaining its ties with Iran and preserving its relations with the West. If the United States and its NATO allies remain united, it seems unlikely that Russia would jeopardize its most valuable economic and security links for the dubious pleasures of positive relations with Iran.

■ Conclusion

For the foreseeable future, Russia will remain an enclave economy in which both its macroeconomic equilibrium and fiscal health will remain disproportionately and dangerously dependent on the price of oil and gas on international markets. As a consequence, Russia finds itself caught between the temptations of high energy prices, which mitigate the urgency of structural reforms, and the dangers of low prices, which threaten the viability of the state itself. This is, of course, the fate of petrostates around the world.

Therefore, both the Russian economy, which has been improving in the past several years, and the Russian state, which has been consolidated to an extent under Putin, remain fragile accomplishments. Linear extrapolation from current economic and political trends ten years down the road seems tenuous. This is especially so since the primary impulses for Russia's recent spurt of economic growth derive from two factors, one of which was a one-time event with diminishing returns (the 75 percent devaluation of the ruble in August 1998 and the spur this gave to domestic manufacturing) and the other an external shift in the terms of trade over which Russia has no real influence (the dramatic increase in the price of oil and gas).

At the same time, the Russian political system remains narrowly and superficially institutionalized, lacking the organizational efficiencies of accountable, consolidated democracies. A neopatrimonial state based on a close nexus of economics and politics and an authoritarian presidency within the framework of a "managed" democracy are the orders of the day. The latent fragility of the Russian political system, however, renders the federal center vulnerable should the terms of trade in global energy markets suddenly turn for the worse. We could then see a return to the situation immediately after the August 1998 crash, when most state power, including control over substantial parts of the armed forces, was wrested from the federal center by regional barons who, unlike the center, were able to pay state officials. The Russian president's ability to maneuver among the country's economic oligarchs, such as it is, depends on a steady stream of oil and gas revenues into state coffers. Russia's rich cannot plausibly threaten to bring the government down by their financial decisions (as they frequently did under Yeltsin) when world energy prices are high and the government is relatively flush with cash (Nikonov 2003). A steady decline in the price of oil and gas, however, could well change the balance of power between the state and the oligarchs, to the distinct disadvantage of the former.

Seen in this light, the most important domestic effect on Russia's standing in the world and on global security ten years from now is the possibility of a destabilizing implosion of the Russian state. To the extent that this is so, a primary task of the West is to address the underlying economic conditions that make this outcome possible, and prepare for the worst if economic insurance fails, by reinforcing the insulation between Russia's multiple nuclear, chemical, and biological archipelagoes and the latent fragility of the Russian state.

The case for treating the Russian-Western relationship as a reciprocal partnership, as distinct from a "take it or leave it" proposition, is not based on providing political rewards for Russia's president or on shoring up a precarious political position at home. Quite the contrary: it was precisely

Putin's independence of the formal agencies of the Russian constitution that allowed him to engineer such a dramatic breakthrough in Russian-US relations. Nor can Russia realistically confront the United States and its allies, even if it wanted to.

Rather, the argument for engaging Russia is based upon a pragmatic consideration of US and Western interests. Russia has the potential to counterbalance Persian Gulf oil as a major supplier of reasonably priced oil and natural gas to the Western world. The West, in turn, has within its power the ability to offer to Russia a degree of price stability that would in turn stabilize the finances of the Russian government and allow for longer-term economic planning and development. Without that stability, Russia will remain in a condition of latent macroeconomic fragility for the foreseeable future. Given the necessity of sustaining Russian governmental control over its nuclear, chemical, and biological complex, as well as over immense stretches of Eurasia itself, the economic prerequisites of Russian governmental stability are in fact of vital interest to the West and to the whole world. One way or another, the West will have to live with Russia, in sickness and in health, just as Russia is constrained, or impelled, to live with the West, for better or for worse. Ironically, in the post–Cold War world, Russian weakness, not Russian strength, poses the greater threat to Western and global security.

■ Bibliography

Ambrosio, Thomas. 2005. "The Russo-American Dispute over Iraq: International Status and the Role of Positional Goods." *Europe-Asia Studies* 57(8): 1189–1210.
———. 2007. "Insulating Russia from a Colour Revolution: How the Kremlin Resists Regional Democratic Trends." *Democratization* 14(2): 232–252.
Arbatov, Alexei G., Karl Kaiser, and Robert Legvold, eds. 1999. *Russia and the West: The 21st Century Security Environment*. Armonk, NY: M. E. Sharpe.
Bank of Finland. 2007a. Institute for Economies in Transition. *BOFIT Weekly,* no. 3, January 19. http://www.bof.fi/bofit_en/seuranta/viikkokatsaus/vuosikirjat/vuosikirjat.htm.
———. 2007b. Institute for Economies in Transition. *BOFIT Weekly,* no. 8, February 23. http://www.bof.fi/bofit_en/seuranta/viikkokatsaus/vuosikirjat/vuosikirjat.htm.
Beschloss, Michael R., and Strobe Talbott. 1993. *At the Highest Levels: The Inside Story of the End of the Cold War*. Boston: Little, Brown.
Black, J. L. 2000. *Russia Faces NATO Expansion: Bearing Gifts or Bearing Arms?* Lanham, MD: Rowman & Littlefield.
Carley, Michael Jabara. 1999. *1939: The Alliance That Never Was and the Coming of World War II*. Chicago: I. R. Dee.
Cohen, Stephen F. 2000. *Failed Crusade: America and the Tragedy of Post-Communist Russia*. New York: Norton.
Donaldson, Robert H., and Joseph L. Nogee. 2002. *The Foreign Policy of Russia: Changing Systems, Enduring Interests*. 2nd ed. Armonk, NY: M. E. Sharpe.

European Commission. 2006. "Russia—Trade Statistics." http://trade.ec.europa.eu/doc lib/docs/2006/september/tradoc_113440.pdf.
———. n.d. "The EU's Relations with Russia: EU-Russia Trade." http://europa.eu .int/comm/external_relations/russia/intro/trade.htm.
Fuller, William C. 1992. *Strategy and Power in Russia, 1600–1914.* New York: Free Press.
Gaddis, John Lewis. 1982. *Strategies of Containment: A Critical Appraisal of Postwar American National Security Policy.* New York: Oxford University Press.
———. 1997. *We Now Know: Rethinking Cold War History.* New York: Oxford University Press.
Garthoff, Raymond L. 1985. *Détente and Confrontation: American-Soviet Relations from Nixon to Reagan.* Washington, D.C.: Brookings Institution.
———. 1994. *The Great Transition: American-Soviet Relations and the End of the Cold War.* Washington, D.C.: Brookings Institution.
Gati, Charles. 1990. *The Bloc That Failed: Soviet–East European Relations in Transition.* Bloomington: Indiana University Press.
Gelb, Bernard A. 2007. "Russian Natural Gas: Regional Dependence." *CRS Report for Congress,* January 5. http://www.fas.org/sgp/crs/misc/RS22562.pdf.
Goldgeier, James M., and Michael McFaul. 2003. *Power and Purpose: US Policy Toward Russia After the Cold War.* Washington, D.C.: Brookings Institution.
Gorodetsky, Gabriel, ed. 2003. *Russia Between East and West: Russian Foreign Policy on the Threshold of the Twenty-First Century.* London: Frank Cass.
Haas, Mark L. 2007. "The United States and the End of the Cold War: Reactions to Shifts in Soviet Power, Policies, or Domestic Politics?" *International Organization* 61(1):145–179.
Hurst, Andrew. 2003. "Russia Has Hill to Climb to Win Investment Grade." *Reuters,* February 7.
Jacobson, Jon. 1994. *When the Soviet Union Entered World Politics.* Berkeley: University of California Press.
Kekic, Laza. 2004. "How Dependent Is Growth on the Oil Price?" *St. Petersburg Times,* February 3.
Kennedy, Paul. 1987. *The Rise and Fall of the Great Powers: Economic Change and Military Conflict from 1500 to 2000.* New York: Random House.
Kotkin, Stephen. 2001. *Armageddon Averted: The Soviet Collapse, 1970–2000.* New York: Oxford University Press.
LeDonne, John P. 1997. *The Russian Empire and the World, 1700–1917: The Geopolitics of Expansion and Containment.* New York: Oxford University Press.
Leffler, Melvyn P. 1992. *A Preponderance of Power: National Security, the Truman Administration, and the Cold War.* Stanford, CA: Stanford University Press.
Legvold, Robert. 2001. "Russia's Unformed Foreign Policy." *Foreign Affairs* 80(5): 62–75.
———, ed. 2007. *Russian Foreign Policy in the Twenty-first Century and the Shadow of the Past.* New York: Columbia University Press.
Lieven, Anatol. 1998. *Chechnya: Tombstone of Russian Power.* New Haven, CT: Yale University Press.
Lipman, Masha. 2007. "Resolving Russia's Paradox." *PostGlobal,* January 21. http:// newsweek.washingtonpost.com/postglobal/.
Lynch, Allen C. 1987. *The Soviet Study of International Relations.* Cambridge, UK: Cambridge University Press.
———. 2001. "The Realism of Russia's Foreign Policy." *Europe-Asia Studies* 53(1): 7–31.

MacKenzie, David. 1994a. *From Messianism to Collapse: Soviet Foreign Policy, 1917–1991.* Fort Worth, TX: Harcourt Brace College Publishers.

————. 1994b. *Imperial Dreams, Harsh Realities: Tsarist Russian Foreign Policy, 1815–1917.* Fort Worth, TX: Harcourt Brace College Publishers.

Malcolm, Neil, et al. 1996. *Internal Factors in Russian Foreign Policy.* Oxford, UK: Oxford University Press.

Malia, Martin. 1999. *Russia Under Western Eyes: From the Bronze Horseman to the Lenin Mausoleum.* Cambridge, MA: Harvard University Press.

Mandelbaum, Michael, ed. 1998. *The New Russian Foreign Policy.* New York: Council on Foreign Relations.

Medvedev, Roy. 2004. *Vladimir Putin: Chetyre goda v Kremle* [Vladimir Putin: Fours years in the Kremlin]. Moscow: Vremia.

Melville, Andrei, and Tatiana Shakleina, eds. 2005. *Russian Foreign Policy in Transition: Concepts and Realities.* Trans. Anna Yastrzhembska. Budapest: CEU Press.

Mendelsohn, Sarah E. 2001. "Democracy Assistance and Political Transition in Russia: Between Success and Failure." *International Security* 25(4): 68–106.

Motyl, Alexander J., Blair A. Ruble, and Lilia Shevtsova, eds. 2005. *Russia's Engagement with the West: Transformation and Integration in the Twenty-First Century.* Armonk, NY: M. E. Sharpe.

Nekrich, A. M. 1968. *June 22, 1941: Soviet Historians and the German Invasion.* Trans. Vladimir Petrov. Columbia: University of South Carolina Press.

Nikonov, Viacheslav. 2003. "Putinizm" [Putinism]. In *Sovremennaia rossiiskaia politika* [Contemporary Russian politics], ed. Viacheslav Nikonov. Moscow: OLMA-PRESS.

Ouimet, Matthew J. 2003. T*he Rise and Fall of the Brezhnev Doctrine in Soviet Foreign Policy.* Chapel Hill: University of North Carolina Press.

Pipes, Richard. 1974. *Russia Under the Old Regime.* New York: Scribner.

Poe, Marshall. 2003. *The Russian Moment in World History.* Princeton, NJ: Princeton University Press.

Ragsdale, Hugh. 1996. *The Russian Tragedy: The Burden of History.* Armonk, NY: M. E. Sharpe.

Reddaway, Peter, and Dmitri Glinsky. 2001. *The Tragedy of Russia's Reforms: Market Bolshevism Against Democracy.* Washington, D.C.: United States Institute of Peace Press.

Sapir, Jacques. 2003. "Is Russian Growth Bound to Disappear?" *Russia and Eurasia Review* 2(2), January 21. http://www.jamestown.org/publications_details.php?volume_id=16&&issue_id=614.

Sestanovich, Stephen. 2002. "Putin Has His Own Candidate for Pre-emption." *New York Times,* October 6.

Shevardnadze, Eduard. 1991. *The Future Belongs to Freedom.* Trans. Catherine A. Fitzpatrick. New York: Free Press.

Simes, Dimitri K. 1999. *After the Collapse: Russia Seeks Its Place as a Great Power.* New York: Simon & Schuster.

Skopin, A. Iu. 2003. *Ekonomicheskaia geografiia Rossii* [An economic geography of Russia]. Moscow: Prospekt.

Socor, Vladimir. 2007. "Shah-Deniz Gas Buttressing Georgia, Azerbaijan Economically and Politically." *Eurasia Daily Monitor* 4(12), January 17. http://www.jamestown.org/edm/.

Stiglitz, Joseph E. 2002. *Globalization and Its Discontents.* New York: Norton.

Talbott, Strobe. 2002. *The Russia Hand: A Memoir of Presidential Diplomacy.* New York: Random House.

Tikhomirov, Vladimir. 2004. "The Future of Russia's Economic Growth: De-Coupling from Oil." In *Slavic Eurasia's Integration into the World Economy and Community*, ed. Tabata Shinichiro and Iwashita Akihiro. Sapporo, Japan: Slavic Research Center, Hokkaido University.

Torbakov, Igor. 2005. "Russia Seeks to Reassert Its Status as a Key Power in the Caucasus." *Eurasia Daily Monitor* 2(113), June 10. http://www.jamestown.org/ edm/.

———. 2006a. "Ivanov Restates Kremlin's Monroe Doctrine." *Eurasia Daily Monitor* 3(9), January 13. http://www.jamestown.org/edm/.

———. 2006b. "Ukraine's Geopolitical Predicament: While Longing for Place in United Europe It Cannot Ignore Russia's Concerns." *Eurasia Daily Monitor* 3(199), October 27. http://www.jamestown.org/edm/.

Trenin, Dmitri. 2001. *The End of Eurasia: Russia on the Border Between Geopolitics and Globalization*. Washington, D.C.: Carnegie Moscow Center, Carnegie Endowment for International Peace.

———. 2006. "Russia Leaves the West." *Foreign Affairs* 85(4): 87–96.

Ulam, Adam B. 1974. *Expansion and Coexistence: Soviet Foreign Policy, 1917–73*. 2nd ed. New York: Praeger.

Vernadsky, George. 1936. *Political and Diplomatic History of Russia*. Boston: Little, Brown, and Company.

Von Laue, Theodore H. 1993. *Why Lenin? Why Stalin? Why Gorbachev?: The Rise and Fall of the Soviet System*. 3rd ed. New York: HarperCollins.

Wallander, Celeste A. 1999. *Mortal Friends, Best Enemies: German-Russian Cooperation After the Cold War*. Ithaca, NY: Cornell University Press.

Washington Post. 2002. "Russia Wondering What It Gets for Backing U.S. Against Iraq: In Moscow's View, Promises of Partnership Not Kept," October 4.

Weafer, Chris. 2003. "Too Much Oil Could Be Bad for Russia's Health." *Financial Times*, April 29.

Wedel, Janine R. 1998. *Collision and Collusion: The Strange Case of Western Aid to Eastern Europe, 1989–1998*. New York: St. Martin's Press.

Wesson, Robert G. 1986. *The Russian Dilemma*. Rev. ed. New York: Praeger.

Zelikow, Philip, and Condoleezza Rice. 1995. *Germany Unified and Europe Transformed: A Study in Statecraft*. Cambridge, MA: Harvard University Press.

Zhurkin, V. V., et al. 2001. *Between the Past and the Future: Russia in the Transatlantic Context*. Moscow.

Zimmerman, William. 2002. *The Russian People and Foreign Policy: Russian Elite and Mass Perspectives, 1993–2000*. Princeton, NJ: Princeton University Press.

7

Ethnicity and Identity

Katherine E. Graney

One of the most significant dimensions of Russia's multifaceted search for viable forms of political, economic, and social organization to replace those of the Soviet era is the attempt to craft a new sense of national identity and community for the citizens of Russia. In addition to its vast territorial and natural resource wealth, contemporary Russia is distinguished by another rich historical legacy bequeathed to it by successive generations of tsarist and Soviet expansion: an exceptionally diverse populace. According to the first post-Soviet census, conducted in October 2002, over 20 percent of Russia's citizenry are not ethnic Russians but instead representatives of nearly 160 other officially recognized ethnic groups.

On the whole, and with some prominent historical and current exceptions that will be discussed in this chapter, Russians and non-Russians share their country peacefully, and have done so for centuries. However, like all modern states with multiethnic populations, Russia is trying to determine the specific balance it should strike between competing ethnic and civic conceptions of national community. Debates over the degree to which the country should be considered the homeland of ethnic Russians alone, as opposed to one that is the civic home of Russia's entire multiethnic population, shape Russian politics in important ways. Two related issues have dominated the discussion about Russia's national character. The first is the issue of how the state should provide for the political and cultural rights of non-Russians in Russia. This debate centers on the question of whether Russia's unique form of ethnofederalism, established during the Soviet era, is still the best way to accommodate minority rights in contemporary Russia. The second major concern is the ongoing tragedy in Chechnya and the entire complex of problems that have arisen from the failure to find a satisfactory resolution to it.

Current debates about Russia's national identity and the future shape of multicultural policies in Russia are legacies of the complex and contradictory policies pursued toward non-Russians by the tsarist and Soviet governments. Moreover, they stem from the fact that for the first time in its history, Russia exists not as an empire but as a more or less "normal" nation-state that is struggling to find a new place for itself in both the European and international communities (Beissinger 1995). Thus in fashioning a new national identity, Russia must grapple not only with the tsarist and Soviet past but also with present European and international norms regarding multiculturalism and minority rights, which present Russian actors with both constraints and opportunities. In general, throughout the post-Soviet period, the Russian state has supported at least a limited form of cultural pluralism, despite the challenges raised by the Chechen conflict and terrorist violence associated with it. For example, in its 1993 Constitution Russia identifies itself as a democratic, civic state that belongs to all the peoples of Russia (Articles 1 and 3) and gives all its citizens the right to determine their own nationality and confessional allegiance (Articles 26 and 28), as well as the right to use their native languages in "communication, education, training, and creative work" (Article 26). The Russian government has also accommodated non-Russian minority rights by maintaining an ethnofederal system of political organization and by passing new legislation that formally protects individual and corporate rights to religious and cultural autonomy. Therefore, a basic framework for the provision of the political and cultural rights of non-Russians exists, and if the European and international communities continue to pressure Russia to maintain its commitments, there is reason to hope that Russia's degree of cultural pluralism could become even deeper in the future. The potential threats to this hope, however, are also addressed here.

This chapter begins with a brief ethnodemographic sketch of Russia and a discussion of the results of the first post-Soviet Russian census. Then, because the historical legacy of tsarist and Soviet policies toward non-Russians so strongly influences contemporary debates about multiculturalism and national identity in Russia, these legacies are examined in some depth. The next section documents the evolution of Russia's ethnofederal system in the post-Soviet period and presents the differing opinions about the utility of that system as a way of providing for minority rights in Russia. The focus then turns to Chechnya, the one great tragic failure of interethnic relations in Russia in the post-Soviet period. Both the trajectory of this conflict itself and the repercussions it has had for Russia's search for a new sense of national identity are addressed in this section. The chapter concludes with some thoughts about the future of Russia as a multicultural state.

■ A Survey of Multicultural Russia

The first post-Soviet Russian census was both highly anticipated and highly contentious. One of the most disputed aspects of the census concerned the best method of determining the country's ethnic makeup. During the tsarist era, census respondents were not asked about their ethnicity, but rather about their language-use patterns. During the Soviet era, citizens were asked to reveal their self-described "nationality" (ethnicity), but the list of nationalities that was officially recognized by the Soviet state was itself subject to intense political pressure according to the ideological needs of party elites and thus varied in number from census to census.[1] Therefore, one of the chief concerns of the Russian government when crafting the October 2002 census guidelines was that the question of ethnicity be handled in a manner that would both yield the most accurate and objective picture possible of the country's ethnic composition and also ensure that individual citizens' rights to declare their own ethnic affiliation freely and without any state interference be fully protected. In the end, the Russian government did develop a list of officially recognized nationalities that census workers were to refer to when interviewing respondents, but citizens were also free to declare themselves affiliated with any nationality, even if it did not appear on the official list. Respondents were not asked about their "native language" but only about their level of facility with the Russian language; nor were respondents asked about their religious affiliation.

The October 2002 census revealed that more than one in five Russian citizens is not an ethnic Russian. Seven different ethnic groups in Russia, including ethnic Russians, had populations numbering over one million (see Table 7.1), while several dozen of the other 150-plus officially recognized nationalities had a thousand or fewer members. The smallest group, the Kaitagtsi, has only five members!

The rate of Russian-language literacy of these non-Russian groups varies from 100 percent to as low as 40 percent, though the vast majority of groups report Russian-knowledge levels of 90 percent or more (see Table 7.1). Three of the ten most populous non-Russian nationalities are Turkic-speaking, Muslim populations (the Tatars and Bashkirs of the Middle Volga region, and the Kazakhs, who hail from the Central Asian steppe borderlands of Russia), while two other of the largest non-Russian groups are Muslim populations whose languages and cultures are indigenous to the North Caucasus region where they live (Chechens and Avars). Ukrainians and Belarusians, whose Slavic languages, Orthodox religion, and ethnic histories are closely related to those of Russians, are also among the most numerous of Russia's ethnic minorities. Rounding out the list of the ten most populous non-Russian groups are two other Middle Volga peoples, the Turkic-speaking Chuvash

Table 7.1 Ten Largest Nonethnic Russian Populations in the Russian Federation

Ethnic Group	Population	Percent of Group with Russian-Language Fluency
Tatar	5,554,601	96.05
Ukrainian	2,942,961	99.76
Bashkir	1,673,389	94.47
Chuvash	1,637,094	96.80
Chechen	1,360,253	82.85
Armenian	1,130,491	98.47
Mordvin	843,350	99.31
Avar	814,473	85.91
Belarusians	807,970	99.80
Kazakh	653,962	98.29

Source: Goskomstat Rossii 2004.

and Finnic-speaking Mordvins, both of whom were converted to Orthodoxy during the tsarist era in Russia, and one final group, the one-million-plus representatives of the world-wide Armenian diaspora that are scattered across Russia.

The census also revealed some significant patterns regarding demographic change among Russia's ethnic minority populations. For example, Russia's Muslim population (derived from information about ethnic affiliation) was calculated to be only about 14.5 million, or about 10 percent of the country's overall population, whereas earlier government estimates regarding the number of Muslims in Russia had been much higher, at about 20 million. Not surprisingly, Muslim leaders in Russia have challenged the census results, arguing that they systematically "undercounted" Muslims in Russia. However, virtually all of Russia's Muslim minority populations showed a demographic increase since the time of the last Soviet census in 1989, with some, like the Ingush, showing incredibly high population growth (91.45 percent). The other populations that showed impressive demographic growth in the post-Soviet period (a 17 percent increase) are the forty-five groups that make up the "small peoples of the North" in Russia. They are ethnically related and otherwise analogous in many ways to the native peoples in the northern regions of Canada and the United States.[2] By contrast, both the overall number of ethnic Russians and the percentage of the country's population that they represent declined during the same period from 119.9 million (81.5 percent of the total population) in 1989 to 115.6 million (79.8 percent of the total) in 2002.

Kazakh men constructing a nomad's tent
for summer quarters (top), and
Kazakh men sitting in a nomad's tent (bottom),
Republic of Altai.

Migration patterns have also affected the multicultural composition of the Russian state in the post-Soviet period. For example, nearly one-fourth of Russia's Ukrainians and one-third of Russia's Belarusians have left the country since 1989 to become citizens of the new independent states of Ukraine and Belarus. Similarly, almost half of Russia's Jewish population has emigrated since 1989 (mainly to Israel, the United States, and Germany), leaving only 230,000 Jews in Russia today. Joining the exodus of Russian citizens to Germany in the post-Soviet period are the almost 300,000 ethnic Germans who have left Russia since the collapse of the USSR (one-third of the Soviet-era total). At the same time, since 1989 Russia has experienced significant immigration of Azerbaijanis (a Turkic, Muslim people), Tajiks (a Persian, Muslim people), and Armenians, mainly because their respective homelands have either suffered civil war or international conflict (for the latter, Armenia and Azerbaijan being the most prominent) during this period.

The picture of Russia as a multicultural entity that emerges from the October 2002 census data reflects important elements of Russia's tsarist and Soviet-era history and provides interesting observations about the future direction of Russia's population growth. The presence of those Slavic populations that were long part of the Russian and Soviet empires but now have their own neighboring homeland states is shrinking in Russia, while other non-Russian groups who were also integrated into the tsarist and Soviet empires but whose new post-Soviet homelands are proving to be less attractive are finding their way back to the former "metropole" in ever increasing numbers. Coupled with the fact that Russia has also become one of the leading destinations for immigrants from countries other than those from the former Soviet Union (mainly from China and Vietnam), these trends suggest that Russia's population will only become more multicultural in the future.

In order to better comprehend the ways in which the Russian government has tried (and not tried) to accommodate the political and cultural needs of its increasingly diverse population in the post-Soviet era, it is first necessary to understand how Russia became a multicultural polity and how previous policies continue to shape contemporary Russian debates about national identity and minority rights.

◼ Making Russia Multicultural: Empire, Statehood, and Nationality in the Tsarist Era

Rulers of premodern forms of government, such as absolutist monarchies and imperial dynasties, invoked both religion and tradition to legitimate their claims to power, while the leaders of the modern nation-states that emerged out of the collapse of the old orders must struggle to craft a sense of national identity that fosters feelings of belonging and loyalty amongst their citizens. Today Russia is in the peculiar and uncomfortable position of being a "latecomer" to the process of nation-building, as the country for the first time is coming to terms with the fact that it is no longer an empire, but rather merely a "normal" nation-state (Beissinger 1995). More problematic still is that the policies pursued by Russia's two imperial predecessors, the tsarist empire and especially the Soviet Union, left uniquely institutional-ized patterns of interethnic relations that continue to influence the search for viable forms of multiculturalism and national identity in contemporary Russia, sometimes in unconstructive ways.

In the middle of the sixteenth century, under the ambitious leadership of Tsar Ivan the Terrible, with ethnic Russian princes having finished "gather-ing the lands of Russia" by consolidating power around a core settlement in Moscow, a process of expansion began that would last three hundred years and eventually encompass over one-sixth of the world's landmass. The Rus-sian tsars first conquered the lands of the former Golden Horde, taking the khanates of Kazan (1552), Astrakhan (1556), and Siberia (1581–1582) in the mid-sixteenth century, then continued to push on steadily north, east, and south into the Far East and Central Asia, while also engaging in an ongoing battle with Sweden and Poland-Lithuania for territory and sovereignty in the west. Using a combination of persuasive means (gifts and titles) and more coercive methods (military force and taxation), the agents of Russia's tsars gathered an increasingly diverse array of subjects into the empire. At its zenith in the late nineteenth century, over half of the tsar's 125 million sub-jects were non-Russians.

For most of its existence, the Russian empire was a classic model of a premodern imperial state, wherein most non-Russian subjects expressed and experienced their identity through religion and language and neither demanded nor received territorial autonomy. During most of the tsarist era, at least some latitude regarding the practice of non-Orthodox religion and non-Russian culture was tolerated as long as all continued to profess and practice loyalty to the tsar (through the payment of taxes, tributes, and in some cases the completion of military service). However, pragmatic con-cerns alone did not govern relations with non-Russian subjects. In fact, var-ious ideological imperatives shaped official policy toward minorities at dif-ferent points in Russian imperial history. Most significantly, Russia was understood first and foremost as an Orthodox empire, the "Third Rome," whose head, the tsar, not only served as the symbolic head of the Orthodox Church, but also had a divine calling to Christianize and civilize non-Russians in the realm.

This missionary spirit was manifested at different times in different ways during the tsarist era, ranging from coercive conversion policies to attacks on non-Orthodox places of worship and clergy to formal policies of tolerance toward non-Orthodox minorities, coupled with heavy state oversight and regulation of their religious practices. The reigns of Tsarinas Anne and Elizabeth, which saw the establishment of the brutal Agency for Convert Affairs in 1740, the legalization of purchase of non-Russian peasants by Orthodox clergy for the purpose of conversion in 1755, and the destruction of over 418 of the 536 mosques in the empire, represented the low point regarding persecution and repression of non-Russians in imperial Russia. In contrast, Catherine the Great's reputation for tolerance toward non-Russians in the latter half of the eighteenth century is to some extent justified. Under Catherine, non-Orthodox minorities were afforded greater religious freedoms, and the much-hated Agency for Convert Affairs was abolished. These gestures were in part motivated, however, by the desire to co-opt Muslims (Volga Tatars in particular) for use in the expansion of Russia's imperial project in Central Asia. Furthermore, as one set of authors has concluded, because of the special and privileged role of the Russian Orthodox Church in the tsarist era, "At all times, religious minorities were in effect second-class subjects of the empire" (Geraci and Khodarkovsky 2001, 7).

By the nineteenth century, two ideological processes were at work in the Russian empire that had important consequences for non-Russians in the realm. On the one hand, as Russia's leaders became more and more invested in their membership in the exclusive club of Western European powers, they also became increasingly convinced that Russia, like other leading states at the time, had an important "civilizing mission," in this case, aimed at the myriad and manifold non-Russians who inhabited the realm. Simultaneously, a growing sense of Russian ethnic awareness, which manifested itself both in Nicholas I's legitimating ideology of "Orthodoxy, Autocracy, and Nationality" and in the growing intelligentsia movement, which was quickly developing a passionate but critical sense of specifically Russian national history and identity, also highlighted the differences between the ethnic Russian core of the empire and its non-Russian subjects. This distinction is represented in the Russian language through the use of two different adjectives, *russkii,* which signifies all things having to do with the ethnic Russian people, and *rossiiskii,* which signifies all things having to do with the Russian empire, implying the multiethnic nature of its subjects. These tendencies are also illustrated by the fact that by the 1860s all non-Russians, regardless of their religion, were categorized by the state as *inorodtsy,* or foreign-born, indicating that the natural, ruling core of the empire was the ethnic Russian people (Werth 2001, 130).

In the waning decades of the tsarist era, the process of linguistic and cultural Russification of non-Russians continued, but was complicated by the rise of forces calling for democratic constitutional reforms and even revolutionary change in the empire. Indeed, non-Russian national consciousness and political activism was greatly invigorated by the rights bestowed through the October Manifesto of 1905, and some non-Russian groups in the realm began to demand territorial autonomy as a way to accommodate their political and cultural needs. Nicholas II's Fundamental Laws of 1906 included assertions of the Russian state's territorial integrity and of the Russian language's primacy in the realm, which were meant to, and effectively did, dampen non-Russian political ambitions, though these demands would reemerge in the tumultuous revolutionary period of 1914–1917.

◼ An Affirmative Action Empire: The Soviet Union

In addition to being an anti-imperial, anticapitalist and antiwar movement, the Bolshevik Revolution of October 1917 was also a specifically anti-Russian revolution. The Bolsheviks did not, as did their Cadet and Octobrist rivals, dream of creating a more democratic and constitutionally based form of Russian statehood out of the crumbling tsarist empire. Instead, inspired by Marx and Engels's summons to "all working men of the world" to unite, the Bolsheviks believed that by founding the world's first socialist state in Russia, they were forging the first link in what they fully expected to be a global chain of internationalist socialist states reaching across Europe and the world. Given this aversion to nationalism and strong commitment to internationalism, some of the most unexpected of the many dramatic changes wrought by the Bolsheviks in the new Soviet Union concerned the non-Russian peoples of the former Russian empire.

The surprisingly powerful ethnonationalist movements that the Bolsheviks encountered across the former tsarist realm led Lenin and his people's commissar of nationalities, Joseph Stalin, to make the idea of national self-determination for ethnic groups a fundamental organizing principle of the new Bolshevik state in Russia. In fact, as author Terry Martin has argued, the new Soviet Union was explicitly constructed as an "affirmative action empire" dedicated to accommodating and even promoting the ethnonational consciousness of its ethnic minorities through a multifaceted system that included the following elements: an ethnofederal political arrangement wherein some of the administrative units of the new Soviet Union were organized as "ethnic homelands" for ethnic minorities; the cultivation and promotion through affirmative action of ethnic elites to staff government, education, and industrial positions in these new homelands; the promotion (in some cases creation) of the native languages of the titular populations of the new ethnofederal units; and the creation of a whole myriad of cultural institutions such as newspapers, journals, opera, theater, and ballet troupes, and museums to support the "national cultures" of these peoples (Martin 2001, 10–13).

The Soviet system of ethnofederalism has often been compared to a set of Russian nesting dolls (called a *matrioshka*), as there were several layers of administration, hierarchically organized according to their respective levels of political and cultural rights. In practice, none of the administrative units had any real political autonomy, and even their rights to cultural expression were directed by the central state (Taras 1997). Thus citizens found themselves not only residents of the new Union of Soviet Socialist Republics, but also simultaneously inhabitants of one of fifteen "union republics," officially known as Soviet Socialist Republics, which included the Russian Republic along with the fourteen homeland republics of the peoples living near the borders of the USSR. Citizens might find themselves further nested within one of the "autonomous republics" (Autonomous Soviet Socialist Republics or ASSRs), homelands for peoples whose territory lay within the confines of a union republic and who enjoyed lesser levels of (theoretical) political autonomy. Further down in the administrative hierarchy were "autonomous oblasts" and "national areas," with correspondingly lower levels of authority.

In addition to effectively creating national homelands or quasi-nation-states for non-Russians within the USSR by institutionalizing and territorializing ethnic identity in the ethnofederal system, Soviet officials also fostered a strong sense of individual ethnic or national identity among its citizens, not only by promoting ethnic affirmative action programs but also by demanding that each person record their ethnicity on the internal passports that all Soviet citizens were required to carry at all times. As author Yuri Slezkine (1994b, 450) has put it:

> Every Soviet citizen was born into a certain nationality, took it to day care and through high school, had it officially confirmed at the age of sixteen and then carried it to the grave through thousands of application forms, certificates, questionnaires, and reception desks.

The Soviet Union thus ended up magnifying, celebrating, and reifying the linguistic and cultural diversity that had existed in the old tsarist empire, while also wedding it for the first time to an explicit sense of ownership over particular territorial units. As such, the "imagined community" that the Soviet people were to pledge loyalty to did not correspond to one particular ethno-national group but rather was the collective and multiethnic "Friendship of Peoples" that made up, and made great, the Soviet Union (Martin 2001, 459).

Given the firm Marxist opposition to ethnic nationalism and commitment to internationalism, where did the Bolshevik impulse to invest so much energy and so many (scarce) resources into this complex and multi-faceted system of managing multiculturalism come from? The answer lies in the way that Lenin understood the relationship between nationalist consciousness (feelings of ethnic or nationalist loyalty) and class consciousness (feelings of class solidarity) and his beliefs about the inevitable historical progression of the communist revolution. According to Lenin, nationalist feelings were a "natural" and indeed "progressive" stage that different peoples (especially more "backward" or "primitive" peoples) had to experience and pass through on the journey to internationalist, proletariat consciousness. By fostering and using ethnonationalist feelings for their own ends, the Bolsheviks would hasten the creation of mature communism in the Soviet Union. As Lenin himself put it when speaking of some non-Russian peoples in 1919, "We are going to help you develop your Buriat, Votiak, etc., language and culture, because in this way you will join the universal culture, revolution, and communism sooner" (Slezkine 1994b, 420). Accordingly, Soviet efforts to support particular national identities followed a specific formula, one that was "national in form," but strictly "socialist in content." Any expressions of national identity that transgressed the narrow boundaries set by the Communist Party according to this formula were quickly and severely punished.

Another crucially important aspect of the Soviet "affirmative action empire" is that it was, as mentioned above, largely an anti-Russian enterprise, particularly in its first two decades. During this time the ethnic Russian nation alone was denied the right to express its national culture or have it supported by the new Soviet state. Instead, the Russian nation was criticized for its tendency toward "great Russian chauvinism" and was "punished" for its exploitation of non-Russians during the tsarist era by having to sacrifice jobs and political power to non-Russians, who became the beneficiaries of the policies of the new state (Martin 2001, 17–25). Ethnic Russians alone were denied a specific homeland in the new USSR; the Russian Republic was expressly not to be interpreted as the ethnic homeland of Russians and was instead to host hospitably within its boundaries the homelands of multiple non-Russian groups (sixteen autonomous republics and five autonomous regions). While the ethnic Russian nation was somewhat rehabilitated beginning in the late 1930s, when it became the "first among equals" in the "Friendship of Peoples" that made up the USSR, and Russian language and culture came more and more to represent the substance, such as it was, of Soviet culture, the Soviet Union was never reconceptualized as a Russian nation-state, and ethnic Russians remained buried "in a federation within a federation" in the USSR (Suny 1993, 129).

It is critical to note, however, that even as Russian ethnic identity was intentionally obscured during the Soviet era, non-Russian nationalities suffered the most under Soviet rule, in particular "punished peoples" such as the Chechens and Kalmyks who were targeted by Stalin for forced migration to Central Asia during World War II (Nekrich 1978). Viewed as a whole, Soviet policies toward the country's non-Russian minorities represented a paradoxical mixture of carrots and sticks that bequeathed a confused and contradictory legacy to the future citizens of the Russian Federation.

■ The Reemergence of Russia: The Russian Federation and the Quest for a New Multicultural Order

In retrospect, it seems at least logical, if not inevitable, that the Soviet policies described above would lead to the deepening of ethnonationalist consciousness among the non-Russian minorities of the Soviet Union. After all, for seventy years the Soviet Union cultivated the impression that non-Russian minorities "deserved" some form of homeland and even provided them with artificial versions of modern nation-states, even if they were more form than function. Among the "punished peoples," the nation-building effects of Soviet affirmative action policies were reinforced by the bitter experience of internal exile and the subsequent desire for national rebirth and reconstruction, not to mention revenge. Even so, Soviet elites continued to assert triumphantly in the late 1970s and early 1980s that they had "solved" the nationalities question and that socialist loyalties had trumped ethnic identities in the USSR. Thus it came as a great surprise to Soviet president Mikhail Gorbachev (and many others) when the national minorities in the Soviet Union, led by the Baltic republics as well as Georgia and Armenia, rapidly and confidently began to use the new freedoms granted during *glasnost* (openness) to press ethnonationalist demands. At first, the non-Russian minorities demanded only that the latent rights they theoretically held according to the Soviet constitution be actualized in practice, but their programs quickly evolved to include demands for outright independence from the Soviet Union, visions that were realized totally with the collapse of the Soviet Union in 1991 (Beissinger 2002; Walker 2003).

For all his faults, Boris Yeltsin intuitively understood the importance of ethnonationalist feelings during the late *glasnost* period. He skillfully maneuvered to use growing feelings of nationalism to his own advantage during his struggle for power with Gorbachev. On the one hand, Yeltsin encouraged the non-Russian minorities in the Soviet Union (including those whose autonomous homelands were nested in his own Russian republic, such as the Tatars, Bashkirs, and Chechens) to "take as much sovereignty" as they could get, thus playing the ethnic card against Gorbachev's reformist communist card. On the other hand, Yeltsin also worked to cultivate a sense of aggrieved Russian nationalism and hence to provoke among ethnic Russians the demand for an independent Russian nation-state, understanding that if he could pull off this trick, he would be the natural leader of such a state. Ultimately, Yeltsin was successful in his quest to depose Gorbachev, becoming president of a new independent Russian state following the collapse of the Soviet Union in December 1991. However the ethnonationalist card that he played so skillfully to achieve this desired outcome would in turn bind Yeltsin's hands and severely complicate his efforts to consolidate power and create a unified legal order in the new Russian Federation.

The new Russian Federation inherited the ethnofederal apparatus that had recently served as the principal means by which the Soviet Union was dismantled and thus had to decide how, if at all, to adapt it to the post-Soviet context. Some ethnic Russian politicians, most notably right-wing leader Vladimir Zhirinovsky, called for the abolition of the ethnofederal system and a return to the tsarist-era system of nonethnically based territorial administrative units (which were called *guberniias*). Predictably, the leaders of the Soviet-era ethnic homelands in Russia (now referred to simply as "national republics"), whose sense of ownership of these territorial units had become quite entrenched over the years, countered with demands that the ethnofederal system be enshrined in the new, ostensibly more democratic Russian political order.[3] In fact, the leaders of some ethnic republics like Tatarstan, Chechnya, and Bashkortostan, even called for the ethnofederal system to be enhanced in post-Soviet Russia, demanding new levels of sovereignty and more trappings of statehood for their "homelands" (Gorenburg 2003; Kahn 2002).

The new Federation Treaty proposed by the Yeltsin government in March 1992 institutionalized the ethnofederal system for Russia. It was now reconfigured as a three-tiered system composed of twenty-one ethnic national republics, eleven ethnically designated autonomous regions (including ten autonomous okrugs and one autonomous oblast), and fifty-seven nonethnic, administrative-territorial formations (among these, forty-nine oblasts, six krais, and two federal cities) (see Table 7.2 and Map 2.10). Despite these accommodations to the national republics, some of them, namely Tatarstan and Chechnya, continued to push for an enhanced ethnofederal system that would give them more rights and privileges, and they refused outright to sign the new treaty. Meanwhile another holdout, the Republic of Bashkortostan, only signed upon the addition of a special "Bashkir Appendix" to the document.

The failure of the Yeltsin administration to persuade Tatarstan and Chechnya to sign the 1992 Federation Treaty (and its willingness to give special privileges to recalcitrant republics like Bashkortostan), encouraged the national republics to continue to press for ever greater levels of political, economic, and cultural autonomy within the new Russian state during the remainder of the Yeltsin era. Tatarstan was the undisputed leader of this trend, according to which nearly all the national republics adopted their own new constitutions, laws, and state symbols, elected their own presidents and legislatures, and sponsored linguistic and cultural revivals within their territories. Chechnya would choose another, ultimately tragic path, declaring outright independence from the Russian Federation and attempting to back up this claim with armed resistance, actions that have led to more than a decade of war, terrorism, and elevated interethnic tensions in Russia. The net effect of these two processes, which are discussed in more detail below, was that by the end of the Yeltsin era, Russia was in a state of "legal chaos." Not only

Table 7.2 National Republics and Autonomous Regions, by Federal District, Before December 1, 2005

Northwestern	Southern	Volga	Urals	Siberian	Far Eastern
Karelia	Adygea	Bashkortostan	Khanty-Mansi A. Okrug	Altai	Sakha (Yakutia)
Komi	Chechnya	Chuvashia	Yamal-Nenets A. Okrug	Buryatia	Jewish A. Oblast
Nenets A. Okrug	Dagestan	Mari-El		Khakassia	Chukchi A. Okrug
	Ingushetia	Mordovia		Tyva	Koryak A. Okrug
	Kabardino-Balkaria	Tatarstan		Aga Buryat A. Okrug	
	Kalmykia	Udmurtia		Evenk A. Okrug	
	Karachay-Cherkessia	Komi-Permyak		Taymyr (Dolgan-Nenets)	
	North Ossetia-Alania	A. Okrug		A. Okrug	
				Ust-Orda Buryat A. Okrug	

Note: Encouraged by Putin, a number of Russia's autonomous okrugs entered into merger negotiations with the larger nonethnic regions to which they had been subordinate during the Soviet era. The first such union occurred December 1, 2005, when the Komi-Permyak Autonomous Okrug joined Perm Oblast to form Perm Krai. In 2007, the Evenk and Taymyr autonomous okrugs merged with Krasnoyarsk Krai, while the Koryak Autonomous Okrug combined with Kamchatka Oblast to form Kamchatka Krai. In 2008, the Ust-Orda Buryat Autonomous Okrug merged with Irkutsk Oblast, and the Aga Buryat Autonomous Okrug united with Chita Oblast to form Zabaikal Krai. Additional mergers are possible.

Bashkir women in traditional dress.

did the laws and constitutions of the national republics openly clash with Russian federal norms, the Russian government had actually signed "treaties" with over half of the national republics. Furthermore, ethnic Russian citizens complained that their rights were being trampled in the new "ethnocracies" that had emerged in some of the national republics, and that Chechnya was a de facto independent state.

■ Creating Legal Chaos: Yeltsin and the Parade of Treaties

After refusing to sign the 1992 Federal Treaty, Tatarstan's leaders continued to press for increased levels of rights and privileges within Russia. Their central demand was that Russia sign a bilateral treaty with Tatarstan, one that would give the republic enhanced economic and political rights and recognize its sovereign statehood. According to Tatarstani leaders, only by rebuilding ethnofederalism in this bottom-up, treaty-based way could the rights of non-Russians to national self-determination really be provided for in the new Russia. Tatarstan also engaged in other state-building efforts, which included adopting a constitution, establishing a Ministry of Foreign Affairs and its own representations in other countries (including the United States), creating new state holidays, and writing new Tatarstani textbooks to

A Tatar woman selling cloth in Kazan.

be used in its schools. Other national republics in Russia followed suit, albeit at a somewhat slower pace than Tatarstan (Gorenburg 2003).

Tatarstan's defiance continued, and it did not support the referendum for the approval of the December 1993 Russian Constitution, despite the fact that the constitution enshrined the principles of cultural pluralism in many significant ways, including the following: the constitution was issued in the name of the sovereignty of the "multinational people" of Russia and not the ethnic Russian nation (Article 3); it did not give the Russian Orthodox Church any special privileges in Russia but rather declared Russia to be a secular state (Article 14); it gave the republics the right to have their own constitutions and state languages (Articles 66 and 68); and it gave the republics significant representation in the upper legislative chamber in Russia, the Federation Council (Article 95). In addition to Tatarstan and Chechnya, eight other national republics also voted down the 1993 Constitution.

However, the referendum was successful at the national level. The reaction of Tatarstan and the other republics, who considered the new Russian constitution to be an infringement on their right to national self-determination, was simply to ignore the parts of the document they objected to, and to continue to pass laws and conduct business according to their own local norms. Tatarstan also demanded that the Yeltsin administration recognize its claims to sovereignty and statehood by signing a separate bilateral agreement with the republic, a request Moscow finally granted in February 1994.

The new Moscow-Tatarstan treaty, which referred to Tatarstan not as a constituent member of but only as being "associated with" the Russian Federation, was greeted in Tatarstan as a huge victory for the republic, the first time since the capture of the Kazan Khanate in 1552 by Ivan the Terrible that the Russian government had truly recognized the right to national self-determination of the ethnic Tatar nation.

Over the next four years, inspired by the prestige, political rights, and economic perks that Tatarstan had received in the February 1994 treaty with Russia, ten more national republics and over thirty ethnic Russian regions of the Federation would sign similar, though less expansive, treaties with the Yeltsin government (Kahn 2002, especially Chapter 6). This "parade of treaties" added even more complexity to the already chaotic legal framework governing federal relations in Russia. There were now at least four sets of legal documents governing federal and interethnic relations in Russia (the 1992 Federal Treaty, the 1993 Russian Constitution, the bilateral treaties, and the republican constitutions), all of which contradicted one another to some degree. Not only did all national republics have more rights than Russian oblasts and krais, but some national republics, namely Tatarstan and Bashkortostan, had more rights than others.

Complicating matters further were the legal agreements that national republics had begun to sign with one another and with ethnic Russian oblasts and krais without the approval or consultation of federal officials, agreements that were aimed at ensuring that the cultural and political rights of their ethnic kin living in other places in Russia were also protected. The federal government in Moscow was also attempting to write national legislation that would regulate the provision of cultural and political rights to non-Russians who lived in Russian oblasts and krais, and to develop a new law on religious practice and freedom in Russia.

While the leaders of Russia's national republics argued that this complex and untidy legal situation represented democratic progress for the young country (a position which may in fact have some theoretical merit), federal officials in Moscow and ethnic Russians living in the national republics complained that it represented legal anarchy at best and ethnic tyranny on the part of non-Russians at worst. Indeed, while national republican leaders such as Tatarstan president Mintimer Shaimiyev attempted to frame the state-seeking efforts of their republics as multiethnic, civic movements for increased democracy, the ethnonationalist overtones of the new republican initiatives kept emerging. For example, Tatarstan's controversial 1994 language law required that all the republic's students, not just ethnic Tatar students, be required to learn the Tatar language along with Russian. In Murtaza Rakhimov's Bashkortostan, non-Bashkirs complained not just of cultural prejudice but of outright physical and political intimidation by the new Bashkir "ethnocracy" (Hale 2003a, 2003b).

The Yeltsin administration remained too weak and apparently too apathetic to tidy up the legal mess it had allowed to emerge since 1991, and it left the task to Yeltsin's more energetic successor Vladimir Putin. At least part of this failure must be attributed to the emergence in late 1994 of a much more serious and militarized conflict between the federal government in Moscow and the national republic Chechnya.

■ Origins and Consequences of the First Chechen War

While Tatarstan has persistently probed the limits of political and economic rights for Russia's ethnic-minority national homelands in the post-Soviet period, it has done so in an entirely peaceful, negotiated way, calibrating its moves carefully to avoid provoking undue rhetorical, political, or military reaction from Moscow, a strategy so successful it has been dubbed the "Tatarstan Model" of bargaining and offered as a blueprint for other ethnically divided societies to follow (Bukharaev 1999). In stark contrast to the Tatarstan Model, beginning in late 1990 ethnic elites in the Republic of Chechnya pursued a confrontational path aimed at securing the absolute independence of Chechnya from Russia by any means necessary, including armed resistance. Chechnya's firm (some would say reckless) stance was met by an equally stubborn response on the part of Yeltsin and his advisers, and in December 1994 over twenty thousand Russian troops entered Chechnya. If the tortured history of Russian-Chechen relations in the tsarist and Soviet eras bears much of the explanatory weight in understanding the reasons behind the ongoing Chechen conflict, the character of the individual leaders of both Chechnya and Russia in the post-Soviet period was also determinative.

The Chechens, who constitute the largest ethnic group in the North Caucasus region, are Sunni Muslims who were converted to Islam beginning in the late seventeenth century. The history of Russian-Chechen interaction is a bloody one. At every stage, Chechens have resisted Russian imperial expansion and have acquiesced only under coercion. The Chechens were leaders of the Caucasian War against Russian colonialism (conventionally dated 1817–1864), while during the revolutionary era the Chechens fought both the Whites (various outlawed political parties, from socialists to monarchists) and the communist Reds until being forcibly integrated (along with the neighboring Ingush people) into an autonomous republic within the Russian part of the USSR. Stalin's paranoia and knowledge of the historical record led him to undertake the wholesale deportation of the Chechens into Central Asia during World War II. Amazingly, the Chechen nation managed to survive and even prosper in exile, due in part to extremely high birth rates among Chechen women and in part because of the Chechens' "sheer determination" to return to their ancestral homeland (Lieven 1998, 321). After Stalin's death, the Chechen community in exile began to demand a return to their historical homeland (still called the Chechen-Ingush Autonomous Republic), a demand to which the Khrushchev administration acquiesced.

From 1991 until Russia launched a full-scale military invasion of Chechen territory on December 11, 1994, a former Soviet air force general named Dzhokar Dudayev spearheaded the first attempt to create a wholly independent Chechen state on the territorial and administrative basis of the former Soviet Chechen-Ingush Republic. Dudayev was an ethnic Chechen who had spent much of his Soviet military career serving in the Baltic states, and who, inspired by the Baltics' quest for independence, returned to Chechnya in 1990 to fulfill what he believed was a personal mission to lead his ethnic homeland to freedom. In rapid succession during the fall of 1991, Dudayev was elected president, declared independence, and formed a Chechen army, known as the Chechen National Guard. Alarmed by the turn of events in Chechnya, Yeltsin declared the "Dudayev revolution" illegal and imposed martial law in the republic. Moscow's heavy-handed actions reinforced the legitimacy of the new Dudayev government, making him a genuine national hero in Chechnya by "reopening dormant hatreds and reviving and reopening traumas of past humiliations and defeats" at the hands of the Russians (Isaenko and Petschauer 2000, 7; Lapidus 1998, 15). Dudayev, however, proved largely incapable of capitalizing on this gift of "instant legitimacy" to build an effective and functioning sovereign state in Chechnya, instead proving to be an ethnocratic, authoritarian, ineffective, and in some cases, blatantly criminal leader.

As such, opposition to Dudayev's regime grew quickly both in the republic and in Moscow. For its part, the Chechen parliament began impeachment proceedings against Dudayev and scheduled a referendum on the question of removing the Chechen president. Russia also began to make more concerted moves toward toppling the increasingly criminalized and embarrassing Dudayev regime and moved closer to a decision to use military force toward this end. An important aspect of this evolution was the deep personal animosity between Yeltsin and Dudayev, which led Yeltsin to avoid any personal contact with Dudayev, contrasting sharply with Yeltsin's ongoing cordial personal meetings during 1992–1994 with Tatarstan's leader Shaimiyev (Dunlop 1998, 183). Two other important factors influencing Yeltsin's decision to use military force in Chechnya were (1) the spread of Chechen gangsterism, hostage-taking, and terrorism to southern Russia, where a series of bus hi-jackings in summer 1994 unnerved Russian authorities and the populace alike; and (2) the ultimately tragically mistaken belief among Russian military elites that a full-scale Russian military incursion into Chechnya would be a "small and victorious war" (Lapidus 1998, 20).

The entry of over twenty thousand Russian troops into Chechnya on December 11, 1994, united the Chechen people in a common cause as the much-reviled Dudayev enjoyed a resurgence in popularity as the symbol of a nation that was again facing possible extermination at the hands of its larger neighbor. Though the Russian military did succeed in killing Dudayev himself in April 1996, even without their leader, the Chechen irregular forces were able to defeat the more numerous and better-supplied Russian forces by summer 1996. Ultimately, the Chechens forced a truce agreement, negotiated between Chechen general Aslan Maskhadov and Russian general Alexander Lebed in the Dagestani city of Khasavyurt in August 1996, which included a complete Russian withdrawal from the republic. The pathetic quality of all aspects of the Russian military effort and the lack of support for the war among the Russian public also contributed to the eventual Russian loss in the first Chechen war (Lieven 1998, Chapters 5 and 8).

The August 1996 Khasavyurt Accords called for the "shelving" of the question of Chechnya's final political and legal status for five years, and were themselves intentionally ambiguous—they only provided that by the end of 2001, Russia and Chechnya were to sign an agreement "demarcating the legal parameters of their relationship" (Blandy 1998, 52). For the victorious Chechens, the agreements were tantamount to Russian recognition of Chechen independence. As one author has put it, the five-year respite provided for in these accords was interpreted by the Chechens as "a face-saving device allowing the Russians to prepare mentally for Chechnya's independence" (Walker 1997). Aslan Maskhadov was elected president by the Chechen people in January 1997 in elections that Tim Guldimann, head of the Chechnya mission of the Organization for Security and Cooperation in Europe (OSCE), described as "exemplary and free" (Evangelista 2002, 48). Over the next two years, however, Maskhadov would prove no more able to build a truly functioning sovereign state in Chechnya than had Dudayev (the only other state that ever recognized Chechnya's independence was the Taliban-led regime of Afghanistan). Instead, Chechnya's economy and political system remained largely nonexistent, while the various clan-warlord factions that had solidified during the war with the Russians (some of whom were now inspired and funded by Islamist ideologies and actors that had made their way to the country during the course of the war from Saudi Arabia, Afghanistan, and Bosnia) competed with one another for military and ideological control over Chechnya. The terrorist acts and irredentist invasions that some of the Islamist-inspired Chechen groups would undertake on Russian territory were the pretext for then prime minister Vladimir Putin's decision to invade Chechnya again in September 1999.

■ The Putin Era: Restoring Order to Chaos or Threatening Non-Russian Rights?

Thus even before he was appointed acting president of Russia by Yeltsin on New Year's Eve 1999, Vladimir Putin had demonstrated that the Kremlin would be taking a much harder line regarding the ongoing efforts of Russia's ethnic national republics to challenge the federal government's central authority. Upon formally taking office as president, Putin referred to the legal chaos that had emerged in Russia during the Yeltsin era as "outrageous" and asserted that restoring the "vertical authority" of the federal executive over the national republics would be a main plank of his "dictatorship of the law" in Russia. In addition to pursuing a military strategy aimed at reintegrating Chechnya into Russia's legal and political system, Putin attempted to use all three branches of the federal government to pursue his attack against the other national republics, such as Tatarstan and Bashkortostan, finding Russia's legislative and judicial branches to be willing partners in this venture.

In May 2000, Putin used his executive authority to create seven large federal districts whose heads reported directly to him and who were charged with reining in "runaway national republics" and increasing the power of the executive in their respective jurisdictions. His administration has also initiated and coordinated efforts by the Interior Ministry, the Prosecutor General's Office, the Federal Treasury, the Press Ministry, and the Russian Foreign Ministry to recentralize control over various policy venues and to clamp down on republican "freelancing" in these areas. The effectiveness of these new executive overtures is disputed, with most scholars arguing that the well-entrenched local elites and local bureaucracies in the republics have been able to resist centralizing overtures to some degree, while a lack of funding and poor administrative coordination further weakens these federal overtures in the national republics (Hahn 2003; Nelson and Kuzes 2003).

The legislative and judicial branches of the federal government have also made moves in support of Putin's recentralizing efforts. In June 2000, the Russian Constitutional Court issued two key decisions that were directly aimed at curbing the national republics' claims to enhanced statehood. The court baldly stated that, "the subjects of the Russian Federation do not possess any state sovereignty, which belongs to the Russian Federation alone." Despite the definitive nature of the court's declaration, national republics such as Tatarstan have challenged this decision on legal grounds, launching appeals both with the Russian court and their own republican constitutional courts, while in practice ignoring the decision and continuing to assert their rights to "sovereignty" (Graney 2001).

Putin's legislative initiatives included a new law that weakens the power of the national republics in the Federation Council, a revised tax code that is less favorable to the republics, and legislation that gives the Russian president the power both to dissolve republican legislatures and to remove regional executives in the event that they are found guilty of violating federal laws. The latter moves, though they were eventually passed by the State Duma, provoked harsh opposition among some republican elites, prompting the president of the Ingush Republic, Ruslan Aushev, to ask, "What kind of federation is it if the president can remove the popularly elected head of a region or disband the regional legislature?" (as reported in *EWI Russian Regional Report* 2000). Even more disturbing to those who see Russia's ethnofederal system as the key to the country's future as a multicultural democracy, in September 2004, in response to the horrific terrorist attack in Beslan and in the name of enhancing Russia's "state security" (see next section), Putin announced that Moscow would henceforth appoint all the heads of the regions and republics, with those nominees to be confirmed by the local parliaments. While the leaders of most national republics, including Tatarstan's Shaimiyev, assented to Putin's proposal, others such as independent State Duma deputy Vladimir Ryzhkov note that having the president appoint regional heads of state "greatly exceeds the boundaries of the constitution and a federative system" (as reported in Khasanova 2004a).

Another Duma initiative that has angered the national republics is the Cyrillic-only bill signed by Putin in December 2002. According to the law, national republics such as Tatarstan must use the Cyrillic script for their native languages (Tatarstan had earlier passed a bill calling for the latinization of the Tatar language, a move the republic had hoped would move it closer to Turkey and the rest of Europe). Tatarstani leaders have vociferously condemned the Duma's actions, with Shaimiyev referring to the bill as "an invasion of human rights." In response to Tatarstan's staunch defense of its right to use the Latin alphabet (which the republic says is guaranteed by its own constitution, the republic's 1994 treaty with Moscow, and Article 68 of Russia's constitution), Putin called for "further dialogue" with Tatarstan on the issue.

The Putin administration also pressured the national republics to begin to harmonize their constitutions and laws with federal legal norms and also has pushed for the abrogation of the treaties that were signed during the Yeltsin era. This drive for harmonization has yielded some successes. By April 2002, about fifty-eight hundred of the over six thousand regional laws that contradicted federal norms had been changed, while most national republics, including Tatarstan and Bashkortostan, had also revised their constitutions to bring them into line with federal legislation (Hahn 2003). However, these constitutional revisions in many cases have failed to clarify completely the division of power and authority between Moscow and the non-Russian regions, and several republics have refused to abrogate the treaties they signed with the Yeltsin administration, asserting that they remain important legal guarantees of their right to national self-determination as ethnic minorities in Russia. Indeed, in October 2004, Tatarstani presidential adviser Rafael Khekimov announced that Tatarstan was engaged in negotiations with Moscow to extend the provisions of the February 1994 treaty between Russia and the republic (Khasanova 2004b). These negotiations were protracted and difficult, especially with respect to oil tax revenues and national language rights for Tatarstan. Although Putin and Shaimiyev finally signed an agreement in October 2005, it was not until February 2007 that the Duma ratified the treaty, only to have it rejected by the Federation Council a few days later (Arnold 2007a; Radio Free Europe/Radio Liberty 2007). Finally, in July 2007, the Federation Council gave its assent to the treaty (Arnold 2007b).

The Putin administration saw the Yeltsin-era treaties, and the asymmetrical division of rights and powers among Russian and non-Russian members of the Russian Federation that resulted from them, as problems that are partly to blame for Russia's continued state weakness and vulnerability to terrorist attacks and as such must eventually be ironed out. In contrast, non-Russian leaders argued that Russia's system of ethnofederalism has provided well for their political and cultural rights in the post-Soviet era and sought to protect and even strengthen those provisions for the future. This fundamental tension, and the continued existence of multiple and contradictory sources of legal authority governing center-periphery relations in Russia, suggests that the battle over the reform of the ethnofederal system will continue to be an important aspect of ethnic minority politics in Russia well into the future.

■ The Second Chechen War and Rising Interethnic Tensions in Putin's Russia

Putin's other major policy initiative, aimed at restoring the authority of the federal center in Moscow over rebellious non-Russian populations, namely the second invasion of Chechnya, has produced similarly mixed results. Russian officials left little doubt about their intentions for the "second Chechen war." Upon the invasion of Chechnya in fall 1999, Russian defense minister Igor Sergeev frankly announced that Russian troops had "come (to Chechnya) to never go away" (*CNN.com* 1999). Russian forces performed much better in the second war, and took the city of Grozny in February 2000, at which time Putin announced that the war had been won and Russia would now begin to restore some semblance of a "normal life" in Chechnya. Toward this end, a Moscow-backed government headed by Chechen mufti Akhmad Kadyrov was installed in June 2000 and subsequently given a veneer of legitimacy by the introduction of a new constitution for the republic (passed in a referendum of dubious legality in March 2003) and the formal election of Kadyrov as president of Chechnya in October 2003.

While the Kremlin claims that it has resolved all questions of Chechnya's legal status (insisting that the republic is fully a part of Russia's political and economic space again), in reality sustained, low-intensity guerrilla warfare in the republic continues to hobble any real progress on restoring normalcy to Chechnya. The assassination of Chechen president Kadyrov in a bombing at the Dinamo stadium in Grozny on May 9, 2004, provided graphic evidence of the severe cleavages (both Chechen-Russian and intra-Chechen) that continue to divide the beleaguered republic. The fact that numerous assailants were able to place a massive bomb directly below where Kadyrov would be sitting indicates further how Russian efforts to establish security and return life to "normal" in the republic remain woefully inadequate. If Russian and pro-Russian Chechen forces are unable to protect the president of the country, who can they protect? In the pessimistic assessment of one author, post-Kadyrov Chechnya is gripped by a civil war in which "there are not two, and not even three sides, but rather a fluctuating multiplicity of conflicting groups," a situation that, pointedly, "provides no realistic opportunities for a negotiated end to the conflict" (Ware 2004).

Furthermore, the horrible and routine abuses of the human rights of Chechen citizens, by both Russian soldiers and forces associated with the Chechen administration (violations that led the Parliamentary Assembly of the Council of Europe to suspend Russia's voting rights for nine months in 2000), also belie Moscow's assertions that the Chechen problem has been solved. More ominously, in addition to fighting the Russian occupation of their republic at home, Chechen fighters have increased terrorist attacks on the Russian heartland itself, such as the tragic hostage drama at Moscow's Palace of Culture theater, in October 2002, and the June 2004 assault on the Interior Ministry building in the city of Nazran, Ingushetia, that killed forty-eight people. In what was perhaps the most horrific of any of these inhumane acts, in September 2004 a group of Chechen terrorists took over one thousand people hostage, mainly children and their parents, at an elementary school in Beslan, North Ossetia. In the end, more than three hundred people, over half of whom were children, were killed in the siege at Beslan.

Despite the setbacks posed by the terrorist violence generated by the Chechen conflict in 2004, developments since 2005 suggest that some modicum of normalcy might actually be returning to Chechnya, as the Russian government has long hoped and claimed is the case. In March 2005 Chechen rebel leader Aslan Maskhadov, who had been in hiding for several years, was killed by Russian forces. Many analysts felt that Maskhadov's killing would only increase feelings of desperation among the most radical Chechen terrorists, namely Shamil Basayev, architect of the Beslan tragedy, thus making Chechen terrorist attacks against innocent civilians in both Russia and Chechnya more likely than before.[4] However, this has not proven to be the case. Instead, Basayev himself was killed by what the Federal Security Service of the Russian Federation (FSB) called a "special operation" in July 2006, while Akhmad Kadyrov's son Ramzan, who was named prime minister of Chechnya in March 2006 and elected president a year later, has imposed a calm of sorts on the republic that has allowed the rebuilding of infrastructure and social services to progress. That this revival is taking place only due to the brutal and capricious "enforcement" of Kadyrov the younger's private army, which has largely relieved the Russian military of its occupying role in Chechnya, does not inspire confidence about the prospects for Chechnya as a peaceful, integrated part of the Russian Federation.

In addition to serving as a pretext for President Putin to move ahead more boldly with his plan to "establish vertical authority in Russia," terrorist attacks such as those in Beslan in turn have spurred the growth of anti-Chechen, anti-Islamic, and xenophobic feelings in Russia. Routine violations of the human rights of any "person of Caucasian nationality" and other Muslims residing anywhere in Russia, along with rising numbers of violent attacks on immigrants from Central Asian countries and foreign students residing in Russia, now threaten the complex multicultural compromises that have been forged in the rest of the country in the post-Soviet period. For example, in just one weekend in March 2005, African, Chinese, and Bangladeshi students studying in St. Petersburg were attacked in three different incidents (Associated Press 2005).

The Russian government has responded to these increased manifestations of ethnic tension, and to poll data that show that fully one-fourth of the Russian population admits to "strongly disliking" people from the Caucasus, with a "Law on Countering Extremist Activities" that was rushed through the Russian parliament in summer 2002 in response to increased interethnic violence. However, some observers say the cure may be as harmful as the disease, as this law gives the government sweeping powers to target legitimate religious and non-Russian cultural organizations along with ethnic Russian neo-Nazi hate-mongering groups.

■ Conclusion: The Future of Multicultural Russia

In September 2003, at the OSCE Conference on Racism, Xenophobia, and Discrimination, in Vienna, Vladimir Zorin, Russia's minister for coordination of nationalities policy, boasted that Russia's ethnofederal system "was unique in all of Europe," representing the most comprehensive and effective policy in all of the OSCE countries for "achieving the equality of rights of representatives of different nationalities, races, ethnic cultures, and religions" (Zorin 2003). He highlighted the fact that Russia's constitution and legislation were explicitly committed to multiculturalism, and offered as evidence of this commitment the fact that over eighty non-Russian languages are taught in Russia's nine-thousand-plus "national" schools, and that there are over two thousand different ethnic organizations at the local level in Russia. Finally, he argued that the recent Chechen terrorist acts and attendant ethnic violence had only redoubled President Putin's commitment to promoting tolerance and preventing extremist violence, leading him to institute new training classes in "the history, culture, customs, and traditions of all the peoples of Russia" for the Ministries of Defense and Internal Affairs in Russia.

These achievements are real, noteworthy, and laudable. However, as this chapter has shown, Zorin has presented only part of the story of multiculturalism in Russia in the post-Soviet period. Notably absent from his speech were any references to the recent battles over the scope of Russia's vaunted ethnofederal system, Putin's recentralization campaigns, or the conflict over alphabets for non-Russian languages in Russia. Russia's history is one in which non-Russians have had to work hard for the right to be able to define and realize their own cultural and political self-determination in their own ways. This is still the case, and this task is perhaps becoming increasingly difficult as the Chechen debacle and its horrific attendant terrorist violence continues. One hopes that continuing to include Russia in a dense web of European and international organizations, such as the OSCE and the Council of Europe, will help to preserve and even to expand the real gains that Russia has made in democratic multiculturalism during the post-Soviet period, even in the face of powerful pressures to the contrary.

■ Notes

1. On the politics of census-taking in general, see Kertzer and Arel (2002). On tsarist, Soviet, and post-Soviet Russian census politics, see Arel (2002); Hirsch (1997); Martin (2001); and Sokolovsky (2002).

2. On the "small peoples of the North" in Russia, see Balzer (1999) and Slezkine (1994a).

3. One of the best discussions of this phenomenon can be found in Chapter 2 of Brubaker (1996).

4. For example, in speaking to Radio Ekho Moskvy (Echo of Moscow) on the day after Maskhadov's killing, Russian commentator Alexei Pushkov argued that the situation in post-Maskhadov Chechnya "may mirror what happened in Iraq, where attacks by isolated rebel groups became more aggressive and harder to trace after the seizure of Saddam Hussein" (Reuters, March 9, 2005).

■ Bibliography

Arel, Dominique. 2002. "Demography and Politics in the First Post-Soviet Censuses: Mistrusted State, Contested Identities." *Population-E* 57(6): 801–828.

Arnold, Chloe. 2007a. "Tatarstan: Power-Sharing Deal Clears Russian Duma." *Radio Free Europe/Radio Liberty,* February 13. http://www.rferl.org.

———. 2007b. "Russia: Federation Council Backs Tatarstan Power-Sharing Bill." *Radio Free Europe/Radio Liberty,* July 11. http://www.rferl.org.

Associated Press. 2005. "African, Asian Students Attacked in Russia," March 28. http://www.msnbc.msn.com/id/7319008/.

Balzer, Marjorie Mandelstam. 1999. *The Tenacity of Ethnicity: A Siberian Saga in Global Perspective.* Princeton, NJ: Princeton University Press.

Beissinger, Mark. 1995. "The Persisting Ambiguity of Empire." *Post-Soviet Affairs* 11(2): 149–184.

———. 2002. *Nationalist Mobilization and the Collapse of the Soviet State.* Cambridge, UK: Cambridge University Press.

Blandy, Charles. 1998. *Chechen Status—Wide Differences Remain.* Sandhurst, UK: Conflict Studies Research Centre of the Ministry of Defense Royal Military Academy.

Brubaker, Rogers. 1996. *Nationalism Reframed: Nationhood and the Nation Question in the New Europe.* Cambridge, UK: Cambridge University Press.

Bukharaev, Ravil. 1999. *The Model of Tatarstan: Under President Mintimer Shaimiyev.* Richmond, UK: Curzon Press.

CNN.com. 1999. "US Urges Peace in Chechnya: Chechens Say Russians Attacked Refugees," October 29. http://edition.cnn.com/WORLD/europe/9910/29/russia.chechnya.03/.

Dunlop, John. 1998. *Russia Confronts Chechnya: Roots of a Separatist Conflict.* Cambridge, UK: Cambridge University Press.

Evangelista, Matthew. 2002. *The Chechen Wars: Will Russia Go the Way of the Soviet Union?* Washington, D.C.: Brookings Institution Press.

EWI [EastWest Institute] *Russian Regional Report.* 2000. "Reaction Strong to Duma Override of Bill Giving President Power to Remove Governors." 5(29), July 26. http://www.isn.ethz.ch/pubs/ph/details.cfm?id=13831.

Geraci, Robert P., and Michael Khordarkovsky. 2001. *Of Religion and Empire: Missions, Conversion and Tolerance in Tsarist Russia.* Ithaca, NY: Cornell University Press.

Gorenburg, Dmitry. 2003. *Minority Ethnic Mobilization in the Russian Federation.* Cambridge, UK: Cambridge University Press.

Goskomstat Rossii. 2004. *Vserossiiskaia perepis' naseleniia 2002 goda* [The 2002 All-Russia population census]. http://www.perepis2002.ru/index.html?id=17.

Graney, Katherine E. 2001. "Ten Years of Sovereignty in Tatarstan: End of the Beginning or Beginning of the End?" *Problems of Post-Communism* 48(5): 32–41.

Hahn, Gordon. 2003. "The Impact of Putin's Federative Reforms on Democratization in Russia." *Post-Soviet Affairs* 19(2): 114–153.

Hale, Henry. 2003a. *The Bellwether Battle for Bashkortostan (Rage Against the Machine).* PONARS Policy Memo 293 (November). http://www.csis.org/ruseura/ponars/pm/.

———. 2003b. "Explaining Machine Politics in Russia's Regions: Economy, Ethnicity and Legacy." *Post-Soviet Affairs* 19(3): 228–263.

Hill, Fiona. 1995. *Russia's Tinderbox: Conflict in the North Caucasus and Its Implications for the Future of the Russian Federation.* Occasional Paper. Cambridge, MA: Harvard University, Strengthening Democratic Institutions Project.

Hirsch, Francine. 1997. "The Soviet Union as a Work in Progress: Ethnographers and the Category Nationality in the 1926, 1937, and 1939 Censuses." *Slavic Review* 56(2): 251–278.

Isaenko, Anatoly, and Peter Petschauer. 2000. "A Failure That Transformed Russia: The 1991–1994 Democratic State-Building Experiment in Chechnya." *International Social Science Review* 75 (1/2): 3–15.

Kahn, Jeffrey. 2002. *Federalism, Democratization, and the Rule of Law in Russia.* New York: Oxford University Press.

Kertzer, David, and Dominique Arel, ed. 2002. *Census and Identity: The Politics of Race, Ethnicity, and Language in National Censuses.* Cambridge, UK: Cambridge University Press.

Khasanova, Gulnara. 2004a. "Ryzhkov: Appointment of Tatar President Violates Russian Constitution." *RFE/RL Tatar-Bashkir Report,* October 20. http://www.rferl.org/reports/tb-daily-report/archive2004.asp.

———. 2004b. "Shaimiev Adviser Believes Tatarstan Will Remain National Republic." *RFE/RL Tatar-Bashkir Report,* October 22. http://www.rferl.org/reports/tb-daily-report/archive2004.asp.

Lapidus, Gail. 1998. "Contested Sovereignty: The Tragedy of Chechnya." *International Security* 23(1): 5–49.

Lieven, Anatol. 1998. *Chechnya: Tombstone of Russian Power.* New Haven, CT: Yale University Press.

Martin, Terry. 2001. *The Affirmative Action Empire: Nations and Nationalism in the Soviet Union, 1923–1939.* Ithaca, NY: Cornell University Press.

Nekrich, Aleksandr M. 1978. *The Punished Peoples: The Deportation and Fate of Soviet Minorities at the End of the Second World War.* Trans. George Saunders. New York: Norton.

Nelson, Lynn D., and Irina Y. Kuzes. 2003. "Political and Economic Coordination in Russia's Federal District Reform: A Study of Four Regions." *Europe-Asia Studies* 55(4): 507–520.

Radio Free Europe/Radio Liberty. 2007. "Russian Upper House Rejects Tatarstan Agreement," February 21. http://www.rferl.org.

Slezkine, Yuri. 1994a. *Arctic Mirrors: Russia and the Small Peoples of the North.* Ithaca, NY: Cornell University Press.

———. 1994b. "USSR as Communal Apartment." *Slavic Review* 53(2): 414–452.

Sokolovsky, Sergei. 2002. "Census Categories Construction in the First All-Russian Census of 2002." Presented at the Russian Census Workshop, Brown University, Providence, RI, March.

Suny, Ronald. 1993. *The Revenge of the Past: Nationalism, Revolution, and the Collapse of the Soviet Union.* Stanford, CA: Stanford University Press.

Taras, Ray. 1997. "From Matrioshka Nationalism to National Interests." In *New States, New Politics: Building the Post-Soviet Nations,* ed. Ian Bremmer and Ray Taras. Cambridge, UK: Cambridge University Press.

Walker, Edward W. 1997. "Constitutional Obstacles to Peace in Chechnya." *East European Constitutional Review* 6(1).

———. 2003. *Dissolution: Sovereignty and the Breakup of the Soviet Union.* Lanham, MD: Rowman and Littlefield.

Ware, Robert Bruce. 2004. "Can Moscow Engineer a Political Solution in Chechnya?" *RFE/RL Newsline* 8(107), June 8. http://www.rferl.org/newsline/.

Werth, Paul. 2001. *At the Margins of Orthodoxy: Mission Governance, and Confessional Politics in Russia's Volga-Kama Region, 1827–1905.* Ithaca, NY: Cornell University Press.

Zorin, Vladimir. 2003. "Statement by Mr. Vladimir Zorin, Member of the Government of the Russian Federation and Minister for the Co-ordination of Nationalities (Ethnic) Policy." Delivered at the Organization for Security and Cooperation in Europe (OSCE) Conference on Racism, Xenophobia, and Discrimination, Vienna, Austria, September 4–5.

8

Population, Health, and Migration

Timothy Heleniak

An appreciation of demographic and health conditions is necessary for an understanding of contemporary Russia. This includes knowledge of fertility, mortality, and migration. Taken together, these trends have an influence on population size and structure, which in turn both influence and are influenced by other aspects of contemporary Russia that are described elsewhere in this book. The size, structure, and health of the Russian population influences both Russia's economic development and its political standing in the world. The size and, more importantly, the spatial distribution of Russia's population have an impact on the country's ability to control what is by far the world's largest country territorially.

Russia currently combines demographic trends characteristic of both developed and developing countries. Fertility fell during the 1990s to some of the lowest levels in the world, placing Russia in a category that includes not only several other postcommunist transition countries but also the advanced industrialized nations of Western Europe. Since 1992 and the beginning of Russia's postcommunist era, the number of deaths in the country has exceeded the number of births, ranking it with a small group of countries experiencing negative natural increase. Life expectancy for Russian males is at levels usually found in less developed countries with incomes far below Russia's. The life expectancy gap between males and females in Russia, currently about 13.5 years, is the largest in the world (Goskomstat Rossii 2006, 101). Against this background of high mortality levels is an HIV/AIDS epidemic that is among the fastest growing in the world. With the breakup of the USSR, Russia has also become a "migration magnet" within the former USSR, much to its consternation. This migration does not just include members of the Russian diaspora migrating to Russia from other states of the former Soviet Union, but also many titular members of those states, in addition to an increasing number of persons from outside the former Soviet Union. Internally, the country has experienced a massive migration from Siberia and the Russian north and a concentration of people in the capital city, Moscow.

In the early 1990s, shortly after the dissolution of the Soviet Union and the onset of economic reforms, many of these demographic trends were not readily apparent. Consumed by the challenge of economic transformation and political intrigue, Russia's leaders paid scant attention to the country's dismal demographic health. This was not surprising, too, given Boris Yeltsin's own poor health during his two terms as president in the 1990s, which mirrored that of many Russian men. More recently there has been both an increasing awareness of Russia's alarming demographic trends and a heightened interest on the part of policymakers to deal with them. How effective these policies will be is uncertain.

The chapter begins with a brief review of Russia's recent demographic history, as many of its current demographic problems are rooted in the country's turbulent past. This is followed by a review of demographic trends in Russia relating to fertility, health, mortality, and life expectancy. From there, the chapter takes a detailed look at international and internal migration. The final section examines projections of the Russian population into the twenty-first century and considers possible implications.

■ Russia's Recent Demographic History

A century ago, Russia had a largely peasant, illiterate, agrarian population. With the serfs only having been freed in 1861, many vestiges of serfdom remained. Even so, the last third of the nineteenth century was a time of rapid industrialization and major social change as the country's urban population more than doubled from 10 percent of the total, in 1867, to 21 percent in 1917. With a birth rate of 49.5 per thousand people in European Russia in 1900, and a death rate of 32.5, the rate of natural increase was 17 per thousand, indicative of a rural economy in the early stages of demographic transition (Pirozhkov and Safarova, 1994, 442). Also indicative of such change, women went from having 7 children, on average, in 1870, to 4.5 in 1900. The first all-Russian population census, conducted in 1897, showed a population of 110 million people, 97 million of whom were peasants. In European Russia, only 36 percent of men and 12 percent of women were literate. Life expectancy was 31.4 years for males and 33.3 years for females (Goskomstat Rossii 1998, 58–63).

Like any country, Russia's current demographic size, structure, and distribution is rooted in its past, setting the parameters for future trends because of the "demographic momentum" that is a part of its age structure. Figure 8.1 shows the country's age-sex structure as of the date of post-Soviet Russia's first population census in October 2002, revealing the turbulent demographic history of Russia's twentieth century (Rosstat 2004, 6–8). The most striking features of Russia's pyramid are the indentations for certain age groups. These reflect not only the country's numerous demographic disasters, which

Figure 8.1 Age-Sex Structure, October 2002

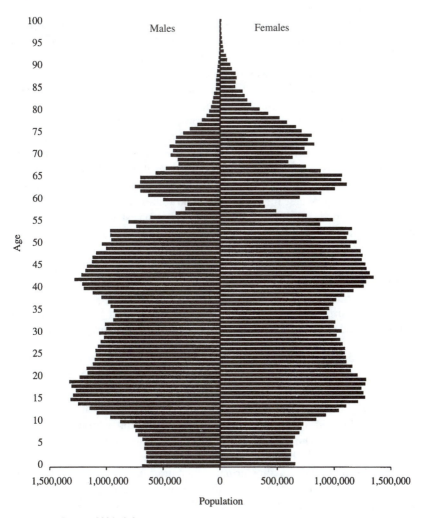

Source: Rosstat 2004, 6–8.

affected the size of certain cohorts, but also the "echoes" that followed a generation later.

World War I (1914–1918), the Bolshevik Revolution (November 1917), and the ensuing Civil War (1918–1920) caused the country's first major indentation of the twentieth century. According to estimates, seventeen to eighteen million people died because of these events, many through famine and disease. The total includes four million casualties to the Russian army in World War I, most of whom were between the ages of twenty-five and forty. Total direct and indirect losses from 1914 to 1920 are estimated at around twenty-five million, including children not born because of these events (Pirozkhov and Safarova, 1994, 443).

The next major demographic calamity was the result of Stalin's forced collectivization of agriculture that accompanied the crash industrialization drive of the first Five-Year Plan (1928–1932), in which national income and industrial production was to be doubled. Launched in 1929, collectivization reflected Stalin's mistrust of the peasantry and his desire to gain control of Soviet agriculture. The initial cost of collectivization to the countryside was great: 1.4 million peasant households were seized, with 6 to 7 million people deported or killed. By 1930, 58 percent of households had been collectivized (Livi-Bacci 1993, 747). The response on the part of more well-off peasants was to slaughter their cattle, sell their stocks and implements, and refuse to plant crops, resulting in a major deterioration of the food supply. The worst hit areas were Ukraine and the North Caucasus, which, combined, produced one-third of the harvest and one-half of all marketed output. The numbers of excess deaths through 1936 reached about 9.5 million. The total demographic deficit was about 13.5 million. Child abandonment was widespread and the major causes of death were typhus and starvation. Life expectancy went from 33 years in 1932 to 11.6 years in 1933, and then back to 38 years in 1934 (Andreev, Darsky, and Kharkova 1994, 429). Births exceeded deaths by about 3 million in 1930, but in 1933 deaths exceeded births by 5.7 million. Infant mortality jumped from about 180 infant deaths per thousand births to 317 in 1933.

World War II is the next major indentation in the age-sex pyramid. The official Soviet figure was 7 million deaths during World War II (Ellman and Maksudov 1994, 671). Various estimates put total war-related losses at 25 to 28 million people. Of these, about 8.1 million were military losses, including 5.2 million who were killed in action, 1.1 million who died from injuries, 0.6 million who died from disease, and 1.2 million others. Even more startling are the 19 million Soviet nonmilitary losses, including deaths in the siege of Leningrad, deaths in German concentration camps, mass shootings of civilians, deaths from famine and disease, and deaths in Soviet camps. An estimated 11.5 million children were not born as result of the war (centered around age fifty-six in Figure 8.1), which would raise the total demographic impact to over 36 million. One estimate of the total demographic losses from 1927 to 1946 is 56 million (Andreev, Darskii, and Khar'kova 1998). From 1926 to 1959, the population could have grown by another 80 million persons (Pirozkhov and Safarova 1994, 450). Over the entire Soviet period, the USSR's population could have grown to 440 million, instead of the 287 million that it had by the time the Soviet Union broke apart (Haub 1994, 4). The Russian Republic alone would not achieve its prewar population size of 111 million until 1955, ten years after the war had ended, before increasing to 117 million in 1959 (Goskomstat Rossii 1998, 32–34). Males suffered the brunt of these demographic disasters. The ratio of males to females was 90 per 100 in 1927. Just after the war, in 1946, it was 75 per 100, and by 1959 had recovered somewhat to 80 per 100. Today, Russia still has the largest excess of females over males in the world, about 86 males per 100 females (Goskomstat Rossii 2006, 43). This is the cumulative result of these demographic events of the past century as well as a persistently wide gap in male-female life expectancy.

In spite of these mortality disasters, Russia continued its demographic transition from high birth and death rates to low birth and death rates as a result of continuing, long-term improvements in welfare and life expectancy, and long-term increases in height, the onset of maturity, and caloric consumption. The birth rate declined from fifty births per thousand in 1927 to twenty-five in 1958, and the death rate declined from twenty-nine deaths per thousand in 1927 to eight in 1958. From 1927 to 1958, life expectancy increased from thirty-four years to sixty-two for males, and thirty-eight to seventy for females (Andreev, Darskii, and Khar'kova 1998, 164–165). The period from the end of World War II until the breakup of the Soviet Union was one of relative calm. The birth rate declined throughout the 1960s and then remained constant. The total fertility rate (TFR) was 2.6 in 1960 and fell to 2.1 by 1964, as Russian women settled into a two-child pattern.

The fertility level stayed at roughly two children per woman until the late 1980s, when there was a brief upswing as a result of a package of pro-birth measures, introduced in 1983 designed to boost the birth rate (see Figure 8.2). One such measure was the introduction of partially paid maternity leave for up to three years. Another was that large families (three or more children) were made eligible for housing, various services, and child allowances. The law was regionally differentiated and designed to stimulate second and third children in European parts of the USSR. This reflected the Soviet leadership's concerns that while most industry was located in labor-deficit central Russia, the highest population and labor force growth region was in Central Asia. The peak fertility years were 1986 and 1987 when the TFR was 2.2. The conclusion of most demographers is that Russian women did not end up having more children as Soviet policymakers had intended, they just had them sooner. Even so, through the end of the Soviet era, natural

Figure 8.2   Number of Births and Total Fertility Rate, 1950–2005

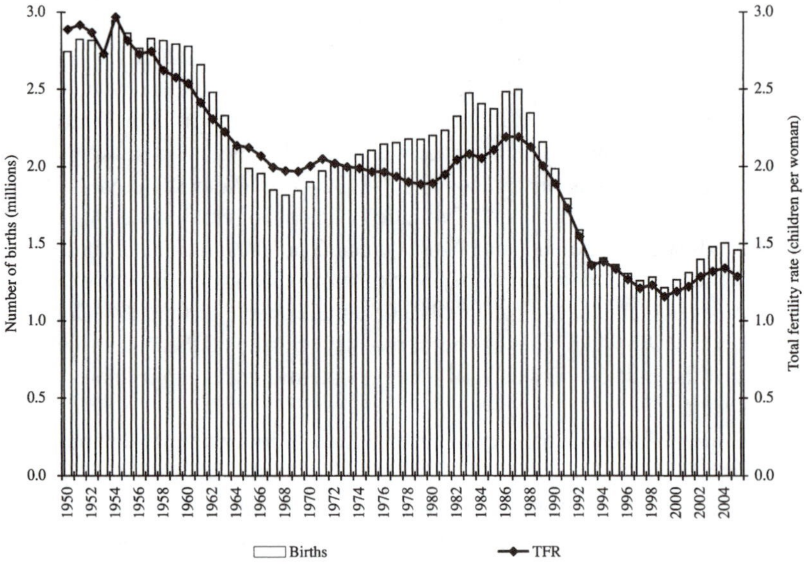

☐ Births   ◆ TFR

Source: Goskomstat Rossii, *Demograficheskii ezhegodnik* (various years).

increase (the combination of births and deaths in a society) remained positive as Russia's population grew from 119 million in 1960 to 148.7 million in 1992 (Goskomstat Rossii 1998, 32–33).

From the mid-1960s through the mid-1980s, the number of births in the Russian Republic exceeded the number of deaths by about eight hundred thousand a year. In the late 1980s, the number of births started to decline and the number of deaths started to increase. In 1992, the number of deaths began to exceed the number of births; ever since, Russia has experienced a negative natural increase, which is expected to continue well into the future because of trends in fertility, mortality, and the country's age structure. For example, in the seven years from 1999 through 2005, the number of deaths exceeded the number of births by eight hundred thousand or more. Although the situation Russia now finds itself in with a negative natural increase began in the first year after the Soviet collapse, the two events are not necessarily related. In fact, Russia's natural decrease in population was expected to occur beginning early in the twenty-first century anyway, regardless of the breakup of the Soviet Union and the economic upheavals that followed, because of an age structure that had fewer people entering childbearing ages than the number who were entering older age cohorts with their higher mortality rates. The same was true for other postcommunist countries, in addition to some of the older West European countries where deaths exceeded births because of a combination of aging populations and decades of below-replacement fertility. Russia's economic transition accelerated this trend, however, not only by causing the birth rate to plunge but also by increasing the death rate. Even so, it is actually the decline in the number of births, more than the increase in the number of deaths, that has brought about this situation of negative natural increase. From 1987 to 1999, the average annual number of births fell by 1.3 million while the average annual number of deaths increased by 0.6 million. The indentation at the bottom of the pyramid from age fifteen and younger, in Figure 8.1, represents the fertility decline of the transition period. The fall in the number of births is reflected in the decline of the total fertility rate to 1.17 in 1999, which recovered slightly to 1.34 in 2005 (Figure 8.2). It is expected to rise only slightly through 2026, according to projections by the Russian Federal State Statistics Service (Goskomstat Rossii 2005a, 102). However, a fertility rate of about 2.1 children per woman over the long run (if there is no migration and mortality is held constant) is required to hold population growth at zero. This is known as "replacement level fertility." According to World Bank projections, Russia's TFR will return to replacement level by 2050. UN estimates are not as optimistic, however, projecting that Russia's TFR in 2050 will be about 1.85.

Birth and death rates combined form one half of total population change in a country, the other half being net migration (Figure 8.3). For most of the Soviet period there was net out-migration from Russia to the non-Russian republics of the USSR. In 1975, this pattern reversed itself, and from 1975 until 1991, the last year of the Soviet Union's existence, there was net in-migration to Russia of about 160,000 persons per year. Following the breakup of the Soviet Union, immigration into Russia increased considerably, rising to a peak in 1994 of just under 810,000. However, this immigration into Russia has not been sufficient to compensate for the excess of deaths over births, and as a result the Russian population has fallen by about 5.7 million from its peak in 1995. This is partly because migration slowed considerably from its mid-1990s peak to 125,000 in 2005, just one-eighth of the 1994 total. One of the most surprising results of the October 2002 Russian census, however, was that the size of the Russian population was larger than expected: 145.18 million people, instead of the 143.85 million estimated at the beginning of 2002 (Heleniak 2003a, 430–431). The bulk of this difference is attributable to unrecorded migration during the 1990s.

■ Factors Influencing Fertility

The USSR had a number of policies that, while not explicitly pro-birth, had that effect. These policies included free education, free health care, and on-site day care. Through the end of the Soviet era, Russia had a fertility pattern

Figure 8.3 Net Migration and Natural Increase, 1960–2005

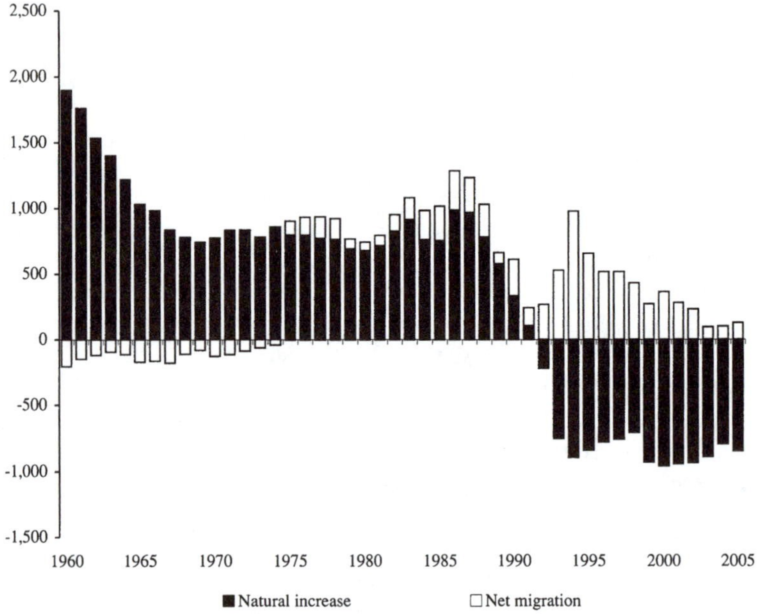

Source: Goskomstat Rossii, *Demograficheskii ezhegodnik* (various years).

that was different from that of Western Europe. This included a high proportion of women marrying, a low mean age at marriage, low percentages of couples who remained childless, early childbearing (typically within the first year of marriage), and short intervals between successive births, all of which resulted in a larger contribution by younger women to the total number of births (DaVanzo and Grammich 2001, 34). At the end of the Soviet period, fertility was also characterized by high rates of female labor force participation, low levels of contraceptive use, and high abortion rates.

Abortion as a means of fertility regulation has a long history in Russia. Even as early as the beginning of the twentieth century, every fifth pregnancy ended in abortion. The Soviet Union became the first country in the world to legalize abortion in 1920. Subsequently, an abortion industry emerged, and it became the cheapest and most readily available form of fertility regulation (Popov and David 1999, 248–249). Contraceptives were not prohibited but their use was not promoted, and several attempts to increase the production of condoms failed. The public health system was adapted to abortion technology and did not provide family planning counseling and supplies. As women entered the labor force, demand for abortions increased.

In the wake of the events of the 1930s, a pro-birth policy was promulgated and abortion was completely banned in 1936 (Avdeev 1994, 131). However, a clandestine abortion industry developed. Abortion was legalized again in 1955 after Stalin's death, but did not lead to a fertility decline. According to recent surveys, Russian women have an average of two to five abortions over the course of their reproductive years (Popov and David 1999, 245). This compares with 0.7 abortions per woman in the United States (Alan Guttmacher Institute 1999).

As mentioned earlier, it is the decline in fertility, more than the well-publicized increase in mortality, that has caused Russia's population to decline so dramatically in recent years. Four variables explain most of the differences in fertility among populations: contraceptive prevalence, the abortion rate, the proportion of females who are married, and the duration of time in which women cannot become pregnant again because of breast-feeding (Bongaarts 1982, 179–189). In Russia during the transition period of the 1990s, these proximate determinants of fertility all moved in a direction to drastically lower the fertility rate.

During the Soviet era the availability of contraceptives was limited, and those that were available were of poor quality (Popov and David 1999, 248–249). The estimated contraceptive prevalence rate (CPR) for 1979 was 34.8 percent and for 1988 was 31.4 percent. Following the breakup of the Soviet Union, however, contraceptives became more readily available. As a result, the CPR more than doubled to 66.8 percent in 1994, with about half of women using modern methods employing intrauterine devices (IUDs). Much of this is with assistance from international donors and nongovernmental organizations (NGOs) that are trying to move Russia from abortion to contraception as the primary means of birth control. So far, they have had success. While during the last three decades of Soviet rule the abortion ratio was near or above 200 abortions per 100 births (Popov and David 1999, 232–233), by 2003 the ratio had fallen to 126 per 100 births (UNICEF 2004). This rate is still extremely high by world standards, however. According to this source, Russia has the highest abortion ratio of the twenty-seven post-communist countries of the former Soviet Union and Eastern Europe. According to the United Nations' latest compilation of data on abortion, only Vietnam, Cuba, Uzbekistan, and Romania have higher rates than Russia (United Nations 1999). Thus, even though the incidence of abortion as a means of birth control has declined, its use remains widespread, further explaining the fertility decline in post-Soviet Russia.

The third major variable affecting fertility is the proportion of females who are married. At one time, marriage was nearly universal, with only 3.7 percent of men and 3.4 percent of women by the ages of forty-five to forty-nine not having been married. Childlessness was rare. Since 1987, however, the number of marriages has declined by 29 percent while the number of divorces has increased by 47 percent (Goskomstat Rossii 2002a, 119; Goskomstat Rossii 2003, 119). At the same time, marriage and pregnancy have become independent.

In 1950, only 4 percent of Russian marriages ended in divorce. This figure climbed to about 40 percent in the 1980s, jumping to 83 percent by 2001. Thus, one of the strongest links to first pregnancies—marriage—has declined considerably. This has been partly compensated for by an increase in births taking place outside of marriage, rising from 13 percent in 1988 to 29 percent in 2001 (Goskomstat Rossii 2002a, 149). The increase in nonmarital fertility, however, is hardly compensating for the decline in marital fertility, as the number of births to married women declined by over nine hundred thousand from 1989 to 2001, while the number of nonmarital births increased by only eighty-six thousand over the same period (Goskomstat Rossii 2002a, 149). In short, Russia is undergoing what is known as a "second demographic transition." Long under way in the West, such a transition is characterized by an increase in consensual unions, a larger contribution of births outside marriage, a later peak childbearing age, and an increase in the average age at marriage, first births, and all births.

Among other factors contributing to the decline in the birth rate is the explosion in the number of sexually transmitted diseases (STDs). The officially reported number of newly registered cases of STDs has nearly doubled from 209,000 cases in 1989 to 415,000 in 2000 (UNICEF 2004). A widespread prevalence of venereal diseases can cause a high prevalence of sterility, further lowering a population's fertility. Figures indicate that five million women and three million men in Russia are infertile (RIA News Agency 2000).

The rapid increase in the cost of having and raising children has also led most couples to postpone childbirth. Food as a share of household expenditures increased from 32 percent in 1990 to 51 percent in 1998 (Goskomstat Rossii 1999, 166–167). While education expenditures dropped from 2.3 percent to just 1 percent over the same period, there is anecdotal evidence that various "under-the-table" payments for education, nominally free in Russia, have risen tremendously. Furthermore, employer-provided day care was among the first benefits to be eliminated under the privatization of state-owned enterprises. The Soviet Union also had a system of monthly child allowances. The value of these allowances as a share of the minimum wage declined from 19 percent in 1993 to 7 percent in 1999 (Goskomstat Rossii 2002b, 165). These factors, coupled with alcoholism and drug abuse among parents, have led to a rise in the number of abandoned children, now estimated at between one and three million (*Oxford Analytica* 2002; RIA Novosti 2002). This represents the third large wave of orphans and street children in Russia in the last century, the first being in the 1920s after the Russian Civil War, and the second after World War II. A recent survey of the health status of 30 million Russian children has shown that 50 percent suffer from health disorders, most common of which are blood diseases due to anemia, bone and muscle tissue diseases, obesity, and digestive tract and circulatory system diseases. Only 34 percent of Russian children can be considered healthy (Rosbalt News Agency 2003).

■ Health, Mortality, and Life Expectancy

In 1897, the year of Russia's first census, life expectancy was twenty-nine years for males and thirty-two for females. By 1939, it had risen only to forty-four for males and fifty for females (Andreev, Darskii, and Khar'kova 1998). In the United States at that time life expectancy was sixty-two for males and sixty-six for females. Thus, after more than twenty years of Soviet rule, the country still had the mortality pattern of a traditional society, that is, high infant and child mortality, a prevalence of infectious and diarrheal diseases, and airborne and food-borne diseases. High infant and child mortality rates accounted for a large portion of the difference between the Soviet Union and United States. Infant mortality was still about one hundred deaths per thousand births in 1950. In the decades after World War II, the Soviet Union invested heavily in social services. School enrollments increased, nutritional status improved, many childhood communicable diseases were prevented, and housing became more available. The result was that the Soviet Union, like other countries, began to follow the general pattern of reductions in mortality from infectious diseases and increases in mortality from degenerative diseases. This was true up through the mid-1960s, when reductions in mortality from infectious diseases reached their maximum gains and could no longer offset increased deaths from chronic diseases and violence.

Even so, the Soviets made such great strides in raising life expectancy that by 1964 life expectancy for males in the USSR was within three years that of the United States, with the same pattern apparent for females (see Figure 8.4). Thereafter, the two began to diverge widely. Unlike in the United States, female life expectancy in the Soviet Union remained stagnant at about 72 to 73 from 1960 through the late 1980s, when it increased to 74.5 for a few years. Soviet male life expectancy, on the other hand, declined steadily from almost 64 years in 1960 to 62 in the late 1970s. The response on the part of the Soviets was to stop publishing data, which they did from about 1973 through 1989. Male life expectancy increased dramatically during the antialcohol campaign (discussed below in more detail) to about 65 in 1987 and then fell rather precipitously during the early years of postcommunist transition to a low of 57.6 in 1994, recovering somewhat by the end of the 1990s before falling again following the 1998 ruble crisis. The death rate

Figure 8.4 Life Expectancy, 1897–2005

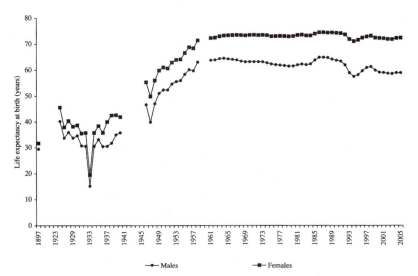

Sources: Andreev, Darskii, and Khar'kova 1998, 164–165; Goskomstat Rossii, *Demografi-cheskii ezhegodnik* (various years).

reached a low of 10.4 deaths per thousand in 1986, the peak year of mortality improvements from the antialcohol campaign. It then rose steadily, peaking at 15.7 per thousand in 1994 before falling until 1998 and then rising again.

According to the Russian Federal State Statistics Service, life expectancy in Russia in 2015 is expected to improve by about three years for both sexes, with the male-female gap in life expectancy remaining at about thirteen years. If these projections hold, Russian males are expected to have a *lower* life expectancy in 2026, 61.9 years, than they had in 1960, 63.8 years (Goskomstat Rossii 2005b). This is completely contrary to the health improvement experience of countries across both the developed and developing worlds.

There is evidence that life-style factors—diet, tobacco and alcohol consumption, lack of exercise, and stress—partly account for the gap between Russian and Western mortality and morbidity patterns (Anderson and Silver 1990, 192). Russia has long had a diet very high in fat and particularly rich in animal food products. By 1990, the energy in over 36 percent of the Russian food supply was from fat, making it one of the richest diets in the world (Popkin et al. 1997, 328). Indeed, diet partially explains the divergence in mortality rates from circulatory system diseases between Russia and the United States and Europe. Alcohol consumption is also a factor.

Throughout the Soviet era, alcohol was a major public health and social problem that resulted in economic losses but at the same time provided the state with a major source of revenue. In the mid-1980s, under Gorbachev, the Soviet Union instituted an antialcohol campaign that included drastic cuts in the production and sale of alcoholic beverages, large price increases, efforts to reduce home production, and the development of facilities for compulsory treatment of alcoholism. Alcohol consumption reached its highest point in 1984, just before the start of the campaign, at 10.5 liters of pure alcohol per person, and then dropped to 3.9 liters in 1987. One effect of the policy was the rapid growth in *samogon* (home-brewed alcohol) production. Even so, decreases in mortality from almost all causes during the campaign contributed to large improvements in both male and female life expectancy. Life expectancy increased by 3.2 years for males and 1.3 years for females. Mortality decreases from injuries and poisonings added 1.8 years for males. Secondary roles were played by the reduced incidence of cardiovascular diseases (0.7 years) and respiratory diseases (0.5 years). The campaign prevented 622,000 male deaths and 310,000 female deaths in the Russian Republic (Shkolnikov and Meslé 1996), showing that the antialcohol campaign did have an impact, although its effects were temporary and are not replicable in a market economy.

Following the end of the antialcohol campaign, and continuing through the post-Soviet economic transition period, life expectancy fell by 7.3 years for males and 3.4 years for females. It reached lows in 1994 of 57.4 years for males and 71.2 years for females. The largest declines were in 1992–1993, which coincided with the period of greatest macroeconomic instability as measured by inflation, when life expectancy fell 3.1 years for males and 1.9 years for females. By 1998, each recovered slightly over half of the decline experienced during 1987–1994. Following the August 1998 ruble crisis, life expectancy again fell, by 2.8 years to 58.5 for males, and by 1 year for females to 71.9. Fluctuations in deaths from external causes (suicide, traffic incidents, homicide, unintentional poisoning by alcohol, and falls) and cardiovascular diseases (predominantly among young and middle-aged men) explain these rises and falls. During the 1990s the increase in mortality led to an estimated 2.5 to 3 million excess deaths among young and middle-aged Russian men, which, according to the census results, is more than the entire population decline over this period (Men et al. 2003, 3–4).

A number of other factors influenced mortality in Russia and the other postcommunist transition countries, including economic outputs that declined by amounts much greater than during the Great Depression in the United States, and triple-digit inflation. Open unemployment also became a reality for the first time. Large-scale privatization caused labor turnover, and the breakup of the Soviet Union caused a rather large movement of peoples around and within Russia. Added to these circumstances was the collapse of the social safety net: education, health care, social protection, guaranteed wages and pensions, and a rewriting of the social contract.

One of the most notable features of the mortality crisis in the former Soviet Union, especially in Russia, is the sharp rise in deaths for middle-aged people and the absence of such an increase for children or the elderly. Deaths by age rose in Russia for every group from fifteen to sixty-four years of age, but declined in the younger groups. Several theories have been advanced to explain why mortality increased so much among postcommunist countries in general and Russia in particular. These include the collapse of health-care systems across the region, poor diets that were worsened by economic recession, increased poverty, high rates of consumption of tobacco and alcohol, the impact of the environment on health, and psychosocial stress.

Looking first at the Russian health-care system, health expenditures declined with the large shift in financing from federal to regional governments without commensurate changes in taxation authority. There have been large increases in informal out-of-pocket payments for health care, which has greatly limited access to health care for various social groups. However, those most affected by the mortality crisis, adult men, are the least frequent users of formal health-care systems. Thus it seems implausible to attribute the surge in adult mortality to the health-care system collapse. Diet too may be a cause, for reasons associated with both affordability and availability, as the cost of food has increased as a share of household expenditures. Even so, the rise in various diseases of poverty (infectious, nutritionally related, and parasitic diseases) was relatively modest. A large increase in poverty and hunger would have affected the biologically vulnerable, and as shown above, it was those in the primes of their lives who experienced the largest increases in mortality. The Russian population did not experience any serious malnutrition, despite a decrease in the consumption of meat and milk products.

There was a surge in alcohol and tobacco consumption, however. A "catching up" hypothesis has often been advanced, which states that alcoholics artificially survived during the 1985–1987 period. This means that the same age groups and causes behind the decline in mortality during the antialcohol campaign account for the subsequent rise when restrictions were lifted. The World Health Organization states that a country is severely affected when alcohol consumption is above eight liters per person per year. It is currently more than twice that in Russia at 18.5 liters (*Pravda.ru* 2003). Furthermore, with the opening of Russia and other postcommunist countries, Western tobacco companies have moved in aggressively with little resistance from advocacy or public health groups. Imports of both raw tobacco and cigarettes more than quadrupled from 1991 to 1993. The 1990s ushered in the creation of many joint ventures between Western tobacco companies and bankrupt firms or factories in Russia, resulting in an increased market share for Western tobacco products, promotion, and advertising. The "Westernization" of the tobacco industry in the former Soviet Union is tied to an escalation in one of the largest risk factors threatening health in the region. Among adult males in Russia, the number of smokers increased from 53 percent in 1985 to 67 percent in 1992. The number of men under forty who smoke is now 70 percent (Corwin 2004). The tobacco situation in Russia is similar to that in the United States prior to the release of the first report of the Surgeon General in 1964. Smoking rates are high, it is socially acceptable throughout the region, and there are no serious governmental efforts to reduce smoking.

The impact of the environment on health is another possible explanation for increased mortality rates. If a factor, environmental causes should have resulted in a higher incidence of deaths from bronchitis, pneumonia, influenza, certain types of tumors, and various genetic disorders. This is not what we have seen, however. In fact, there has been a decrease in the emission of harmful substances, commensurate with the decline in industrial pollution resulting from the drop in industrial production during the 1990s. Thus, although environmental degradation still may be a long-term factor in keeping life expectancy lower in Russia than in the West, it cannot be used to explain mortality trends so far in the postcommunist era.

The conclusion of most researchers is that mass psychosocial stress seems to be the primary cause of increased mortality (Cornia and Pannicia, 2000). Open unemployment, rapid labor turnover, increased job insecurity, growing family instability, increased social stratification, and "distress migration" all became realities, combined with, or laid on top of, a country and society that had significant demographic problems to begin with. The periods of highest increases in standardized death rates (SDR) were the years of highest inflation and macroeconomic instability. As inflation fell and countries introduced stabilization measures, the SDR fell. The increase in mortality in Russia and other European former Soviet states was greatest among the least educated, namely, those with fewer options and weaker coping skills than those more educated.

■ Mortality and HIV/AIDS

Compared with much of the rest of the world, the HIV/AIDS epidemic came rather late to Russia. However, because of its peculiar epidemiological pattern, and official neglect until recently, the disease has the potential to be crippling for Russia, demographically, socially, and economically. The first Russian case of HIV/AIDS was diagnosed in 1987 in Moscow. During the next eight years, the epidemic progressed very slowly, totaling only 1,072 HIV/AIDS cases at the end of 1995 (see Figure 8.5). In 1996, however, the number of new HIV cases increased exponentially, eight times the number of cases diagnosed in 1995, and has continued increasing ever since. By 2005, a

Figure 8.5 HIV Incidence and Deaths, 1987–2005

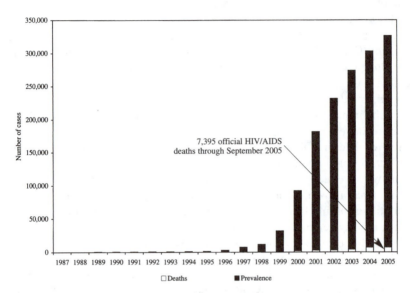

Source: Federal'nyi nauchno-metodicheskii tsentr (2005 figure is through September 30).

cumulative total of 319,000 people had been diagnosed with HIV. Because of the recent arrival of the epidemic to Russia, however, only 190 people were living with AIDS in mid-2002, and only 816 total AIDS deaths had occurred by mid-2003 (Eberstadt 2003b). Even so, the rapid spread of the disease in Russia places it among the highest prevalence countries in the world, along with several other former Soviet states. Of the cumulative 229,000 people diagnosed with HIV at the end of 2002, a quarter had been diagnosed with the disease in that year alone. Given the usual latency period between diagnosis of HIV and the onset of AIDS, and extremely high levels of HIV prevalence in the country, by 2010 the full force of the epidemic will start to be felt.

Changes in the modes of transmission are fueling the recent upsurge in new HIV cases. During the early period of the epidemic in Russia, through 1995, the majority of new HIV cases were attributed to homosexual or heterosexual contacts. The most frequently reported risk factor was having unprotected sex with foreigners. In 1996, a new trend appeared when intravenous drug users (IDUs) became widely involved in the epidemic through the sharing of unsterilized needles and other drug paraphernalia (Vinokur et al. 1999). The proportion of cases attributed to intravenous drug use drastically increased from virtually nothing in 1993 to 66.1 percent in 1996. However, by 2002 the epidemic began to leak back into the general population when HIV-positive persons from the IDU subculture began having unprotected sex with others. The percent of new HIV cases attributable to intravenous drug use fell to 36 percent, from over 90 percent in 2000, and the share attributable to heterosexual transmission increased to over 12 percent (Transatlantic Partners Against AIDS 2003, 4). The HIV profile in Russia is young because the majority of drug users are young. At the end of 2001 those infected were predominantly young males: 78 percent of the total, with 62 percent of male cases being between ages twenty and thirty (Rühl, Pokrovsky, and Vinogradov 2002). There are currently half a million registered intravenous drug users in Russia, with estimates of the true number ranging from 2.5 to 4 million. Thus the potential for further spread from this subpopulation is quite high. The figures given above for HIV prevalence are based on official counts. Most people analyzing the HIV epidemic in Russia apply some multiplier to this figure to get at the true number. Estimates range from 500,000 to 1.5 million people (Eberstadt 2003b). This compares with about 900,000 HIV-positive persons in the United States through the end of 2001, a country with roughly double the population of Russia (UNAIDS 2003).

In addition to IDUs, other high-risk groups for HIV in Russia include commercial sex workers, prisoners, and homosexuals. Each of these groups now serve as bridge groups for the spread of HIV into the rest of the population. The prison population in Russia has often been cited as a source for the rapid spread of HIV as well as tuberculosis (TB), which is a common opportunistic infection that HIV-positive people contract. One source states that over 4 percent of the prison population in Russia may be HIV-positive and about 10 percent have tested positive for TB. Tuberculosis incidence in Russia has risen from 55,469 in 1989 to 130,685 in 2000 (UNICEF 2004). With the lack of success of DOTS ("Directly Observed Treatment, Short-Course," the most commonly accepted program for the treatment of TB) and other programs that have proven effective elsewhere in the world, the number of TB deaths increased from 13,784 in 1992 to over 29,000 in 1999 and 2000 (Goskomstat Rossii 2002a, 215). There has been a recent overhaul in the Russian prison system reducing the number of inmates from 1.1 million in 2000 to 850,000 in 2003 (Lukashina 2003). The release of such a large number of people with HIV and/or TB will fuel the spread of these diseases throughout the general population.

Given the current HIV situation, it is not surprising that projections of the disease in Russia are dire. The US Census Bureau projects life expectancy in Russia without the effect of HIV/AIDS to rise from its current 67 years to 72.5 in the year 2025. With this as a baseline, under three scenarios of a mild, intermediate, or severe epidemic, life expectancy would fall to 69, 63, and 56 years respectively (Eberstadt 2002). The cumulative number of HIV-positive persons in 2020 would range from 5.4 million to 14.5 million people, and the annual number of HIV/AIDS–attributable deaths in 2020 would range from 250,000 to 650,000. Compare this to 15,000 HIV/AIDS deaths in 2001 in the United States. The baseline US Census Bureau projection also calls for a slight increase in the working-age population from 101 million people in 2000 to 102 million in 2010 before falling to 89 million in 2025 (Eberstadt 2003b). Under the three scenarios, with the effects of the epidemic included, the working-age population would range from 86 million to 78 million, or between 3 to 9 million below the baseline.

If there are any bright spots in the HIV/AIDS epidemic in Russia, and there appear to be few, it is that there now seems to be official recognition at the highest levels of the potentially crippling effects of the disease on an already demographically sick country. In his May 2003 address to the Federal Assembly, President Putin stated that HIV/AIDS represents a threat to Russian national security and that new epidemics such as drug abuse and AIDS are exacerbating already high rates of illness from accidents, poisonings, and injuries (Bernstein 2003). The amount of funding currently allocated from the federal budget for prevention and treatment of the disease, $4 million, is paltry given the enormity of the task. Perhaps indicative of how seriously the country's leaders are beginning to take this problem, Russia recently decided to borrow $150 million from the World Bank for TB and AIDS control after initially choosing not to implement a $60 million loan that already had been approved by the Bank's board of directors (World Bank 2003). In addition to this loan, there seems to be no lack of interest on the part of numerous international and nongovernmental organizations to assist Russia, given the possibly destabilizing impact on the international community of a large HIV/AIDS epidemic in that country. However, with the epidemiological momentum of HIV/AIDS in Russia already well under way, it will take all of these resources and more to prevent a catastrophe.

■ Migration

Before discussing migration trends in the post-Soviet period, it is useful to review Russia's migration experience as it relates to the expansion of the Russian empire and the USSR. Ivan the Terrible's defeat of the Tatar Khanate at Kazan in 1552 is viewed by many as the symbolic starting point of the Russian empire. This imperial expansion project lasted for the next four centuries, beginning in earnest with the exploration of Siberia and the first crossing of the Ural Mountains in about 1580. The Russian empire expanded first east, then west, and then finally south. Russia's eastward expansion across the Urals, through Siberia, to the Pacific coast was achieved with remarkable speed. By 1689 Russia laid claim to the entire region from the Urals to the Pacific Ocean north of the Amur River. By about 1700, native peoples of this vast region had become a demographic minority with the migration of some two hundred thousand Russians across the Urals. The Russian empire stretched out into Asia in successive waves of expansion from 1796 to 1914.

During the 1800s five million Russians crossed the Urals into Siberia. Construction of the Trans-Siberian Railway started in 1891 and was instrumental in further settling and asserting Russian control over the region. Between 1897 and 1911 another 3.5 million made the journey into Siberia, often with state-supported reduced fares. As for Russia's southern expansion, all of the Caucasus was brought into the Russian empire by 1878 and Central Asia by 1895. Of 140 million persons in the Russian empire at the time of the first All-Russian census in 1897, 65 million were non-Russians.

Migration and the mixing of nationalities played important roles in the histories of the Russian empire and the USSR, and in the breakup of the Soviet system. At the time of its collapse, the USSR possessed fifty-three different ethnic homelands, dating from the early Soviet period and based on the results of the 1926 census in which ethnographers identified 172 different ethnic groups (Hirsch 1997). The original eighty-nine regions of post-Soviet Russia included thirty-two ethnic homelands: twenty-one republics, ten autonomous okrugs, and one autonomous oblast. The other fifty-seven regions are regular administrative units, including Moscow and St. Petersburg, which have the status of federal cities, and thus are not based on ethnicity. Because of decades of in-migration of Russians and other ethnic groups, in only eight of the Russian Federation's ethnic homelands does the titular nationality constitute a majority (Harris 1993b). These tend to be peripheral areas with few key resources to attract migrants. In eighteen of the thirty-two ethnic regions, Russians are the majority nationality. In most of these, the titular group is less than 25 percent of the population in their homeland. The most extreme examples are the two oil and gas regions of West Siberia, the Yamal-Nenets and Khanty-Mansi autonomous okrugs, where the titular nationalities make up only 5.2 and 1.9 percent of the total population respectively.

In 1897, 93 percent of Russians resided in the western regions of the empire, the traditional areas of settlement (Chinn and Kaiser 1996). By 1970, only 78 percent of Russians resided in these regions, marking the maximum extent of distribution for Russians across either the Russian empire or the Soviet Union. In the mid-1970s, the migration pattern shifted back toward European Russia. The percent Russian in the non-Russian Soviet republics went from 10 percent, in 1926, to a peak of 20 percent in 1970, before declining to 18 percent in 1989 (Harris 1993a). With the Soviet Union's collapse, the existence of this 25.2-million-person ethnic Russian diaspora was of great concern for the Russian Federation and the other fourteen newly independent former Soviet states.

Forty-five percent of this diaspora (nearly 11.4 million Russians) lived in Ukraine, 6 million were in Kazakhstan, and another million each lived in Belarus, Latvia, Kyrgyzstan, and Uzbekistan. Three republics with the largest shares of Russians were Kazakhstan (38 percent), Latvia (34 percent), and

Estonia (30 percent). In both Ukraine and Kyrgyzstan, Russians made up 22 percent of the population. The smallest Russian share was in Armenia, at 1.6 percent. Russians, however, made up larger shares of the urban populations than their shares of the total population in all republics, and Russians also made up larger shares of the capital cities than they did in urban areas in general. For instance, the Kazakh capital, Almaty, was 59 percent Russian and 22 percent Kazakh, while the Kyrgyz capital, Bishkek, was 56 percent Russian and 23 percent Kyrgyz. Because of such enclaves, ethnic Russians' knowledge of the titular languages was very low, with only 19 percent speaking the titular language as a second language. Thus, the capitals and other large cities of the non-Russian Soviet republics were Russian exclaves where Russians could enjoy their traditional cultural life, speak their language freely, and never have to learn the local language. Consequently, in the post-Soviet era ethnic Russians have had a difficult time meeting the language requirements that many of these states have imposed to qualify for citizenship, obtaining jobs in the public sector, or gaining entrance to higher education. Russians, however, have enjoyed a privileged occupational status, making up disproportionate shares of industrial enterprise managers, scientists, professors, engineering-technical specialists, and other high-wage, high-prestige professions (Goskomstat Rossii 1994, 16–19).

Since the 1989 census there has been a net migration of 3.5 million ethnic Russians to Russia, representing 13.8 percent of the diaspora population. A clear regional grouping emerges. From Armenia, Tajikistan, Azerbaijan, and Georgia, half or more of the Russian populations have left. Significant shares of the titular populations also have fled from these states because of deteriorating economic conditions. From Moldova and the Baltic states only 10 to 13 percent of the Russian diaspora populations have left despite the restrictive citizenship policies of two of the three Baltic states, Estonia and Latvia. Only small portions of the Russians living in the other two Slavic states, Belarus and Ukraine, have migrated to Russia. Part of what these numbers reveal is that despite what seems to be a large-scale migration of Russians to Russia, most, about eighteen million, have chosen to stay in the non-Russian Soviet successor states (Heleniak 2004, 113).

A number of factors have influenced migration patterns for post-Soviet Russia (Heleniak 2001b). Not surprisingly, the greatest influence on international migration was the breakup of the Soviet Union into fifteen successor states. This event turned what had been internal migration within a tightly controlled political system into international migration across increasingly porous national boundaries. Because the USSR broke apart along its ethnic seams, a large portion of post-Soviet migration, although certainly not all, consisted of people moving to their ethnic homelands. This included a portion of the Russian diaspora population residing in the non-Russian former Soviet republics.

Economic factors also have influenced migration. Under the USSR's centrally planned economy most prices were administratively set and, as a result, differences in the cost of living from one region or republic to the next were small. Soviet planning also included a set of regional wage coefficients designed to induce people to migrate to work in priority sectors of the economy. Price liberalization and the removal of most subsidies in Russia in 1992 caused a rapid uneven rise in income distribution and greatly increased differences in the cost of living across regions. In Russia's market economy, open unemployment became a reality and for the first time became a factor influencing migration. With the opening up of the Russian economy also came increased involvement with the outside world, including foreign direct investment, which further exacerbated differences among regions, increased awareness of economic and migration opportunities abroad for Russians, and increased such opportunities for outsiders in Russia. There has also been a large increase in temporary, cyclical, and seasonal migration, whereas during the Soviet era much of the migration was long-term and permanent.

During the 1990s, Russia became a "migration magnet" for residents of the non-Russian former Soviet states. The fact that Russians and other ethnic groups are choosing to emigrate to Russia should come as no surprise, given the economic divergence of these states during the post-Soviet period. Of the fifteen Soviet successor states, only the three small Baltic states have a higher per capita gross national income than Russia. Most of the Central Asian and Transcaucasus states, as well as Ukraine and Moldova, have incomes half, or less than half, that of Russia.

The 2002 Russian census showed a net population gain from immigration of 5.6 million. From 1975, when Russia's migration balance with the non-Russian Soviet republics became positive, until the breakup of the Soviet Union at the end of 1991, net migration into Russia averaged about 160,000 annually. Net migration to Russia rose rapidly following the breakup of the Soviet Union, peaking at 809,614 in 1994. In 2002, net migration to Russia was only 77,927, less than 10 percent of the 1994 figure (Goskomstat Rossii 1995, 400–403).

The patterns of migration for Russia by country since 1989, both for the Soviet successor states and the so-called far abroad (that is, countries outside the former USSR), have been driven in part by the nationality composition of those migration streams (Figure 8.6). Three countries account for the bulk of people migrating from Russia to the far abroad: Germany with about 61 percent, Israel with 23 percent, and the United States with 11 percent. These flows have consisted mainly of three groups: Germans, Jews, and Russians.

Russia has had a positive migration balance, however, with all the other former Soviet states except for Belarus. Between Russia and the non-Russian Soviet successor states, the three with the largest Russian diaspora populations—Ukraine, Kazakhstan, and Uzbekistan—account for the largest shares of immigration. Ukraine and Kazakhstan each are responsible for a quarter

Figure 8.6 Net Migration by Country, 1989–2005

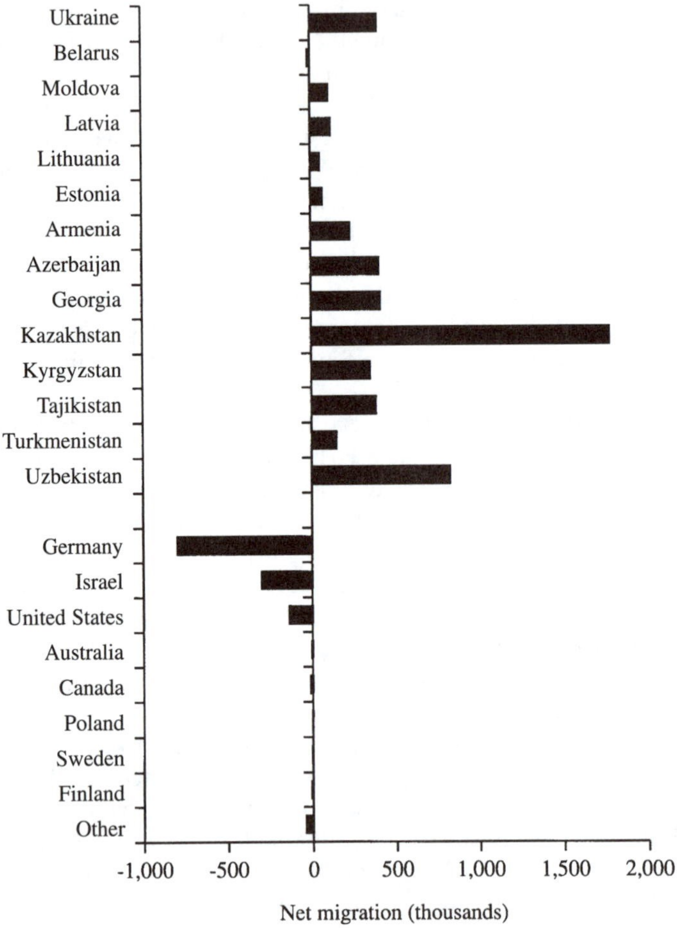

Net migration (thousands)

Source: Goskomstat Rossii (selected publications).

of all Russian immigration, and Uzbekistan 11 percent. Overall, the Central Asian states, including Kazakhstan, have been the source for about half of all migrants to Russia, and the three Transcaucasus states 15 percent.

There have been numerous reports about the "brain drain" during the 1990s (*BBC News* 2002; Sacks 1998, 246). While Russia may indeed have lost a large number of people among select, highly specialized occupations, overall, the country has actually increased the educational level of its population through migration during the post-Soviet period, largely at the expense of the other former Soviet states. Russia is a net recipient of migrants across the age spectrum but disproportionately among those twenty to fifty who tend to be more educated and highly skilled than older individuals. Since 1994 a clear pattern has emerged of migration from each of the fourteen non-Russian titular nationalities of the Soviet successor states to Russia. This is a pattern similar to that experienced by other empires as they broke apart, such as Algerians following the French to France, and Indians following the British to Britain. Tajiks, Armenians, Georgians, and Azeris all significantly increased their numbers in Russia through migration. The common denominator among these groups was the episodes of violence during the post-Soviet period in their ethnic homelands, which, in addition to bloodshed and displacement, was accompanied by economic downturns that were more severe than those experienced by the other successor states.

As to internal migration, the predominant flow in Russia during the transition period has been out of Siberia and the Far East toward central Russia (Map 8.1). Eight regions have had population increases of greater than 10 percent. These include the city of Moscow, several regions in the

Map 8.1 Net Migration by Region, 1989–2006

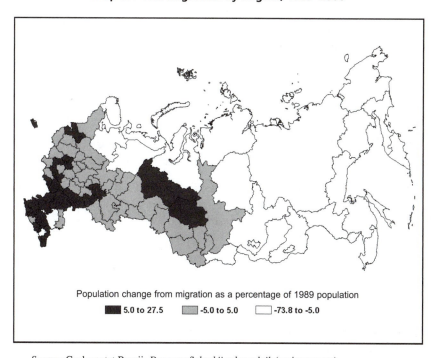

Population change from migration as a percentage of 1989 population

■ 5.0 to 27.5   ▨ -5.0 to 5.0   □ -73.8 to -5.0

Source: Goskomstat Rossii, *Demograficheskii ezhegodnik* (various years).

North Caucasus, and the natural gas region of Khanty-Mansi in West Siberia. At the same time, forty regions have experienced net out-migration. Most of the regions with large population declines were periphery regions in Siberia, the Far East, and the European north. This included nineteen regions that lost more than 10 percent of their populations to out-migration, and ten that lost more than 20 percent. At the extreme were Magadan Oblast and Chukchi Autonomous Okrug, both in the distant northeast across the Bering Strait from Alaska, which had migration losses of 57 and 74 percent respectively.

Although many have regarded Siberia and the north as being overpopulated, a majority of Russia's crucial raw materials are located in its northern periphery. During the Soviet period a unique set of development practices existed to exploit the resources of the northern regions, including financial and other incentives for people to move to and work in the north, and the construction of large urban agglomerations (Heleniak 1999). The result was that Russia had a much more densely populated north than other countries with comparable high-latitude regions. While many areas of Alaska, the Canadian north, and the northern regions of Scandinavia are similarly well-endowed with natural resources, these countries have developed and exploited these resources differently than Russia, relying on smaller permanent settlements and temporary labor forces. There are about ninety-five persons per one hundred square kilometers in the Russian north, which makes it about two and a half times as densely populated as Alaska and roughly fifty times as populated as the Canadian north and Greenland. Altogether, there are eleven cities with more than two hundred thousand people in the northern regions of the world. Ten of them are Russian. The eleventh is Anchorage, Alaska, with a population of 250,000.

One unintended consequence of Russia's transition to a market economy has been a massive out-migration from its vast northern periphery. Since 1989 (the year of the last Soviet census), nearly 10 percent of the population has migrated out of the sixteen regions classified by the Russian government as being part of the "Far North" (*Krainii sever*). Those who have left the Far North have tended to be younger and more highly educated, leaving behind many older and less able people who lack the means to migrate. The major causes of out-migration have been price liberalization (which makes the cost of fuel, food, and other consumer goods in the north more expensive), fiscal decentralization (which has shifted the burden of local revenue and expenditure responsibility away from the central government in Moscow to financially hard-pressed northern regions), and a shift in the country's approach to the development of its Arctic and sub-Arctic regions. In short, Russia is neither willing nor able to sustain the scale and scope of development that was promoted during the Soviet era in its northern periphery. As a result, the Russian government has borrowed $80 million from the World Bank to assist in the voluntary resettlement of persons from three northern regions (Vorkuta, Norilsk, and Magadan) and may expand the project to include the entire north.

Russia's Far Eastern periphery poses its own particular challenges. The vast distances between the region and central Russia have always meant that incorporating the Far East into the rest of the economy, be it free market or planned, is difficult. The Russian Far East is a classic example of a periphery region where inexpensive raw materials are extracted and sent to the core in exchange for expensive finished products. The Far East produces over 60 percent of Russia's gold, 90 percent of its diamonds, 65 percent of its fish products, and 30 percent of its forest products. Traditionally a major food-deficit region, the Far East is forced to import a majority of its foodstuffs to support its large population (Tikhomirov 1997). With the withdrawal of transport and other subsidies in the post-Soviet era, the food supply situation has become even worse. As a result, many of its inhabitants have left and many of those who remain have seen their standard of living plummet. Attempts to tie the region to the more prosperous Pacific Rim countries, such as Japan and the United States, have not produced the desired results, and the regional economy continues to stagnate. Overall during the 1990s the population of the Far East declined by 15 percent, nearly all due to out-migration (Heleniak 2001a).

As a result of this depopulation of the Far Eastern periphery, along with the opening up of Russia's borders, some fear a large-scale Chinese immigration into the region that could ultimately result in the eventual annexation of parts of the Russian Far East by China. This fear is based on the simple demographic fact that there are 5 million people in the Russian regions bordering China in the Far East, and 110 million Chinese in the three regions bordering Russia. Unproven estimates provided by local officials claim that up to 2 million Chinese already live illegally in the southern reaches of the Far East. Some Russian policymakers favor increased Chinese migration into the region, citing the fact that Chinese shuttle traders serve an important economic role through their imports of inexpensive food, clothing, and other consumer goods, and also fill an important labor market niche by taking unskilled jobs in construction and agriculture. These policymakers maintain that the demographic imbalance in the region is unnatural, and that increased migration is unavoidable and necessary in order to develop further the resources of the Far East. Those opposed to additional Chinese migration underscore the fact that the Far East is a crucially important region, being Russia's naval outlet to the Pacific and a vast storehouse of strategic minerals. They allege that if migration continues, there may be as many as 8 to 10 million Chinese residing in Russia by 2010, which would make the Chinese Russia's second-largest ethnic group. Such estimates are wildly exaggerated, however, and more careful assessments based on discussions with local officials, analyses of data from local migration offices, and eyewitness accounts, place the total closer to one hundred thousand to three hundred thousand

Chinese in the region, most arriving under rather closely monitored labor contracts (Alexseev 2001). For its part, the 2002 census claims that only thirty-five thousand Chinese live in Russia (Goskomstat Rossii 2004). Contrary to the fears of some, it appears that the Chinese are more interested in shuttle trade than in long-term residence.

One final element influencing Russia's internal migration is the unusual rank-size distribution[1] of its urban areas (Hill and Gaddy 2003). This is partially the result of decades of central planning and attempts by Soviet leaders in search of the "optimal" city size to control internal population movements by placing limits on the growth of certain urban areas. Russia deviates from the general "rank-size" rule in two respects. First, there is the absence of medium-sized cities. At the time of the 1989 census, Moscow and Leningrad (now St. Petersburg) were rather large cities with 8.9 and 5 million inhabitants respectively. After these two cities, the next largest Russian city was Novosibirsk, at 1.4 million. In most countries that deviate from the general rank-size rule, it is because the largest, or primate, city is larger than predicted by the rule. The Soviet case, however, did not follow this pattern, leading to its second deviation from the rule: namely, that Soviet-era Moscow should have been even larger than it was.

Not surprising to those who live or travel there, the population of Moscow has grown precipitously since the end of Soviet rule. The 2002 census revealed that the population of Moscow was 10,358,000, an increase of almost 1.5 million, or 16.6 percent, since the 1989 census. In post-Soviet Russia, investment and economic growth has been highly concentrated in a few select regions and cities, with Moscow leading in both respects. The 2002 census confirms that people are following suit and concentrating in the capital along with money and economic opportunity. Thus, little more than a decade away from central planning, the rank-size distribution of Russian cities seems to be adjusting to a more normal pattern. According to the census, a larger share of the Russian population now resides in Moscow than at any time since the country's first census in 1897 and perhaps at any other time in Russian history. Moscow's share has grown from 2.2 percent in 1926 to 7.1 percent in 2002, despite repeated efforts during both the Soviet and post-Soviet eras to restrict entry into the capital. At the other end of the urban spectrum is the increasing number of Russian ghost towns. These are villages that were supposed to contain people and were included in the official list of populated places, but when the census takers came they found nobody living in them. These 13,032 abandoned villages constituted 8.4 percent of all villages in Russia. Another 34,803 had fewer than ten people residing in them. Thus, nearly a third of Russian villages are either dead or soon will be. Many of these empty villages continue to be supplied with electricity, gas, and other services, representing a costly drain on the Russian state budget (Heleniak 2003a).

◼ Russia's Population in the Twenty-First Century

This final section looks at projections of the future size and composition of the Russian population and recent government population policy. The Russian Federation's population grew steadily from 119 million in 1960 to 148 million in 1992. Since then it has fallen to 145.1 million, according to the 2002 census, and is expected to fall further. Goskomstat projections high (147 million in 2026) and low (125 million in 2026) bracket the range of estimates derived by others (Figure 8.7). The Goskomstat medium scenario projects 134 million in 2015 and 94 million in 2050. The United Nations projects the population of Russia to range between 135 and 92 million (United Nations 2005, 372–373). Most of these projections do not incorporate the impact of possible AIDS mortality in Russia. Thus, despite the higher than expected census count, the population of Russia has fallen and is expected to continue to decline well into the future.

It is difficult to see and understand the possible implications of Russia's declining population when walking the streets of Moscow, as the population of Russia's prosperous capital city has grown considerably during the intercensus period. Even so, the 2002 census confirms that Russia, the world's largest country territorially, has fallen to seventh place in terms of population, behind China (1.285 billion), India (1.025 billion), the United

Figure 8.7 Historical and Projected Population, 1960–2050

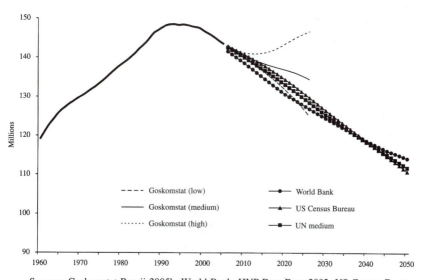

Sources: Goskomstat Rossii 2005b; World Bank, HNP Data Base 2002; US Census Bureau, International Data Base n.d.; United Nations 2005.

States (286 million), Indonesia (215 million), Brazil (173 million), and Pakistan (146 million). Of the world's twenty largest countries, only Russia's population is declining. If the most recent UN population projections hold, Russia will fall to seventeenth in the world by 2050, just behind Japan, Iran, and Uganda (United Nations 2003, 34). The implications of this for economic growth and Russia's overall place in the world are difficult to determine, as a population decline of such a magnitude for a country of this size is unprecedented, and raises the question of whether Russia will be able to continue to maintain effective control over the world's largest landmass. That Russia will remain a great power forty years from now seems increasingly remote.

Added to this scenario is the graying of Russia's population. Although like much of the rest of the developed world, in that all will confront financial and health issues as a result of rapid population aging, Russia and some of the other transition countries face a more dire situation with fewer resources because of the economic downturns of the 1990s as well as peculiarities in their pension and health-care systems. The percent elderly in Russia (defined as males aged sixty and over and females fifty-five and over) has increased from 18.5 to 20.5 between the 1989 and 2002 censuses and is expected to make up 26 percent of the population in 2025. At the other end of the age structure, the slowdown in birth rates has meant that the percent young (that is, those who are fifteen and under) in Russia has declined from 24.5 to 18.1 percent. Russia has a pay-as-you-go pension system where current workers are taxed to pay the social security of current retirees. With the number of births peaking in Russia in 1987, smaller cohorts will soon start entering the labor force, leaving Russia with fewer workers supporting each retired person.

Studies investigating the feasibility of replacement migration easing this burden have found that in order for Russia to maintain the population size it had in 1995, there would have to be a net migration of 24.9 million in the first half of the twenty-first century (United Nations 2000). For the size of the working-age population to stay the same, there would have to be a net migration of 35.8 million. Even the lower figure assumes the migration to Russia of the entire remaining Russian diaspora in the non-Russian former Soviet states. Such hopes must be looked at in the context of recent peak migration of almost 810,000 in 1994 and the drastically reduced 2002 net migration of just under 78,000. While it appears likely that Russia's migration balance will continue to be positive, much of the post-Soviet migration potential appears to have been exhausted.

Thus, the possibilities of maintaining the current demographic balance through migration appear slim, unless Russia wants to begin recognizing and assimilating the large illegal population that currently resides in the country. Most countries with long histories of immigration have had difficulty pulling off similar feats. For Russia to do so would put a quite different literal and figurative face on the Russian population. Russia appears unwilling to do this, as we will see below.

Throughout his presidency, Putin demonstrated an acute awareness of Russia's dire demographics. In July 2001, in his first state-of-the-nation address, he stressed that Russia would be threatened with extinction if present trends persisted and cautioned that the country could become a "senile nation." The chair of the Duma's health committee warned that

> Russia may simply disappear as an independent state before the end of the twenty-first century. The nation is shrinking for the fourth time since the start of the twentieth century. It is not just that the population of Russia is dwindling. Worse still, depopulation, meaning extinction, has hit above all the titular nation, meaning Russians. (Bekker 2000)

The recent census backs his claim, showing that the ethnic Russian population has declined from 81.3 to 79.8 percent of the total population of Russia, its lowest level since the first Soviet census in 1926 (Goskomstat Rossii 2004; Harris 1993a).

Even as the general fear of population decline is dominating discussion of demographic issues in Russia, it may be unfounded, associated as it is with notions that link population size, military might, and economic strength. Indeed, population size is just one factor that contributes to a country's relative strength and position in the world, others being land size and location, level of technology, and form of government. Furthermore, Russia is neither the first country to deal with the issue of population decline, nor is this the first time in either Russian or Soviet history that it has had to confront the question. Russia's population fell following the two world wars and rebounded each time. Though the current decline is due to more fundamental, underlying causes, even if predictions hold, by mid-century Russia's population will be about 100 million, hardly a small country.

At the same time, migration policy has shifted from one of welcoming the Russian diaspora, to counter the country's demographic shortfall, to one of combating illegal migration. There will be continued pressure for migration from the southern-tier states of the former Soviet Union (the eight states of Central Asia and the Caucasus), which are growing rapidly as the population of Russia declines. In 1950, these states had 25 million people versus Russia's 102 million. Russia currently has double the population of these countries, but with the shrinking Russian population combined with the growing populations of Central Asia and the Caucasus, these southern-tier states will nearly equal Russia's population by 2050. Although now in separate countries, these former Soviet republics continue to share the same landmass and common historical ties. Combined with diverging rates of economic growth, the population pressures in Central Asia and the Caucasus will give impetus to migration, both legal and illegal to Russia.

Russia's current demographic policy is contained in a document titled *Conception of Russia's Demographic Policy Through 2015* and in various pieces of legislation. Taken together, these legislative initiatives and public policy pronouncements indicate that the country's demographic future is of considerable concern. The Duma has proposed or debated legislation on a number of issues, including increasing funding for school lunches, reducing the incidence of abortion as a means of fertility regulation, providing housing grants to stimulate the birth rate, and enacting measures to curb smoking and alcohol consumption. Russia's HIV/AIDS problem also seems no longer taboo.

That Putin raised these issues is a step in the right direction. Yeltsin was either unaware of them or had no desire to deal with them. Although the assessment that Russia will eventually cease to exist as a nation is probably premature, the country does face a number of demographic dilemmas that will affect almost every aspect of its domestic and foreign affairs. While all projections point to a vastly smaller Russian population in the future, if the United Nations' "medium" scenario of 112 million in 2050 comes to fruition, Russia will still have a sizable population, even by world standards. In the next fifty years the Russian population probably will become smaller, older, and more diverse. Russia's leaders should take steps to adjust to this new reality, focusing their efforts on increasing the quality of the population, both in terms of health and education. Although Russia's demographic problems are numerous, it still has ample human capital in the form of many highly educated, highly skilled people. The country should use this capital to its advantage. Even so, the Russian government needs to take immediate steps to address what could potentially be a devastating HIV/AIDS epidemic, and it must introduce measures to prevent premature adult mortality before its human capital deteriorates further. Furthermore, even though many among Russia's political and policy-making elite now seem to be aware of the country's demographic problems, what is missing is any large public outcry in response to the dire demographic and health situation, as one might expect in the United States or Europe (Eberstadt 2003a). In the United States, it was partly public pressure that prompted government to take measures to reduce smoking, improve food quality, and in general promote healthier life styles. In Russia, public outcry concerning individual health issues would signal a level of personal responsibility that the majority of the population does not yet possess.

Note

1. Rank-size distribution is a mathematical law found to apply across most countries where the largest city in a country is twice as large as the second-largest city, three times as large as the third-largest city, four times as large as the fourth-largest, and so on.

▓ Bibliography

Alan Guttmacher Institute. 1999. "Sharing Responsibility: Women, Society and Abortion Worldwide (1999, Special Report)." http://guttmacher.org/sections/abortion.html.

Alexseev, Mikhail A. 2001. "Socioeconomic and Security Implications of Chinese Migration in the Russian Far East." *Post-Soviet Geography and Economics* 42(2): 122–141.

Anderson, Barbara A., and Brian D. Silver. 1990. "Trends in Mortality of the Soviet Population." *Soviet Economy* 6(3): 191–251.

Andreev, E. M., L. E. Darskii, and T. L. Khar'kova. 1998. *Demograficheskaia istoriia Rossii: 1927–1959* [A demographic history of Russia: 1927–1959]. Moscow: Informatika.

Andreev, Evgeny M., Leonid E. Darsky, and Tatiana L. Kharkova. 1994. "Population Dynamics: Consequences of Regular and Irregular Changes." In *Demographic Trends and Patterns in the Soviet Union Before 1991,* ed. Wolfgang Lutz, Sergei Scherbov, and Andrei Volkov. Laxenburg, Austria: International Institute for Applied Systems Analysis.

Avdeev, Alexandr. 1994. "Contraception and Abortions: Trends and Prospects for the 1990s." In *Demographic Trends and Patterns in the Soviet Union Before 1991,* ed. Wolfgang Lutz, Sergei Scherbov, and Andrei Volkov. Laxenburg, Austria: International Institute for Applied Systems Analysis.

BBC News. 2002. "Russian Brain Drain Tops Half a Million," June 20. http://news.bbc.co.uk/1/hi/world/europe/2055571.stm.

Bekker, Alexander. 2000. "Russian Socio-Economic Situation: Outlook Bleak." *Vedomosti,* September 20. In *Johnson's Russia List,* no. 4528, September 20. http://www.cdi.org/russia/johnson/4528.html.

Bernstein, Jonas. 2003. "Statistics Bear Out Putin's Concerns over Demographic Trends." *Radio Free Europe/Radio Liberty (RFE/RL) Russian Political Weekly* 3(21), May 29. http://www.rferl.org/reports/rpw/.

Bongaarts, John. 1982. "The Fertility-Inhibiting Effects of the Intermediate Variables." *Studies in Family Planning* 13(6/7): 179–189.

Canning, Mary, Peter Moock, and Timothy Heleniak. 1999. *Reforming Education in the Regions of Russia.* World Bank Technical Paper Series, number 457. Washington, D.C.: World Bank.

Chinn, Jeff, and Robert Kaiser. 1996. *Russians as the New Minority: Ethnicity and Nationalism in the Soviet Successor States.* Boulder, CO: Westview Press.

Conquest, Robert. 1990. *The Great Terror: A Reassessment.* New York: Oxford University Press.

Cornia, Giovanni Andrea, and Renato Pannicia. 2000. "The Transition Mortality Crisis: Evidence, Interpretation and Policy Responses." In *The Mortality Crisis in Transitional Economies,* ed. Giovanni Andrea Cornia and Renato Pannicia. New York: Oxford University Press.

Corwin, Julie A. 2004. "Popularity of Smoking Continues Rising." *RFE/RL Newsline* 8(1), January 5. http://www.rferl.org/newsline/.

DaVanzo, Julie, and Clifford Grammich. 2001. *Dire Demographics: Population Trends in the Russian Federation.* Santa Monica, CA: Population Matters, RAND.

Eberstadt, Nicholas. 2002. "The Future of AIDS." *Foreign Affairs* 81(6): 22–45.

———. 2003a. "The Demographic Factor as a Constraint on Russian Development: Prospects at the Dawn of the Twenty-first Century." National Defense University Institute for National Strategic Studies. http://www.ndu.edu/inss/Repository/

INSS_Proceedings/Russian_Power_Apr03/RussianPower_Eberstadt_AY02-03.pdf.

———. 2003b. "The Fight Against AIDS in Russia: A Status Report." Unpublished trip report.

Ellman, Michael, and S. Maksudov. 1994. "Soviet Deaths in the Great Patriotic War: A Note." *Europe-Asia Studies* 46(4): 671–680.

Federal'nyi nauchno-metodicheskii tsentr po profilaktike i bor'be so SPIDom [Federal Scientific-Methodological Center for the Prevention of AIDS]. n.d. http://www.hivrussia.org/.

Feshbach, Murray, and Albert Friendly Jr. 1992. *Ecocide in the USSR: Health and Nature Under Siege.* New York: Basic Books.

Goskomstat Rossii. 1994. *Chislennost' i sotsial'no-demograficheskie kharakteristiki russkogo naseleniia v respublikakh byvshego SSSR* [size and sociodemographic characteristics of the Russian population in the republics of the former USSR]. Moscow: Goskomstat Rossii.

———. 1995. *Demograficheskii ezhegodnik Rossii* [Demographic yearbook of Russia]. Moscow: Goskomstat Rossii.

———. 1998. *Naselenie Rossii za 100 let: 1897–1997* [Population of Russia: 1897–1997]. Moscow: Goskomstat Rossii.

———. 1999. *Sotsial'noe polozhenie i uroven' zhizni naseleniia Rossii* [The social situation and standard of living of the population of Russia]. Moscow: Goskomstat Rossii.

———. 2001. *Chislennost' naseleniia Rossiiskoi Federatsii po polu i vozrastu na 1 ianvaria 2001 goda* [Population of the Russian Federation by age and sex on January 1, 2001]. Moscow: Goskomstat Rossii.

———. 2002a. *Demograficheskii ezhegodnik Rossii* [Demographic yearbook of Russia]. Moscow: Goskomstat Rossii.

———. 2002b. *Sotsial'noe polozhenie i uroven' zhizni naseleniia Rossii* [The social situation and standard of living of the population of Russia]. Moscow: Goskomstat Rossii.

———. 2003. *Rossiia v tsifrakh 2003* [Russia in figures 2003]. Moscow: Goskomstat Rossii.

———. 2004. *Broshiura "Osnovnye itogi Vserossiiskoi perepisi naseleniia 2002 goda"* [Brochure "Main results of the All-Russian population census of 2002"]. Moscow: Goskomstat Rossii.

———. 2005a. *Demograficheskii ezhegodnik Rossii* [Demographic yearbook of Russia]. Moscow: Goskomstat Rossii.

———. 2005b. *Predpolozhitel'naia chislennost' naseleniia Rossiiskoi Federatsii do 2026 goda* [Projections of the population of the Russian Federation to 2026]. Moscow: Goskomstat Rossii.

———. 2006. *Demograficheskii ezhegodnik Rossii* [Demographic yearbook of Russia]. Moscow: Goskomstat Rossii.

Harris, Chauncy D. 1993a. "The New Russian Minorities: A Statistical Overview." *Post-Soviet Geography* 34(1): 1–28.

———. 1993b. "A Geographical Analysis of Non-Russian Minorities in Russia and Its Ethnic Homelands." *Post-Soviet Geography* 34(9): 543–597.

Haub, Carl. 1994. "Population Change in the Former Soviet Republics." *Population Bulletin* 49(4). Washington, D.C.: Population Reference Bureau.

Heleniak, Timothy. 1999. *Migration from the Russian North During the Transition Period.* Social Protection Discussion Paper, number 9925. Washington, D.C.: World Bank.

————. 2001a. "Demographic Change in the Russian Far East." In *The Russian Far East: Prospects for the New Millennium,* ed. Michael Bradshaw. Richmond, UK: Curzon Press.

————. 2001b. "Migration and Restructuring in Post-Soviet Russia." *Demokratizatsiya* 9(4): 531–549.

————. 2002. "Migration Dilemmas Haunt Post-Soviet Russia." *Migration Information Source* (October). http://www.migrationinformation.org/feature/display .cfm?ID=62.

————. 2003a. "The 2002 Census in Russia: Preliminary Results." *Post-Soviet Geography and Economics* 44(6): 430–442.

————. 2003b. "The End of an Empire: Migration and the Changing Nationality Composition of the Soviet Successor States." In *Diasporas and Ethnic Migrants: German, Israel and Russia in Comparative Perspective,* ed. Rainer Munz and Rainer Ohliger. London: Frank Cass Publishers.

————. 2004. "Migration of the Russian Diaspora After the Breakup of the Soviet Union." *Journal of International Affairs* 57(2): 99–117.

Hill, Fiona, and Clifford Gaddy. 2003. *The Siberian Curse: How Communist Planners Left Russia Out in the Cold.* Washington, D.C.: Brookings Institution Press.

Hirsch, Francine. 1997. "The Soviet Union as a Work in Progress: Ethnographers and the Category *Nationality* in the 1926, 1937, and 1939 Censuses." *Slavic Review* 56(2): 251–278.

Kingkade, W. Ward. 1989. "Content, Organization, and Methodology in Recent Soviet Population Censuses." *Population and Development Review* 15(1): 123–138.

Krassinets, Eugene. 1998. *Illegal Migration and Employment in Russia.* International Migration Papers, no. 26. Geneva: International Labour Organization.

Livi-Bacci, Massimo. 1993. "On the Human Costs of Collectivization in the Soviet Union." *Population and Development Review* 19(4): 743–765.

Lukashina, Vita. 2003. "Russia Set to Overhaul Its Prison System." *Gazeta.ru,* October 23. http://www.gazeta.ru/2003/10/23/Russiasettoo.shtml.

Men, Tamara, et al. 2003. "Russian Mortality Trends for 1991–2001: Analysis by Cause and Region." *British Medical Journal* 327.

1989 USSR Population Census CD-ROM. 1996. Minneapolis, MN: East View Publications.

Oxford Analytica. 2002. "Street Children in Russian Federation," April 14.

Pirozkhov, Sergei, and Gaiane Safarova. 1994. "Demographic Regularities and Irregularities: The Population Age Structure." In *Demographic Trends and Patterns in the Soviet Union Before 1991,* ed. Wolfgang Lutz, Sergei Scherbov, and Andrei Volkov. Laxenburg, Austria: International Institute for Applied Systems Analysis.

Popkin, Barry, et al. 1997. "Nutritional Risk Factors in the Former Soviet Union." In *Premature Death in the New Independent States,* ed. Jose Luis Bobadilla, Christine A. Costello, and Faith Mitchell. Washington, D.C.: National Academy Press.

Popov, Andrej A., and Henry P. David. 1999. "Russian Federation and USSR Successor States." In *From Abortion to Contraception: A Resource to Public Policies and Reproductive Behavior in Central and Eastern Europe from 1917 to the Present,* ed. Henry P. David. Westport, CT: Greenwood Press.

Pravda.ru. 2003. "Alcohol Makes Russians an Extinct Nation," December 19. http://english.pravda.ru/main/18/90/359/11593_alcoholism.html.

RIA News Agency. 2000. "Russia: Birth Rate Down, Death Rate Up, Smoking and Drinking to Blame," October 24. In *Johnson's Russia List,* no. 4599, October 25. http://www.cdi.org/russia/johnson/4599.html##2.

RIA Novosti. 2002. "Number of Street Children in Russia Close to 3 Million," February 19. In *Johnson's Russia List,* no. 6087, February 20. http://www.cdi.org/russia/johnson/6087.htm.

Rosbalt News Agency. 2003. "Over Half of Russian Children Suffer from Functional Health Disorders," April 23. http://www.rosbaltnews.com/2003/04/23/62334.html.

Rosstat. 2004. *Vozrastno-polovoi sostav i sostoianie v brake. Itogi Vserossiiskoi perepisi naseleniia 2002 goda. Tom 2* [Age-sex structure and marital status. Results of the 2002 All-Russian population census. Vol. 2]. Moscow: Statistika Rossii.

Rühl, Christof, Vadim Pokrovsky, and Viatchslav Vinogradov. 2002. *The Economic Consequences of HIV in Russia.* http://www.worldbank.org.ru/ECA/Russia.nsf/ECADocByUnid/56435B1EA108E164C3256CD1003FBE54.

Sacks, Michael Paul. 1998. "Privilege and Prejudice: The Occupations of Jews in Russia in 1989." *Slavic Review,* 57(2): 245–265.

Schwartz, Lee. 1986. "A History of Russian and Soviet Censuses." In *Research Guide to the Russian and Soviet Censuses,* ed. Ralph S. Clem. Ithaca, NY: Cornell University Press.

Shkolnikov, Vladimir M., and France Meslé. 1996. "The Russian Epidemiological Crisis as Mirrored by Mortality Trends." In *Russia's Demographic "Crisis,"* ed. Julie DaVanzo. http://www.rand.org/publications/CF/CF124/index.html.

Slavin, V. S. 1972. *The Soviet North: Present Development and Future Prospects.* Moscow: Progress Publishers. As cited in Michael J. Bradshaw, 1995, "The Russian North in Transition: General Introduction," *Post-Soviet Geography* 36(4): 195–203.

Staines, Verdon S. 1998. *A Health Sector Strategy for the Europe and Central Asia Region.* Washington, D.C.: World Bank.

Tikhomirov, Vladimir. 1997. "The Food Balance in the Russian Far East." *Polar Geography* 21(3): 179–180.

Transatlantic Partners Against AIDS. 2003. *On the Frontline of an Epidemic: The Need for Urgency in Russia's Fight Against AIDS.* New York: EastWest Institute.

Tsentral'noe statisticheskoe upravleniii SSSR. 1984. *Chislennost' i sostav naseleniia SSSR: po dannym Vsesoiuznoi perepisi 1979 goda* [size and composition of the population of the USSR: According to data from the 1979 population census]. Moscow: Finansy i statistika.

Vinokur, Anatoly, et al. 1999. *Russia: TB, HIV/AIDS, and STIs: Portrait of a Crisis.* Washington, D.C.: World Bank.

UNAIDS (Joint United Nations Program on HIV/AIDS). 2003. *AIDS Epidemic Update: 2003* (December). http://www.unaids.org/Unaids/EN/Resources/Publications/corporate+publications/aids+epidemic+update+-+december+2003.asp.

UNICEF (United Nations International Children's Emergency Fund). 2004. Innocenti Research Centre (Florence, Italy). *TransMONEE Database.* http://www.unicef-icdc.org/resources.

United Nations. 1999. Department of Economic and Social Affairs. Population Division. *World Abortion Policies: 1999.* New York: United Nations.

———. 2000. Department of Economic and Social Affairs. Population Division. *Replacement Migration: Is It a Solution to Declining and Aging Populations?* ESA/P/WP.160, March 21. New York: United Nations.

———. 2005. Department of Economic and Social Affairs. Population Division. *World Population Prospects: The 2004 Revision.* Vol. 1 of *Comprehensive Tables.* New York: United Nations.

United States Census Bureau. n.d. International Data Base. http://www.census.gov/ipc/www/idbnew.html.

World Bank. 2002. World Bank Health, Nutrition, and Population Data Base. "Demographic Projections." http://devdata.worldbank.org/hnpstats/dp.asp.

————. 2003. "World Bank Helps Tackle Tuberculosis and HIV/AIDS in Russia: Approves $150 Million Loan." Press Release, April 4. http://www.worldbank.org.ru/ECA/Russia.nsf/ECADocByUnid/F85139A466195762C3256D0B00 287EF6.

Walsh, Nick Paton. 2003. "Low-Birth Russia Curbs Abortions. Women Denounce Law Reducing Reasons for Legal Terminations." *Guardian,* September 24.

9

Environmental Problems

Philip R. Pryde

The quality of life in any country is as much a function of its environmental health as it is of its economic well-being. Indeed, the two are interdependent. The expenses of securing environmental quality are most easily met in a healthy economy, and in turn economic vitality requires clean and healthy surroundings and workplace environments. Unfortunately, neither condition tended to be met in the Soviet Union. During the Soviet era, for political reasons, myths were perpetrated by the government that there could be no unwise use of natural resources under socialism. This meant, so they said, that any visible pollution was well within desirable public health norms, and that in any event pollution levels in the USSR were much lower than in Western countries (Pryde 1972).

As it turned out, none of these claims were true. It is now universally understood that not only did the Soviet Union have some of the world's highest levels of pollution but that there was an ongoing campaign to conceal this fact from both the outside world and its own citizens (Feshbach and Friendly 1992; Komarov 1980; Massey Stewart 1992; Peterson 1993; Pryde 1991; Ziegler 1987).

Unfortunately, the change in governments in 1991 did not instantaneously improve the Russian environmental picture. Currently, environmental problems in the Russian Federation remain numerous, severe, and widespread. They are of sufficient magnitude that they are restraining post-Soviet advancement in Russia in both the social and economic spheres (Pryde 1995). In this chapter, these problems will be examined under three major headings: pollution, biotic preservation, and radioactive contamination.

■ Pollution

Air Pollution

Air quality in any country is first and foremost a matter of public health, and only secondarily concerns aesthetics. Most industrial processes and motor vehicles inherently produce air pollutants that are potentially harmful to human health. Commonly, governments require that measures be taken to greatly reduce these potential harmful effects. The Soviet Union, for its part, did have a large number of antipollution laws on the books. However, in general they were either weak or poorly enforced, and as a result pollution levels were often very high (Komarov 1980).

In the Soviet Union, two other factors besides poor enforcement combined to produce these high pollution levels. First, the USSR placed paramount importance on rapid industrial expansion, generally at the lowest possible investment cost. This often meant minimizing, or completely ignoring, environmental safeguards. Second, as previously noted, Soviet authorities and bureaucrats believed that somehow socialist factories would be inherently cleaner than capitalist ones, a belief that unfortunately had no basis in reality. One result was air pollution levels in industrial regions that threatened public health and were reflected in respiratory diseases and weakened resistance to other ailments (Feshbach and Friendly 1992).

The worst Soviet air pollution conditions were in cities with factories that employed inherently dirty processes. Examples include steel mills, petroleum refineries, pulp and paper mills, nonferrous (copper, lead, zinc, and nickel) smelters, petrochemical factories, and fossil-fuel power plants. The Norilsk Nickel plant has been charged with being the single worst polluter in the country. Public health there is poor, and dead forests extend outward from the city for dozens of miles (Bond 1984). Large factories were not the only sources of pollution, however. Many small enterprises also put out uncontrolled emissions that, cumulatively, produced significant amounts of pollution. The burning of trash and even forest fires were also widespread sources of air pollution as were motor vehicles.

By the 1980s, hazardous industrial wastes and pollution from improper handling and storage of nuclear wastes had to be added to the list. The result was that several major industrial regions, such as the Donets coal basin in Ukraine, the southern Ural Mountains, the Kuznets coal basin in West Siberia, much of eastern Kazakhstan, and many individual cities such as Norilsk, Lipetsk, Magnitogorsk, Omsk, Angara, Monchegorsk, Ufa, and Bratsk suffered from air pollution concentrations that were well above safe norms (see Table 9.1). Even parts of Moscow suffer from contaminated air (Bityukova and Argenbright 2002).

Unfortunately, after the dissolution of the Soviet Union in 1991, funds were not available to improve air quality. In recent years, foreign entrepreneurs and

During the Soviet era, large factories such as this one,
the Ust-Ilimsk pulp and paper mill in East Siberia,
were significant sources of air pollution.

corporations have been willing to invest in Russia and are building more modern plants, or cleaning up older ones, so that some improvement is being realized. Nevertheless, air quality is still poor in many regions. The Russian government reported in 2003 that two hundred industrial cities in Russia have air pollution levels that exceed health standards by 400 percent or more, resulting in about thirty million people breathing polluted air. Air pollutants caused the incidence of bronchitis among adults to increase by 70 percent from 1997 to 2002, and by 50 percent among children (ITAR-TASS 2003a).

As already noted, some improvement in air quality has been realized since 1991 due to the modernization of plants either by their new Russian owners or, frequently, by outside money from industrial partners in other countries. But the main cause of reduced air pollution in Russia during the 1990s was simply the shutting down of numerous older, inefficient, and highly polluting Soviet-era factories. As the new Russian economy picks up steam in the twenty-first century, some of these mothballed factories may reopen, and if so, air quality will see corresponding instances of local deterioration.

A significant problem that has come to the fore in the past decade is global warming, which has severe implications for many parts of the world, including vast areas of both North America and Russia. Although the causes

Table 9.1 Russian Cities with Highest Emission Levels

City	Stationary Sources	Mobile Sources	Total Emissions (thousand metric tons)
Norilsk	2,400.1	25.9	2,426.0
Moscow	369.1	841.5	1,210.6
Novokuznetsk	892.9	55.8	948.7
Magnitogorsk	871.4	28.5	899.9
Lipetsk	722.1	61.6	783.7
Nizhniy Tagil	685.2	26.7	711.9
Cherepovets	671.7	—	>671.7
St. Petersburg	254.1	371.9	626.0
Omsk	479.4	143.4	622.8
Chelyabinsk	446.7	86.5	533.2
Angarsk	466.8	15.2	482.0
Ufa	349.1	126.4	475.5

Source: Bond 1991, 407.
Note: 1987 data is used here because no more recent comparable data has been encountered.

of global warming are unclear, there is no question that it is occurring, and that the melting of polar ice may cause the oceans to rise. The implications for certain coastal cities from increases in sea level due to global warming are enormous, especially for such low-lying cities as Venice, New Orleans (tragically confirmed in 2005), and St. Petersburg. St. Petersburg has been flooded many times over the centuries from storm surges in the Gulf of Finland. Any increase in sea level would only make the flooding threat that much worse. Another major disaster for Russia from global warming would be the melting of large areas of Siberian permafrost, which could destroy structures built on such permafrost and increase flooding on Siberian rivers (Agence France Presse 2003a). A further prediction is that climate change could increase aridity in some regions, adversely affecting agricultural productivity.

Global warming is believed to be partially the result of emissions into the atmosphere of certain types of air pollutants, particularly carbon dioxide and methane, which are often termed greenhouse gases. Russia is a major producer of these greenhouse gases (Oldfield 2005, 55). The most worrisome threat is that global warming might release vast quantities of methane that have been securely frozen in Siberian permafrost since the last ice age. Since methane is twenty times more powerful a greenhouse gas than carbon dioxide, the implications for global warming of such a release could be tremendous (Sample 2005). During the 1990s an international agreement was devised, called the Kyoto Protocol, which laid out steps that industrial nations should take to reduce these types of emissions. The only two major industrial nations that refused to sign this protocol were Russia and the United States (Holley 2003b). However, in 2004, Russia reconsidered its position and became a signatory to the agreement. Significantly, with the addition of Russia, enough countries were participating for the protocol to go into effect.

Water Pollution

The pollution of a nation's freshwater supplies is primarily viewed as a public-health problem, particularly where drinking water supplies are concerned. However, it is frequently also an industrial problem, as many industries require clean water for their manufacturing operations. In both cases, it quickly translates into an economic problem. Fortunately, achieving clean water is not technically difficult. What is difficult is finding the political will, and establishing the economic priorities, in order to allocate sufficient funds to accomplish the task. This has been the main problem in Russia.

Water pollution problems are easily traced to the Soviet era, and summaries of the problem in the USSR in the 1970s and 1980s can be found in the references in the bibliography for Komarov (1980), Pryde (1991, Chapter 5), and ZumBrunnen (1984). The discharge of untreated municipal and industrial wastes directly into rivers has always been the most expedient option and was a common practice both before and during the Soviet period. Unfortunately, the situation has improved only marginally in the post-Soviet era.

As noted in the preceding section on air quality, certain types of industries have inherently dirty processes that tend to generate pollution of various types, including water pollution. Industries that tend to be highly water polluting include steel mills, pulp and paper mills, textile mills, nonferrous smelters, dairy and beef cattle operations, and petrochemical industries. In addition, fossil-fuel and nuclear power plants (and many industrial operations) generate thermal discharges that can also harm or kill marine life in bodies of water.

In the USSR, new industrial plants were required to have wastewater treatment facilities, but often the factory would begin operations with the treatment plant either unfinished or working imperfectly. But industrial pollutants are not the only problem. A recurring problem is oil pollution from pipeline accidents. Soviet crude petroleum pipelines were not built to the safety standard levels used elsewhere. Breaks and other accidents along pipeline corridors, especially in West Siberia, are common (Tavernise 2003; Vilchek 2002). It is estimated that more than eight hundred thousand hectares (over three thousand square miles) of West Siberia have been polluted from pipeline oil leaks (*Kommersant* 2004).

Of course, there is also the universal problem of adequately handling human wastes. As with industrial wastes, standards and norms existed, but plants did not always perform as required. Also, the rapid growth of many

Soviet cities sometimes outpaced the ability of wastewater treatment plants to expand in kind. Wastes that pollute drinking water supplies are the greatest concern. This is still a problem in many regions, with water quality problems in such major rivers as the Volga, Ob, Oka, Irtysh, Yenisey, and others being frequently reported. The majority of large Russian cities, for historical reasons, tend to be situated on large rivers such as these. The river that for decades has generated the most concern is the Volga and its tributaries (Komarov 1980; Pryde 1991). The Volga basin was one of the earliest centers of industrial development in both the tsarist and Soviet eras, and by the late twentieth century it was heavily polluted. Efforts to clean it up have had some success, but a significant water quality problem still exists in portions of the Volga.

Rivers are not the only water bodies of concern. Lakes and even coastal waters are also often at risk. Two prominent examples are Lake Baikal and the St. Petersburg dike. The threat of polluting Lake Baikal is probably the best known of all Soviet, and now Russian, environmental problems. The threat to the lake from timber cutting near its shores and two pulp mills that process the timber has been the subject of international concern for over forty years. This concern reflects the exceptional physical and biological attributes of Baikal, which, among other things, is both the deepest and largest volume freshwater body in the world (Mackay, Flower, and Granina 2003). Baikal's greatest depth of 1,637 meters (5,371 feet, or a little more than a mile) easily surpasses that of Lake Superior, the greatest of North America's Great Lakes, at a depth of 406 meters (1,332 feet). In terms of volume, Baikal holds 20 percent of the world's freshwater, slightly more than all the Great Lakes combined.

The threat of its pollution caused Lake Baikal to be the first Soviet environmental problem to gain worldwide attention. The resulting international outcry eventually reduced the potential of major pollution greatly, but did not entirely eliminate it; the threat of pollution from one of the pulp and cellulose mills remains (Loginova 2003b). In a partial response, both the Soviet and Russian governments created new national parks and other protected preserves along its shoreline.

In the twenty-first century, however, there is a new threat to Lake Baikal. An oil pipeline from East Siberia to China has been proposed, which would partly lie within the basin on the south side of the lake and cross one or more of the new nature reserves. Worse, this is a highly seismically active region, and it would be easy for a major earthquake to crack a pipeline. Despite forty years of discussion and plans, the unique resources of Lake Baikal remain at risk.

The problem of the St. Petersburg dike is a textbook case of poor environmental planning and inadequate impact assessment. Construction on this huge dike across the Gulf of Finland a few miles west of the city of St. Petersburg

Philip R. Pryde

The shoreline of Lake Baikal.

began in the 1980s. It was planned to be both a flood-control barrier and the route of a superhighway that would bypass the city center, both worthy urban-planning objectives. But there was a potentially serious problem. The dike might create a stagnant "lake" immediately adjacent to the center of the city, in which pollutants could accumulate to intolerable levels. The dike's proponents assumed that ship passage facilities utilizing gates in the dike would permit enough water to flow through and circulate inside the "lake" to keep it clean. Not until billions of rubles had been spent on the dike was construction stopped because of fears that the amount of water circulation would be inadequate to prevent gross pollution of the harbor area. The Russian government believes, however, that flood control takes precedence and ordered completion of the dike, using a large measure of foreign financial assistance (Walsh 2003). Assurances that the pollution problem would be adequately taken care of have not been convincing to St. Petersburg environmentalists.

■ Biotic Preservation

For many, the name *Russia* brings forth an image of snow-covered forests and Muscovites bundled up against the winter cold. While this image may have some validity for a portion of the country over a part of the year, it ignores other equally valid images of Russia, such as the vast steppe regions covered with spring wildflowers, or mountain slopes and meadows containing a vast array of vegetation and wildlife. Indeed, the Russian Federation as a whole contains a mosaic of significant biological regions that have considerable importance for planetary biodiversity (Knystautas 1987). One might guess that this would be the case based on the country's huge size alone, and a brief survey of Russia's natural heritage will confirm it to be an accurate impression.

The Russian Federation by itself (setting aside all the other portions of the former Soviet Union) is an area far larger than the United States, and it is the country in the world that comes closest to being self-sufficient in terms of economically important natural resources. For this reason, the USSR gave paramount importance to the development of this industrial potential. In the process, biotic resources, while not entirely ignored, generally lost out in any direct conflict with desired economic expansion.

In the post-Soviet era, Russia's natural resources have become a focus of increasing international interest regarding their development. As both domestic and international interest in Russia's oil, timber, and other natural resources intensifies, the potential for deterioration of the country's biological wealth also increases. This is particularly true in Siberia and the Russian Far East (Pryde 1995; Rodgers 1990). In contrast to the situation during the Soviet era, both foreign and domestic actors now play a role in promoting natural-resource conservation in Russia.

During the Soviet era, federal ministries regulated the exploitation of commercial biotic resources, such as forests, fisheries, and furbearing mammals (Pryde 1972). An effort was made to regulate the extraction or "take" of these resources in such a way that they would not become depleted, so that their use would be sustainable over the long run. No such systematic protection existed for noncommercial species, however. The preservation of noncommercial species was generally left up to the managers of the nation's network of protected natural areas, and outside of them supervision was often almost nonexistent. The only major exceptions were endangered "charismatic" species that held popular appeal, such as the Siberian tiger, Siberian cranes, and the European bison.

Contemporary Russia, like the Soviet Union before it, utilizes three main types of protected areas: national parks, limited access nature reserves, called *zapovedniki,* and natural preserves, termed *zakazniki* (Center for Russian Nature Conservation 2003; Pryde 1991). The national parks are managed in a manner similar to their counterparts in the United States (Chebakova 1997). The *zapovedniki* are often referred to as "strict nature reserves," meaning that normally they are not open to the general public for recreational uses and instead are intended for biological protection and scientific research. The *zapovedniki* are the most highly protected category of all Russian natural areas. There were slightly over 100 *zapovedniki* in existence in 2003. The *zakazniki*

An entrance into the Kavkaz Zapovednik
(Caucasus Nature Preserve) in the North Caucasus.

enjoy a lesser degree of protection, often seasonal in nature or otherwise limited. Hunting is often permitted in them.

In general, under the USSR, wildlife protection outside the *zapovedniki* was poor. Not only did economic development have priority but it was often carried out in a manner that harmed wildlife. For example, the rapid development of oil fields often left pools of oil on the ground that trapped migratory birds. The construction of hydroelectric dams on the Volga eliminated valuable sturgeon and other fish runs on the river. Overuse of long-lived pesticides killed millions of birds, as well as the predators that fed on them. Even the regulated commercial species did not always fare well, as overharvesting was often reported. In addition, poaching, the illegal taking of fish and wildlife, has always been a problem.

As with pollution, the situation with poaching has not improved much in the post-Soviet period. The problem is that the depressed economy in rural parts of the country, combined with the loss of the tight controls of the Soviet government, has resulted in a great increase in poaching. Also, the contemporary private-entrepreneur nature of the economy, which lacks adequate governmental supervision and regulation, has resulted in additional losses of forests and wildlife. For example, poor management of the Volga's resources in both the Soviet and post-Soviet periods has resulted in the loss of 90 percent of that river's valuable sturgeon resources, the source of caviar. Poaching

is equally a problem on the high seas as it is on internal rivers, and regulatory efforts rarely succeed (Borisova 2003).

The *zapovedniki* system has never had an easy time. Under the USSR it
was constantly threatened with decimation by Stalin and others to allow economic exploitation of resources (Pryde 1972; Weiner 1999). After Stalin's
death the system eventually expanded, especially during the last three
decades of the twentieth century (see Table 9.2). Since 1991, however, the *zapovedniki* and other protected natural areas in Russia have fallen on hard economic times. The main reason has been large reductions in governmental
financial support for them, which has necessitated significant personnel cutbacks. As suggested above, a related problem has been an upswing in poaching in the parks and preserves. These problems call into question Russia's
ability to protect its biotic resources under current conditions.

The country's financial situation notwithstanding, a number of new *zapovedniki,* twenty-eight in all, have been established in Russia since 1991.
These twenty-eight new preserves collectively take in over eleven million
hectares (more than forty-two thousand square miles), of which the vast
majority (about 98 percent) are in Siberia and the Russian Far East, where
large reserves are more easily created (Pryde 1997). Because the eastern *zapovedniki* tend to be larger than those in European Russia, wildlife protection is somewhat better in Siberia than in western Russia (with the exception of the Siberian tiger, discussed later).

A unique approach to nature conservation also was initiated in Russia during the 1990s when, for the first time since before the Bolshevik Revolution,

Table 9.2 Development of the *Zapovedniki* System

	Number of *Zapovedniki*		Hectares of *Zapovedniki*	
Year	USSR	Russia	USSR	Russia
1937	37	n.a.	7,138,300	—[a]
1951	128	n.a.	12,500,000	—[a]
1952	40	19	1,466,000	—[a]
1988	155	63	18,886,223	ca. 15,700,000
1991	ca. 170	73	ca. 23,000,000	ca. 19,900,000
1997	>200	94	n.a.	30,843,358
2006	>200	101	n.a.	ca. 32,000,000

Sources: For 1937, 1951, 1952: Pryde 1972; for 1988: Pryde 1991; for 1991: Pryde 1995;
for 1997 and 2006: Center for Russian Nature Conversation 2003 and 2007.

Notes: a. Exact number of hectares in Russia prior to about 1960 unknown. In 1966 these
19 reserves totaled 2,425,000 ha., but many were enlarged between 1952 and 1966.
   n.a. indicates data not available.

a private nature reserve was established. This first private reserve was inaugurated in 1994 in East Siberia along the Amur River's floodplain, south of the city of Blagoveshchensk. The project is named Muravyovka Park, after a nearby village, and takes in 5,207 hectares (a little more than twenty square miles). Among the protected species at Muravyovka are cranes, which have great symbolic importance in Russian and Chinese culture. Two crane species nest in this region, one of which, the red-crowned (or Japanese) crane, is endangered (Pryde 1999). Assistance in paying for the initial lease on the park's land was provided by the International Crane Foundation (ICF) and a private Japanese corporation. Various environmental organizations such as the ICF, World Wildlife Fund, and Audubon Society provide help with the ongoing administrative and maintenance costs at Muravyovka.

In the years that have passed since the creation of Muravyovka Park, considerable progress has been realized, so much so that the park was recognized in 1997 with a Distinguished Service Award from the Society for Conservation Biology. It has also become an international center for crane preservation, hosting experts from China, Korea, Japan, and the United States. It will be interesting to see whether in years to come Muravyovka Park can be a model for similar enterprises elsewhere in Russia.

Despite the problems mentioned above, Russia, like most other countries, values its biological resources, and at least in principle desires to conserve them. Nevertheless, these problems have resulted in some species becoming severely depleted to the point that they are threatened with extinction. These are referred to in Russia and most other parts of the world as endangered species and in Russia are described and cataloged in what are termed "Red Books" (Eliseev 1983).

Endangered wildlife species are not uniformly distributed across Russia. Within the Russian Federation, there are concentrations of endangered species in both the North Caucasus and the Russian Far East (Pryde 1987). In the latter region, many of the endangered species are marine mammals and sea birds. Across the former Soviet Union endangered species tend to be most highly concentrated along the mountainous southern borderlands. The main reason for this is that alpine regions often have relatively small, isolated eco-regions where limited wildlife populations can be easily reduced, and where detrimental human activities such as agriculture, settlements, recreation, and poaching will magnify adverse effects. Among Russia's endangered animals are numerous species of birds, several species of marine mammals, and a large number of land mammals and reptiles. The list of mammals is headed by three large felines: the highly endangered Amur leopard, the snow leopard, and the Siberian tiger.

The Siberian tiger has garnered the most international attention. There appears to be rough agreement that the number of tigers in the Russian Far East has been decreased to between 360 and 450. Russian biologists generally

A Siberian tiger in captivity.

express concern that the tiger population continues to decline, though a few feel their numbers are stable. No one believes they are increasing. Poaching is the major problem, with perhaps as many as sixty tigers (15 to 20 percent of the entire population) having been illegally shot during the 1990s (Solovyova 2003). A significant step on behalf of tiger conservation was taken in 2007 with the formation of two new large preserves in the Russian Far East, the Zov Tigra and Udege Legend national parks (World Wildlife Fund 2007). Their creation brings the total number of national parks in Russia to thirty-nine. Besides protecting tigers, the Udege Legend National Park also safeguards the homeland and forests of the indigenous Udege people. In addition to wildlife, a large number of plant species are also listed as endangered in Russia. In the case of plants, the primary problem is generally not illegal harvesting, but large-scale economic activities, such as timber harvesting and agriculture.

Russia belongs to most international conservation treaties that work to preserve flora and fauna, such as CITES (Convention on International Trade in Endangered Species). However, the enforcement aspect of these treaties is generally left up to the individual countries, and Russia, along with numerous other nations, does not have a good record in this regard.

Poor forest management is also a concern. Its problems include the approval of large-scale commercial timber-harvest contracts, illegal timber cutting, and inadequate forest-fire prevention. Seeking additional income, the Russian government has offered long-term timber-harvesting contracts to foreign companies, giving rise to complaints that these contracts frequently disregard environmental safeguards. So too are the rights and needs of indigenous peoples often ignored. On occasion, only international opposition has ensured that these needs are taken into account. The illegal cutting of forests by Russians for private economic gain is also considerable. Given the modest resources available for enforcement, such violations are difficult to deter. To make matters worse, timber poachers sometimes deliberately set forest fires in an effort to cover their tracks (Holley 2003a).

Even without poachers, forest-fire prevention in Russia is a challenge, because of inadequate road networks and insufficient fire-fighting resources, especially in the more remote areas of Siberia. The scale of Russia's forest-fire losses is sometimes staggering: in the first eight months of 2003 alone approximately two million hectares, or about 7,700 square miles, of forest were destroyed by fire (ITAR-TASS 2003b).

Economic encroachments, which are often accompanied by land and water pollution, are a major threat to wildlife. Perhaps the best example is the massive amount of oil and natural gas development that is occurring in such areas as the West Siberian lowlands and around Sakhalin Island (*The Banker* 2003). Mining for coal and other valuable minerals is an equal threat to wildlife. Many areas are also negatively affected by nuclear energy facilities. There have been massive releases of radiation at various Siberian facilities, and the problem of abandoned nuclear submarines on the Kola Peninsula near Norway has received widespread publicity. These types of problems will be examined in more detail in the next section.

As noted above, Russia has long cataloged its threatened species of plants and animals, but it is highly expensive to set in place a national program to address the problem. The political motivation to do this is lacking at present. As a result, Russia has no effective equivalent of the United States' Endangered Species Act. But lack of funding is hardly the only problem. Environmental groups are sometimes harassed by government agencies, and there is a major problem of bureaucratic corruption, which most commonly involves officials ignoring, or even participating in, environmental law-breaking. Both in the Soviet and post-Soviet periods, media accounts of regulators accepting bribes and similar circumvention of laws and their enforcement have been commonplace. Although Russian officials have indicated they intend to take action against such practices, little change has been observed at the time of this book's publication.

Can the problems that have emerged since the collapse of the USSR, with its strong centralized control mechanisms, be corrected? Most likely they can, but the pace of improvement will not be swift. This is because the emphasis on economic development is almost as great in Russia as it was under the USSR, and as noted above, effective governmental restraints over polluting or rapacious forms of economic development seem to be unavailable or inadequate at present.

The Russian Far East is an area of particular concern, as it lies close to other economically attractive areas on the Pacific Rim, and hence is viewed as ripe for significant development (Rodgers 1990). It is currently also an economically depressed region, and hence there is a strong desire to assist economic development there. Unfortunately, it is also an area of unusual biological importance. The push to develop oil and timber harvesting in the Russian Far East has been noted, and it can only be hoped that this can be accomplished with a minimum of environmental damage (Agence France Presse 2003b).

In order to ensure the future of Russia's outstanding wildlife, flora, and natural systems, improvements are needed in the management of the country's natural resources. The problems listed above are correctable, but must be taken seriously by a national government that views biotic preservation as a priority. It is convenient to blame governmental inaction in the area of biotic protection on the rocky state of Russia's economy, but it is not a convincing excuse. No country can provide adequately for its economic future if it permits the deterioration of its natural resource base. Russia need look no further than to the history of its own predecessor state, the Soviet Union, to see the truth of this proposition.

■ Radioactive Contamination

Radioactive contamination is a well-known major public health and environmental problem in contemporary Russia. Although the Chernobyl explosion is the best-known incident, it was not, as will be shown later, the USSR's largest uncontrolled release of radiation. The adverse effects of the overall radiation situation on human health, agriculture, and water quality are well understood and appreciated, but the monetary resources needed to correct the various problems are currently beyond the country's budgetary capabilities. This section will summarize the radioactive waste problems in the Russian Federation at present.

Immediately after World War II, the United States was the only nuclear power. This was unacceptable to the Soviet leadership. As such, the Soviet Union began a crash program to obtain a strategic nuclear capability at any cost, and by 1949 the USSR possessed an atomic bomb. However, the USSR wanted not one but thousands of nuclear devices, and thus a huge, secret network of mining, processing, manufacturing, testing, and disposal sites was created across the country (Map 9.1). Because speed was deemed essential, these facilities were often built with less than adequate safety procedures. The long-run result was radioactive contamination that in places greatly

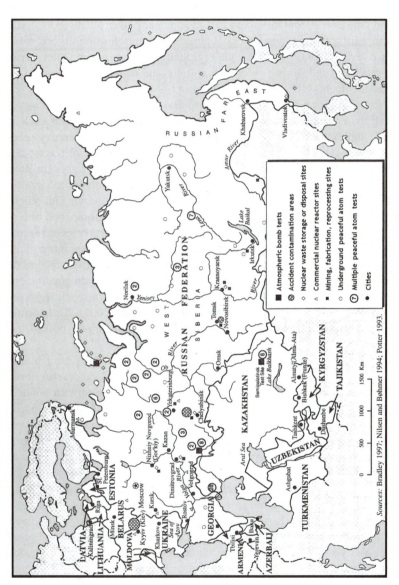

Map 9.1 Radioactive Waste and Contamination Locations in the Russian Federation

Sources: Bradley 1997; Nilsen and Bøhmer 1994; Potter 1993.

exceeded human health limits. This legacy remains today in post-Soviet Russian society and is well documented in such works as Bradley (1997).

Radioactive contamination can occur at any stage of producing or using nuclear fuels. Specific areas within the Soviet Union that have experienced radioactive contamination include nuclear power plants (both civilian and military), factories that concentrate and enrich uranium ore, sites used for testing atomic weapons, underground nuclear explosion sites, areas of reprocessing and storing used nuclear fuels, and regions contaminated by nuclear accidents, such as around Chernobyl (Pryde 2003).

First, let us look at the commercial nuclear power program. Most Soviet nuclear power plants were built within the Russian Federation. Ten nuclear power complexes exist, which collectively contain thirty-one operating reactor units (see Table 9.3). Of these, fifteen utilize the same type of reactor design found in US nuclear plants, termed pressurized-water reactors (in Russian, VVER reactors). Eleven of the remainder are called graphite-moderated reactors (RBMK type), which is the design used at Chernobyl. The others include four very small reactors in the Siberian town of Bilibino, and one in the Urals at the city of Beloyarsk. The Beloyarsk facility is a breeder reactor and thus yields fissionable uranium, which can either produce more commercial reactor fuel or serve as the start-up material for the manufacture of nuclear weapons (Pryde and Bradley 1994). In 2007 the Russian government announced a plan to expand the number of new, commercial nuclear power plants by as many as twenty-six by the year 2030 (Weir 2007). At the same time, an expansion plan announced in 1993 has been largely unfulfilled (Marples 1993).

It is not commonly known that all commercial nuclear power plants store their radioactive wastes on-site, at least initially. Used reactor cores must be kept well isolated from human contact, as they contain what is termed high-level radiation. The treatment and storage of Russia's high-level wastes is conducted near the cities of Dimitrovgrad and Kyshtym. Radioactive materials that are not so dangerous, called low- and medium-level wastes, are treated and stored in various ways at a number of locations throughout the country.

The work of processing uranium for nuclear weapons, and building them, was carried out at a number of "secret cities," which were not even shown on public maps (Rowland 1996). Since 1991 these secret cities have been opened up and visited by specialists from the United States and elsewhere. Many operate nuclear research centers or process nuclear wastes and some engage in disassembling nuclear warheads (Bradley 1997). Some of the most significant radiation releases have occurred at facilities near certain of these cities, such as Kyshtym and Tomsk.

Although the explosion at the Chernobyl nuclear reactor occurred in the neighboring country of Ukraine, the accident was not far from the Russian

Table 9.3 Nuclear Power Plants in the Russian Federation

Name of Complex	Site (nearest town)	Reactor Type[a]	Units Operating	Units Shut Down	Units Planned or Under Construction	Reactor Size (megawatts)	Year 1st Unit on Line
Balakova	Balakova	VVER	4		2	1,000	1985
Beloyarsk	Zarechny	LMFBR	1	2	1	600	1964
Bilibino	Bilibino	LWGR	4			12	1973
Kalinin	Udomlia	VVER	3			1,000	1984
Kola	Polyarnye Zori	VVER	4		2	440	1973
Kursk	Kurchatov	RBMK	4		1	1,000	1976
Leningrad	Sosnovy Bor	RBMK	4			1,000	1973
Novovoronezh	Novovoronezh	VVER	3	2	2	1,000; 440	1964
Rostov	Volgodonsk	VVER	1			1,000	2001
Smolensk	Desnogorsk	RBMK	3			1,000	1982

Sources: Adapted from Pryde and Bradley 1994, table 2; Bradley 1997, 587–588; International Nuclear Safety Center 2005.
Notes: The table does not include proposed complexes where planning or construction has been stopped at Arkhangelsk, Bashkir, Gorky, Kostroma, Rostov, Tatarstan, Volgograd, and Voronezh.
a. VVER, pressurized-water reactors; RBMK, graphite-moderated reactors; LWGR, light water–cooled graphite reactors; LMFBR, liquid metal fast-breeder reactor.

border, and contamination occurred over a large adjacent area of the Russian Federation. This area includes portions of the provinces of Bryansk, Orel, Tula, Kaluga, and Kursk. Radiation was released into the atmosphere for over a week, and fell out as far away as Scandinavia (OECD 1995). Questions still remain concerning human health problems and long-term contamination of land and water in regions receiving fallout.

No credible figure of fatalities within Russia from the Chernobyl accident is available, but as many as fifty thousand persons may have been evacuated from fallout regions in Russia alone, some not until years after the accident occurred. The safety of clean-up crews was often slighted (Marples 2004). Illnesses associated with the accident include a sharply increased incidence of thyroid cancer in children since 1989 in adjacent areas of Russia, and in Ukraine and Belarus as well (Bradley 1997). Concerns about radioactive contamination of soil has curtailed agricultural activities, and water supplies in some regions must be constantly tested for high radiation readings.

Several major nuclear facilities are located in the central Ural Mountains region, which is the portion of the Russian Federation most contaminated by nuclear radiation. The nuclear facilities are situated near two of the former "secret cities," which are now called Ozersk and Snezhinsk, and are located about 100 kilometers northwest of Chelyabinsk. Ozersk is the site of the Mayak Production Association, which is the main site in Russia for reprocessing atomic wastes. Unfortunately, a number of major accidents have occurred here that, collectively, have released more high-level radiation than the Chernobyl incident (Monroe 1992).

The first, in the 1950s, was the dumping of millions of cubic meters of nuclear wastes directly into the Techa River, which drains into, and therefore contaminated, the larger Tobol and Ob rivers. The second crisis occurred in September 1957. Kept secret for many years, it involved a chemical explosion in a high-level waste-storage tank, which released about two million curies of radiation that were blown downwind hundreds of kilometers. As a result of this accident 7,500 residents had to be evacuated from twenty nearby villages, and large areas of forests were destroyed by radiation (Medvedev 1979).

The third large release of radiation at Mayak involved high-level wastes in a storage pond known as Lake Karachai. The filling of Lake Karachai began in 1951, but the main radiation release at the lake occurred in 1967 when, after a drought, winds picked up radioactive dust from the exposed shoreline and deposited it up to seventy-five kilometers (more than forty-six miles) away. The lake has since been stabilized, but it remains as the major radiation concern at the troubled Mayak facility (Bradley 1997).

In all, at least 130 million curies of radioactivity have been discharged into the environment from the incidents at Mayak. This represents about two and a half times the amount of radiation released at Chernobyl. It has been estimated that about five hundred thousand people have been exposed to high radiation doses from the Mayak accidents, and about eighteen thousand have been relocated. Over 2,000 workers at the plants have suffered occupational radiation sickness, 935 people have been diagnosed with chronic radiation sickness, and 37 cases of leukemia have been reported (Bradley 1997).

Siberia, like the Ural Mountains, became a preferred location for secret nuclear activities due to its remoteness. Several of the most important facilities were located near the cities of Tomsk and Krasnoyarsk. These facilities store the world's most extensive deposits of uncontained radioactive wastes, which include an estimated 1.45 billion curies of liquid wastes alone (Bradley 1997). "Uncontained" means susceptible to being released into the atmosphere or water bodies.

The former secret complex "Tomsk-7" (now Seversk) houses the Siberian Chemical Combine, which reprocesses and stores high-level radioactive wastes. Scientists at the complex have stated that about 127,000 metric tons of solid wastes and 33 million cubic meters of liquid wastes have been stored underground at Tomsk-7. Some liquid wastes have been discharged directly into the Tom River. Tomsk-7 became known to the world in April 1993, when a chemical explosion in a uranium processing tank at the Siberian Chemical Combine sent a highly radioactive plume into the atmosphere. Although not as large as the Chernobyl or Mayak accidents, the Tomsk incident did contaminate approximately 123 square kilometers (about 47 square miles), fortunately in a lightly populated area (Bradley 1997). Children were evacuated from the nearby village of Georgievka, but not until more than a week after the explosion.

Even larger nuclear complexes exist at two secret cities near Krasnoyarsk along the Yenisey River. One, now called Zheleznogorsk, produced plutonium and lies partly in vast subterranean chambers that include a tunnel over two kilometers (about 1.25 miles) long under the Yenisey River. Over a million curies of radiation have been released into the Yenisey River from the atomic reactors at Zheleznogorsk (Bradley 1997) and could create future problems. Much of this radiation has settled into the bottom sediments, but these sediments are subject to scouring in large floods.

Further to the north, there are several locations of nuclear contamination in the Arctic region, especially on Novaya Zemlya Island and the Kola Peninsula. On the Kola Peninsula near the cities of Murmansk and Severomorsk, and on Andreev Bay, are several locations where decommissioned nuclear submarines and reactor components are stored (Bradley 1997). These obsolete submarines are slowly being dismantled and their radioactive components relocated, but they will represent a potential pollution problem for years to come. Some of the subs are old and leaky and two have sunk, one with a significant loss of lives.

The large Arctic island of Novaya Zemlya was the main Soviet nuclear weapons testing base during the Cold War. A total of 132 tests were conducted here, including 86 in the atmosphere, 43 underground, and 3 under the ocean. Two-thirds of the underground explosions vented radiation into the atmosphere. In 1961, the largest hydrogen bomb ever built (fifty-eight megatons) was exploded over Novaya Zemlya, and resulted in fallout all around the Northern Hemisphere.

In addition to the terrestrial contamination, nuclear wastes, at least four scuttled ships with nuclear reactors, and thousands of individual waste containers were deposited in the ocean at about eleven sites in adjacent portions of the Kara Sea (Pryde and Bradley 1994). Russian Federation officials have acknowledged that the USSR deposited high-level radioactive wastes at many sites in the Barents and Kara seas from 1964 to 1986 in violation of the London Convention, which prohibits the ocean dumping of nuclear wastes.

Radiation reaches the Kara Sea not only from these and other Russian sites, but also from foreign sources, such as the British Sellefield Facility and the French plant at La Hague. As a result, there is concern for the overall condition of the Kara Sea, a rich fisheries region. Most of the wastes deposited offshore from Novaya Zemlya are either in containers or in the sea-bottom sediments, and pose no immediate danger. The concern is over possible future disturbances to these sediments or containers, and subsequent ecological effects to oceanic food chains.

Further east, there are several nuclear facilities along the coastline of the Russian Far East. Similar to the Kola Peninsula, submarine and other nuclear wastes are stored here, often improperly. At least one serious accident has taken place, a 1985 explosion in a submarine's nuclear reactor at the Chazhma Ship Repair Facility. Radioactivity was spread over a distance of several kilometers.

In addition to the testing on Novaya Zemlya, the Soviet Union's other atmospheric nuclear test site was in Kazakhstan just west of Semipalatinsk (now renamed Semey). It is the most highly contaminated location in Kazakhstan: 467 nuclear tests were carried out there, including atmospheric explosions from 1949 to 1963 (Bradley 1997). This site was sufficiently close to Russia (see Map 9.1) that on twenty-two occasions, measurable fallout was recorded in Russia's adjacent Altai Territory. The government of the newly independent nation of Kazakhstan shut down the test facility in 1991.

Starting in 1965, the Soviet Union carried out 115 so-called peaceful underground nuclear explosions at numerous locations in Russia and four of the other USSR republics (Bradley 1997; Scherbakova and Wallace 1993). Most of these subsurface detonations were for economic reasons, such as stimulating oil or natural gas production. Although these tests did not produce significant contamination, some did vent radiation to the surface, either at the time of the blast or subsequently.

In summary, in their efforts to heighten national security during the Cold War, the leaders of the USSR created a landscape with vast areas of serious radioactive contamination problems. The consequences can be grouped under three main headings: (1) the immediate economic costs of isolating and cleaning contaminated areas, (2) the costs of addressing the resulting human health problems, and (3) the long-term environmental problems of contaminated soils and water bodies. Since these economic costs are beyond the means of the Russian treasury, considerable foreign assistance will be needed, and is currently being provided, to remedy the most pressing problems.

It was suggested earlier that a fundamental cause of these problems was the tendency of the USSR not to fund sophisticated safety measures in both their military and civilian nuclear programs. Improvements will be difficult due to limited financial resources, inadequate regulatory mechanisms, the inertia of Soviet-era officials still in office, the continued operation of the flawed RBMK reactors, and the departure of skilled nuclear workers for various reasons. The Chernobyl-style RBMK reactors are no longer produced, but as Table 9.3 indicates, many are still in use. New VVER-type reactor units currently being built must now have containment domes and redundant safety features similar to those used at US and other foreign nuclear power plants.

The old Soviet penchant for secrecy is still flourishing, too. Russian citizens who sought to play a "whistleblower" role by reporting nuclear dangers that might embarrass the government have been harassed and even jailed. The most highly publicized cases were those of Alexander Nikitin and Grigory Pasko, who were arrested by the Federal Security Service (or FSB) on spurious "spying" charges when they reported threats of radioactive contamination from deactivated Soviet submarines and other sources (Loginova 2003a).

At the start of the new century, the health of millions of people in Russia and the other former republics remains at risk, and the Russian people will have to live with these problems for decades to come. The USSR has, unfortunately, taught other nations the high price of developing nuclear programs with inadequate levels of safety and waste control.

■ The Environment, Public Health, and Prospects for the Future

At various points in this chapter, the connection between environmental deterioration and public health has been noted. Decreased life expectancy and increased infant mortality have unfortunately become commonplace, and while there are more causes than just environmental deterioration, it is unquestionably a major factor. Pollution-related illnesses are a serious problem in contemporary Russia and have been well documented statistically, particularly in the book by Feshbach and Friendly (1992) cited in the bibliography to this chapter.

The environmental situation in Russia at the start of the twenty-first century must be characterized as acute. During the 1980s and 1990s, Russian geographers mapped the USSR, and smaller portions of the Russian Republic as well, in terms of environmental quality. Of the sixteen regions that were designated as being in the worst category, regions termed "critical environmental areas," ten were in what is now the Russian Federation, the capital city of Moscow among them (Pryde 1994). Although almost all these problem areas were inherited from the former Soviet Union, the current Russian government must now find some way to address them.

What can be done to correct these troubling environmental situations? There is no instant cure. A number of factors must change or improve significantly. First and foremost, there needs to be concerned political leadership. This means that the government must recognize the importance of enhancing Russia's environmental quality above its unimpressive current levels and take appropriate actions. The Soviet government often paid only lip service to environmental issues. Many Soviet-era bureaucrats remain firmly entrenched in office and still tend to like huge projects, central control, and secrecy, or at least minimal public input. Throughout the Russian bureaucracy there remains a tendency to make speeches on behalf of environmental improvement, with minimal effective follow-up. The reality is that corruption, graft, and profiteering are still widespread. At the same time, the concept of sustainable development needs to be understood and embraced (Oldfield, Kouzmina, and Shaw 2003).

The Russian government needs to do much more than it is, but there is reason to question its resolve. As one notable example, in May 2000, Putin announced the abolishment of the State Committee for Environmental Protection, the agency that had been responsible for pollution control and sustainable natural resource management. Its functions were transferred to the Russian Ministry of Natural Resources, a ministry historically devoted to resource exploitation and economic development (Peterson and Bielke 2001; Oldfield, 2005). It remains to be seen how this reorganization will affect the quality of Russia's environment and natural resources over the long term.

The Russian public needs to play a larger and stronger role in the nation's environmental affairs. Support, and indeed demand, for environmental improvements must come from the public, if the administration and representatives to the State Duma are to be moved. But this is difficult in a country whose older generations faced prison for engaging in what the Soviet government termed "volunteerism," that is, acts of citizen involvement, which in Western countries would be viewed as desirable public engagement in the affairs of a participatory democracy. Older Russians still remember the KGB all too well. Simply put, the majority of Russian citizens, especially older ones, generally do not become personally involved with environmental problems and often either deny or ignore them. In addition to the passivity of much of the Russian public, the work of environmental groups, as noted earlier, is undermined by periodic harassment by the so-called *siloviki,* the power ministries and agencies of the Russian state (Loginova 2003a).

Nevertheless, citizen environmental groups have existed and indeed proliferated in Russia beginning in the late 1980s. The largest is the nationwide Socio-Ecological Union. Groups such as the SEU are linked electronically to similar organizations in the rest of the world (DeBardeleben 1992; Mezhdunarodnyi n.d.). To encourage participation in such citizen activist groups, a broader and more sophisticated level of environmental education in the schools would also be a desirable step forward.

Economic limitations have been mentioned throughout the chapter. As the Russian economy improves, hopefully more money will be made available for environmental improvements. As noted, though, Russia's resources are nowhere near adequate to clean up all the environmental messes inherited from the Soviet Union. A large measure of both financial support and diplomatic pressure from the world community will be needed as well. It will need to come from both governmental agencies and from private enterprises that do business in Russia.

Certainly, there is tremendous outside interest in the potential integration of Russia and its resources into the greater world economy. This is particularly true with regard to its "frontier" areas of Siberia and the Russian Far East (Kotkin and Wolff 1995; Mote 1998; Newell 2004; Rodgers 1990). All parties need to understand and agree that a part of that integration needs to include adequate environmental protection measures.

Although it will take much time and vast resources to clean up all the sites and sources of residual pollution in Russia, the task is not impossible. If the Russian state were to assign a high priority to the mission, and if other nations continue to be ready to assist, Russia could eventually join the ranks of the world's leaders, not only as a military and economic power but as a country that values the environmental health of its land and its people.

■ Bibliography

Agence France Presse. 2003a. "Global Warming Could Turn Siberia into Disaster Zone," October 2.
———. 2003b. "Sakhalin Energy Project a Threat to Russian Environment, Ecologists Say," November 1.

The Banker (Financial Times). 2003. "Energy Boost," October 6. http://www.the banker.com/news/fullstory.php/aid/735/Energy_boost.html.

Bityukova, Viktoria R., and Robert Argenbright. 2002. "Environmental Pollution in Moscow: A Micro-Level Analysis." *Eurasian Geography and Economics* 43(3): 197–215.

Bond, Andrew. 1984. "Air Pollution in Norilsk: A Soviet Worst Case?" *Soviet Geography* 25(9): 665–680.

———, ed. 1991. "Panel on Siberia: Economic and Territorial Issues." *Soviet Geography* 32(6): 363–432.

Borisova, Yevgenia. 2003. "Auctions Provide Incentive to Poach." *Moscow Times,* July 17.

Bradley, Don J. 1997. *Behind the Nuclear Curtain: Radioactive Waste Management in the Former Soviet Union,* ed. David R. Payson. Columbus, OH: Battelle Press.

Center for Russian Nature Conservation. 2003. *Russian Conservation News* (Special issue: The Transformation of Protected Areas in Russia, A Ten-Year Review) 33 (Summer).

———. 2007. *Russian Conservation News* 42 (Winter).

Chebakova, I. V. 1997. *National Parks of Russia.* Moscow: Biodiversity Conservation Center.

DeBardeleben, Joan. 1992. "The New Politics in the USSR: The Case of the Environment." In *The Soviet Environment: Problems, Policies, and Politics,* ed. John Massey Stewart. Cambridge, UK: Cambridge University Press.

Eliseev, N. V., et al., eds. 1983. *Krasnaia kniga RSFSR* [Red book of the RSFSR]. Moscow: Rosselkhozizdat.

Feshbach, Murray, and Alfred Friendly. 1992. *Ecocide in the USSR.* New York: Basic Books.

Holley, David. 2003a. "Russian Officials See Shadow of Illegal Loggers in Forest Fires." *Los Angeles Times,* June 29.

———. 2003b. "Russia Will Not Sign the Kyoto Treaty." *Los Angeles Times,* December 3.

International Nuclear Safety Center. 2005. United States Department of Energy. "Maps of Nuclear Power Reactors: Russia." http://www.insc.anl.gov/pwrmaps/map/russia.php.

ITAR-TASS. 2003a. "President's Agency Reports High Water, Air Pollution Levels in Russia," November 18. In *BBC Monitoring International Reports,* November 18.

———. 2003b. "Russia Loses Vast Area of Forest to Fires in 2003." In *BBC Monitoring International Reports,* September 16.

Knystautas, Algirdas. 1987. *The Natural History of the USSR.* New York: McGraw-Hill.

Komarov, Boris [Ze'ev Wolfson]. 1980. *The Destruction of Nature in the Soviet Union.* White Plains, NY: M. E. Sharpe.

Kommersant. 2004. "Russian Companies Will Need 100 Years to Fully Restore Polluted Land." February 10.

Kotkin, Stephen, and David Wolff, eds. 1995. *Rediscovering Russia in Asia: Siberia and the Russian Far East.* Armonk, NY: M. E. Sharpe.

Loginova, Viktoria. 2003a. "Russian Environmentalists Face Indifference, Harassment." Agence France Presse, August 30.

———. 2003b. "World Bank Loan Could End Baikal Pollution, but Ecologists Have Doubts." Agence France Presse, August 14.

Mackay, Anson, Roger Flower, and Liba Granina. 2003. "Lake Baikal." In *The Physical Geography of Northern Eurasia,* ed. Maria Shahgedanova. Oxford, UK: Oxford University Press.

Marples, David R. 1993. "The Post-Soviet Nuclear Power Program." *Post-Soviet Geography* 34(3): 172–184.

———. 2004. "Chernobyl: A Reassessment." *Eurasian Geography and Economics* 45(8): 588–607.

Massey Stewart, John. 1992. *The Soviet Environment: Problems, Policies, and Politics.* Cambridge, UK: Cambridge University Press.

Medvedev, Zhores. 1979. *Nuclear Disaster in the Urals.* New York: W. W. Norton.

Mezhdunarodnyi sotsial'no-ekologicheskii soiuz [International Socio-Ecological Union]. n.d. http://www.seu.ru.

Monroe, Scott D. 1992. "Chelyabinsk: The Evolution of Disaster." *Post-Soviet Geography* 33(8): 533–545.

Mote, Victor L. 1998. *Siberia: Worlds Apart.* Boulder, CO: Westview Press.

Newell, Josh. 2004. *The Russian Far East: A Reference Guide for Conservation and Development.* 2nd ed. McKinleyville, CA: Daniel & Daniel.

Nilsen, Thomas, and Nils Bøhmer. 1994. *Sources of Radioactive Contamination in Murmansk and Arkhangel'sk Counties.* Oslo: Bellona Foundation.

OECD (Organization for Economic Cooperation and Development). 1995. Nuclear Energy Agency. *Chernobyl Ten Years On: Radiological and Health Impact: An Assessment by the NEA Committee on Radiation Protection and Public Health.* Paris: OECD Publications. http://www.nea.fr/html/rp/chernobyl/chernobyl-1995 .pdf.

Oldfield, Jonathan D. 2005. *Russian Nature: Exploring the Environmental Consequences of Societal Change.* Aldershot, UK: Ashgate.

Oldfield, Jonathan D., Anna Kouzmina, and Denis J. B. Shaw. 2003. "Russia's Involvement in the International Environmental Process: A Research Report." *Eurasian Geography and Economics* 44(2): 157–168.

Panyushkin, Valery. 2003. "Half Our Children Won't Live to Retirement Age." *Kommersant,* June 2. In *Current Digest of the Post-Soviet Press* 55(22), July 2.

Peterson, D. J. 1993. *Troubled Lands: The Legacy of Soviet Environmental Destruction.* Boulder, CO: Westview Press.

Peterson, D. J., and Eric K. Bielke. 2001. "The Reorganization of Russia's Environmental Bureaucracy: Implications and Prospects." *Post-Soviet Geography and Economics* 42(1): 65–76.

Potter, William C. 1993. *Nuclear Profiles of the Soviet Successor States.* Monterey, CA: Program for Nonproliferation Studies, Monterey Institute of International Studies.

Pryde, Philip R. 1972. *Conservation in the Soviet Union.* Cambridge, UK: Cambridge University Press.

———. 1987. "The Distribution of Endangered Fauna in the USSR." *Biological Conservation* 42(1): 19–37.

———. 1991. *Environmental Management in the Soviet Union.* Cambridge, UK: Cambridge University Press.

———. 1994. "Observations on the Mapping of Critical Environmental Zones in the Former Soviet Union." *Post-Soviet Geography* 35(1): 38–49.

———, ed. 1995. *Environmental Resources and Constraints in the Former Soviet Republics.* Boulder, CO: Westview Press.

———. 1997. "Post-Soviet Development and Status of Russian Nature Reserves." *Post-Soviet Geography and Economics* 38(2): 63–80.

———. 1999. "The Privatization of Nature Conservation in Russia." *Post-Soviet Geography and Economics* 40(5): 383–394.

———. 2003. "Radioactive Contamination." In *The Physical Geography of Northern Eurasia,* ed. Maria Shahgedanova. Oxford, UK: Oxford University Press.

Pryde, Philip R., and Don J. Bradley. 1994. "The Geography of Radioactive Contamination in the Former USSR." *Post-Soviet Geography* 35(10): 557–593.

Rodgers, Allan L., ed. 1990. *The Soviet Far East.* London: Routledge.

Rowland, Richard. 1996. "Russia's Secret Cities." *Post-Soviet Geography and Economics* 37(7): 426–462.

Sample, Ian. 2005. "Warming Hits 'Tipping Point': Siberia Feels the Heat." *Guardian,* August 11.

Scherbakova, Anna, and Wendy Wallace. 1993. "The Environmental Legacy of Soviet Peaceful Nuclear Explosions." *CIS Environmental Watch* 4 (Summer): 33–56.

Solovyova, Yulia. 2003. "Paw Prints Disappearing for Siberia's Amur Tiger." *Moscow Times,* October 8.

Tavernise, Sabrina. 2003. "Pollution Gets a Shrug as Production Booms." *International Herald Tribune,* October 6.

Vilchek, Gregory. 2002. "Environmental Impacts of Oil and Gas Development." In *The Physical Geography of Northern Eurasia,* ed. M. Shahgedanova. Oxford, UK: Oxford University Press.

Walsh, Nick P. 2003. "St. Petersburg in Race to Hold Back Rising Waters." *Guardian,* July 29.

Weiner, Douglas R. 1999. *A Little Corner of Freedom.* Berkeley: University of California Press.

Weir, Fred. 2007. "Russia Plans Big Nuclear Expansion." *Christian Science Monitor,* July 17.

World Wildlife Fund. 2007. "Russia Declares Parks for Tiger Conservation." *Focus* 29(5).

Ziegler, Charles E. 1987. *Environmental Policy in the USSR.* Amherst: University of Massachusetts Press.

ZumBrunnen, Craig. 1984. "A Review of Soviet Water Quality Management: Theory and Practice." In *Geographical Studies on the Soviet Union: Essays in Honor of Chauncy D. Harris,* research paper no. 211, ed. George J. Demko and Roland J. Fuchs. Chicago: University of Chicago, Department of Geography.

10

Women in a Changing Context

Sarah L. Henderson

Those who have navigated the transition from the Soviet Union to an independent Russian Federation have weathered attempted coups, corrupted elections, financial crashes, social upheaval, and civil war. The collapse of communism launched a revolutionary set of changes in political, economic, and social institutions in Russia that transformed the daily lives of almost everyone. However, the change has posed different and in some ways more severe challenges for Russia's women. Although elections have, in general, opened up the political process to a variety of new actors, most of the key political players have been men. Once ensured significant though often not meaningful political representation, women have struggled to establish a political voice in the new Russia. Economically, Russia's citizens have endured a wrenching process of transition since the late 1980s. Women have suffered disproportionately; wage gaps between men and women have soared as men have come to dominate the financially lucrative sectors of the economy. Furthermore, in the face of a retreating state and an erratic economy, women have come under increasing pressure to "hold things together" at home.

This chapter considers the many challenges facing women in today's Russia, and the ways in which their experiences—in an age of great political, economic, and social change—diverge from those of men. Many of the problems confronting women in contemporary Russia are not new. In fact, their experiences are the latest expression of enduring historical patterns of gendered divisions of labor in politics, economics, and society. As such, the chapter begins with a brief overview of the conditions women faced during the imperial era, followed by a discussion of the Soviet period. In both eras government policies were male-dominated and class-oriented. Whereas the tsarist state provided a few special benefits and limited employment opportunities to upper-class women, Soviet policies offered more options for working-class and peasant women. In both of these eras, however, women were treated as second-class citizens and paid a high price for their progress (Hutton 1996, 63). As was true during the imperial and Soviet periods, women in post-Soviet Russia have borne the brunt of the costs of political, economic, and social change. Further, throughout these three eras, women's rights have often taken a back seat to what have been deemed as "more pressing" political and economic issues.

It is important to note, too, that when speaking of "Russian women," one must be careful to avoid overly simplistic generalizations. Women are joined by their gender but also separated by large class, cultural, and ethnic differences. There is no single "woman's experience" in any of the three eras surveyed here. Thus, although the chapter provides an overview of many of the challenges that have confronted and continue to confront women in Russia, it is by no means exhaustive.

■ Women in Imperial Russia

It is difficult to discuss women in imperial Russia without starting off with a qualification. Elite women and peasant women lived markedly different lives, and when we speak of "women in imperial Russia," for the most part we are speaking of the experiences of a small percentage of women (Engel 2004). Although the majority of women were peasants, we know less about their lives because most peasant women could not read or write. As a result, they left behind few clues as to their thoughts, feelings, and experiences. In addition, because serfdom ended relatively late in Russia, and industrialization did not begin until late in the nineteenth century, peasant women tended to be less affected by the broader economic, social, cultural, and political developments that were changing elite women's lives. Indeed, throughout the imperial era (1700–1917), the lives of Russia's peasant women remained remarkably same in that they were primarily a source of labor, and their lives were similarly punctuated by arranged marriages, childbearing, child rearing, and labor in the home and in the fields. Thus, the story of women in imperial Russia as relayed in this chapter is really a commentary on the lives of upper-class women.

The lives of elite women began to change under Peter the Great (reigned 1682–1725), whose reforms, at least in part, sought Russia's absorption of European norms and customs. In pre-Petrine Russia, women had little to no role in the public realm. Women were valued for what they could add to the household in terms of family connections and labor, both in terms of production and reproduction. In upper-class families, women were often secluded and lived in their own special quarters, known as the *terem* (Engel 2004, 6). The most dominant institution in a woman's life (besides her marriage) was the Orthodox Church, which stressed women's physical and moral weakness in comparison to men's, and their duty to submit to the authority and guidance of the male head of the household. For thousands of women (many of them widows with grown children), the most virtuous path in life was one that led them to the convent (Clements 1991, 3–5).

Peter the Great's effort to "Europeanize" Russia impacted women. As was the custom in Europe, they were now expected to mingle in public and serve as public accessories to their husbands. To encourage this unique form of state service, women were forbidden from entering monastic life during their reproductive years (Engel 2004, 13). Catherine the Great (reigned 1762–1796) further broadened the opportunities available to women by founding the first state-supported school for girls. Housed in a former monastery, the Smolnyi Institute provided an education for about nine hundred elite women during Catherine's reign, including not only daughters of the nobility but also daughters of mid-ranking military officers and civil servants (Stites 1978, 4). Much in line with Peter the Great's vision, Catherine's interest in advancing the educational opportunities of young women fit within the larger goal of supporting a male-dominated state. Thus, education at Smolnyi focused primarily on ensuring that women would make adequate spouses and mothers of state servitors. Despite this limitation, increasing access to education was one of the most significant developments for women during the imperial era.

The small sphere of opportunity for elite women was further enlarged by Alexander II (reigned 1855–1881), who implemented a variety of liberalizing reforms. In addition to affecting the lives of women directly, these reforms unleashed numerous debates, including one that was referred to simply as the *zhenskii vopros,* or the "woman question." In sum, this question asked what the role of women in society was to be, and in what ways the state could better prepare women to live meaningful and productive lives. Initially, discussions revolved around upgrading the type of education women received so that they were prepared to function beyond their traditional roles as wives and mothers. During this era of Great Reforms, educational opportunities for women gradually expanded. On this question and others, however, Alexander II's record was mixed. For instance, in 1858, he established provincial secondary schools for girls, but poorly funded them (Hutton 1996, 64). In 1859, women were allowed to attend lectures at Russian universities, but were excluded from regular university study. Thus, a small percentage of Russian women enrolled in university in Zurich, Switzerland, to complete their educations, often with great success (Stites 1978, 55). Given that women could not travel without the permission of their fathers or husbands, several women gamely embarked on fictitious marriages in order to gain an education. Sofia Kovalevskaia, for example, contracted such a marriage so that she might study in Heidelberg, Germany, eventually becoming the first woman in Europe to earn a doctorate in mathematics and the first to hold a university chair position (Engel 2004, 78).

Although the government continued to exclude women from regular university study, in 1872 it established a four-year course of study to train women midwives. Four years later, another year of education was added to the program, now known as the "Women's Medical Courses" (Engel 2004, 77). These reforms were launched, at least in part, in response to demands to keep young Russian women at home in Russia, and thus away from the radicalizing influences of Zurich. The regime also tolerated increases in the number of women in careers, such as the medical and educational professions, that were not already overcrowded by men (Hutton 1996, 64). Despite these developments, educated women were still the exception, not the rule. Even by 1894, only 1 percent of all females were in school. For that matter, only 3.9 percent of all boys were in school, an indication of the vast divide between the peasantry and the upper and middle classes in Russia (Stites 1978, 166).

However, education did have spillover effects. Access to education for some women also meant access to radicalizing ideas, and in the process of their studies a few women joined some of the small, underground movements pushing for political change in Russia. In 1878, for example, Vera Zasulich shot and seriously wounded General Trepov, the governor general of St. Petersburg. Women made up one-third of the leadership of the People's Will, the organization that successfully plotted the assassination of Alexander II in 1881 (Clements 1991, 9). Women joined the ranks, too, of other radicalized intelligentsia to push for political change. If the government was hoping to control what women learned, and to dampen the rising expectations that education often fed, it was failing miserably.

In the wake of this emergent radicalism, Tsar Alexander III (reigned 1881–1894) attempted to roll back the reforms launched by his father. Women's access to higher education was one of the first reforms to be jettisoned in his new, counterreform regime. The medical courses were discontinued. In addition, efforts launched by reformist civil servants to revise marital law to expand the grounds for divorce to include spousal abuse were rebuffed by a more assertive Russian Orthodox Church (Engel 2004, 109). However, even the tsar could not contain the effects of industrialization and the changes wrought on society. These changes, such as an increasingly literate population and an emerging individualist culture, picked up momentum under Nicholas II (reigned 1894–1917) as a weakening political system met the growing demands of an increasingly mobilized populace.

At the turn of the twentieth century, even though elite women were increasingly educated and mobilized, there were few institutionalized means through which they could utilize their education. Women who graduated from women's higher courses received only a certificate, not a degree. Only with a degree in hand could a person qualify for state examination, and thus state employment, ensuring that state service remained the realm of men. As a result, despite their education, women had few career options beyond teaching primary school (Engel 2004, 116). The exclusion of women from state service meant that they had scant ability to influence government decisions except as wives, sisters, or mothers. This gap between training and opportunities fueled their frustration and sense of relative deprivation. This situation became increasingly difficult to maintain as more women gained access to education.

While a small contingency of radical women had agitated for reform throughout the latter half of the nineteenth century, there was no genuine women's movement until 1905, when Nicholas II implemented a slew of reforms to further modernize Russia. Very quickly, two different kinds of women's activism emerged. One, a feminist strand, diverging from the nineteenth-century tradition of philanthropic activism, focused on winning women's suffrage. The other, a socialist strand, focused on workers' issues and on recruiting women to the larger socialist cause. Both were led by women of the intelligentsia. Both attempted to expand to the growing class of women workers and servants (Stites 1978, 160). While neither type of activism on the part of women was widespread, both were indicative of the increasing volatility of Russian society as it headed into World War I.

World War I (1914–1918) served to increase the mobility of women, at the same time further eroding the authority of the tsar. Russia's war effort mobilized 14.6 million men into service, many of whom had been the family breadwinner (Engel 2004, 128). The transfer of so many men from the country's factories to the front created new job opportunities for women, although factory owners viewed them mainly as cheap and temporary sources of labor (Goldman 2002). Indeed, the percentage of women workers in industry rose from about a third of the labor force in 1914, to about half in 1917 (Stites 1978, 287). The influx of women, as well as increasing levels of general political agitation, fostered increased labor activism on the part of women, who called for day care, maternity leave, and nursing breaks. The issue of equal pay for equal work was not an issue on the negotiating table, however, as most women sought improvement in their lives as mothers, not as workers (Engel 2004, 119). During the war, too, elite women who had gained access to university courses finally won the right to teach in secondary schools (Engel 2004, 131).

The abdication of Nicholas II in March 1917, and the installation of a provisional government soon after, led to new political and economic opportunities for women. The small but vocal women's movement, which had first emerged in the wake of the 1905 revolution, successfully pushed for women's suffrage. Women also gained equal rights with men for employment in the civil service, and women lawyers won the right to serve as attorneys and represent clients in court. Women also won the right to wage war. Partially in the hope that it would shame men into a more enthusiastic commitment at the front, the Provisional Government approved the formation of the all-female Petrograd and Moscow Battalion of Death (Stites 1978, 295–300; Stockdale 2004).

Unlike their counterparts in Russia's upper and middle classes, few lower-class women were at the forefront of political action. Even as some lower-class women took advantage of their newly won rights and opportunities, none assumed leadership positions in the revolution being made partly in their name. Although comprising over half of the labor force, women were poorly represented in trade-union factory committees. Of the few examples of organized action, women tended to frame their demands as economic, rather than political, and based their claims on their status as wives and mothers, rather than as citizens (Engel 2004, 135–140).

In the midst of this time of political upheaval, a small, relatively unknown political faction emerged that appealed directly to women for their votes, promising to equalize relations between the sexes. Calling themselves the Bolsheviks, this revolutionary party proposed socializing housework by handing the tedious task over to paid workers, thus enabling women to join the paid labor force. In so doing, the Bolsheviks argued, women would be earning incomes, thus freeing themselves from marrying out of economic necessity and no longer having to exchange domestic and sexual services for a man's financial support.

▓ The Soviet Woman

After seizing power in November 1917, the Bolsheviks attempted to turn their rhetoric of equality for women into reality, seeking not only to recruit women to new economic and political roles but also to redefine the family and to alter deeply ingrained cultural values, attitudes, and behaviors. At the time, it was the most far-reaching attempt to radically transform the position and status of women in a society (Lapidus 1978, 3). In 1918, the new Soviet government enacted a family code that promised to alter traditional norms and customs within family life. Marriage was removed from the control of the church. Married couples could choose either partner's surname. Illegitimate children were granted the same legal rights as legitimate ones. Divorces became easily obtainable by either spouse. Working women were granted eight weeks paid maternity leave before and after childbirth. In separate legislation, abortion, if performed by a physician, was legalized. In addition, the government launched ambitious education campaigns to bring literacy to women, particularly those in remote rural areas.

In 1919, the Bolshevik Party Central Committee formed the *zhenotdel,* or Woman's Bureau, to better coordinate party work among women. Originally formed for the relatively mundane task of linking the party's message with a female constituency, the *zhenotdel* soon became involved in women's affairs in all spheres of life by setting up child-care centers and communal dining halls, launching literacy campaigns, and mobilizing female factory workers to help women balance their multiple political, economic, and social responsibilities (Engel 2004, 143). In all spheres, the Bolsheviks intimated, the status of women was equal to that of men.

Despite this initial outburst of revolutionary idealism, the Soviet regime, throughout its history, was always more progressive in rhetoric than in deed. While the law could mandate gender equality, only the Soviet state could enforce it. While the communist regime implemented policies that allowed women to make advances in terms of political representation, job opportunities, and social status, these halting steps forward were often met with great resistance from men and required great sacrifices on the part of women. At times, too, the state reversed its progressive rhetoric by implementing policies and procedures that fostered a much more traditional view of women and their "appropriate" roles in society. In many instances, the support for women's rights was often sacrificed in the face of other, "more important" tasks in the drive to make the Soviet Union economically, politically, and socially powerful on the world stage. Thus, even though women were often told that they were equal, they were in fact bearing terribly unequal burdens in politics, at work, and at home. Although the lives of women did radically change during this period, the reality of their existence rarely matched the ideal presented by the Bolsheviks in 1917.

Women and the Making of the Soviet System

In the years following the Bolshevik Revolution, women activists confronted a shifting political landscape as the party transitioned from revolutionary rule to the routine governance of the new Soviet state. On the one hand, the proportion of women among the Bolshevik Party's rank and file nearly doubled in a decade, increasing from 7.5 percent to just over 13 percent by the end of the 1920s. Women also increased their representation in regional soviets, from the low single digits in the early 1920s to about one-third in 1934. Nonparty women, too, were increasingly mobilized in party-organized activities. By 1928, more than two million women were participating in *zhenotdel*-sponsored internships, workshops, and gatherings. On the other hand, women could not break through to the upper echelons of the party. In the early 1920s, for instance, as the party consolidated its power and created its key decision-making bodies, many prominent women, including Bolshevik luminaries Alexandra Kollontai, Inessa Armand, and Lenin's wife, Nadezhda Krupskaia, were elbowed aside. In 1930, after almost fifteen years of Soviet rule, women comprised just under 3 percent of the membership of the Central Committee (Nechemias 1996, 18–19). In the same year, Stalin declared the "woman question," the resolution of which had been a critical component of early Bolshevik policy, "solved." The emancipation and advancement of Soviet women now took a backseat to Stalin's ambitious economic goals, which called for the country's rapid economic development. Instead of transforming the role of women in politics and society, women were exhorted to fill low-paying, low-skilled jobs in the labor sector while at the same time producing baby Soviet citizens on the home front. One sign of this shift in policy came with the Soviet government's decision in the late 1920s to abandon its efforts to organize women within trade unions, followed in 1930 by the abolishment of the *zhenotdel,* thus effectively extinguishing the government's official link to women and their demands as workers and destroying the network that had linked Soviet women to the party (Goldman 2002, 68).

The Soviet state also chose not to enforce a policy of equal opportunity. In the factories, men opposed the advancement of women at almost every turn, reacting with hostility toward their female colleagues. Managers resisted hiring more women. Women who had gained employment during World War I were sent back to the home, as the share of women in the labor force dropped from 45 percent in 1918 to less than 30 percent in 1928, a figure roughly equal to prewar tsarist-era levels (Engel 2004, 153). When women were hired, they filled low-paying, low-skilled jobs in such fields as textiles and food processing. On the newly collectivized farms of the early 1930s, women comprised the majority of farm laborers and supplied most of the backbreaking work (Hutton 1996, 67–72). Instead of sharing an equal role in the development of the Soviet economy, women were ghettoized in the worst jobs, which often involved strenuous physical labor.

In addition to exhorting women to join the work force as low-paid, low-skilled laborers, Stalin called upon women to step up their commitment to their reproductive responsibilities. A series of reforms were launched to strengthen the family unit and return to more traditional visions of marriage and family. In a new family code passed in 1936, abortion, except to save the life or preserve the health of the mother, was once again banned. Divorce became more complicated and expensive. Contraceptives were removed from sale, and women were given bonuses for having more than six children (Engel 2004, 178–179). The state also churned out propaganda to encourage the new desired results. In propaganda posters, male workers were portrayed as big, muscular, capable men. Women were encouraged to fulfill their "natural destiny," which presumably was to have children, care for the home, and act the loving wife. These were no longer admirable personal skills. They now were imbued with the legitimacy of serving the Soviet state in its drive to industrialize. Joseph Stalin was portrayed as the all-knowing, all-seeing patriarch at the top of the giant, happy, Soviet family.

The reality was much different, however, as women were now working feverishly to meet the increased demands of a Stalinist system that wanted increased production in the factories and reproduction at home. Yet this same system was doing relatively little to help women balance the double burden of work in the public and the private realms. For example, while day-care institutions increased ten-fold between 1928 and 1936, supply was nowhere near demand. In addition, women were spending as much time on housework as they were at their jobs, thus creating a work week that had no beginning and no end. At the same time, the Soviet state continued a propaganda campaign that portrayed their policies as the most progressive and humane in the world.

The one clear advancement of the day was in women's access to higher education, as the share of women grew from 31 percent of all students in 1926 to 43 percent in 1937 (Engel 2004, 175). Thus, women enjoyed some increased social mobility, but at a much slower and more uneven pace than either anticipated or promised in the heady days of 1917 revolutionary Russia.

World War II presented a brief hiatus in the drive to reinforce traditional family values and divisions of labor as women played critical roles in the war effort. They filled the factories that produced the weapons of war, and as the overwhelming majority of the agricultural labor force, they kept the country fed. Women also waged war. By war's end, more than a million women had performed military service on all fronts and in all branches of service, accounting for 8 percent of the total of all Soviet forces (Engel 2004, 214). They served on the front as doctors, field surgeons, medical assistants, and nurses. Yet even before the war ended in 1945, traditional divisions of labor returned. A new family code passed in 1944 made divorce even more complicated and difficult to obtain. The distinction between legitimate and illegitimate children was restored, and the cult of motherhood reached new proportions. Women were expected to heal the wounds, actual as well as metaphysical, of a war-torn nation. At the same time, the Soviet government desperately needed them to work, not only at home but in the workforce. Once again, the state asked women to perform heroic tasks both at home and at work, while lagging behind on policies that would help women carry out these tasks.

After Stalin's death in 1953, the Soviet leadership admitted that the system had fallen short in matching its rhetorical commitment to women's equality with policies that could nurture such a development, and they attempted to close this gap. In 1956, at its Twentieth Congress, the party elected a woman, Ekaterina Furtseva, to the Central Committee Secretariat. She was also elected to the Presidium (as the Politburo was then called) as a candidate, or nonvoting, member. A year later, she attained full, voting membership. Even after running afoul of Nikita Khrushchev a few years later, with the result that she lost both her Presidium and Central Committee Secretariat posts, she was appointed minister of culture, a post she held until her death in 1974 (Pavlenko 1990). Although this position lacked the political clout of many of the other ministries, Furtseva's appointments to high party and government posts represented the first time since the 1920s that a woman had been in the Soviet leadership. Under Khrushchev, the state also made an effort to reestablish lines of communication cut by Stalin between women and the party by reviving the network of *zhensovety,* or women's councils (Engel 2004, 234–235).

Still, women had little access to significant political power in the Soviet system. In fact, women reached their zenith of formal political influence in August of 1917, when they formed over 9 percent of the membership of the Central Committee, at a time when less than 8 percent of party membership was female (Lapidus 1978, 217). This figure was never again reached during the Soviet era. In 1952, the year before Stalin's death, only 3.1 percent of the members of the Central Committee of the Communist Party of the Soviet Union (CPSU) were women. In 1961, several years into Khrushchev's tenure as party leader, the figure stood at 3.3 percent. Female representation was higher in political institutions that had relatively little power. Thus, women made up 27 percent of the deputies to the USSR Supreme Soviet in 1959. At the regional and local levels, female representation was even higher. Despite this, in comparison to their male counterparts, women were more often seen than heard, frequently serving only a single term. Women were also underrepresented in the party, comprising less than 20 percent of the overall membership (Nechemias 1996, 21–23). If women did serve in government-appointed positions, they tended to be "ghettoized" into areas that were considered women's domains, such as issues concerning youth, the family, and of course, women.

Women also continued to occupy low-status, low-paying jobs in every area of the economy. Their willingness to work for low pay in light industries such as textiles helped subsidize the entire industrial economy. In agriculture, even though women represented two-thirds of the labor force in the collectives, they were the ones who toiled away in the most physically demanding and poorly paid positions, while men dominated administrative positions (Engel 2004, 235). The Soviet leadership acknowledged the secondary status of women in official speeches to the Supreme Soviet. In 1958, Khrushchev pledged to make sectors of the economy dominated by women "more productive, and this means more highly paid, too" (as quoted in Engel 2004, 236). Policy was slow to materialize, however, while progress was slow and halting. Despite the leadership's professed desire to improve the condition and status of women, it simultaneously could not afford to address the economic inequality of women. Simply put, economic growth in the Soviet system depended on the willingness of women to work the most poorly paid jobs.

Even so, the state was willing to push forward a variety of social reforms that helped women manage their private lives and balance the demands of reproduction, hearth, and home. In 1955, the government reversed itself, legalizing abortion. The government also bolstered its package of incentives to encourage women to have more children by extending paid and unpaid maternity leave. In the late 1960s, birth control became more accessible, although it was never widely available during the Soviet era. The state also promised to address the ongoing problem of day-care options. By 1965, there were spaces for 22.5 percent of eligible children, which was progress from the previous decade (Engel 2004, 238). The government also took steps to give women more control in marriage. Divorce procedures were simplified and costs reduced. This collection of family legislation, although not fundamentally altering women's working and social conditions, did improve their lives somewhat (Noonan 1996, 81).

Despite such strides, women still labored under a heavy double burden. Housework was much more time consuming in the USSR than in the United States. Soviet women did not have access to consumer products, such as washing machines, vacuum cleaners, and other time-saving devices. They had to stand in long lines at a variety of stores in order to put together meals for the family. Cooking and cleaning was further complicated by the fact that even in the mid-1950s, two-thirds of Soviet families in urban areas lacked running water. Thus, women spent as much time on housework as they did at their paying jobs. The regime tried to respond to these problems. At the Twenty-First CPSU Congress in 1959, Khrushchev promised that the Soviet leaders would turn their attention to the production of consumer goods and domestic appliances, the first time the Soviet system had made such a commitment since the 1930s. Although it took time for this policy to take effect and change the lives of most women, by the 1970s, half of all Soviet families had refrigerators and two-thirds had washing machines (Engel 2004, 237–239, 242). These small strides helped women reduce the burden of juggling work and family.

Women and the Decline of the Soviet System

Even as women began to benefit from the increased availability of consumer goods, other factors were in play that were reshaping the way women responded to the state's promise of providing the ideal Soviet family life. By the mid-1970s, the proportion of women in higher education institutions was just over 50 percent (Lapidus 1978, 150). At the same time, rural women were deserting small towns for the cities. Across the country, women were choosing to have fewer children. More educated than ever, women were becoming increasingly dissatisfied with their lives and with the gap between the ideal and the reality of the Soviet system. Small pockets of dissent formed and disturbed the calm face of highly stylized Soviet propaganda. In 1969, Natalia Baranskaia published a short story entitled "A Week Like Any

Other" in the liberal journal *Novyi mir* (*New World*). In describing the day-to-day life of a woman struggling to juggle family, work, and party commitments, Baranskaia publicly revealed the reality of Soviet women's triple burden, and the state's failure to produce an ideal society for half its citizens. Thus, even though it would be another decade and a half before the launching of sweeping reforms intended to make good on the Soviet system's promises to its people, women had already realized that socialism had failed to resolve "the woman question."

Mikhail Gorbachev's ascension to power in 1985 began a revolutionary period of intense political, economic, and social reform for all Soviet citizens. Although his economic and political reforms were quite radical by Soviet standards, his policies toward women were much less so. When discussing women's issues, Gorbachev spoke mainly in terms of needing to help women achieve their traditional roles as mother, homemaker, and child rearer, so that they could "return to their purely womanly mission" (as quoted in Noonan 1996, 84). In 1987, the Soviet leaders launched a series of pronatalist policies, but neglected to provide effective mechanisms for their enforcement. They increased the amount of paid maternity leave, but did not obligate the federal government to pay for these benefits. Instead, it became one more economic responsibility for enterprises to cover at a time of increasing economic dislocation. Responsibility for day care was transferred from the federal to the local level, with no provision for funding. As a result, spaces for children decreased as costs soared (Engel 2004, 258).

Others in the Soviet leadership echoed the motherhood theme, framing the push to send women back home as an emancipatory choice that women should be entitled to make. Initially, many women responded positively to this rationale. After all, they slaved away at work, then at home, and wished to have more time to spend with family. Soon it became clear that women were not really given a choice, as many were forcibly made redundant by the dramatic economic downturns produced by Gorbachev's policies.

At the same time, women were becoming more vocal about exposing the inadequacies of the Soviet system in improving the lives of women. At the 1987 All-Union Conference of Women, Valentina Tereshkova, the USSR's first female cosmonaut and outgoing chair of the conference, underlined the harsh realities faced by Soviet women. The media, too, in the more permissive environment of *glasnost* (openness), began to report, with brutal honesty, on the daily lives of women. The yawning gap between the happy propaganda promoted by the Soviet state and the daily grind of work, more work, and less pay, grew ever wider. Media coverage, however, portrayed a schizophrenic vision of the lives of Soviet women. At the same time that it shone a spotlight on the realities confronting women, the increasingly vocal media also borrowed a page from Western commercialism by spreading a new, glamorous, and often unrealistic portrait of the way women could live in a capitalist fairy tale. They touted beauty pageants, published magazines that emulated Western publications such as *Vogue* and *Elle,* and flouted women's bodies in pages of advertising and on newly erected billboards. Not only were women's real lives worsening, but they were being exposed to an increasingly unattainable and overly romanticized vision of what they "should" be (Bridger 1992, 185–187; Buckley 1992, 220–222; Sperling 1999, 64–78).

At the same time, women were losing even their token representation in politics. In 1989, Gorbachev experimented with the concept of limited democracy when he introduced semicontested elections for a new legislative body, the Congress of People's Deputies of the USSR. However, he also abandoned the old quota system, which had traditionally reserved a third of the seats in the Soviet legislature for women. Rather, a new quota system was introduced, in which a third of the seats were reserved for party-affiliated organizations. Women mainly gained seats through their affiliation with the Soviet Women's Committee, which was allotted seventy-five seats. However, the final result marked a significant drop for women's representation as the share of women deputies dropped from 33 to 16 percent (Kochkina 2001, 45). In similar elections held in 1990 for the new Congress of People's Deputies of the Russian Republic, similar quotas for women were also dropped, with the result that representation for women tumbled even further, to 5.4 percent (Sperling 1999, 116).

▪ Women in Post-Soviet Russia

The USSR's dissolution in December 1991 ushered in a period of tumultuous political, economic, and social change. In the ensuing decade, Russia's president, Boris Yeltsin, presided over an economic transformation that moved the bulk of the economy from the hands of the state to those of private investors, a political transformation that created a new constitution with new institutions, rules, and players, and a social transformation in which old Soviet models of the welfare state were eroded and new Westernized images of society were introduced.

How did women fare in this process? It is important to acknowledge that nearly everyone, men and women, faced a dramatic decline in their standards of living. A small percentage of elites managed to benefit from the changes, but for most of Russia's citizens the 1990s were a time of upheaval more severe than the worst years of the United States' Great Depression. Even so, women suffered disproportionately, and in different ways, from men. Economically, women have struggled to reposition themselves in a capitalist system, which has tended to magnify preexisting Soviet-era gender inequalities. Politically, they have watched their representation tumble precipitously in the absence of the Soviet quota system. Socially, they have also paid a high price in the transition. As caretakers of the household, they continue to shoulder primary responsibility for maintaining their families in the face of constantly declining social benefits.

Women have not sat by passively as this has happened, however, as they form the backbone of a newly emerging citizen activism as leaders of nongovernmental organizations (NGOs). A very few women, too, have chosen to express their dissatisfaction with the direction of Russian policy, specifically with regard to the war in Chechnya, through terrorism.

Women and the Economy

The economic transition from state socialism to free-market capitalism was disastrous for nearly every citizen of Russia. From 1992 through 1996, during the height of privatization, the country's gross domestic product declined every year, dropping by almost 40 percent. Industrial production plummeted, inflation skyrocketed, and many citizens lost their jobs. Signs of a recovery by 1997 were reversed with an economic crash in 1998, and although the Russian economy has been growing steadily ever since, much of this growth, as James Millar notes in Chapter 5, is based on advantageous oil and natural gas prices.

Even though economic restructuring negatively affected the vast majority of Russians, the process and outcome of this transformation has been deeply gendered. While women managed to avoid the massive layoffs and high unemployment that some experts predicted during the 1990s, the gender inequalities of the Soviet-era labor market either persisted or worsened in the new capitalist economy. Although a high percentage of women remained employed, they continued to work predominantly in low-paying positions or were squeezed out of fields they had once dominated. As caretakers of households, women struggled to feed and clothe their families in the face of high inflation, rising unemployment, and price liberalization (Bridger, Kay, and Pinnick 1996, Chapters 4–7). Thus, in the midst of economic transformation, preexisting norms regarding "appropriate" gender roles remained intact, exacerbating the disadvantageous economic position of women.

During the early years of reform, many feared that women's participation in the labor force would drop dramatically and that women overwhelmingly would be the first fired and last rehired (Bridger, Kay, and Pinnick 1996; Posadskaya et al. 1994). While this dire prediction did not come to pass, the effects of economic reform have not improved the economic status of women. In 1991, the year of the Soviet Union's breakup, women accounted for 53 percent of the labor force. In 1995, the proportion of women in the labor force dropped to 51 percent (USAID 1997). By 1999, the figure was 47 percent (CEDAW 1999, 7). Even as their share of the labor force has declined, 66 percent of working-age women remain employed, which is still one of the highest rates of female employment in the world.

Nevertheless, these figures mask deep inequalities in how men and women participate in the post-Soviet labor market. Women are still segregated in low-prestige, low-paying sectors of the economy (USAID 1997). In fact, they comprise over 80 percent of all workers in education, health care, and social services. In some sectors, women have lost ground. For example, in industry, where the pay is higher, women's participation dropped by almost 50 percent between 1990 and 1998 (Snezhkova 2004, 86). Other areas of the economy, such as trade, finance, lending, and insurance, previously employed more women than men. As these fields became more critical and better paying, women were squeezed out of these jobs (CEDAW 1999, 7). The transition to the market also failed to raise women's wages vis-à-vis men's. Indeed, Soviet-era wage gaps continued, with women's earnings being between 66 to 95 percent that of men's (Glinskaya and Mroz 2000). Interestingly, this discrepancy cannot be explained by a lack of skills on the part of women, for even though they are paid less, Russian women are, on average, better educated than Russian men (CEDAW 1999, 7). Even as women have not suffered disproportionately in terms of finding employment, the gender gap in the quality of jobs has widened (Gerber and Mayorova 2006).

Women's work doesn't stop at the end of the work day, either. As mentioned earlier, women also spend long hours buying food for their families, cooking and cleaning in the household, and caring for children and other family members. As prices for food, clothing, housing, and medical care have exploded, the burden of managing these rising costs in the face of diminishing wages has fallen primarily on the shoulders of women. In many respects, dealing with the social consequences of economic reform has been primarily women's work. Further, many of the state programs that helped women join the labor force were drastically reduced during the 1990s. Day care, for instance, which was instrumental in allowing women to work, was radically restructured as the government cut back on its funding, effectively reducing its availability and increasing the costs to the consumer (CEDAW 1999, 10).

Prevailing gender norms greatly influence the unequal economic status of women in Russia. Survey research indicates that both sexes believe that men should be the "breadwinners" while women should be responsible for the home. When it comes to employment opportunities, employers and employees alike internalize these norms about "proper" jobs for men and women. Women are more likely to accept work that is lower paying and replicates their household caregiving duties. They are also more likely to take time off from work to tend to sick relatives. Even as these gendered expectations have in some ways hurt the economic status of women, they have also unexpectedly given women the advantage in surviving the negative effects of economic restructuring. Indeed, it seems that the traditional household roles women play inadvertently help them endure hard times by providing a sense of meaning to their lives. Expected to be breadwinners, men are more susceptible to alcoholism, illness, and early death as they struggle to adapt to new economic norms and realities. The strain of this effort is believed to be one of the reasons for the dramatic decline in male life expectancy in Russia. Women may be financially worse off than men, but they live, on average, an additional thirteen to fourteen years (Ashwin 2006; see also Timothy Heleniak in Chapter 8 of this volume).

Women and Politics

As this chapter has stressed, the Soviet system was stronger on rhetorical support for women's political participation than in deed. While women were granted a quota of one-third of the seats in the USSR Supreme Soviet, this generous number was more a testament to the lack of real power this governing body held than in the regime's faith in women. In truth, women held little significant political power under the Soviet regime. The Supreme Soviet served as a legislative rubber stamp for decisions made by the party's leading organs, the Central Committee, Politburo, and Secretariat. These were the real holders of political power, and women were rarely present. Even in the Supreme Soviet the status of women was not high, as they accounted for 72 percent of the body's nonparty deputies. Most were recruited from the working class, not the professions. Rarely were they reappointed for a second or third term, further limiting their abilities to build experience or clout (Kochkina 2001, 50).

Few were prepared for the dramatic decline in representation that took place in 1989 with Gorbachev's political reforms. Two decades later, this pattern of declining representation and power for women shows few signs of reversing, despite the presence of a few prominent women politicians. While there is no shortage of qualified, experienced women to hold political office, this has not resulted in a similar proportion of female candidates at election time. Women's issues are not stressed by political parties, women candidates are not promoted, and women's organizations and society at large seem relatively untroubled by this political trend.

Following the collapse of the Soviet Union in 1991, Russian president Boris Yeltsin chose to keep the old political system while focusing on economic reform. However, after facing a rebellion from the Russian Congress of People's Deputies in 1993, he dissolved the body, and called for elections under new rules to a new legislative body, the Duma.

At first, it seemed the new system would be woman friendly. Russian voters in Duma elections would be presented with a double ballot, in which they were asked to cast two votes, one for a party list in which candidates would gain office through a system of proportional representation (PR), and another for an individual candidate who would be elected through a plurality vote in a traditional single-member district (SMD). This new system, similar to one used in Germany, was, on its face, considered favorable to women for two reasons. First, because voters would have two selections to make, they would be less likely to think they were "wasting" a vote on a woman. Second and related to this, because half of the Duma's seats would be filled through proportional representation, women would have a better chance of being elected because they would not have to win their seats outright as in single-member district races. Instead, a woman would simply need to earn a spot high enough on a party list to win her seat (Rule and Shvedova 1996, 42–44). For this reason, political scientists have long argued that proportional representation should increase the number of women elected to legislative bodies (Norris 1993; Norris and Lovenduski 1995; Rule 1994). In practice, many systems that use proportional representation also have higher percentages of female parliamentarians. For example, of the ten countries that have the highest percentages of women legislators, nine use a proportional representation electoral system (Inter-Parliamentary Union 2005).

Such has not been the case in Russia, however. In the four Duma elections held under this system (1993, 1995, 1999, and 2003), the share of seats won by women was relatively low. In the 1993 elections, women actually got off to a pretty good start, gaining 13.7 percent of the seats in the Duma. In the 1995 election, their numbers dropped to 10.1 percent, and in 1999 fell to 7.8 percent (Moser 2003, 159). In the December 2003 elections, women rebounded somewhat, winning about 9 percent of the seats (OSCE/ODIHR 2004, 19).

Women have fared even worse in Russia's upper house, the Federation Council, where two deputies are appointed by the legislative and executive branches of each subject of the Federation. Under Yeltsin, the executive branches' "seats" were filled by the governors. Because most governors were men, few women made it into the upper house. In 1997, for instance, the only female senator was Valentina Bronevich, the governor of the Koriak Autonomous Okrug. Not long after Vladimir Putin's election as president in 2000, however, the Federal Assembly passed legislation prohibiting provincial governors from serving in the Federation Council. Under the new law, each governor now nominates a candidate to fill the regional executive's Federation Council seat. As a result of this change, women's representation in the Federation Council has increased slightly to 3.4 percent (UNDP 2006, 381).

Proportional representation has not helped women gain elected office in Russia to the extent that it has elsewhere, especially in Western Europe. A close look at Table 10.1 provides details of women's election rates on both sides of the ballot in the first four Duma elections (1993 through 2003). Why was Russia unusual in this regard? Why did women fare so poorly in the proportional representation races? Scholars agree that Russia does not lack qualified candidates. Russian women are highly educated, highly trained, and have positions of power and responsibility in other areas of society. Much of the problem lies with Russia's parties. On party lists, parties have tended to place women toward the bottom, ensuring that most of their female candidates have little hope of actually being assigned a seat in the Duma.

In contrast, in the single-member district races, women were able to turn weak party identification among voters to their advantage. Because more than two legitimate candidates normally ran in the single-member districts, the winner often only needed to receive a plurality, rather than a majority, of the vote. Because many candidates ran as independents in these races, parties had a harder time imposing discipline on their own candidates. As such, parties tended to invest less money and energy in these races, inadvertently helping women win office. Furthermore, Russian male and female politicians came from varied backgrounds. While men often came from the economic elite or economic management positions, women were more likely to have had experience as the heads of schools or hospitals (Nowacki 2003, 189–191), which gave women more "face recognition" with local constituencies.

This experience is now moot, however, because of legislation signed into law by Putin in May 2005 that eliminated all single-member district seats in the Duma (beginning with the 2007 election) in exchange for a system based entirely on proportional representation. The same law also raised the threshold required for parties to gain seats in the Duma from 5 percent to 7 percent of the popular vote (Levada Center and CSPP 2007). Despite concerns that these changes might hurt women, the proportion of women now serving in the Duma as a result of the 2007 election is higher than at any time under the previous system (see Table 10.1). Although good news, the Russian figure, 14 percent, is still low in comparison with PR systems in Western Europe, where women commonly hold a third or more of the seats. As was the case under the Duma's original election law, the key to success for women under the new system will be the willingness of parties to place them higher on their party lists. Of the four parties that cleared the 7 percent threshold in the 2007 election, only one party, A Just Russia, made a concerted effort to promote women in its ranks. Of its thirty-eight Duma deputies, 28.9 percent are women. In comparison, only 14 percent of United Russia's deputies are women. Totals for the Liberal Democratic Party of Russia (LDPR) and the Communist Party of the Russian Federation (CPRF) are even lower at 10.2 and 7.0 percent (Gosudarstvennaia Duma 2008).

In response to the lack of female representation in Russia's political parties in the early post-Soviet era, a group of women formed their own party, Women of Russia, a merger of three organizations, the former Soviet Women's Committee (now renamed the Union of Women of Russia), the Union of Navy

Table 10.1 Number of Women Elected to the Russian Duma, 1993–2007

Election Year	Number (and Percentage) of Women Elected in Single-Member Districts		Number (and Percentage) of Women Elected in Proportional Representation Races		Total Number (and Percentage) of Women Elected	
1993	26	(11.6)	34	(15.0)	60	(13.7)
1995	31	(13.8)	15	(6.7)	46	(10.1)
1999	20	(8.9)	15	(6.7)	35	(7.8)
2003	20	(8.9)	21	(9.3)	41	(9.1)
2007	—		63	(14.0)	63	(14.0)

Sources: Moser 2003, 159; OSCE/ODIHR 2004, 19; Gosudarstvennaia Duma 2008.

Women, and the Association of Women Entrepreneurs. Founded in 1993, Women of Russia strongly emphasized the "traditional" roles of women as mother and caretaker. In their party platform, they promised to "assert the interests of women, children, families, pensioners, and the depressed strata of the population." They also mixed traditionalist rhetoric with calls for political and economic equality. In addition, they promised

> to promote greater involvement of women in the country's social and political life and to increase their proportion in power structures to achieve a genuine realization of the constitutional principle of equal rights and opportunities for women and men in all spheres of public life. (*Russia Journal* 1999)

Initially, Women of Russia received substantial support from a small but vital constituency. In their first election in 1993, the movement was quite successful, receiving just over 8 percent of the party list vote and twenty-two seats in the Duma (Salmenniemi 2003). In the Duma, they translated their platform into a centrist voting-bloc position, voting for measures that would maintain or restore the tattered social safety net, while expressing support for progressive democratic reforms.

However, the movement could not repeat the success of the 1993 election. In the 1995 and 1999 Duma elections, it failed to clear the 5 percent hurdle needed to gain seats apportioned by the proportional representation side of the ballot. This was particularly devastating in 1995, when Women of Russia fell short of the mandatory 5 percent barrier by only 0.39 percent (Kochkina 2001, 47). Even so, Women of Russia did have an impact as it forced other parties to put women higher on their lists and to include women on lists for single-member district seats.

More recently, a well-known network of NGOs that draws heavily on themes of women's activism and motherhood has tried to formalize its movement into a political party. However, changes in federal laws on parties and elections have made this transition difficult. Founded in 1989, the Committee of Soldiers' Mothers was created to protect the rights of young men in Russia who, during the course of their two years of compulsory military service, are often subjected to hazing and other severe human rights violations. The start of an especially brutal war in Chechnya in 1994 further spurred their activities, which currently include helping parents keep their sons out of the military, locating their missing sons, fighting for better conditions for all conscripts, and advocating an end of compulsory military service. After more than a decade of working to influence politics as an NGO, the group decided that it could be more effective as a political party. Thus, in November 2004, representatives from the Union of Soldiers' Mothers Committees met to transform their social movement into a viable political party. The result was the creation of the United People's Party of Soldiers' Mothers, with plans to participate in the 2007 Duma elections (Yablokova 2004).

However, this new party has struggled to find a political niche in an environment regulated by two new federal laws on parties and elections. The first, a revised law on parties signed by Putin in December 2004, increased membership and branch requirements for parties wishing to contest seats in the Duma. These revisions, outlined by Michael Bressler in Chapter 4, make it more difficult for small parties to get on the ballot. A second law, approved five months later, eliminated all single-member district seats in the Duma in favor of a system based entirely on proportional representation. Although such an electoral system normally would benefit small parties, which rarely win single-member district races, the new law also increased the threshold required to win party list seats from 5 to 7 percent. Together, the two laws meant that even if a small party were to satisfy the more stringent registration requirements stipulated by the revised-parties law, its chances of winning seats in the Duma would be slim. Given the electoral dominance of pro-Putin United Russia in 2007, an already daunting task became even more so for small parties.

Unable to compete as an independent organization, the fledgling United People's Party of Soldiers' Mothers formed alliances, first, with the Republican Party, which the Supreme Court subsequently dissolved for failing to satisfy the requirements of the revised-parties law, and later with Yabloko, which was on the ballot for the 2007 Duma elections but managed to receive only 1.6 percent of the vote, well short of the 7 percent required to win seats. By gathering under Yabloko's political umbrella (along with a number of other prodemocracy, pro–human rights organizations), the United People's Party of Soldiers' Mothers hoped to gain institutionalized access to the political system and at the same time improve Yabloko's chances of clearing the

7 percent hurdle (Radio Mayak 2007). Having failed to achieve its aims, this new women's party remains outside the formal structures of Russia's political system.

Despite this, a few women have achieved national prominence in other political parties. Galina Starovoitova, for example, a prodemocracy politician based in St. Petersburg, rose to prominence as an outspoken proponent of reform under Gorbachev. She served in the USSR Congress of People's Deputies from 1989–1991, and in 1990 was elected to the Russian Republic Congress of People's Deputies in 1990. A psychologist and ethnographer by profession, she served as an adviser to Yeltsin on ethnic relations and nationality affairs. She cofounded the Democratic Russia movement, and in 1995 was elected to the Duma, defeating twenty-three rivals to win her seat. She also contemplated a bid for the presidency in the 2000 elections. In November 1998, however, Starovoitova and her legislative aide were gunned down

Galina Starovoitova during a November 1997 visit to the United States.

Watson Institute for International Studies, Brown University

outside her apartment in St. Petersburg. Although no group claimed responsibility for the act, her death was not an isolated incident. She was the sixth
member of Russia's Duma to have been murdered since 1993, either for political or business motives (Dhue 1998). Despite the public outcry over her
assassination, the pace of the official investigation was slow. Finally, in June
2005, a St. Petersburg court handed down two convictions and four acquit-
tals in the case. Of the two men convicted, one was found guilty of being the
trigger man, while the other was found guilty of organizing the killing. Although the court ruled that Starovoitova's murder was "political" in nature,
the precise reasons behind her death remained a mystery. So too, at the time
of the court's verdicts, was the identity of the person who ordered her assassination (Bigg 2005).

Another well-known female politician is Irina Khakamada, cofounder of
the SPS, the Union of Rightist Forces. A prominent advocate for liberal reform, Khakamada rose to the position of deputy speaker in the Duma. Her
prominence in Russian politics was not enough to guarantee her seat in the
Duma, however, when, in the 2003 elections, the SPS failed to clear the 5
percent barrier on the proportional representation side of the ballot. In the
same election, Khakamada ran for a seat in a single-member district race,
but also lost. Following these losses, she launched an unsuccessful bid for
the presidency in the 2004 race. Most recently, she has formed the Free Russia Democratic Party.

It is unclear what effect this small number of women is having on Russian politics. In studies on the role of women in legislatures, scholars have
argued that the representation by women often engenders greater concern
for social policy. One study of Duma proceedings found that women
deputies expressed attitudes that reflected supposedly female values (such
as pacifism, compassion, and concern for people's health) with greater fre-
quency than their male colleagues. Women have also voiced opposition to
the death penalty and spoken out in favor of improving nuclear safety and
environmental protection. Such views are not necessarily reflected in the
voting records of women deputies, however, except in issues unrelated to
party affiliation, such as women's health (Shevchenko 2002, 1201). Thus,
as a potential bloc of votes in the Duma, women have not had a consistent
impact on legislation, despite pockets of support for such influence.

Women are not a strong presence in the executive branch either, further
supporting what one scholar refers to as a "gender power pyramid," meaning
that the higher one climbs, the fewer women one sees with political power
(Kochkina 2001, 50). Women's leadership here is even rarer. Indeed, one can
count the number of high-profile women patrolling the halls of political power
on the fingers of one hand. Only one of Russia's eighty-three regions had a
woman at the top in 2008 as this book went to press: Valentina Matvienko, the
governor of St. Petersburg. Another woman, Natalia Partasova, served as

prime minister of the Republic of Chuvashia from December 2001 through April 2004. One other woman, Valentina Bronevich, was governor of the Koryak Autonomous Oblast from November 1996 through December 2000 (Rulers.org 2008a). The situation is not much better for women at the federal level in Moscow. Only two women have held the post of deputy prime minister. One, St. Petersburg's Valentina Matvienko, served five years (1998–2003) as a deputy prime minister. The other, Galina Karelova, spent less than a year in the post, after which she became chairperson of the Russian government's Social Insurance Fund. Compare this with the sixty-six men who have served as deputy prime ministers since the USSR's dissolution in 1991. Through 2008, only four women have been cabinet ministers. Three of the four have served in ministries traditionally thought of as involving issues that "naturally" concern women: the Ministry of Healthcare and Social Development and the Ministry of Culture and Mass Communications. Only one woman has held the top post in one of the more prominent ministries: Elvira Nabiullina, the current minister of economic development (Rulers.org 2008b).

To the extent that women have an impact on policymakers at the federal level, it tends to come through their participation in government advisory bodies that deal with issues affecting women. Some of these advisory bodies include the Commission of Women's Affairs of the Federation Council, and the Duma Committee on Women, Family, and Youth. Others include Duma committees on Education, Health Care, and Labor and Social Policy. Women's organizations also work with ministries that design and implement policies affecting women. These include the Ministry for Labor and Social Policy, the Ministry for Public Health and Medical Industry, the Ministry of Public Education, and the Department on Migration Policy (Moscow Center n.d.). Women's groups work with government by serving as experts on issues affecting women and by providing gender analyses of the impact of legislation on the social and economic status of women. These groups tend to be most effective on issues that fit Russian cultural norms on the caring roles of women. For example, women were more effective in helping draft and pass new Family Code legislation than they were in influencing guidelines for the implementation of the constitutional clause on equal rights and opportunities (Caiazza 2002).

Women and Society

Even though women in Russia rarely climb to the top of the pyramid of political or economic power, they are extraordinarily active in a wide array of NGOs that energetically push for change. Few women in Russia, however, organize around issues that are often associated with women's movements in the West, such as advocacy for greater political representation, less job discrimination, or control over reproductive rights. Instead, women in Russia tend to involve themselves in issues that are traditionally perceived to be within women's spheres of influence. Furthermore, despite this activism, it is important to note that Russia's women are most active in a realm that has had relatively little impact on bringing about political change.

Most NGOs in Russia today are products of the post-Soviet era. Although a wide array of organizations existed during the Soviet period, ranging from the Pioneers (akin to the Boy Scouts and Girl Scouts) and women's councils to stamp collector clubs and sports leagues, these associations of people were formed, supported, and controlled by the state. Independent organizations were not allowed until 1990, late in the Soviet era. Eventually, after the Soviet system's collapse, additional legislation was passed in 1993 and 1995, further outlining the parameters of NGOs in Russia. With this legislation, the right to form independent associations was codified into law, rather than dependent on the whims of a reformist regime. Since 1990, hundreds of thousands of organizations have formed representing a wide array of issues and interests. In 2003, according to one source, approximately 570,000 NGOs were operating in Russia (Hudson 2004, 2). These organizations form what is often referred to as the "third sector," the realm of organizations separate from the state and business. NGOs also form a part of the broader theoretical space known as civil society, where citizens gather to formulate and express their interests independent of the state.

Women form the backbone of this nonstate sector in Russia, covering a broad range of organizations, including political parties, crisis centers, surviving Soviet-era women's councils, business women's groups, charitable associations, and a small feminist contingent. Despite the great breadth of these activities, the vast majority of women's groups have as their aim the pragmatic objective of providing services that the state no longer can secure for Russians in an era of social and economic dislocation. Thus, most women active in the third sector do not primarily identify their activism as motivated by concerns about gender inequality. Instead, they are mobilizing on issues that are traditionally perceived as important to women (Henderson 2003).

Thus, many women active in NGOs draw on their roles as "mothers" and "caretakers." For example, the network of groups that comprise the Committees of Soldiers' Mothers have drawn most explicitly on the symbol of motherhood as caretaker to address the larger societal issues of war and peace. As one activist explained, "[o]ur women's organization is concerned especially with men's problems which worry women/mothers. . . . The basis of our work has lain in the egotistical mother instinct—the protection of our sons." Another activist noted, "you are struck by the steadfastness and optimism of our women . . . ready to unselfishly help one another, taking on their shoulders worries about friends, aged parents, and often unemployed men" (Henderson 2003, 98). In short, these women mobilize to protect the quantity and quality of life of society's most vulnerable citizens, such as children, retired people, and the disabled. In the late 1990s, as many as two-thirds of women's organizations were involved in issues of "social rights" (Abubikirova et al. 1998). Thus, the themes that resonate with women are those that impact women but are not solely focused on women.

When women do mobilize to protect their own diminishing status in Russia, it tends to be on issues directly related to the welfare of women. These issues are often related to the retraction of government services, such as preschool, day care, and health care, in the face of state penury and spiraling costs. In response, many women's groups serve as self-help organizations, formed in response to such things as cutbacks in state funding for maternity wards and clinics. Other groups try to help women overcome the difficulties of unemployment. The late 1980s and early 1990s, for example, witnessed a mushrooming of women's organizations that served as small-scale cooperatives in which women assembled products for sale. Still other organizations seek to help pensioners, the majority of whom are women, cope with steep declines in their standards of living as the state struggles to maintain anything resembling its former cradle-to-grave welfare system (Henderson 2003).

A women's movement per se, in which groups organize to advocate for women's equality or women's issues, has yet to take root in Russia. The few organizations that do have an explicitly Western feminist orientation are small in size and number. Their membership consists of the women who work for the organization. They are often supported by Western donors, however, who have been active in funding projects that advance the position and status of women in Russian society.

A few of the organizations in Russia that work explicitly on women's issues are the Moscow Center for Gender Studies (www.gender.ru), the Women's Consortium of Nongovernmental Organizations (www.wcons.org .ru/ru/main.php), Open Women Line (www.owl.ru), and Femina (www.femin .ru). Many of these organizations were formed in the early 1990s and staffed by women academics interested in feminism, women's studies, and the status and position of women in Russia. These groups often explicitly employ terms and concepts of Western feminism in their promotion of gender equality and the prevention of discrimination against women. In furthering their cause, they conduct research, publish studies, and work behind the scenes on a variety of government commissions to advocate for women's concerns. They are also active participants globally, working with women's organizations around the world and participating in international conferences, such as the Fourth World United Nations Conference on Women held in 1995 in Beijing. Although well-networked internationally, and tireless in their publication of research on gender issues, feminist organizations in Russia have thus far been unsuccessful in reaching a mass audience and attracting Russian women to their cause.

Why has a women's movement failed to take shape in post-Soviet Russia? Certainly, it is not for a lack of problems facing women. As this chapter shows, women have achieved little in terms of political or economic influence as a result of the collapse of communism. Even so, issues that have mobilized women in other societies, such as job discrimination or a lack of political representation, have provoked relatively little reaction on the part of Russian women.

Part of the explanation certainly lies in their exhaustion with the prowoman, proequality rhetoric of the Soviet era. From early on, women were told they were equal to men and that the Soviet state would provide them with advantages that would afford them higher standards of living than experienced by their counterparts trapped in the capitalist West. Reality was very much at odds with the official myth, however, as the rhetoric of women's equality translated into long work days on the job, followed by equally weighty responsibilities in the home. Furthermore, the heightened, yet essentially symbolic, political status of women simply loaded them down further as they faced a triple burden of work, home, and public life. Consequently, many women, particularly those old enough to remember the communist era, do not respond to the Western feminist rhetoric of equality as it merely echoes the empty promises of the Soviet past.

In addition, many women who grew up in the drab uniformity of the Soviet period reacted positively to the new consumerist culture of postcommunist Russia. Many women initially embraced makeup, high heels, and tight clothing as a welcome change from the Soviet era. Thus, Western feminist concerns about social pressures on women to look beautiful fell on deaf ears. Moreover, one mobilizing factor for the women's movement in the West—a woman's right to choose to have an abortion—did not exist in Russia. As Heleniak discusses at some length in Chapter 8, women during much of the Soviet era could choose to terminate their pregnancies with an abortion. Furthermore, Soviet women enjoyed generous maternity-leave benefits. Thus, many of the issues that mobilized women in the West either did not exist in Russia, or were subverted by Soviet ideology, thus making it difficult for a new wave of women activists to appropriate the rhetoric of feminist principles.

Another factor hindering the development of a women's movement in contemporary Russia is that few women have had the time, income, or energy to advocate for an improvement in their immediate conditions or to think about such issues as self-expression, gendered divisions of labor, and quality of life. Overburdened by work at home and on the job, Russia's women have had little to give to a movement that in the West often gained momentum when a critical mass of middle-class women found the time and energy to mobilize on women's issues.

In addition, all Russian NGOs, not only those dealing with women's issues, have had trouble attracting broad-based memberships. Despite the large number of NGOs, they are thinly stretched across the country's vast landmass. One reason for such anemic development is rooted in Russia's overall economic environment. Although the economic climate of the 1990s provided the impetus for organization, it simultaneously kept groups from developing a stable presence for lack of financial support. Despite recent more encouraging economic trends, NGOs continue to struggle financially as many people are either unable or unwilling to give them money. In a country where even checkbooks do not exist, checkbook activism, the backbone of nonprofit development in other countries, is slow to develop. The absence of tax incentives, for businesses or individuals, to donate time and money to organizations complicates the search for funds. International sources of funding are shifting, too, as several donor organizations have begun to pull out of Russia, are scaling back their commitment, or are setting new priorities, affecting some 5 to 10 percent of NGOs that receive financial support from the West (Borovikh 2004).

Russians are also hesitant to join independent associations. While they have deserted their former Soviet-era organizations, they have tended not to join new ones. Russia's rate of "associationism," at 0.65 organizations per person, is low, even for postcommunist countries, which, as a bloc, have the lowest rates of organization among democratizing countries (Howard 2002, 159).

The reasons for this are several. First, some people may be weary of organizational membership after years of forced participation in "voluntary" communist-era activities. Second, scandals in the 1990s, in which organized crime or others formed front nonprofit associations to import and export alcohol and cigarettes, or in which pyramid schemes were touted as charitable funds, have not aided public relations between legitimate NGOs and the public. Third, citizens are unfamiliar with many of the larger theoretical concepts supporting democracy. A 2001 survey, for instance, revealed that only 16 percent of Russians were familiar with the term "civil society" (Oslon 2001, 6–13). Thus, even as specific factors impede the emergence of a Russian women's movement, broader forces are at work, too, that are hindering the development of an active and organized third sector at large.

Finally, unlike Yeltsin, who did not take a particular interest in NGOs, NGO development, or civil society at large, President Putin implemented a variety of policies that critics argue will create a "managed" civil society that parallels Russia's "managed" democracy. He publicly questioned the legitimacy and efficacy of foreign aid to foster civil society development, resulting in increased scrutiny of some NGOs by law enforcement and the tax authorities. Proposed draft amendments to the tax code (which eventually failed) imposed registration requirements on all types of grants, which would have further complicated the work of foreign donors and recipient NGOs (Mereu 2005). Moreover, in December 2005, the Duma voted overwhelmingly in favor of legislation that increases state oversight (or, as some argue, control) over nongovernmental organizations. The law created a new agency to monitor the registration, financing, and activities of NGOs. This agency also has the power to determine if an NGO should be shut down for violating domestic regulations. While supporters of the law point out that previous legislation regulating the sector was so poorly drafted that NGOs were often used as money-laundering fronts (thus, hindering legitimate nonprofit efforts to raise money), critics fear that the new law will be enforced selectively to muzzle organizations critical of Kremlin policies and politics. Many of these same NGOs, among them several women's groups, rely on Western financial support for their survival. As such, they are at risk of investigation by the state.

In one prominent case, the Committee of Soldiers' Mothers, long a critic of the Putin administration, was temporarily targeted by the Justice Ministry's newly created Federal Registration Service. Although the case was eventually dropped, the court initially ruled that the committee should be shut down on the grounds that it had not filed the appropriate paperwork to register its existence. While the committee was at fault in that it had failed to submit the routine paperwork necessary to maintain its registered status, many feared that the case was intended primarily as a signal to opposition groups that they and their activities were being monitored by the Russian state (Medetsky 2006). The case against the committee illustrated another point as well: even as many women's groups perform social services that are viewed as "valuable" by the government, the few groups that pursue explicitly political aims can expect further scrutiny from the state.

Despite this potential threat, women, by forming the bulk of the leadership of Russia's nongovernmental organizations, have found alternative ways of expressing their concerns and interests. As remarkable as these efforts are, this activism is relegated primarily to the nonprofit realm, a sector that has relatively little political power and even less economic influence. Thus, even when women do assume leadership roles, these tend to be in the least-valued and least-powerful sectors in society. For Russia's women, there is not only a glass ceiling but a sticky floor.

Women and War

On the evening of August 24, 2004, two commercial airliners that had departed forty minutes apart from Moscow's Domodedovo Airport were destroyed within minutes of each other in midair explosions, killing ninety people. Less than a week later, a suicide bomber killed nine people and wounded an additional fifty-one outside a subway station in northeastern Moscow (*CNN.com* 2004). Both incidents, predictably, shook Russia's population. However, it was not just the terrorist acts that mesmerized and horrified the public; the suicide bombers were women.

Not all of Russia's women have chosen to express their opinions through such institutionalized means as peaceful protests, voting, or organizing and leading NGOs. In response to the seemingly endless, brutal war being waged by Russia in Chechnya, a small, well-publicized contingent of Chechen women has resorted to terrorism to pressure the Russian government to bring an end to the deadly conflict. The August 2004 bombings were not the first times women had taken such action.

In 2001, a woman drove a truck bomb into a Russian military compound near the Chechen capital, Grozny. The following year, almost two dozen women terrorists took part in the hostage crisis in Moscow's Palace of Culture theater, during a performance of the Russian patriotic musical *Nord-Ost*. The siege ended when Russian officers stormed the building, killing 130 of the 800 hostages and executing all of the hostage takers (Weir 2003). In 2003, two Chechen women blew themselves up at a summer outdoor rock concert, killing fourteen (*CNN.com* 2004). A few months later, in December, two women blew themselves up a few yards from the Kremlin, killing five and injuring twelve. Less than two weeks after the August 2004 plane crashes and the Moscow subway bombing, women terrorists reportedly were involved in the Beslan crisis in which an entire school was taken hostage. Since the resumption of fighting in Chechnya in 1999, women have been involved in at least fifteen terrorist attacks (Myers 2004). This trend in terrorism presents a new problem for the Kremlin as it continues its war in Chechnya.

Because almost all of the terrorists have died while carrying out their attacks, it has been difficult to discern their underlying motivations. The media quickly labeled them "black widows," and claimed that these women were drawn to terrorism after their Chechen husbands, and often other relatives as well, had been killed by Russian forces (McLaughlin 2003). Alternatively, news sources have referred to them as *shakhidy,* the Russian variant for the Arabic word for "holy warriors" who sacrifice their lives (Myers 2004). Many dress head to toe in black, wearing the so-called martyr's belt filled with explosives.

Neither label quite fits the profiles of many of the suicide bombers, however, or accurately captures the complexity of the Chechen crisis. The bombers do not fit a single profile. While some had lost close friends or family members, others were divorced, with all family members alive. Nor do Chechen terrorists use rhetoric similar to that of Palestinians in the West Bank and Gaza, insurgents in Iraq, or militant groups such as Al-Qaida. Chechnya's imams, too, are leaders of a moderate branch of Islam in an outwardly secular society. The cult of religious martyrdom is neither fostered nor embraced by segments of society (Myers 2004; Weir 2003).

The Russian government has portrayed the women as helpless pawns, brainwashed and drugged by male terrorist leaders. The government bases this assessment on interviews with Zarema Muzhakhoyeva, a would-be Chechen suicide bomber, who was unable to set off the 1.5 kilograms of plastic explosive she had brought with her to a Moscow cafe on July 9, 2003

(Groskop 2004). A desperately poor young woman from a region devastated by war, Muzhakhoyeva claims that she had to perform a suicide mission after being unable to repay a loan. In addition, she says, she was drugged. She described a realm in which women were "forced, blackmailed, or brainwashed to their deaths" (Groskop 2004). Others posit that women are recruited after having been raped. In a traditionalist culture such as Chechnya's, this is enough to dishonor a woman's family, and the women cooperate with terrorists because they feel they have no choice.

Doubtless, the female terrorists' motivations are complex and varied. Women are often acting on elements of choice as well as coercion, perhaps provoked by larger feelings of hopelessness and despair after a decade of destruction. Many Chechen women, after years of war, have few options facing them in the future. Engaging in the conflict may seem preferable to continued war, poverty, and lack of opportunity. For terrorists, too, women are often useful recruits. Societal stereotypes of women as peaceful and nonaggressive ensure that police and military forces are less likely to search them carefully at security checkpoints. Furthermore, women tend to elicit less suspicion from citizens, who are more apt to look at men as potential terrorists.

This is not the first time women have resorted to terrorism in Russian history. Women were active in underground terrorist organizations in the latter half of the nineteenth century in opposition to the tsarist system. A striking contrast, however, is that while the female terrorists of more than a century ago were relatively well educated and from middle- to upper-class families, today's women terrorists come primarily from poor families with few options. One thing the two share, though, is frustration with a political regime's unwillingness to change course on policies that promise them and their people no future.

■ Conclusion: The Prospects for Russian Women

During the twentieth century, Russia's women were presented with scenarios that offered unparalleled opportunities. Socialism and capitalism both promised emancipation. The reality, however, has always been much more complex. While the Soviet Union succeeded in providing numerous educational opportunities for women, women still, in many ways, were second-class citizens. Economically, they swelled the ranks of the lowest-paid jobs. Politically, they occupied positions that were more symbolic than influential, rarely advancing to significant positions of power. The collapse of the Soviet Union launched Russia into a transition that promised to open new doors for women, but in truth more often erected new barriers. Gendered divisions of labor predominated in the market economy, in politics, and in society. Contemporary Russia resembles a pyramid, with men mostly occupying positions of power.

While a few high-profile women have benefited from economic reforms, many more tumbled to the bottom, forming small businesses as merchants in bazaars. Politically, men have dominated the structure of power, occupying almost all key positions in the federal government and political parties. Women, by contrast, disproportionately have filled leadership positions in nongovernmental organizations, which struggle to influence policy. While women face numerous new challenges, their position reflects a larger ambivalence that has surfaced throughout Russian history about the appropriate role of women in economics, politics, and society.

■ Bibliography

Abubikirova, N. I., et al. 1998. *Zhenskie nepravitelstvennye organizatsii Rossii i SNG* [Women's nongovernmental organizations in Russia and the CIS]. Moscow: Eslan.

Ashwin, Sarah, ed. 2006. *Adapting to Russia's New Labor Market: Gender and Employment Strategy.* New York: Routledge.

Atkinson, Dorothy, Alexander Dallin, and Gail Warshofsky Lapidus, eds. 1977. *Women in Russia.* Stanford, CA: Stanford University Press.

Baranskaia, Natalia. 1990. *A Week Like Any Other: Novellas and Stories.* Trans. Peita Monks. Seattle, WA: Seal Press.

Bigg, Claire. 2005. "Two Convicted of Starovoitova Murder." *Radio Free Europe/ Radio Liberty (RFE/RL) Russian Political Weekly* 5(26), July 11. http://www .rferl.org/reports/rpw/2005/07/26-110705.asp.

Borovikh, Alexander. 2004. Interview by Sarah L. Henderson. June 3. NGO Support Center, Moscow, Russia.

Bridger, Sue. 1992. "Women and Agricultural Reform." In *Perestroika and Soviet Women,* ed. Mary Buckley. Cambridge, UK: Cambridge University Press.

Bridger, Sue, Rebecca Kay, and Kathryn Pinnick. 1996. *No More Heroines?: Russia, Women, and the Market.* London: Routledge.

Buckley, Mary, ed. 1992. *Perestroika and Soviet Women.* Cambridge, UK: Cambridge University Press.

Caiazza, Amy. 2002. *Mothers and Soldiers: Gender, Citizenship, and Civil Society in Contemporary Russia.* New York: Routledge.

CEDAW (Convention on the Elimination of All Forms of Discrimination Against Women). 1999. *Russian Federation,* fifth periodic report. CEDAW/C/USR/5. http://www.un.org/womenwatch/daw/cedaw/reports.htm#r.

Clements, Barbara Evans. 1991. "Introduction: Accommodation, Resistance, Transformation." In *Russia's Women: Accommodation, Resistance, Transformation,* ed. Barbara Evans Clements, Barbara Alpern Engel, and Christine D. Worobec. Berkeley: University of California Press.

CNN.com. 2004. "Russia's 'Black Widows' Wreak Terror," September 3. http://www .cnn.com/2004/WORLD/europe/09/01/russia.widows/index.html.

Dhue, Laurie. 1998. "Politician's Murder Stuns Russia." *CNN Worldwide,* November 21 (Transcript no. 98112102V18).

Engel, Barbara Alpern. 2004. *Women in Russia, 1700–2000.* Cambridge, UK: Cambridge University Press.

Gerber, Theodore P., and Olga Mayorova. 2006. "Dynamic Gender Differences in a Post-Socialist Labor Market: Russia, 1991–1997." *Social Forces* 84(4): 2047–2075.

Glinskaya, Elena, and Thomas A. Mroz. 2000. "The Gender Gap in Wages in Russia from 1992 to 1995." *Journal of Population Economics* 13(2): 353–386.

Goldman, Wendy Z. 2002. *Women at the Gates: Gender and Industry in Stalin's Russia.* Cambridge, UK: Cambridge University Press.

Gosudarstvennaia Duma. 2008. "Sostav i struktura Gosudarstvennoi Dumy: Fraktsii v Gosudarstvennoi Dume po sostoianiiu na 7 fevralia 2008 goda" [Composition and structure of the State Duma: Fractions in the State Duma as of 7 February 2008]. http://www.duma.gov.

Groskop, Viv. 2004. "Chechnya's Deadly 'Black Widows.'" *New Statesman* 133 (4704): 32–33.

Hemment, Julie. 2007. *Empowering Women in Russia: Activism, Aid, and NGOs.* Bloomington: Indiana University Press.

Henderson, Sarah L. 2003. *Building Democracy in Contemporary Russia: Western Support for Grassroots Organizations.* Ithaca, NY: Cornell University Press.

Howard, Marc Morjé. 2002. "The Weakness of Postcommunist Civil Society," *Journal of Democracy* 13(1): 157–169.

Hudson, Gerry. 2004. "Determinants of the Effectiveness of Civil Groups in Russia: Individual and Group Level Factors." Paper presented at the Annual Meeting of the American Association for the Advancement of Slavic Studies, Boston, MA, December 4–7.

Hutton, Marcelline. 1996. "Women in Russian Society from the Tsars to Yeltsin." In *Russian Women in Politics and Society,* ed. Wilma Rule and Norma C. Noonan. Westport, CN: Greenwood Press.

Inter-Parliamentary Union. 2005. "Women in National Parliaments." http://www.ipu.org/wmn-e/classif.htm.

Kochkina, Elena V. 2001. "Women in Russian Governmental Bodies." *Russian Social Science Review* 42(2): 44–59.

Lapidus, Gail Warshofsky. 1978. *Women in Soviet Society: Equality, Development, and Social Change.* Berkeley: University of California Press.

Levada Center and Centre for the Study of Public Policy (CSPP). 2007. *Duma Election Law: Details.* http://www.russiavotes.org/duma/duma_election_law.php.

Lovenduski, Joni, and Pippa Norris, eds. 1993. *Gender and Party Politics.* London: Sage Publications.

Matloff, Judith. 2000. "Russia's Powerhouses of Dissent: Mothers." *Christian Science Monitor,* February 24.

McLaughlin, Daniel. 2003. "Bombing Shocks Russians: Muscovites Aghast at 'Black Widow' Attacks." *Vancouver Sun,* July 7.

Medetsky, Anatoly. 2006. "Soldiers' Mothers in the Crosshairs." *Moscow Times,* April 20.

Mereu, Francesca. 2005. "Duma Gives Nod to Tough NGO Bill." *Moscow Times,* November 24.

Moscow Center for Gender Studies. n.d. "History of Moscow Center for Gender Studies." http://www.gender.ru/english/index.shtml.

Moser, Robert G. 2003. "Electoral Systems and Women's Representation: The Strange Case of Russia." In *Women's Access to Political Power in Post-Communist Europe,* ed. Richard E. Matland and Kathleen A. Montgomery. New York: Oxford University Press.

Myers, Steven Lee. 2004. "From Dismal Chechnya, Women Turn to Bombs." *New York Times,* September 10.

Nechemias, Carol. 1996. "Women's Participation: From Lenin to Gorbachev." In *Russian Women in Politics and Society,* ed. Wilma Rule and Norma C. Noonan. Westport, CT: Greenwood Press.

Noonan, Norma C. 1996. "The Bolshevik Legacy and Russian Women's Movements." In *Russian Women in Politics and Society,* ed. Wilma Rule and Norma C. Noonan. Westport, CT: Greenwood Press.

Norris, Pippa. 1993. "Conclusions: Comparing Legislative Recruitment." In *Gender and Party Politics,* ed. Joni Lovenduski and Pippa Norris. London: Sage Publications.

Norris, Pippa, and Joni Lovenduski. 1995. *Political Recruitment: Gender, Race, and Class in the British Parliament.* Cambridge, UK: Cambridge University Press.

Nowacki, Dawn. 2003. "Women in Russian Regional Assemblies: Losing Ground." In *Women's Access to Political Power in Post-Communist Europe,* ed. Richard E. Matland and Kathleen A. Montgomery. New York: Oxford University Press.

O vnesenii izmenenii v Federalnyi zakon "O politicheskikh partiiakh" [On the insertion of changes into the Federal law "On political parties"]. 2004. Rossiiskaia Federatsiia Federalnyi zakon N 168-FZ [Russian Federation Federal law No. 168-FZ], December 20. http://www.akdi.ru/GD/proekt/095698GD.shtm.

Oslon, A. 2001. "Predvaritel'nye zametki" [Preliminary notes]. In *Pogovorim o grazhdanskom obshchestve* [Let's talk about civil society]. Comp. E. Petrenko. Moscow: Institut Fonda "Obshchestvennoe mnenie."

OSCE/ODIHR (Organization for Security and Cooperation in Europe/Office for Democratic Institutions and Human Rights). 2004. "Russian Federation Elections to the State Duma, 7 December 2003: OSCE/ODIHR Election Observation Mission Report," January 27. http://www.osce.org/odihr-elections/documents .html?lsi=true&limit=10&grp=231.

Pavlenko, V. N., comp. 1990. *Politbiuro, Orgbiuro, Sekretariat TsK RKP(b)—VKP (b)—KPSS* [Politburo, Orgburo, Secretariat CC RCP(b)—AUCP(b)—CPSU]. Moscow: Politizdat.

Posadskaya, Anastasia, et al. 1994. *Women in Russia: A New Era in Russian Feminism.* Trans. Kate Clark. London: Verso.

Radio Mayak. 2007. "Yabloko Spokesman Outlines Manifesto on Russian State Radio," September 17. In *BBC Monitoring Former Soviet Union,* September 19.

Rule, Wilma. 1994. "Women's Underrepresentation and Electoral Systems." *PS: Political Science and Politics* 27(4): 689–692.

Rule, Wilma, and Norma C. Noonan, eds. 1996. *Russian Women in Politics and Society.* Westport, CT: Greenwood Press.

Rule, Wilma, and Nadezhda Shvedova. 1996. "Women in Russia's First Multiparty Election." In *Russian Women in Politics and Society,* ed. Wilma Rule and Norma C. Noonan. Westport, CT: Greenwood Press.

Rulers.org. 2008a. "Rulers: Russia. Administrative Divisions." http://rulers.org/russ div.html.

———. 2008b. "Rulers: Russia. Ministries, Political Parties, etc." http://www.rulers .org/russgov.html.

Russia Journal. 1999. "'Women of Russia' Factions Now on Their Own," March 8.

Russian Life. 2005. "Mothers' Party: Defense Ministry to Take on Russia's Mothers," 48(1): 8.

Salmenniemi, Suvi. 2003. "Democracy Without Women? The Russian Parliamentary Elections and Gender Equality." Aleksanteri Institute, November 7. http:// www.balticdata.info/russia/elections/russia_elections_suvi.htm.

Shevchenko, Iulia. 2002. "Who Cares About Women's Problems? Female Legislators in the 1995 and 1999 Russian State Dumas." *Europe-Asia Studies* 54(8): 1201–1222.

Shvedova, Nadezhda. n.d. "The Challenge of Transition—Women in Parliament in Russia." International IDEA Women in Politics: Women in Parliament: Case Studies. http://archive.idea.int/women/parl/studies2a.htm.

Snezhkova, Irina A. 2004. "Ethnic Aspects of Gender Social Inequality." *Sociological Research* 43(3): 85–96.

Sperling, Valerie. 1999. *Organizing Women in Contemporary Russia: Engendering Transition.* Cambridge, UK: Cambridge University Press.

Stites, Richard. 1978. *The Women's Liberation Movement in Russia: Feminism, Nihilism, and Bolshevism, 1860–1930.* Princeton, NJ: Princeton University Press.

Stockdale, Melissa K. 2004. "'My Death for the Motherland Is Happiness': Women, Patriotism, and Soldiering in Russia's Great War, 1914–1917." *American Historical Review* 109(1): 78–116.

UNDP (United Nations Development Programme). 2006. *Human Development Report 2006.* New York: Palgrave Macmillan.

USAID (United States Agency for International Development). 1997. Office of Women in Development. "Country Gender Profile—Russia." Washington, D.C.: United States Agency for International Development.

Weir, Fred. 2003. "Chechen Women Join Terror's Ranks." *Christian Science Monitor,* June 12.

Yablokova, Oksana. 2004. "Soldier's Mothers Form a Party." *Moscow Times,* November 9.

11

Religion

Olga Kazmina

Religion has traditionally played a significant role in the social life of Russia. Even seventy years of the promotion of atheism and the suppression of religious beliefs by the Communist Party could not eradicate religion. To understand the contemporary religious situation, and even more broadly the specifics of some important cultural, social, and political processes, it is necessary to examine major moments from the history of church-state relations and religious development in general. After outlining the history of the country's leading religious denominations, this chapter will address the contemporary religious situation, the relationship between religion and identity, and the status of religious freedom in Russia.

■ **Religion in Russia from Ancient Times to the Demise of the Soviet Union**

Christianity in Russia

Russian Orthodoxy. Although Christianity is believed to have arrived early in Russia (according to legend the Apostle St. Andrew visited the Russian lands in the first century), its initial impact was slight. Indeed, through the late ninth century, Christianity was restricted to the higher aristocracy of Kievan Rus. There were some Christians among the bodyguards of Grand Duke Igor (reigned 913–945), and in 955 Igor's widow, Olga, (reigned 945–962) was baptized. But only in 988 was Christianity established as the state religion by Grand Duke Vladimir (reigned from about 980 to 1015).

Christianity came to Russia by way of the Byzantine Empire and thus was Eastern Orthodox in form. As in Byzantium, church and state in Russia were tightly connected, and religion was incorporated into the state ideology. The Orthodox doctrine of a "symphony" between church and state mandates close cooperation between these institutions.

From its founding the Russian Church was under the jurisdiction of Constantinople, one of the main seats of Eastern Orthodoxy. Even so, the Russian Church had substantial autonomy. In 1448 the church began electing its own leaders or metropolitans separately from Constantinople. It would not be until 1589, however, that the Russian Church would officially be granted its autocephaly, or independence, by the patriarch of Constantinople. With this act, the metropolitan of Moscow became patriarch of the Russian Church.

As Figes (2002, 305) notes, "religious rituals were at the heart of the Russian faith," with the result that church reform was a source of great controversy. In the second half of the seventeenth century, Patriarch Nikon oversaw changes in some church rituals and liturgical texts to bring them more into line with the Greek originals. Some clergy and laity so opposed these innovations that they broke away from the church and formed a branch of Russian Orthodoxy known as the "Old Believers" or "Old Ritualists." To

The Church of the Transfiguration at Kizhi on Lake Onegin represents the culmination of traditional Russian wooden church architectural style and construction.

this day Old Believers claim that they alone have preserved real Russian faith, culture, and traditions, and even true Russian consciousness.[1]

Despite the bitter differences between Old Believers and church reformers, the two sides in the conflict held one important thing in common: both, as Billington (1970, 158) points out, opposed any notion of "the church as a subordinate institution of a secularized state." Even so, at the time Old Believers and reformers were locked in battle, secular forces grew stronger, such that by the early eighteenth century Peter the Great (reigned 1682–1725) could make crucial changes in the church's organization. A Westernizing reformer, Peter adopted many German practices into the Russian experience, including the German Lutheran model of church-state relations. For the Russian Church this meant setting up a synodical system and abolishing the patriarchate. With this, the tsar in fact proclaimed himself to be the head of the church, and the new Holy Synod was counted as little more than another state ministry, such as the treasury or the military. In removing what autonomy the church had, Peter's reforms ran contrary to Eastern Orthodoxy's conception of symphony between church and state, which held that the "ultimate functions" of church and state, even if in harmony, should remain separate (Meyendorff 1978, 170).

Although it had lost its autonomy, the Russian Orthodox Church would remain the largest and most influential denomination in the country. With around 100 million members at the beginning of the twentieth century, 50,000 priests, and some 95,000 monks and nuns in more than 950 monasteries, it was also the world's largest national church (Tsypin 2000, 132). More importantly, as the established church, it enjoyed many privileges other denominations did not. Even so, its activities were closely regulated and controlled by the state.

When the tsarist state eventually weakened, however, as it came under fire from radicals and reformers during the period that spanned the 1905 and 1917 revolutions, a movement arose within the church that called for the restoration of the Moscow patriarchate, independence from the state, and the launching of church reforms. In August 1917, less than six months after Tsar Nicholas II's abdication, the first All-Russian Church Council convened, and in November of that year elected Tikhon, the metropolitan of Moscow, patriarch of the Russian Church. About that same time, however, the Bolsheviks seized power in Petrograd, interrupting the development of religious freedom in Russia.

The Bolsheviks were Marxists and thus saw religion as the "opiate of the masses." In the view of the Bolsheviks, the Orthodox Church could not have been more closely associated with the old regime. The Russian tsars had ruled in the name of God and had enjoyed a God-like status among the Russian people; Russian Orthodoxy thus enjoyed special status as the state church. Seeing no place for it in the new society they were creating, the Bolsheviks disestablished the church in January 1918. Soon thereafter, the Russian Orthodox Church became a target of Soviet repression, as did other religious denominations some time later. Millions of Orthodox believers, both clergy and laity, as well as people of other faiths, were killed, imprisoned, or exiled. In 1937 alone, the most cruel year of the repression, nearly 137,000 members of the Orthodox clergy were arrested. Of that number, more than 85,000 were killed (*Rossiiskie vesti* 1996). Churches were closed and sometimes destroyed, icons and religious books were burned, members of the clergy were denied civil rights, and children of priests were prevented from receiving higher education.

The Russian Orthodox Church faced a crisis of another sort after the death of Patriarch Tikhon in 1925, when the Soviet government refused to allow the bishops to convene the church council to elect Tikhon's successor. The 1927 declaration of Metropolitan Sergii (then the acting head of the church) further weakened it, by affirming that "[w]e wish to remain Orthodox and at the same time to recognize the Soviet Union as our civil fatherland whose joys and successes are our joys and successes and whose misfortunes are our misfortunes" (quoted in Spinka 1956, 66). Such a declaration provoked schisms in the church, some of which persist to this day.[2] However, it also permitted the church to retain its status as a legally permitted institution, without which it would have been forced to go underground.

In 1925, in accordance with the state policy of promoting atheism, the Union of Militant Atheists was formed. In 1932, this union adopted a Five-Year Plan to close all places of worship of all denominations and to end all religion by 1937 (Tsypin 1994, 103). In 1929, the adoption of the decree "On Religious Associations" further restricted religious activities. Naturally, under such conditions, people had few opportunities to openly profess their religious beliefs. Nevertheless, the level of religiosity remained high, as attested to by the 1937 census, the only Soviet census that measured the denominational composition of the population. Even though many were afraid to declare their belief in God, more than half of the adult population identified themselves as believers, mostly Orthodox (*Vsesoiuznaia* 1991, 106).

Despite this, the Russian Orthodox Church as an institution was on the brink of extinction. In 1917 the church had 163 serving bishops. In 1938, it had only four bishops living freely and running their dioceses. The others had been imprisoned or killed, or had emigrated and now belonged to the Russian Orthodox Church Abroad. Of the fifty-four thousand churches, twenty-five thousand chapels, and twelve thousand convents and monasteries that had been operating in 1917, only four hundred churches remained; all of the Russian Orthodox Church's convents and monasteries were closed (Bezborodov 2005, 72; Tsypin 1994, 106; Zeide 1988, 345–346). In some cities, especially the new ones that were being built to support the country's industrialization drive, there were no churches at all. These "God-less" cities, as they were called in the Soviet press, reflected the ideological underpinnings of the new system, which saw religion as a relic of the past (Anderson 1944, 17–18).

The Russian Orthodox Church's status changed during World War II. Immediately following the German invasion of Soviet territory in June 1941, the church took an active patriotic position. As Russian historian M. Shkarovskii observes, the old national and patriotic traditions of Russian Orthodoxy turned out to be stronger than Soviet ideology (Shkarovskii 2000, 119). Whereas Stalin did not address the Soviet people until the twelfth day of the war, Metropolitan Sergii sent a patriotic message to all parishes the first day of the German invasion. Hundreds of priests served in the Red Army, including many who had spent time in Soviet prisons or camps. Churches all over the country collected money and goods to support the war effort (Tsypin 2005, 68). Wartime documents reveal a significant increase of religiosity across the country, including high-ranking officers in the military (Bezborodov 2005, 76; Shkarovskii 2000, 122–137).

The Nazis, hostile toward Christianity at home, for tactical reasons allowed the reopening of churches in the occupied territories. German reports at the time spoke of the strong profession and practice of religious faith and belief in these regions (Buss 1987, 31). The Soviet government reacted to such measures by improving conditions for religious organizations in territory still under its control. The USSR was concerned, too, about its public image abroad, especially leading up to the Tehran Conference (convened November 28 through December 1, 1943), the first of three great meetings between Stalin and the leaders of the Soviet Union's main wartime allies, the United States and the United Kingdom (Chumachenko 2007, 89).

As a result, many churches were reopened (as were some monasteries and convents), a number of priests and bishops were released from prison, and the Russian Orthodox Church was finally allowed to elect a patriarch. By 1946, the number of functioning churches had tripled in comparison with prewar figures. In the years immediately following the war, atheism was no longer a major policy objective of the Soviet state, and thus, at least for a time, believers, especially older ones, faced few obstacles in practicing their faith (Tsekhanskaia 2001–2002, 19).

In the late 1950s and early 1960s, however, Soviet leader Nikita Khrushchev led a new antireligious campaign that included a renewal of atheistic propaganda, the discrediting of clergy, mass church closures, and other efforts to hinder the church in its operations (Tsekhanskaia 2001–2002, 19–20). Khrushchev, determined to lead the country to full communism, "spoke of showing the last Christian on television by 1980" (Davis 1995, 34). In contrast to Khrushchev's aggressive approach, the Brezhnev era that followed (1964–1982) was one of "slow erosion" with respect to the Russian Orthodox

Church: there were no more large-scale church closings, "but the losses of the Khrushchev attack were not reversed and additional losses accumulated" (Davis 1995, 46).

Relations between the Soviet state and religion only began to change for the better in the late 1980s when the political reforms of Mikhail Gorbachev permitted greater freedom of speech and association for all citizens, including religious believers. In 1988, in the midst of Gorbachev's reforms, the Millennium of Christianity in Russia was celebrated as a national festival. In real terms, this step toward tolerance marked the end of the Soviet repression of religion.

Roman Catholicism. Small groups of Catholics, descendants of settlers from Western Europe, appeared in Russia in the eleventh and twelfth centuries. Early on, there was no real antagonism between Western Catholicism and Eastern Orthodoxy in Russia. Relations between the two Christian faiths began to deteriorate, however, with the fall of Constantinople to the crusaders in 1204. Subsequent German attempts to "Christianize" Slavic peoples by force, and Swedish and Danish invasions of the Russian lands of Novgorod and Pskov, further worsened relations between the two churches (Mchedlov 2003, 334–335). Not until Peter the Great and his turn toward Western Europe did Russia's relations with the Roman Catholic Church improve. As part of his reformist effort, Peter introduced the principle of tolerance toward Catholics on the part of the authorities, conditioned on their loyalty to the Russian state. This principle held until the Bolsheviks came to power in 1917 (Trofimchuk 2002, 282).

The number of Catholics living in the Russian empire increased significantly following Peter's reforms. Catherine the Great (reigned 1762–1796) invited large numbers of Europeans, including many Catholics, to settle in Russia. Such was the openness to Catholics during Catherine's reign, that when the Jesuit Order was suppressed by Pope Clement XIV in 1773, no similar moves were taken by Catherine. Indeed, the Jesuits would not be expelled from Russia until 1820 during a time of nationalist reaction (Bolshakoff 1950, 145–146). During Catherine's reign the Russian empire also acquired land through three partitions of Poland. These newly won Polish territories were inhabited by adherents of the Roman Catholic Church. Gradually, Catholicism came to be seen as the religion of certain ethnic groups who lived in Russia, namely Poles, Lithuanians, and Germans. As such, the very notion of ethnic Russians converting to Catholicism was inconceivable. Thus, Catholic missionary work among non-Catholic ethnic groups was prohibited. As a "foreign" religion, Catholicism was also strongly associated with West European culture, statehood, and policy. Indeed, its spread in Russia coincided with periods of reform and modernization. The first ethnic Russian conversions to Catholicism occurred in the early nineteenth century during the reforms of Alexander I (reigned 1801–1825). Most of these new converts came from the upper classes of Russian society (Filatov and Vorontsova 1999, 96). However, when the political climate changed, becoming more reactionary and nationalistic late in Alexander's reign, Russian Catholics were forced to flee the country or keep their conversions a secret. In fact, Russian law prohibited leaving the Russian Orthodox Church for another faith but was ignored during the period of Alexander I's reforms. During the 1830s and 1840s, conversions to Catholicism often represented a form of protest against the reactionary regime of Nicholas I (reigned 1825–1855) (Tsimbaeva 1999, 147).

Renewed interest in Catholicism came at the beginning of the twentieth century, which was also a period of reform and modernization. This time it resulted in the establishment of ethnic Russian Catholic parishes and even the creation of the Russian Catholic Church of the Eastern Rite in 1907. This followed the 1905 adoption of the Act of Toleration, which finally permitted conversions from Russian Orthodoxy.

The Russian Catholic Church of the Eastern Rite was disbanded in the 1920s, however, in the face of Bolshevik repression. Almost all Latin Rite Roman Catholic parishes were also closed in the Russian Republic by 1940. Two churches, one in Moscow and one in Leningrad, remained open only because they were officially registered as institutions of the French Embassy. The restoration of Catholic parishes began only after Mikhail Gorbachev came to power in 1985. One of the turning points in this shift in policy was his audience with Pope John Paul II, in Malta, in 1989.

Protestantism. Appearing quite early in Russia, the first Lutheran congregation formed in Moscow in 1559. Fifty years later, a Lutheran community was created in the city of Nizhny Novgorod in the Volga region. Not long after, Lutheranism spread in Ingria, a territory around the current location of St. Petersburg that had come under Swedish control in 1617. With Sweden's acquisition of this territory, many Finns (Finland belonged to Sweden at this time), who were Lutherans, moved to Ingria, providing an opportunity for active, though unsuccessful, attempts to convert the local Orthodox population to Lutheranism. In the early eighteenth century, as a result of another war between Russia and Sweden, these lands reverted to Russia, but the Finnish Lutheran population stayed put, with their religious rights secured by the Peace Treaty of 1721 (Kazmina and Shlygina 2001–2002, 60).

Under Peter the Great's rule the number of Lutherans in large Russian cities also increased. These were mostly German specialists invited by Peter to come to Russia. A new influx occurred under Catherine the Great, when at her invitation many German peasants, among them Lutherans, migrated to Russia. Throughout, the status of the Lutheran Church in the Russian empire was quite stable. Because it was an ethnic church there was little concern that

Orthodox believers would convert to Lutheranism. The Lutheran Church even received financial assistance from the tsar's court and immediate members of the tsar's family. This was partly due to the large number of German nobles in aristocratic circles close to the tsar, but also because a number of the tsars' and grand dukes' wives had been Lutherans prior to marriage. Although they converted to Orthodoxy upon marriage into the royal family, they continued to support the Lutheran Church. Furthermore, some of the tsar's residences in the region around St. Petersburg were located in districts where many Lutheran Finns lived, which also positively influenced attitudes at court (Shlygina and Kazmina 1999, 185).

During the Soviet period, however, the Lutheran Church, like other denominations, endured very hard times. Moreover, as a result of events surrounding World War II, ethnic groups professing Lutheranism (Germans, Finns, Latvians, and Estonians) were subjected to purges and deportations. The Lutheran Church actually ceased to exist officially in the Russian Republic, though it continued some of its activities underground. Active restoration of the Lutheran Church took place only in late 1980s.

Lutherans were not the only Protestants in Russia. In the second part of the eighteenth century, another Protestant group, the Mennonites, appeared in the country. Like many Lutherans, they moved there from Prussia at the invitation of Catherine the Great, who granted them some privileges, including exemption from military service, which was crucial to the Mennonites because of their pacifist beliefs. After the 1917 Bolshevik Revolution, a significant portion of the Mennonite community emigrated from Russia. Those who stayed were subjected to repression in 1930s and 1940s. Since the late 1980s many Mennonites have taken advantage of better relations with the West to emigrate to Germany.

Baptists represent yet another Protestant denomination in Russia, first arriving in the country in the middle of the nineteenth century. Initially, the only Baptists in Russia were Germans, but soon this faith spread to other ethnic groups. In 1870, the Evangelical Christian movement, which closely resembled the Baptists, also came to Russia. During the first decade of Soviet rule, when the state concentrated mostly on its struggle against the Russian Orthodox Church, Evangelicals remained relatively free to operate and in the process gained many converts. By the late 1920s, however, Soviet antireligious purges hit them too (Bolshakoff 1950, 119–120). Baptists and Evangelical Christians in Russia made a number of attempts to unite in the late nineteenth and early twentieth centuries. But only in 1944 did they form the Union of Evangelical Christians-Baptists. In 1945–1947 some Mennonites and Pentecostal congregations also joined the union. In 1961, the Council of the Churches of Evangelical Christians-Baptists broke away from the union, accusing its leadership of violating core Baptist principles and of collaborating with the Soviet authorities. The Council of Churches remained underground until 1988 when changes in policy under Gorbachev finally allowed it to operate in the open.

Another Protestant denomination, the Pentecostals, appeared in Russia not long before World War I. The first Pentecostal preachers were former Evangelical Christians who were converted to Pentecostalism by missionaries from the United States with the first Pentecostal congregation forming in St. Petersburg in 1913. At first, Pentecostals pursued their missionary work among Baptists and Evangelical Christians, but then extended their efforts to include the followers of other denominations as well.

In the early 1920s, after the Russian Civil War, their numbers grew dramatically, spurred on in part by the more open atmosphere of the NEP (the New Economic Policy). Importantly, the Soviet authorities were so preoccupied with their struggle against the Russian Orthodox Church that they did little to hinder the Pentecostals and their work. Such was the success of Pentecostals, that when they applied to Lenin for permission to open a church in Petrograd (formerly St. Petersburg), their wish was granted (Lunkin 2002, 343). However, beginning in 1929, with the enactment of new antireligious legislation, the Pentecostals, too, would become targets of repression. Ultimately, during the 1930s, many would die in Stalin's camps. In reaction to this repression, the Pentecostal doctrine of baptism through suffering appeared. After World War II, however, when the Soviet government was more tolerant of religion, Pentecostalism experienced a revival with the creation of numerous illegal and unregistered communities. Eventually, the Soviet state responded to the growth of Pentecostalism in two different ways. First, the authorities worked hard to create an image in people's minds that Pentecostals were a dangerous sect, and therefore to be avoided. At the same time, in contradiction to this message, they simply tried to pretend that these Pentecostal communities did not exist.

Islam in Russia

Islam is Russia's second largest religion. Its history in the country can be considered in four parts: first, Muslim states from the tenth through the sixteenth centuries that occupied territories that are now part of contemporary Russia; second, Islam in the Russian Orthodox state from the sixteenth to the early twentieth century; third, Islam under Soviet rule; and finally, Islam in post-Soviet Russia (Trofimchuk 2002, 436).

Muslims made their first forays into lands that eventually became part of Russia in the seventh century with the Arab invasion of Dagestan. Although Arabs did not manage to keep Dagestan for very long, the Islamization of this territory began a process that would last centuries. The development of Islam in the region resumed in the tenth century and continued through the thirteenth with the acceptance of Islam by many of the ethnic groups of southern Dagestan followed by the conversion to Islam of the region's largest ethnic group, the Avars, in the fourteenth century. In the fifteenth and sixteenth centuries, Islam spread to the territory of Chechnya, and by the seventeenth century it had penetrated the western part of the North Caucasus. In some cases Islam replaced Christianity as the dominant religion, but in others it was interwoven with the pre-Islamic beliefs of the local peoples.

As successful as the spread of Islam was in the North Caucasus region, it enjoyed its greatest success in the Volga region with the founding of full-fledged Muslim states. The first came in 922, with the acceptance of Islam as the state religion of the Volga Bulgars (which covered a territory that now includes the republics of Tatarstan and Chuvashia, and the Ulyanovsk and Samara regions of the Russian Federation). The acceptance of Islam set apart and distinguished the Volga Bulgars from neighboring states. Even though they were defeated by the Mongols (or Tartars) in 1236–1238, the region remained a center of Muslim culture.

The cultural and religious centers of the Volga Bulgars were incorporated into the Mongol Golden Horde, which included a number of other territories, namely, the Crimea, the North Caucasus, the lower Volga region, the southern Urals, western Siberia, and northern Kazakhstan. The rulers of the Golden Horde were religiously tolerant and as a result Islam spread easily within its territory. In the late thirteenth century, the khan of the Golden Horde, Berke (reigned 1260–1277), accepted Islam. His successors would return to their traditional religion, Shamanism, but not long after, under Khan Uzbek (reigned 1312–1342), Islam became the established religion of the Horde. In the fifteenth century, the Golden Horde split into the Kazan, Siberian, Crimean, Astrakhan, and a number of other, smaller khanates (Urazmanova and Cheshko 2001, 79–80). Of these the Kazan Khanate would become the center of Islam in the Volga region and adjacent areas. The khanate remained sovereign from 1438 until 1552, when its capital city, Kazan, now the capital of the Republic of Tatarstan, was captured by the troops of Ivan the Terrible (reigned 1533–1584), and the khanate was incorporated into the Russian state. The Russians followed this with the defeat and incorporation of the Astrakhan Khanate in 1556.

After the victory of Russian forces over the remnants of the Golden Horde, there were numerous attempts to Christianize the Muslim population of the Volga region. Such actions had a strong political component, as Moscow sought to integrate these new lands into Russia and secure their political loyalty. Although Muslims who devotedly served the Russian tsar enjoyed some religious tolerance and could preserve their faith, discrimination was the norm. In particular, Muslims were prohibited from building new mosques, and old mosques could be preserved only in areas where there were no Christians. Muslims who converted to Christianity, however,

The rebuilt Qol Sharif Mosque, Kazan.
The original mosque was destroyed in 1552 following
the Russian conquest of the city. Construction on the new mosque
began in 1996. The largest mosque in Russia, it opened in 2005.

not only were granted privileges but also were much more likely to win promotion in state service. Thus, Tatar rulers who swore allegiance to the tsar usually converted to Orthodox Christianity.

The position of Russia's Muslims changed, however, under Catherine the Great. One of the elements of her religious policy was the protection of Muslims (as well as those who confessed other faiths). Motivated by a desire for greater stability during a time of open rebellion in the countryside (see Steven Marks's discussion of the Pugachev Rebellion in Chapter 3), Catherine, in 1773, signed the Edict of Toleration to All Beliefs, which recognized Islam as an official religion of the Russian empire (Silant'ev 2005, 16). So, too, when the Crimean Khanate was incorporated into Russia in 1783 (thus increasing the number of Muslims in the empire), Catherine's manifesto confirmed the rights of Muslims to profess their faith. Muslims were also permitted to construct new mosques. At about the same time, in 1782, a muftiat, or Muslim spiritual and administrative body, was founded in the city of Ufa, hence establishing the Muslim clergy as a separate class. Not long after, in 1784, the Tatar and Bashkir upper classes were granted the rights of the Russian nobility. In 1788, with the creation of the Muslim Spiritual Meeting, Russia's Muslims possessed a central structure to which all Muslim religious communities were subordinated (Trofimchuk 2002,

445; Urazmanova and Cheshko 2001, 142), strengthening the position of Islam as a religious institution in Russia. Later on, an unwritten rule was negotiated between the Orthodox Christian and Muslim hierarchies to the effect that the Russian Orthodox Church would not try to use its privileged position as an established church in Muslim regions to proselytize there, and in turn, Muslims would not proselytize the Orthodox population in these same regions. In general, Catherine the Great's regulations determined the situation for Muslims until 1917, when the February Revolution forced Tsar Nicholas II from power.

With this end to tsarist rule, the Muslim movement became very active. In May and July 1917, All-Russian (that is, nationwide) Muslim congresses were held. These congresses planned the further development of the Muslim movement in Russia, but the Bolsheviks' seizure of power in October 1917 prevented the realization of these plans. Interestingly, most of Russia's Muslims supported the establishment of Soviet power because they thought conditions would get better. Indeed, during the early 1920s, when the Bolsheviks' religious policies concentrated on their struggle with the Russian Orthodox Church, the position of Islam did improve. Muslim primary schools continued to exist, *sharia* (that is, Islamic law) courts persisted in some places, and mosques could own real estate. Representatives of the Muslim clergy could even be members of the Bolshevik Party (Trofimchuk 2002, 449).

In the mid-1920s, however, the new Soviet state altered its attitude toward Islam and began to oppress Muslim religious life. A certain kind of relief came during World War II when some mosques were allowed to reopen, but during the antireligious campaign of the 1960s, many of them were closed again. Nevertheless, because Islam already had been incorporated into the everyday life and ethnic culture of various national groups in the USSR, the Soviet authorities failed to eliminate Islam as a religion.

Islam experienced a period of renewal in the late 1980s as a result of Gorbachev's reforms. New mosques were built and new madrassas (schools or colleges) opened. In another break with Soviet practice, believers were free to go on the hajj (pilgrimage) to Mecca. Indicative of this new relationship between Islam and the Soviet state, in 1989 celebrations were held in Tatarstan and Bashkortostan to commemorate the bicentennial of the formation of the Muslim Spiritual Meeting and to honor the 1,100th anniversary of the acceptance of Islam by the Volga Bulgars (Silant'ev 2005, 32–33).

Buddhism in Russia

In Russia there are three traditional Buddhist regions: Buryatia, Kalmykia, and Tyva. In each of them Buddhism is represented by its Vajrayana, or esoteric, tradition, in its Dge-lugs-pa, or Yellow Hat, school. The status of Buddhism in these regions, historically, has been directly connected with the politics of the Russian state. At the same time the state declared Buddhism a recognized religion in these regions, it sought to undermine the close ties Buryat and Kalmyk Buddhists had with Tibet and Mongolia by promoting the formation of separate Buryat and Kalmyk Buddhist *sanghas* (communities of Buddhist monks and nuns). Also, even as the political and economic interests of the Russian empire demanded the recognition of Buddhism to appease significant ethnic groups, the government sought to limit the influence of Buddhism and keep open possibilities for Christianization and Russification in the Buddhist regions.

The Buddhist *sangha* in the Trans-Baikal region (located in what is now the Republic of Buryatia and the Aga Buryat Autonomous Okrug) was created in cooperation with the Tibetan and Mongolian *sanghas,* but with the active participation of the Russian state (Trofimchuk 2002, 384). The incorporation of Buryatia into the Russian empire and the beginning of the conversion of Buryats to Buddhism from Shamanism occurred in the seventeenth century. In 1741 the Empress Elizabeth (reigned 1741–1761) signed an edict regulating the religious life of Buryat Buddhists. In particular, this edict designated Buddhist lamas as a separate class and hence recognized Buddhism as a religion in the Russian empire. Conversion to Orthodox Christianity was strongly encouraged, however. Such converts, for instance, were freed from taxes for several years (Mchedlov 2003, 365). Nevertheless, the number of lamas in the Trans-Baikal region increased and Buddhism spread to neighboring territories, much to the dismay of the Russian authorities. In 1853 the government adopted the Regulations on the Lamaist Clergy, which restricted the number of lamas in eastern Siberia. Furthermore, candidates for the head of the lamaist clergy would have to be approved by a special department of the Ministry for Internal Affairs. This regulation remained in force until the 1920s.

As for Kalmykia, the formation of the Buddhist *sangha* there dates to the seventeenth century and the migration of Kalmyks to Russia from northwestern Mongolia and Djungaria, a territory of northwestern China. All legal acts that regulated relations between the Buddhist *sangha* and the state were determined by the Russian government. The Kalmyk Khanate was formed in the 1660s and 1670s as a dependent state within Russia, but both this state and its Buddhist *sangha* had great autonomy. In the eighteenth century the Russian government constantly tried to limit the autonomy of this khanate and to promote the conversion of Kalmyks from Buddhism to Orthodox Christianity, giving various privileges to such converts. A 1744 edict turned the Kalmyks into serfs, who could be bought and sold like slaves, with the result that in 1771 most Kalmyks left the Volga steppes and migrated back to Djungaria. This demographic change weakened both the Kalmyk Khanate and Buddhism in the region. In the same year, the khans lost their autonomy and the Kalmyk Khanate became just another province of Russia (Zhukov-skaia and Mokshin 1998, 295). Interestingly, until 1771 the Kalmyk khans were appointed by the Dalai Lama. Though the khanate was eliminated, Buddhism in Kalmykia continued to be recognized by the Russian state.

Buddhists, as well as adherents to other non-Orthodox Christian faiths, enjoyed more religious freedom after the Act of Toleration of 1905. The first years of Soviet rule were also relatively favorable for active religious life for Buddhists, although many Kalmyk clergy left Russia during the civil war of 1918–1920. Having seen the dramatic deterioration of relations between the new authorities and the Russian Orthodox Church, Buddhist renovationists, or reformers, immediately declared their loyalty to Soviet power. This gave them a chance to preserve their legal existence in the Soviet system but provoked internal conflicts between renovationists and traditionalists. In 1927, the All-Union Congress of Buddhists established a Representative Office of Buddhist Clergy in the USSR. It would be housed in Leningrad's Buddhist temple. Built in 1915, this Buddhist temple was the first ever constructed in Europe. (Burdo and Filatov 2005, 235).

The situation for Buddhists changed in 1929, when lamas were declared to be "capitalist elements," and in accordance with the new decree, On Religious Associations (1929), were denied civil rights. Religious schools were closed (Trofimchuk 2002, 407–408), and more repression followed in the 1930s. With the deportation of Kalmyks in 1943 (who, like many other minority peoples in the European USSR during World War II, were suspected of disloyalty by Stalin and deported from their ethnic homelands to remote regions of the Soviet Union), the Kalmyk *sangha* ceased to exist. It was registered again only in the late 1980s after Gorbachev came to power. By contrast, Buddhism in Buryatia (located far from the war zone) fared much better during World War II, experiencing some improvement in its position. After the war, in 1946, Buryat Buddhists even got permission to restore two monasteries, one in Buryatia, and one in the Aga Buryat Mongolian National Okrug (now known as the Aga Buryat Autonomous Okrug). The Central Spiritual Board of Buddhists in the USSR was also restored and located in Buryatia.

With respect to Tyva (also known as Tuva), Buddhism long predated the region's 1944 incorporation into the USSR, having arrived during the thirteenth century (Burdo and Filatov 2005, 277). Buddhists there were under the Mongolian Buddhist *sangha*. Under constant pressure from both China and Russia, Tyva became a Russian protectorate in 1914. It declared its independence in 1921, only to come under heavy Soviet influence in 1929 with the coming to power of a Moscow-trained local communist, Solchak Toka. Taking a hard Stalinist line, the new leader launched attacks on Tyva's Buddhist monasteries (Rupen 1975, 151–152). By the end of the 1940s, with Tyva now a part of the Soviet Union, every Buddhist temple and monastery had been closed (Trofimchuk 2002, 384, 411). Through the late 1980s, not a single Buddhist community was registered in the region, with the result that Buddhism continued to function only in some rituals of everyday life. The restoration of Buddhism in Tyva, as well as Kalmykia, began only in the late 1980s with Gorbachev's reforms.

Judaism in Russia

Jews first appeared in the territory of contemporary Russia in the first century when they settled in the Greek colonies along the Black Sea coast. In the eighth century Judaism became the established religion of the Khazar Khanate, which encompassed the territory between the Volga and Dnieper rivers, the North Caucasus, and a part of Crimea, and existed until the end of the tenth century. There were also Jewish communities in Kiev and other cities of Old Kievan Rus. In the central Moscow Principality (that is, Muscovy) there were very few Jews. The number of Jews in the Russian empire increased sharply only in the late eighteenth century when Russia acquired the eastern territories of Poland.

In the Russian empire, the rights of Jews were strictly regulated and severely limited by law. Initially assigned by the Russian government to the merchants' estate, Jews, unlike peasants, were free to move about the country. Settling in cities and towns throughout the empire, Jews competed successfully with ethnic Russian merchants for business. Unhappy with this situation, Russian merchants eventually filed a complaint with the state council with the result that in 1791 the Russian government introduced the notorious "Pale of Settlement." The Pale defined and limited the areas where Jews could settle, prohibiting them from living in the interior of Russia. Jews were also required to pay higher taxes (Trofimchuk 2002, 418–419). Those who converted to Christianity, however, were exempt from these laws.

In the late eighteenth century, Hasidism (a mystical movement in which more attention is paid to praying than to studying the Torah) spread in many Jewish communities in Russia. Over time, Hasidic synagogues and yeshivas appeared. Hasidic leader Shneur Zalman (1747–1812) lived in the territory of Belorussia and founded the Habad movement in Hasidism. His descendants later became spiritual leaders of the Lubavitcher Hasidim, which is now headquartered in New York City.

The position of Jews improved to some extent in the early nineteenth century under Alexander I (reigned 1801–1825). In 1804, the Russian government officially recognized two Jewish movements in Russia, Orthodox and Hasidic, and confirmed Jewish community self-government. At the same time, rabbis and community heads had to be approved by regional governors (Trofimchuk 2002, 419). The government also approved a special regulation pertaining to the status of Jews and their religious life. This regulation, among other things, expanded the Pale of Settlement and defined rules for short-term travel by Jews within Russia. This law also permitted Jewish children to study in private high schools and universities in the Pale of Settlement.

However, the situation for Jews worsened again under Nicholas I (reigned 1825–1855). In 1827, military duty was levied on Jews with stricter regulations than for other groups (Mchedlov 1999, 141). Previously, Jewish communities paid a special tax so that their members did not have to serve in the army. The aim of state policy toward Jews now, however, was to convert them to Christianity and to integrate them into Russian culture. In 1835, the building of synagogues near Christian Orthodox churches was prohibited. In 1844, a special tax for wearing Jewish clothing was introduced and community self-government was ended.

Beginning in the mid-nineteenth century, during the reign of Alexander II (reigned 1855–1881), some changes were made in the regulations that determined the Pale of Settlement, one of which was that merchants, industrialists, those with higher education, and some other categories of people were permitted to live outside the Pale. Thus, Jewish communities gradually formed in the internal European provinces of Russia and in Siberia, and synagogues were built in many cities of the Russian heartland. At the same time, however, limits on access to education were introduced, and in 1890 the voting rights of Jews were limited.

In imperial Russia, a special structure, the Rabbi Commission, regulated Jewish religious affairs. This commission also advised the Ministry for Internal Affairs, and was, to a certain extent, an arm of the Russian state (Mchedlov 1999, 142–143). In the late nineteenth and early twentieth centuries, the world's largest Jewish community was in Russia (Kozlov 2000, 3). The Act of Toleration (1905) officially improved the position of Judaism as well as that of other religions in Russia. After 1905, however, anti-Semitic ideological and political tendencies increased, which led to violent pogroms (that is, organized massacres) of Jews. As a result, many Jews emigrated from Russia.

After the February 1917 Revolution, Jews gained a respite when all legal restrictions on them were lifted by the more democratic Provisional Government. As we know from Steven Marks's discussion in Chapter 3, however, the Provisional Government did not last long, as it was removed from power by the Bolsheviks in October 1917. In a Russia now under Soviet rule, the repression of Judaism began as early as 1919, with the prohibition of the teaching of Hebrew. Even so, in 1925, two new synagogues were opened in Moscow (Burdo and Filatov 2005, 19). Repression would not begin in earnest until the late 1920s when many synagogues were closed, rabbis were persecuted, and religious schools were shut down (Trofimchuk 2002, 429).

During World War II, almost two million Soviet Jews died at the hands of the Nazis. On Soviet territory not occupied by the Germans, some synagogues were allowed to reopen as part of Stalin's more tolerant wartime policy toward religion. These synagogues were closed again during the antireligious campaign of the 1960s. By the early 1970s, however, a movement arose among Soviet Jews, especially among religious believers, that called upon the Soviet state to allow them to emigrate to Israel. Although the initial response on the part of the Soviet leaders was further repression, under pressure from international organizations and Western governments, they eventually began allowing Jews to emigrate from the Soviet Union. Whereas only 99 Jews were allowed to emigrate in 1970, by the end of the decade the annual figure stood at 667,000 (Trofimchuk 2002, 433). One effect of this emigration, however, was the further weakening of Jewish religious life in the USSR as most of the country's believers left. Those who emigrated had no chance to return as they were forced to give up their Soviet citizenship.

As a result of Gorbachev's reforms, Jewish emigration further increased. A new feature of this period, however, was that return immigration was permitted, allowing Jews to move back and forth between Israel and the Soviet Union and to visit religious centers. As a result of Gorbachev's reforms, too, an All-Union Council of Jewish Religious Communities was formed in 1990. Up to that point synagogues in the USSR had lacked any common coordinating structure (Kozlov 2000, 17).

Other Religions in Russia

Russia is also home to numerous smaller religious denominations. For instance, approximately thirty thousand people living in the Altai, in southern Siberia, profess Burkhanism. This is a "syncretic" religion, combining elements of Shamanism and Vajrayana Buddhism. It came into being in 1904. Traditional ethnic faiths also still exist in Russia. They can be found foremost among some northern and Siberian peoples such as the Chukchi, Koryaks, and Nivkhs. Followers of traditional faiths also can be found among some peoples of the Volga region, predominantly among the Mari.

■ Religion in Post-Soviet Russia

The Advent of Religious Freedom

A new era in the history of Russian religious life began with the USSR's demise in the fall of 1991. The early post-Soviet era presented many challenges as Russia's people faced disillusionment with the past, loss of previous frames of reference, spiritual vacuum, and vague expectations of what the future might hold. This period also showed, however, that despite all the efforts of the Soviet authorities to stamp out religion, latent religiosity remained in the population. Even before the USSR's collapse, Gorbachev's reforms, combined with this latent religiosity, stimulated a religious revival in the late 1980s and early 1990s. For the first time in seventy years, people in Russia and elsewhere in the Soviet Union could openly profess their religious beliefs.

The first liberal law, On Freedom of Conscience and Religious Organizations, was adopted on October 1, 1990, by the USSR Supreme Soviet. Not long after, with the decentralizing effects of Gorbachev's political reforms already in full swing, the Russian Republic (RSFSR), on October 25, 1990, passed its own law, On Freedom of Beliefs. The Russian law further developed the main ideas of the new USSR law, lifting all restrictions on the activity of religious organizations. It also guaranteed equal rights for all denominations in Russia, permitted religious instruction in nonstate schools, and forbade the interference of government authorities in the affairs of religious organizations. This law did not make any distinctions between, or grant any preferences in legal status to, any religious organization.

For the population at large, the experience of growing up in a system hostile to religion shaped the religious situation of the early 1990s. Most Soviet citizens lacked any form of religious instruction, were ungrounded in religious doctrines and practices, and had few ties with religious organizations. With the advent of religious freedoms, however, almost all of the country's denominations, traditional and new, increased their followings. It was during this period, too, that the overwhelming majority of new denominations began to appear in Russia (Filatov 2002, 471). These denominations either came from abroad or were indigenous, newly minted sects.

An unusually high level of mobility among denominations also marked this early period of religious freedom, as many of the newly faithful converted from one denomination to another, experimenting and trying to find the religious organization that suited them best. The lack of religious knowledge within Russia's population also produced an interest in so-called alternative beliefs. Astrological forecasts were given widespread exposure in the mass media, and some people experimented with nontraditional medicine and magic. Another feature characteristic of this period was the existence of "omnibeliefs," meaning that a person, for instance, might profess Christianity as their faith, but at the same time believe in astrology, poltergeists, interplanetary aliens, reincarnation, and occult phenomena.

Because Russia was traditionally a country where the overwhelming majority of the population professed Orthodox Christianity, Christian denominations in general saw the "re-Christianization" of the population as one of the major tasks of the early 1990s. The Russian Orthodox Church was not the only player in this field. Many Western Evangelicals came to

Russia, as did the Roman Catholic Church. All sought to mobilize those who had become religiously inactive, inert, or ignorant of religious beliefs during the communist era. Because of a lack of religious training and undefined religious beliefs, many people identified themselves not as adherents of some particular denomination but simply as Christians (Byzov and Filatov 1993, 37). This vagueness about religious affiliation facilitated the appearance in Russia of various Western Christian denominations.

The early 1990s also saw a particular interest in Roman Catholicism on the part of many ethnic Russians (especially younger people) who, because they were not members of traditionally Catholic ethnic groups, lacked a traditional Catholic background. Some ethnic Russians even converted to Catholicism. Various scholars have attributed this early interest in Catholicism to the fact that Russia had once again entered a time of reform and modernization (Filatov and Vorontsova 1999, 96). One might wonder, however, why Catholicism, rather than Protestantism, with its very active missionary work, was more attractive in Russia. A number of explanations abound. Traditionally, Roman Catholicism was the faith that most Russians associated with Western values, and it was these values that were popular in Russia during the early 1990s. In addition, the Roman Catholic Church was respected for its history of strong anticommunist positions. Also, people may have had difficulty in choosing among the various Protestant denominations and had trouble associating specific denominations with Protestantism in general, whereas the Roman Catholic Church was well known. The fact that in the late Soviet period the main antireligious struggle was aimed at Protestant denominations (especially Baptists), which were treated as sects, also may have created some residual negative stereotypes and prejudices. However, even as popular as Roman Catholicism was in the early 1990s, Protestant missions were numerous, and their services, often held in large stadiums, attracted many people.

In such an atmosphere, religious denominations found themselves in competition with each other. The Russian Orthodox Church felt particularly frustrated by this emerging post-Soviet reality. Decades of restrictions imposed on Russian Orthodoxy by the communist regime had achieved at least one goal: although religiosity among the people had remained strong during the Soviet era, the church in effect had become a captive in its own sanctuaries. Simply put, it had lost its experience in missionary work and had forgotten how to conduct community activities outside the church. By contrast, Protestant Evangelicals from the West were very skilled in these types of activities. This unequal contest created tensions between the Russian Orthodox Church and Western Christian denominations.

These tensions were aggravated by differences in viewpoints between the Russian Orthodox Church and Protestant denominations on the questions of evangelism, missionary work, and proselytism. As Witte (1999, 21) observes,

> Evangelicals assume that, in order to be saved, every person must make a
> personal, conscious commitment to Christ—to be born again, to convert.
> Any person who has not been born again, or who once reborn now leads a
> nominal Christian life, is a legitimate object of evangelism—regardless of
> whether the person has already been baptized.

In this vein, Evangelicals hold that their missionaries may be sent anywhere
in the world, even if another Christian denomination is already present.
Thus, for Evangelicals, missionary work in Russia was legitimate not only
because of the country's many nonbelieving and religiously inert people but
also because of the many who associate themselves with Russian Orthodoxy out of tradition, but who do not follow the faith in practice.

The Russian Orthodox Church, while agreeing that every person must
come into a personal relationship with Christ, believes that this relationship
comes through the sacraments, services, and the like, and step by step, this
relationship will grow stronger. According to Russian Orthodoxy, most of
the people of Russia are under its spiritual protection because they, or at
least their parents, were baptized in the Russian Orthodox Church. Therefore, Russia is not an open field for the missionary work of Evangelical denominations. Patriarch Aleksii II, in his report to the 1997 Bishops Council
in Moscow, went so far as to declare that the Russian Orthodox Church
considers missionary activity destructive when it is aimed at persons who
were baptized in the Orthodox Church or are linked to Orthodoxy historically (Aleksii II 1997). The Orthodox Church also cites the words of the
Apostle Paul in its defense: "It has always been my ambition to preach the
gospel where Christ was not known, so that I would not be building on
someone else's foundation" (Romans 15:20, New International Version).
Thus, what was legitimate missionary work in the minds of Evangelicals
seemed like illegitimate proselytism in the eyes of the Russian Orthodox
Church.

The Moscow patriarchate's question and challenge to Western Christians in early 1990s was the following:

> Do you recognize us, Orthodox, as Christians or not? If you do, then in-
> stead of trying to outwit and outmaneuver us . . . you ought to help the
> Russian Orthodox Church in this dire moment of economic collapse,
> shortage of clergy and theological schools. . . . You ought to help the Or-
> thodox Church to successfully carry out its mission on its native soil.
> (Pospielovsky 1995, 56)

During the early 1990s many so-called new religious movements also
appeared in Russia. Among these were groups of foreign origin (the Unification Church founded by Reverend Sun Myung Moon, AUM Shinrikyo,
Sri Chinmoy, Scientologists, and others) as well as indigenous ones (for example, the Vissarionists). Each aggressively promoted its activities.

Despite the religious diversity and openness of society to all religious denominations in the early 1990s, the Russian Orthodox Church was the institution the population trusted the most. According to sociological surveys conducted at the time, the church rated higher than the government, the president, the prime minister, the courts, and the mass media. Only the army outpolled the church in some years (White and McAllister 1997, 240). Throughout the 1990s, according to data of the All-Russia Center for the Study of Public Opinion, the Russian Orthodox Church consistently was rated as the social institution Russians most trusted. Other surveys, conducted by the Russian Academy of Sciences' Institute of Social and Political Studies, for the period 1996–1999, reveal similar results regarding societal trust, with the Russian Orthodox Church and the Russian army earning the highest marks. In 2000, only President Putin out-polled the church (Tul'skii 2000).

The Politicization of Religion in the Mid-1990s: The New Restrictive Law on Religion

The Russian Orthodox Church's anxiety over the activities of foreign religious organizations, as well as fears in Russian society over the existence of so-called totalitarian sects, prompted calls in the Supreme Soviet as early as 1993 for a new law on religion. Appeals for new legislation intensified late in that year out of concern for the lack of oversight in the existing 1990 law, On Freedom of Beliefs. As written, primary responsibility for implementation of the law was assigned to local legislative assemblies. With the dissolution of these local councils following the demise of the Supreme Soviet and the Congress of People's Deputies in the fall of 1993, the main control mechanism for the 1990 law ceased to exist.

Russian public opinion had begun to change, too, as the initial euphoria over Western values began to give way to more nationalistic tendencies (Filatov 2002, 471–472). In the religious sphere this meant greater interest in Orthodox Christianity and other traditional religions. Indeed, the very phrase "traditional religions" became widespread in its use during this period, as did its antonyms, "totalitarian sects" and "destructive cults."

The mid-1990s also witnessed the growing politicization of religion as various political forces and state bodies began trying to use religion to suit their own ends. With public confidence in governmental bodies and political parties so low, and the prestige of the Russian Orthodox Church so high, many Russian politicians and officials sought to enhance their standing by demonstrating their loyalty to the church. Often, government officials would be seen standing in church, with candles in hand, in television broadcasts of Christmas and Easter services. Many of Russia's political parties were also interested in gaining the support of the country's largest religious denomination. Even communists, who considered a belief in God to be incompatible with Marxist-Leninist ideology, and who had struggled against religion for several decades, began pretending hypocritically to be defenders of Russian Orthodoxy. During the nationwide election campaigns of 1995 and 1996, almost all of the big political blocs tried to play upon the prestige of the church to gain votes (Verkhovskii, Pribylovskii, and Mikhailovskaia 1998, 176). Political leaders of different orientations also tried to appeal to public sentiments by using any opportunity to denounce foreign missions, totalitarian sects, and destructive cults. At the same time, the general population remained quite tolerant. A sociological survey conducted by Russian and Finnish scholars in 1996 reported that 70 percent of Russia's population "completely agreed" or "agreed to some extent" with the statement that "all religions should have equal rights in Russia" (Kääriäinen 1998, 143).

Such was the domestic political background for the adoption of the new law on religion. At the same time, on the international front, Russia was in the process of joining the Council of Europe, which requires member states to commit to the protection of religious freedom. Clearly, Russia faced two contradictory imperatives. To satisfy internal pressures, the state wanted a law that would restrict the activities of nontraditional denominations. To meet the expectations of external actors, the Russian state was interested in demonstrating its neutrality toward religion. Finally, after heated debate, the Federal Assembly adopted a new law on religion, effective October 1, 1997.

This law, On Freedom of Conscience and Religious Associations, had the potential to change the religious situation in Russia dramatically. It put religious organizations that already had been in operation in Russia for at least fifteen years in a more favorable position than those that had come later. All religious organizations had to undergo a new registration process, but only the pre-1982 organizations could obtain the status of a legal entity upon renewed registration. Those that arrived or were created after 1982 would have fewer rights as religious associations, including the freedom they had to conduct missionary work. This law also gave state bodies grounds to interfere in the religious life of believers.

Although the new law is clearly discriminatory, it has never been fully enforced. In fact, some of its more restrictive terms (including the provision that engendered the harshest criticism, the fifteen-year clause) have been mitigated by constitutional-court rulings, suggesting that the law's adoption was more a political statement than a legal act. At the same time, even though the 1997 law does not deny Russia its religious plurality, it nevertheless favors the Russian Orthodox Church and Russia's other traditional faiths as they seek to enhance their standing in Russian society.

Conceptually, the 1990 and 1997 laws were based on radically different notions of the nature of religion and religious belief. Whereas the 1990 statute viewed religion as a question of individual choice, and thus a private matter of the person, the 1997 law rooted religious life in the historical context and cultural traditions of the population. For its part, the Russian Orthodox Church, in its competition with nontraditional denominations during the mid-1990s, issued public proclamations that were more political and cultural than theological. Notable among these statements was the contention that foreign denominations would divide Russian society and destroy Russian culture and traditions (Filatov 2002, 481). Such arguments tended to be accepted by Russians, most of whom by this time had lost interest in the new denominations. Interestingly, theological statements by the church tended to be reserved for interfaith dialogue.

Initially on the defensive in its competition with nontraditional denominations, the Russian Orthodox Church since the mid-1990s has paid much more attention to promoting its own missionary activities. In 1995 it adopted the "Concept of the Rebirth of Missionary Activity of the Russian Orthodox Church" (see Kontseptsiia 1999, 11–16), followed ten years later by its approval of the "Concept of the Missionary Activity of the Russian Orthodox Church for 2005–2010" (see Missionerskii otdel 2005).

Not surprisingly, the Russian state, too, has undergone a transformation of its own in its attitude toward religion and religious organizations. In contrast with the early 1990s, when the state practiced strict neutrality in its relationship with organized religion, by the end of the decade it demonstrated clear solidarity with the Russian Orthodox Church. Under Putin, the relationship between the church and the Russian state grew even closer, so much so that the church has reclaimed its position as a vital symbol of Russian culture, power, and tradition.

■ The Contemporary Religious Makeup of Russia's Population

Statistics on religion are very complicated and difficult to interpret, because there is no single criterion for affiliating a person with a particular denomination. Figures vary greatly depending on whether one counts those who associate themselves with a certain denomination or just those who are practicing believers. Another problem is the absence of reliable data on religious membership in Russia. Most of the available figures are based on partial sociological surveys. Nevertheless, the estimates below provide at least a rough sense of the contours of religious affiliation in Russia today.

In 2002, 58 percent of Russia's population identified itself as Christian Orthodox (including 1 percent as Old Believers), 1 percent as Protestant (including 0.3 percent Pentecostal or Charismatic, 0.3 percent Baptist, and 0.2 percent Lutheran), 0.6 percent as members of the Armenian Apostolic Church, 0.3 percent as adherents of marginal Protestant faiths, 0.2 percent as Catholic, 8 percent as Muslim, 0.4 percent as believers of traditional ethnic faiths, 0.3 percent as Buddhist, 0.1 percent as Jewish, and 31 percent as nonbelievers.[3]

Two things especially stand out in these figures. First, nearly a third of Russia's population is made up of nonbelievers. This is not too surprising in a country where atheism had been official policy for over seventy years. Second, the overwhelming majority of believers are Christian Orthodox. Most Orthodox believers are ethnic Russians. The majority of Karelians, Komi, and other Finno-Ugric peoples residing in the northern regions of European Russia (excluding Ingrian Finns), many Volga region peoples (except for Tatars, Bashkirs, and Kalmyks), and the majority of Ossetians are also adherents of Orthodoxy. The many peoples of Siberia (Yakuts, Khakas, Western Buryats, Mansi, Khanty, and many others) who are Christianized combine Orthodoxy with the indigenous beliefs of their regions. Ukrainians, Belarusians, Moldavians, and Georgians living in Russia, as well as some others, are also followers of Orthodoxy. Over the last few decades a number of Jews, too, have converted to Orthodoxy, according to some estimates as many as 30 percent (Burdo and Filatov 2004, 30; Tabak 1999, 149).

Russia's few Latin Rite Roman Catholics are settled in both the European and Asian parts of the country. For the most part, Roman Catholicism in Russia is associated with Poles, although other ethnic groups also can be found among Russia's Catholics (Lithuanians, some Belarusians, and others). In 1990–1991, the Vatican reorganized the structure of the Catholic Church in Russia to establish an apostolic administrator for Latin Rite Catholics of European Russia, based in Moscow, and an apostolic administrator for Latin Rite Catholics in the Asian part of Russia, based in Novosibirsk. In 2002, however, this structure was replaced by four Catholic dioceses. Although the names of these new dioceses do not contain territorial affiliations, this reorganization angered the Russian Orthodox Church, which interpreted it as an attempt by the Roman Catholic Church to expand its base in Russia. Not until 2006 did relations between the two churches begin to improve.

In 1991, the Russian Greek Catholic Church (Byzantine Rite Catholics), which was shut down during the 1920s, began to function again in Russia. This Uniate Church is very small, however, having only about three thousand members. Most Greek Catholics in Russia (about half a million) are ethnic Ukrainians who migrated to Russia beginning in the 1970s and are members of the Ukrainian Greek Catholic Church (Johnstone 1993, 467).

Protestantism is represented in contemporary Russia by several different denominations, including Lutherans, Reformed, Mennonites, Baptists, Pentecostals, Seventh-Day Adventists, and others. Considering the experience of the early 1990s, the number of Protestants in contemporary Russia may appear unexpectedly low. There are several explanations for this besides the increasingly nationalistic mood of the population described earlier. First, many Protestants in Russia were ethnic Germans or Finns who emigrated to their ethnic homelands during the 1990s. Second, other Protestants also emigrated, among them ethnic Russians. This exodus included many pastors and large numbers of theological students, who, when sent abroad to study, chose not to return (Johnstone and Mandryk 2001, 543). Third, foreign Protestant missions lost some of their potential members because they often did not know, or did not take into consideration, the ethnic and cultural traditions of the population, did not know much of the history and literature of the country, and were not proficient in the Russian language. Often, they were simply trained for generic, nonspecific, cross-cultural experiences, regardless of their mission (Elliot and Deyneka 1999, 203).

Significant changes in the denominational structure of Protestantism also occurred in Russia during the 1990s. Whereas Baptists once were the largest Protestant denomination in Russia, now they are slightly outnumbered by Pentecostals, together with Charismatics. As in other countries, Pentecostals in Russia are divided into different movements. Because of their active missionary work, however, these various movements have been able to increase their number of adherents.

Other Protestant denominations have also seen some growth due to missionary work. The two main Lutheran denominations in the Russian Federation are the Evangelical Lutheran Church in Russia, Ukraine, Kazakhstan, and Central Asia (uniting Germans, predominantly), and the Evangelical Lutheran Church of Ingria (the church organization of Ingrian Finns). The majority of Latvians and Estonians living in Russia are also Lutherans. Early in the 1990s a few Russians and members of other ethnic groups converted to Lutheranism, with the result that these Lutheran churches became more ethnically pluralistic. Several Russian-Korean Protestant churches (mostly Presbyterian and Methodist) also function in Russia. They pursue their missionary work not only among Russian Koreans but also among other ethnic groups, especially in Siberia and the Far East. Another dynamic Protestant denomination in Russia is the Seventh-Day Adventist Church. In addition to the Protestant denominations already mentioned, many others not typical to Russia before 1991 appeared in the country. Among these were Anglicans, the Salvation Army, and Quakers.

Islam is, as before, the second largest religion in Russia. The overwhelming majority of Russia's Muslims are Sunnis, mostly of Hanafi and Shafii *madhhabs* (*madhhabs* are schools of law that were founded by Sunni Muslim jurists in the eighth and early ninth centuries), although in the last decade the Wahhabi sect of the Hanbali *madhhab* has also appeared in the country, mainly in Dagestan and Chechnya. In Russia, Sunni Muslims predominate among Tatars, Bashkirs, the majority of peoples of the North Caucasus, and immigrants from Central Asia. Azerbaijanis living in Russia are mostly Shia Muslims. The role of Islam in traditionally Muslim regions has grown since late 1980s. This growing role is evident both in the appearance of Muslim parties and in the inclusion of religious statements in the programs of numerous cultural and political organizations.

Historically, Russia's Buddhists come from specific ethnic groups, as outlined above. Since the late Soviet era, however, small groups of followers of different schools of Buddhism have formed in the ethnic Russian population in many of Russia's big cities (Moscow, St. Petersburg, Vladivostok, Ekaterinburg, Novosibirsk, and others). In these cases, Buddhist affiliation is not limited by the Vajrayana movement. Unlike Buddhism as it is practiced in its traditional regions, here Buddhism has been adapted somewhat to Western culture, transforming some of its concepts. In many Russian cities, the marginal neo-Buddhist totalitarian sect AUM Shinrikyo pursued very active missionary work in 1990s. It was banned in Russia, however, after its March 1995 sarin gas attack on the Tokyo subway system, thus forcing it underground.

As to adherents of Judaism, their numbers have decreased in the post-Soviet period because of emigration. Among Russian Jews, too, were many nonbelievers. The rise of religious freedom since the late Soviet era, however, has brought some back to Judaism. In 1993, the Congress of Jewish Religious Communities and Organizations was held, which embraced both Orthodox and Reform Jewish organizations. In 1996 the leadership of the congress initiated the establishment of the Russian Jewish Congress (Kozlov 1999, 5–6), which was later joined by Conservative Jewish communities. Another movement in contemporary Russian Judaism is Lubavicher Hasidism. In 1999, Hasidic communities formed the Federation of Jewish Communities of Russia (Kozlov 2001–2002, 36).

Nontraditional religions in Russia include Hare Krishnas and the followers of the Baha'i faith (numbering in the several thousands). Intensive missionary work is also being conducted by various other nontraditional sects, namely, Jehovah's Witnesses (who first came to Russia in the 1940s), the Unification Church (active in Russia since the late 1980s), and Mormons (who have operated in Russia since the 1990s). One other characteristic feature of religious development in post-Soviet Russia has been the revival of traditional pre-Christian and pre-Islamic beliefs among some Christianized or Islamized ethnic groups.

When using statistics concerning the religious makeup of Russia's population, one must remember that there is a big gap between the number of those who consider themselves to be believers and those who actually practice their religious beliefs (that is, attend religious services, pray, and observe religious doctrine and direction). According to surveys conducted by Mchedlov during the 1990s, only 5 to 7 percent of respondents reported that they were actively involved in institutionalized religious activities (Zaluzhnyi et al. 2002, 45). Such figures are similar for most of Russia's traditional denominations. Moreover, there are also those who do not call themselves believers but associate with a specific denomination for cultural and historical reasons. Religion is often considered more a part of cultural heritage than it is an opportunity to develop a relationship with God. The cultural component of religion is most understandable for those who have grown up in a highly secular society.

◼ Religion and Identity

One of the challenges facing Russia is that it is both a multiethnic and a multiconfessional country. Religious and ethnic identities are often interconnected. In the atmosphere of the crisis of old identities and of the spiritual vacuum following the Soviet Union's collapse, many individuals and groups have created new positive identities grounded in history, culture, and traditions, with the religious factor becoming a meaningful component of identity. For the entire post-Soviet period, ethnic groups typically have seen their traditional religions as unifying factors.

For many of Russia's citizens, Orthodox Christianity has cultural meaning, rather than theological meaning (although those taking a more theological view are increasing in numbers), and thus is seen as a potential symbol of national identity. For ethnic Russians in particular, the religious component, more precisely its cultural dimension, is becoming more meaningful regarding identity. When one asks, "What is your religion?" the response frequently will be, "I am Russian, hence I am Orthodox." Since Orthodoxy has been the historical faith of Russia for more than a thousand years, it is deeply ingrained in Russia's culture, traditions, and common memory. It is even an important element of identity for nonbelievers. That is why one can hear some ethnic Russians say, "Ia neveruiushchii iz pravoslavnykh," which may be roughly translated as "I am a nonbeliever of Orthodox heritage."

Thus, Russian Orthodoxy once again has become a symbol of the country's national identity as the term "Orthodox Rus" (Rus pravoslavnaia) has reentered public discourse. But there is a contradiction here. On the one hand, the conjoining of "Russian ethnic identity" and "Christian Orthodox faith" is very strong. On the other hand, the Russian Orthodox Church is not strictly an ethnic church. Its adherents include many who are not ethnic Russians. For their part in fact, Orthodox believers, according to sociological surveys, tend to be quite tolerant both in ethnic and religious terms. For instance, in one survey, whereas 48.2 percent of believers reflected very positive attitudes toward people from other ethnic groups, only 12 percent of nonbelievers did the same (Verkhovskii, Pribylovskii, and Mikhailovskaia 1998, 177).

The question of religious and ethnic identity also affects Russia's Muslims. Religious rhetoric has been employed by Muslim political and cultural organizations. Related to this is an "ethnicization" of Islam, which is

Evidence of a multiconfessional Russia on display in the
Kazan Kremlin. The onion-shaped domes of the Russian Orthodox
Cathedral of the Annunciation are on the left, and the
minarets of the Qol Sharif Mosque are on the right.

seen as one of the reasons for splits in Russia's Muslim community, with many Muslim ethnic groups creating their own separate organizational structures in place of the previously centralized ones. While during the Soviet era only two such organizations existed in what is now the Russian Federation, today there are about forty, each based either on ethnicity or territory.

The role of the religious factor in ethnic identity is especially obvious for ethnic minorities who differ from the surrounding population in their religious affiliation. This religious "otherness" reinforces ethnic self-consciousness and often becomes the main component in ethnic identity. Religious affiliation helps such groups prevent their assimilation into the broader culture and to remain a community. For example, for Ingrian Finns, the Evangelical Lutheran Church is not only a religious organization but also the center of their culture. Indeed, belonging to the church for this group is a more important source of ethnic identity than are knowledge of the Finnish language or the observance of Finnish rituals and traditions. Interestingly, but perhaps not surprisingly, the level of religiosity of Ingrian Finns in Russia is much higher than that of Finns in Finland. Whereas 74 percent of Ingrian Finns attend Sunday church services, only 4 percent of Finns do in Finland (Ylönen 1997, 204).

Another feature of the contemporary scene in Russia is the revival of traditional pre-Christian and pre-Islamic beliefs as reflections of ethnic identities. The persistence of such traditional beliefs is typical for the peoples of Siberia and the Volga region (both Finno-Ugric and Turkic). During the last decade there were attempts to revive traditional pre-Christian beliefs, not only where they had always remained popular, for example, among the Mari (an ethnic group in the Volga region), but also among strongly Christianized peoples, such as the Mordovians. The leaders of ethnic cultural organizations and nationalist movements among the Mari, Chuvash, Udmurts, and to a lesser extent of Mordovians, search for their ethnic identities in these traditional beliefs. They contrast them with the Russian Orthodox Church, an institution that they associate with the Russification policies of the Russian empire.

Another factor in the mix in the Volga region is the missionary work of the Evangelical Lutheran Church of Ingria among Finno-Ugric peoples. This activity is strongly supported by the Finnish Evangelical Lutheran Church and is even more intensive among the Karelians, another Finno-Ugric people very close to the Finns both in language and geographic proximity, but who profess Orthodoxy as their faith. This missionary work is based on a statement of the Finnish Evangelical Lutheran Church that suggests that the conversion to Orthodoxy of a number of Finno-Ugric peoples was not natural, and that these groups therefore should become Lutheran, even though they had never been Lutherans, having converted directly to Orthodox Christianity from paganism. Whereas this missionary work has brought some results in Karelia, which borders Finland, it has been unsuccessful in the Volga region.

■ Conclusion

The experience of the post-Soviet era raises a few more questions about the condition and influence of religion in contemporary Russia. During the 1990s, one heard much talk of a religious rebirth in the country because of the sharp increase in the number of religious organizations and activity that came with the end of Soviet rule. Although the use of the term "rebirth" is not entirely apt, because despite the Soviet system's best efforts religion never really died in Russia, it is true that the breaking of the CPSU's monopoly on political power provided religious organizations of all sorts the opportunity to participate openly and energetically in the lives of the Russian people.

Religious organizations in Russia have thus gained experience in living and working with each other. It must be noted, however, that dialogue and cooperation has been most fruitful primarily among Russia's traditional religions: Orthodox Christianity, Islam, Buddhism, and Judaism. In 1999 they formed the Inter-Religious Council of Russia. Representatives of these religions have worked together, for example, in organizing several antidrug bus tours aimed at Russia's youth. At the same time, cooperation between the Russian Orthodox Church and other Christian denominations has been more problematic because of proselytism. Despite these tensions, church leaders on both sides have begun to focus more on what their denominations have in common, such as their views on morality.

Many of Russia's religious organizations have sought to integrate certain aspects of social service and charity into their overall mission. Within the Russian Orthodox Church, for instance, there is a significant group of local priests who focus on meeting the needs of their parishioners by providing health care, education, and social work. James Billington refers to these priests as "pastoralists" and sees in their work one way to promote the development of democracy and civil society in Russia (Kennan Institute 2004). Activists of many Protestant denominations are also intensely involved in social and charitable work in their local communities. Such activity on the part of religious organizations has strong public support (Ovsienko, Odintsov, and Trofimchuk 1996, 220).

Religious organizations have also endeavored to influence public attitudes and elite opinion on a range of issues. The Russian Orthodox Church's issuing of its "Social Concept" in August 2000 represents one such effort (*Informatsionnii bulleten* 2000), as is the adoption of special social doctrines by other religious denominations. Having adopted the "Social Concept," which expressed its general opinion on policy, the Russian Orthodox Church tends not to pronounce on narrow questions of politics. However, it does pronounce on government policy that affects the larger population. Such was the case in January 2005 when the Russian government launched far-reaching social reforms that substituted direct social benefits (including health care, public transportation, and the like) with a nonequivalent monetary allowance for certain categories of the population. Patriarch Aleksii II declared that these reforms were unfair, insisting that the government should not deprive anyone of the real possibility of using public transportation, having access to medical care and medicine, and keeping their housing (*Kommersant* 2005).

Given that the Russian Orthodox Church seeks to influence public policy, one might wonder what its current relationship is with the state. Although Eastern Orthodoxy has a tradition of close ties to the state, relations between the Russian Orthodox Church and the Russian state have often been strained. Although at times the church has enjoyed the benefits of being the "established" religious institution of Russia, more often than not, as this chapter suggests, the church has been subject to efforts by the state to control it and use it for its own purposes. In its "Social Concept," the church makes clear what it believes its relationship with the state should be. While on the one hand, "the Church should not assume the prerogatives of the state," on the other hand, "the state should not interfere in the life of the Church." The same document recognizes that "in the contemporary world, the state is normally secular and not bound by any religious commitments. Its co-operation with the Church is limited to several areas and based on mutual non-interference in each other's affairs" (*Informatsionnii bulleten* 2000).

Thus, despite the Orthodox Church's efforts to discourage the development of nontraditional religions in Russia, it seems to lack any aspirations of becoming the "established" church. With such status would come greater dependence on the state. Instead, the Orthodox Church seems to want its place in Russian society to be based not on the granting of unique status by the state, but rather on its place in Russian culture and history, and on the large number of its followers and their traditions.

Given the great diversity of religious life in Russia, the state for its part seems disinclined to grant the Orthodox Church a status above that of any of the country's other traditional religions. Indeed, even as often as high-ranking state officials try to associate themselves with the Orthodox Church, this seems more a recognition of the church's prestige in Russian society than as part of an attempt one day to declare Russian Orthodoxy the official state religion. Indeed, state officials have repeatedly affirmed that Russia is a secular state and seem uninterested in undermining these declarations in any substantive way.

In sum, the role of religious organizations has increased greatly in Russian society since the late 1980s. Although many challenges continue to face the development of religion in Russia, religious believers now possess a degree of freedom to practice and express their faiths unparalleled in Russian history.

▓ Notes

1. The Old Believers themselves were not united for long. By the end of the seventeenth century they too had divided into "priestly" and "priestless" Old Believers. In turn, both of these divisions broke up into smaller churches, concords, and movements. Before the February 1917 Revolution, Old Believers made up about 10 percent of Russia's population. Today they comprise only 1 percent of the total.

2. The most damaging split, between the Russian Orthodox Church and the Russian Orthodox Church Abroad, was overcome only in May 2007 when the two branches of Russian Orthodoxy signed the Act on Canonical Communion.

3. Author interview with Pavel I. Puchkov, member of the Russian Academy of Natural Sciences, Honored Scientist of the Russian Federation, D. Sc., professor,

Moscow State Linguistic University, and counselor of the Institute of Ethnology and Anthropology, Russian Academy of Sciences, June 15, 2005, Moscow, Russia.

■ Bibliography

Aleksii II. 1997. *Doklad Sviateishego Patriarkha Moskovskogo i vseia Rusi Aleksiia II, Arkhiereiskii Sobor 1997 goda. Razdel 11: Mezhkonfessionalnye i mezhreligioznye otnosheniia. Uchastie v deiatelnosti mezhdunarodnykh khristianskikh organizatsii* [Report of His Holiness Patriarch of Moscow and All Russia Aleksii II to the 1997 Bishops Council. Section 11: Interconfessional and Interfaith Relations; Participation in the Activities of International Christian Organizations]. Moscow, February 18–23. http://www.sedmitza.ru/index.html?sid=50& did=40.

Anderson, Paul B. 1944. *People, Church, and State in Modern Russia.* New York: Macmillan.

Bezborodov, Aleksandr. 2005. "Vera i patriotizm v gody Velikoi Otechestvennoi voiny" [Belief and patriotism in the years of the Great Patriotic War]. *Zhurnal Moskovskoi Patriarkhii* 5: 72–76.

Billington, James H. 1970. *The Icon and the Axe: An Interpretive History of Russian Culture.* New York: Vintage.

Bolshakoff, Serge. 1950. *Russian Nonconformity: The Story of "Unofficial" Religion in Russia.* Philadelphia: Westminster.

Burdo, M. (Bourdeaux, Michael), and S. B. Filatov, eds. 2004. *Sovremennaia religioznaia zhizn Rossii* [Contemporary religious life of Russia]. Vol. 1. Moscow: Logos.

―――. 2005. *Sovremennaia religioznaia zhizn Rossii* [Contemporary religious life of Russia]. Vol. 3. Moscow: Logos.

Buss, Gerald. 1987. *The Bear's Hug: Christian Belief and the Soviet State, 1917– 1986.* Grand Rapids, MI: William B. Eerdmans.

Byzov, L., and S. Filatov. 1993. "Religiia i politika v obshchestvennom soznanii sovetskogo naroda" [Religion and politics in the mass consciousness of the Soviet people]. In *Religiia i demokratiia: Ha puti k svobode sovesti* [Religion and democracy: On the path to freedom of conscience]. Comp. A. R. Bessmertnyi and S. B. Filatov, ed. S. B. Filatov and D. E. Furman. Moscow: Progress.

Chumachenko, T. A. 2007. "V rusle vneshnei politiki sovetskogo gosudarstva: Moskovskaia patriarkhiia na mezhdunarodnoi arene v 1943–1948 gg." [In the foreign policy channels of the Soviet state: The Moscow Patriarchy on the international scene, 1943–1948]. *Vestnik Rossiiskogo universiteta druzhby narodov* 1: 89–99.

Davis, Nathaniel. 1995. *A Long Walk to Church: A Contemporary History of Russian Orthodoxy.* Boulder, CO: Westview.

"Deklaratsiia o pravakh i dostoinstve cheloveka" [Declaration on Human Rights and Dignity]. 2006. *Zhurnal Moskovskoi Patriarkhii* 6: 77–78.

Elliot, Mark, and Anita Deyneka. 1999. "Protestant Missionaries in the Former Soviet Union." In *Proselytism and Orthodoxy in Russia: The New War for Souls,* ed. John Witte Jr. and Michael E. Bourdeaux. Maryknoll, NY: Orbis Books.

Figes, Orlando. 2002. *Natasha's Dance: A Cultural History of Russia.* New York: Metropolitan Books.

Filatov, S. B. 2002. "Posleslovie: religiia v postsovetskoi Rossii" [Afterword: Religion in post-Soviet Russia]. In *Religiia i obshchestvo: Ocherki religioznoi zhizni sovremennoi Rossii* [Religion and society: Essays on religious life in contemporary Russia), ed. S. B. Filatov. Moscow: Letnii Sad.

Filatov, Sergei, and Lyudmila Vorontsova. 1999. "Russian Catholicism: Relic or Reality?" In *Proselytism and Orthodoxy in Russia: The New War for Souls,* ed. John Witte Jr. and Michael E. Bourdeaux. Maryknoll, NY: Orbis Books.

Informatsionnii bulleten, otdel vneshnikh tserkovnykh sviazey Moskovskogo Patriarkhata. 2000. "Osnovy sotsialnoi kontseptsii Russkoi Pravoslavnoi Tserkvi" [Fundamentals of the social concept of the Russian Orthodox Church], 8: 5–104.

Johnstone, Patrick. 1993. *Operation World.* Grand Rapids, MI: Zondervan.

Johnstone, Patrick, and Jason Mandryk. 2001. *Operation World: When We Pray God Works.* Waynesboro, GA: Paternoster USA.

Kääriäinen, Kimmo. 1998. *Religion in Russia After the Collapse of Communism: Religious Renaissance or Secular State.* Lewiston, NY: Edwin Mellen Press.

Kazmina, Olga, and Natalia Shlygina. 2001–2002. "The Evangelical-Lutheran Church of Ingria and Its Role in the Life of Finnish Ingermanlanders." *Anthropology & Archeology of Eurasia* 40(3): 56–74.

Kennan Institute. 2004. "Reflections on Orthodoxy and the Construction of Civil Society and Democracy in Russia." *Meeting Reports,* March 25. http://www.wilsoncenter.org/index.cfm?topic_id=1424&fuseaction=topics.publications&doc_id=68602&group_id=7718.

Kommersant. 2005. "Tserkov otkrestilas ot gosudarstva" [The church disavowed the state], January 14.

Kontseptsiia vozrozhdeniia missionerskoi deiatel'nosti Russkoi Pravoslavnoi Tserkvi [Concept of the rebirth of missionary activity of the Russian Orthodox Church]. 1999. In *Pravoslavnaia missia segodnia. Sbornik tekstov po kursu "Missiologiia."* Sostavitel' Vladimir Fedorov [The Orthodox mission today. A collection of texts for a course in "missionology." Comp. Vladimir Fedorov]. St. Petersburg: Apostolskii gorod.

Kozlov, S. Ia. 1999. "Evrei Moskvy v 90-e gody XX veka: Deistvitelno li proiskhodit religioznii renessans?" [Moscow Jews in the 1990s: Is the religious renaissance real?]. *Issledovaniia po prikladnoi i neotlozhnoi etnologii* 125: 3–25.

———. 2000. "Iudaizm v sovremennoi Rossii: Osnovnye struktury i napravleniia" [Judaism in contemporary Russia: Basic structures and trends]. *Issledovaniia po prikladnoi i neotlozhnoi etnologii* 137: 3–27.

Kozlov, Semen Ia. 2001–2002. "Russian Jews: The Confessional Situation in the Late Twentieth Century." *Anthropology & Archeology of Eurasia* 40(3): 31–55.

Loginov, Andrey. 1997. "Religioznaia situatsiia v Rossii i priniatie zakona 'O svobode sovesti i religioznykh obedineniiakh'" [The religious situation in Russia and the adoption of the law "On freedom of conscience and religious associations"]. *Politiya* 6(4): 83–94.

Lunkin, R. 2002. "Piatidesiatniki v Rossii: opasnosti i dostizheniia 'novogo' khristianstva" [Pentecostals in Russia: The dangers and achievements of the "new" Christianity]. In *Religiia i obshchestvo: ocherki religioznoi zhizni sovremennoi Rossii* [Religion and society: Essays on religious life in contemporary Russia]. Ed. and comp. S. B. Filatov. Moscow: Letnii Sad.

Mchedlov, M. P., ed. 1999. *Religii narodov sovremennoi Rossii: Slovar* [Religions of the peoples of contemporary Russia: A dictionary]. Moscow: Respublika.

————, ed. 2003. *Rossiiskaia tsivilizatsiia* [Russian civilization]. Moscow: Akademicheskii Proekt.

Meyendorff, John. 1978. "Russian Bishops and Church Reform in 1905." In *Russian Orthodoxy Under the Old Regime,* ed. Robert L. Nichols and Theofanis George Stavrou. Minneapolis: University of Minnesota Press.

Missionerskii otdel Moskovskogo Patriarkhata [Missionary Department of the Moscow Patriarchy]. 2005. Kontseptsiia missionerskoi deiatel'nosti Russkoi Pravoslavnoi Tserkvi na 2005–2010 gody [Concept of the missionary activity of the Russian Orthodox Church for 2005–2010]. http://www.religare.ru/print 16807.htm.

Ovsienko, F. G., M. I. Odintsov, and N. A. Trofimchuk, eds. 1996. *Gosudarstvenno-tserkovnye otnosheniia v Rossii: Opyt proshlogo i sovremennoe sostoianie* [State-church relations in Russia: Past and present]. Moscow: RAGS.

Poslanie Vsemirnogo sammita religioznykh liderov [Message of the World Summit of Religious Leaders]. 2006. *Zhurnal Moskovskoi Patriarkhii* 8: 59–61.

Pospielovsky, Dimitry V. 1995. "The Russian Orthodox Church in the Postcommunist CIS." In *The Politics of Religion in Russia and the New States of Eurasia,* ed. Michael Bourdeaux. Armonk, NY: M. E. Sharpe.

Robson, Roy R. 1995. *Old Believers in Modern Russia.* DeKalb: Northern Illinois University Press.

Rossiiskie vesti. 1996. "Trudno sniat' s kresta raspiatykh dvazhdy" [It's difficult to remove from the cross those who have been crucified twice]. May 7.

Rupen, Robert A. 1975. "The Absorption of Tuva." In *The Anatomy of Communist Takeovers,* ed. Thomas T. Hammond. New Haven, CT: Yale University Press.

Shkarovskii, M. V. 2000. *Russkaia Pravoslavnaia Tserkov' pri Staline i Khrushcheve* [The Russian Orthodox Church under Stalin and Khrushchev]. Moscow: Krutitskoie Patriarshee Podvor'e Obshchestvo liubitelei tserkovnoi istorii.

Shlygina, Nataliya, and O. Ye. Kazmina. 1999. "Ingrian Finns of the Parish of Holy Trinity Church (Moscow)." In *Ingrians and Neighbors: Focus on the Eastern Baltic Sea Region,* ed. Markku Teinonen and Timo J. Virtanen. Helsinki: Finnish Literature Society.

Silant'ev, Roman. 2005. *Noveishaia istoria islamskogo soobshchestva Rossii* [A new history of the Muslim community in Russia]. Moscow: Ikhtios.

Spinka, Matthew. 1956. *The Church in Soviet Russia.* New York: Oxford University Press.

Tabak, Yuriy. 1999. "Relations Between Russian Orthodoxy and Judaism." In *Proselytism and Orthodoxy in Russia: The New War for Souls,* ed. John Witte Jr. and Michael E. Bourdeaux. Maryknoll, NY: Orbis Books.

Trofimchuk, N. A., ed. 2002. *Istoriia religii v Rossii* [A history of religion in Russia]. Moscow: RAGS.

Tsekhanskaia, Kira V. 2001–2002. "Russia: Trends in Orthodox Religiosity in the Twentieth Century (Statistics and Reality)." *Anthropology & Archeology of Eurasia* 40(3): 10–30.

Tsimbaeva, E. N. 1999. *Russkii katolitsizm: zabytnoe proshloe rossiiskogo liberalizma* [Russian Catholicism: The forgotten past of Russian liberalism]. Moscow: Editorial URSS.

Tsypin, Vladislav. 1994. *Istoriia Russkoi Pravoslavnoi Tserkvi, 1917–1990* [History of the Russian Orthodox Church, 1917–1990]. Moscow: Khronika.

————. 2000. "Russkaia Pravoslavnaia Tserkov v sinodalnuiu epokhu, 1700–1917" [The Russian Orthodox Church in the synod era, 1700–1917]. In *Pravoslavnaia entsiklopediia: Russkaia Pravoslavnaia Tserkov* [The Orthodox encyclopedia:

The Russian Orthodox Church], ed. Aleksii II, Patriarch of Moscow and All Russia. Moscow: Pravoslavnaia Entsiklopediia.

———. 2005. "Russkaia Pravoslavnaia Tserkov v Velikuiu Otechestvennuiu voinu" [The Russian Orthodox Church in the Great Patriotic War]. *Zhurnal Moskovskoi Patriarkhii* 5: 66–71.

Tul'skii, Mikhail. 2000. "Rol' tserkvi v zhizni rossiiskogo obshchestva" [The role of the church in the life of Russian society]. *Nezavisimaia Gazeta,* 9 August.

Urazmanova, R. K., and S. V. Cheshko, ed. 2001. *Tatary* [Tatars]. Moscow: Nauka.

Verkhovskii, Aleksandr, Vladimir Pribylovskii, and Ekaterina Mikhailovskaia. 1998. *Natsionalizm i ksenofobiia v rossiiskom obshchestve* [Nationalism and xenophobia in the Russian society]. Moscow: Panorama.

VTsIOM. 2007. "Religiia v nashei zhizni" [Religion in our life]. Press release no. 789, October 11. http://wciom.ru/arkhiv/tematicheskii-arkhiv/item/single/8954 .html?no_cache=1&L%5.

Vsesoiuznaia perepis naseleniia 1937 g. Kratkie itogi [1937 all-union census of the population: Brief results]. 1991. Moscow: Nauka.

White, Stephen, and Ian McAllister. 1997. "The Politics of Religion in Postcommunist Russia." *Religion, State & Society* 25(3): 235–252.

Witte, John, Jr. 1999. "Introduction." In *Proselytism and Orthodoxy in Russia: The New War for Souls,* ed. John Witte Jr. and Michael E. Bourdeaux. Maryknoll, NY: Orbis Books.

Ylönen, Kaarina. 1997. *Inkerin kirkon nousu kommunistivallan päätyttyä* [The rise of the Ingrian church after the communist era]. Tampere, Finland: Kirkon Tutkimuskeskus.

Zaluzhnyi, A. G., et al., eds. 2002. *Mnogonatsionalnaia Rossia: Dialog religii i kultur; rol religioznykh obedinenii v mirotvorcheskoi deiatelnosti, ukreplenii mezhreligioznogo soglasiia i druzhby narodov* [Multiethnic Russia: A dialogue of religions and cultures; the role of religious associations in peacemaking, the strengthening of interreligious harmony and friendship among peoples]. Moscow: Gotika. http://www.anr-org.ru/Ass_Byulleten.htm.

Zeide, Gernot. 1988. "Russkaia Pravoslavnaia Tserkov Zagranitsei" [The Russian Orthodox Church abroad]. In *Iubileinii sbornik v pamiat 1000-letiia Kreshchenia Rusi, 988–1988* [Anniversary anthology in memory of the millenium of the baptism of Russia, 988–1988]. Jordanville, NY: Holy Trinity Monastery.

Zhukovskaia, N. L., and N. F. Mokshin. 1998. *Ot Karelii do Urala: Rasskazy o narodakh Rossii* [From Karelia to the Urals: Stories about the peoples of Russia]. Moscow: Nauka.

12

Literature and Film

Adele Barker

For most who seek an introduction to Russia's cultural history, the literary sphere is defined by its two nineteenth-century masters, Fyodor Dostoevsky and Lev Tolstoy. From the nineteenth century, when Russia's writers were tackling the major philosophical and religious questions of the day, through the Soviet era, when Alexander Solzhenitsyn declared the writer a "second government," Russian literature occupied a position of unique moral authority. Even for Lenin, architect of a revolution that had as its goal the sweeping away of the old order to make way for the creation of a new society and culture, it was important to take into account a prerevolutionary literary tradition that had earned Russia a place on the world stage and defined for generations of Russians the formative role of literature in their lives.

Although its roots are not as deep in Russian history, film similarly played a defining role in twentieth-century Russian and Soviet culture, where it initially helped bring the new Soviet social order to the masses. Playing an increasingly important role during the Soviet era, film has, since the collapse of the Soviet Union, taken on many of the former functions of literature, becoming the venue through which many of the most pressing questions regarding national identity and "Russianness" are being worked out today.

■ Nineteenth-Century Russian Literature

No study of twentieth-century Russian and Soviet literature can afford to ignore the nineteenth-century Russian literary tradition. One of the most prominent nineteenth-century literary figures, whose works and literary persona have transcended both time and ideology, was Alexander Pushkin. Arguably Russia's greatest poet, Pushkin has proved difficult to classify. He mastered numerous genres—the lyric, dramatic sketches, drama, the *poema* (or long narrative poem), and stories, often combining genres and styles. Among the most beloved of his works are his *poema The Bronze Horseman* (*Mednyi vsadnik*, 1833), about the irreconcilability of the lives of individuals with the grander sweep of imperial design and fate; his novel *The Captain's Daughter* (*Kapitanskaia dochka*, 1836), an account of the Pugachev Rebellion in the 1770s that offers a commentary on Catherine the Great's Russia; a collection of short stories titled *The Tales of Belkin* (*Povesti Belkina*, 1830); and his masterful *The Queen of Spades* (*Pikovaia dama*, 1833), a tight psychological drama infused with gothic elements whose plot turns on a secret to winning at cards. As Pushkin experimented with various literary phases, he conflated styles, often parodying convention. His *Eugene Onegin* (1833), which he termed "a novel in verse," has come to be regarded as nothing less than an encyclopedia of Russian life. Covering the years 1819–1825, the work chronicles the fortunes of its hero, Onegin—urbane, sophisticated, and infected with the boredom of the era—and Tatiana Larina, the provincial maiden who loses her heart to him only to be rejected. Years later, now married into high society, Tatiana encounters Onegin again, and this time it is she who rejects his declaration of love. The novel speaks of bittersweet loss, the price one pays for one's freedom from emotional entanglements, and the fallacy of living one's life through literature. While it is a compendium of the conventions of the era, it also takes up Pushkin's own poetic and emotional journeys in the frequent digressions that frame the story.

Pushkin's life and works were mythologized both in the nineteenth century and in the more recent Soviet period. For some, his death in a duel (at the hands of a foreigner at that!) transformed him into a poet-martyr. In the twentieth century, his image was routinely dragged out by the Communist Party and the Writers' Union on jubilees, anniversaries, and the like. The less able Soviet ideology was to answer the public's need for deep and coherent myths that could bind the country together, the greater the necessity felt by the Communist Party to rely on images and figures from the past that resonated deeply with the population. The Soviet people, however, did not always respond to the old mythology in exactly the way the party wished. Particularly during Stalin's purges of the 1930s, Russians increasingly sought in Pushkin's works examples of how one could persevere and find spiritual sustenance during impossible times (Debreczeny 1993, 61).

Pushkin's Onegin typified an increasingly common male type in nineteenth-century Russian literature known as the superfluous man (*lishnii chelovek*). These were men of talent and intelligence who often wished to change society but were alienated from their surroundings and thus unable

One of Russia's many monuments to Alexander Pushkin. This one is in St. Petersburg in front of the Russian Museum.

Elizabeth A. Smith

to act. Often they possessed sufficient independent means to enable them to live a life of comfort without need of a profession. Oblomov, the epony- mous hero of the novel published by Ivan Goncharov in 1859, dreams of improvements and innovations he is going to make on his estate, and yet ul- timately he is unable to do even so much as get out of bed in the morning. His inability to bestir himself gave birth to the term *oblomovshchina,* coined by the Russian critic Nikolai Dobroliubov in 1859 to describe the uselessness of the entire Russian gentry. In the works of writers such as Alexander Griboyedov, Mikhail Lermontov, and Ivan Turgenev, the theme of the superfluous man seems to spill off the pages. In his novels *Diary of a Superfluous Man* (*Dnevnik lishnego cheloveka,* 1850), *Rudin* (1856), and *Fathers and Sons* (*Ottsy i deti,* 1862), Turgenev develops the theme of men of acute consciousness who are ultimately unable to bring their ideas to fruition and who often, as a result, suffer untimely deaths.

It is no accident that the image of the superfluous man was so prevalent among Russian writers in the nineteenth century, as it was during this period that the country entered into a time of great political and social ferment. In 1825, a group of army officers known as the Decembrists were arrested and sentenced to internal exile (and in some cases hanged) for their revolt against the monarchy, serfdom, and the lack of promised liberal reforms. Even though the rebellion failed, it raised the consciousness of other members of Russia's intelligentsia of the necessity of fundamental social and political change.

Among literary critics, a new school of thought arose known as social criticism, the leaders of which were Vissarion Belinsky, Nikolai Chernyshevsky, and Nikolai Dobroliubov. They argued that literature no longer had the leisure to give itself over to plots and characters divorced from real life, but instead should deal with the political and social realities of the day, pointing the way to social change and transformation.

One of the areas that came under greatest attack was the institution of the landowning gentry. In his *Family Chronicle* (*Semeinaia khronika,* 1856), Sergei Aksakov looked at life on a Russian country estate far removed from the centers of power and contemplated the despotism to which landowners were prone in the absence of checks on their power. Nadezhda Khvoshchinskaia, writing under the male pseudonym of V. Krestovsky, provided further condemnation of such tyranny, on the eve of the emancipation of the serfs, in her novel *In Hopes of Something Better* (*Vozhidanii luchshego,* 1860). Perhaps the most stunning indictments of the landowning class, however, were provided by Mikhail Saltykov-Shchedrin in his novel *The Golovlev Family* (*Gospoda Golovlevy,* 1872–1876), which depicts a family ruined by its own despotism, greed, and spiritual emptiness, and Nikolai Gogol in his novel *Dead Souls* (*Mertvye dushi,* 1842), a lively, often comic denunciation of Russia's moral vacuousness. *Dead Souls* takes shape through the adventures of a swindler named Chichikov who travels throughout Russia's countryside buying up the landed gentry's dead serfs, or souls as they were known, whose deaths had not yet been officially documented by the state. In addition to providing a devastating, if humorous, critique of rural life under Nicholas I, Gogol, at the end of the first volume of the novel, provides one of the more evocative images of Russia in which he compares the country to a troika driven by a team of horses soaring into the distance with no clear direction.

The tendency among writers to critique institutions ranging from serfdom to the autocracy itself was similarly felt in the works penned by women writers. For many years Russia's nineteenth-century women writers did not receive the critical attention they deserved. Contemporary critics often dismissed their works as trivial, as being concerned exclusively with hearth and home. Many of the women who wished to pursue a literary career lived in the provinces and thus had limited access to the major literary journals of the day. Moreover, not all their writing fit neatly into the category of what was expected, namely that writers write about social ills. Yet many wrote precisely about these problems, specifically about their own suffocation by a deeply entrenched patriarchal system. Avdotiia Panaeva in her novel *A Woman's Lot* (*Zhenskaia dolia,* 1862) was the first to take an explicit stand against the fate of gentry women trapped in dynastic marriages. While Panaeva argued against these arranged marriages, she also questioned the wisdom of the domestic emancipation of women without securing their civil rights. The issues facing women were clear: they were fighting to be able to work, to receive an education, and to liberate themselves from domestic oppression. For instance, Nadezhda Khvoshchinskaia's powerful story "The Boarding School Girl" ("Pansionerka," 1861) is almost a love story, but instead confounds and pleases expectations by showing a young woman from the provinces who, instead of succumbing to a traditional romance, rejects it, moves to St. Petersburg, finds work, and supports herself. More nuanced in her critique of a system that kept women socially immobilized was Nadezhda Sokhanskaia, whose story "An After-Dinner Visit" ("Posle obeda v gostiakh," 1858) complicates the issues of women's domestic subordination and emancipation in a way that was rare for the times.

The mid-nineteenth century also ushered in the age of the "realistic" novel in Russian literature. Turgenev, Goncharov, and Aksakov were part of this tradition that sought to depict life as it really is, as were the two most acclaimed Russian writers of the period, Fyodor Dostoevsky and Lev Tolstoy. Not unlike some of his predecessors, most notably Gogol, Dostoevsky in his early work showed a special interest in the downtrodden of Russian society. His first novel, *Poor Folk* (*Bednye liudi,* 1845), became a time-honored defense of the "little man" in Russian literature, crushed by poverty and loneliness, and unable to better his situation. Beginning with his second novel *The Double* (*Dvoinik,* 1846), which ostensibly deals with social issues, Dostoevsky introduced a psychological dimension into his writing that placed the reader inside the tortured minds of lonely, alienated, and morbidly sensitive individuals. Such became the hallmark of his later works, including his famous *Notes from the Underground* (*Zapiski iz podpolia,* 1864). Dostoevsky called himself "a realist in a higher sense," referring to his concern less with physical portrayal and background than with psychological realism, the ability to probe the complex inner world of his characters. In his interest in the psychological realm, Dostoevsky was greatly influenced by his near execution in 1849 for his membership in the radical Petrashevsky Circle. Instead of being executed, he was sent to Siberia for four years of hard labor and another three of internal exile. There, his thinking also acquired a strong religious element that would take shape in the novels he wrote following his return. His greatest novels, *Crime and Punishment* (*Prestuplenie i nakazanie,* 1866), *The Idiot* (1868), *The Possessed* (*Besy,* 1872), and *The Brothers*

Karamazov (*Bratia Karamazovy,* 1880), all deal with a murder, but on a higher level investigate the nature of good and evil and the existential dilemma of those who have denied God.

Like Dostoevsky, Lev Tolstoy dealt with what came to be known as "the cursed questions" (*prokliatye voprosy*), which meant taking on the burning political and religious issues of the day. His characters ponder the meaning of God and human existence. Unlike Dostoevsky, Tolstoy was a product of the landed nobility and could trace his lineage back to the thirteenth century. If he wore peasant garb on his estate, Yasnaya Polyana, it was not through economic necessity but in accordance with his belief that the closer to the land one lived and the further away from the corrupting influences of society, the city, and the established church, the closer one came to finding the Kingdom of God that for Tolstoy lay within. For his unorthodox interpretation of God and the Kingdom of Heaven, Tolstoy was excommunicated from the Russian Orthodox Church in 1901.

His two greatest novels, *War and Peace* (*Voina i mir,* 1869) and *Anna Karenina* (1877), plunge the reader into the everyday life of the nobility and the gentry of nineteenth-century Moscow and St. Petersburg. Such was his attention to realistic detail that one can easily draw a picture of a room or a character in a Tolstoy novel in a way one cannot in Dostoevsky. *War and Peace,* which took him over four years to write, is at once a historical novel, set against the years 1805–1812 just prior to and during Napoleon's invasion of Russia; a bildungsroman, that is, a novel of the personal development of specific people (in this case, charting the fortunes of two families, the Rostovs and the Bolkonskys); and a philosophical novel, narrating the psychological and moral journeys of two characters, Andrei Bolkonsky and Pierre Bezukhov.

Anna Karenina takes a somewhat different turn. In it, Tolstoy interweaves three plots that provide judgment and commentary on each other. Alternating between city and country—the high society of St. Petersburg, life in Moscow, and the countryside he held dear—Tolstoy is philosophically drawn to the rural setting where, far removed from social, political, and ecclesiastical institutions, his characters have the greatest chance of finding their true selves.

During the late 1870s, Tolstoy experienced a deep religious crisis that led him to reject what he saw as a lack of moral and religious purpose in his earlier writings, including his two great novels. His works during the last thirty years of his life took on a decidedly moralistic tone and for that reason are generally considered less artistically successful than his earlier literary output. The one exception to this is his short novel *The Death of Ivan Ilych* (*Smert Ivana Ilycha,* 1886), which recounts the death of a civil servant whose entire life had been defined by social standing and living for himself. Ivan Ilych's fear of death disappears when he finally recognizes the truth of the life he has lived and begins, on his death bed, to think of others. If, for Dostoevsky, salvation was found in a traditional Christian God, for Tolstoy, God lies in the possibilities his characters have to invest meaning in their lives.

By the end of the nineteenth century, the era of the Russian novel was waning. In poetry, the influence of European Symbolism was making itself felt in the work of such authors as Valery Bryusov, Zinaida Gippius, Alexander Blok, and Andrei Bely. At the same time, the tomes of Dostoevsky and Tolstoy were replaced with the short stories of Anton Chekhov, a doctor by training, whose lightness of touch and suggestion through detail more closely resembled a work of impressionist art than it did the moralistic yearnings of his predecessors. Whether describing a nine-year-old boy sending a letter to his grandfather that the old man will never receive ("Vanka"), a provincial schoolteacher fearful of any kind of emotional involvement or change ("Man in a Case"/"Chelovek v futliare"), or a soldier at a ball who inadvertently receives a kiss in a dark room that henceforth transforms his life ("The Kiss"/"Potselui"), Chekhov found the extraordinary in the ordinary, describing it with understated sympathy and pathos in the hundreds of short stories he wrote. Chekhov was also keenly aware of the broader world around him, as the old regime in Russia moved closer to its end. His last play, *The Cherry Orchard* (*Vishnevyi sad,* 1903), ends with the sound of a cherry orchard being cut down with an axe offstage, signaling the end of a way of life for his characters, and more importantly the end of an era.

The Soviet Period

Literature and Culture Under Lenin and the New Economic Policy

When Lenin and the Bolsheviks took power in 1917, one of the questions facing them was how to treat the culture of the past and the writers whose works represented a philosophy and a way of life antithetical to everything they were trying to achieve. At the same time, the Bolsheviks were confronted by a kind of cultural dualism in which the intellectual elite of the country (including most of the revolutionary leaders themselves) was a product of the high culture of the past, while the peasants and workers enjoyed a popular culture that many who led the new order found vulgar and philistine (Barker 1999, 22). How were they to create a new culture that would raise the cultural level of the peasants and workers, preserve the richness of Russia's cultural heritage, and yet reflect the values of the new socialist order? How were they to find a workable place for the past in the present?

In the first few years after the Bolsheviks came to power, much of the country's literary and cultural life continued as it had before. Indeed, the early Soviet period under the NEP (the New Economic Policy, 1921–1928) was a time of great experimentation. Although the heyday of Symbolism had passed, the new proletarian poets still drew on many Symbolist forms. At the same time, the Serapion Brotherhood, formed in 1921, consisted of a group of writers (most prominent of whom were Boris Pilnyak, Evgeny Zamyatin, and Mikhail Zoshchenko) who advocated freedom for the artist, independent of ideological control. As was true before the revolution, Russian writers wanted the freedom to experiment with new forms and ideas.

The Stalin Era and Socialist Realism

After Lenin's death in 1924, however, cultural policy, now influenced by Stalin, slowly began to change. With Stalin's consolidation of power in 1928, and with it the end of the NEP and the beginning of the Five-Year Plans, the world that Soviet artists and writers had known was no more. Under Stalin, the censorship apparatus functioned with much more vigor, denying publication to those writers whose works did not conform to the official party mandate. Just what that mandate was became clear in 1934 when the doctrine of Socialist Realism was presented at the First Congress of the Soviet Writers' Union. Socialist Realism attempted to bring together the ideological designs of the state, the elitist art of the past, and the folk and workers' culture of the present. On paper, this remained the official canon to which all the arts—literature, film, dance, music, and painting—were expected to conform until *glasnost,* or openness, was proclaimed by Gorbachev in 1986.

According to Socialist Realism, literature had to adhere to three basic principals: *partiinost* (party-mindedness), *narodnost* (the values and viewpoints of the *narod,* or people), and *ideinost* (ideological correctness). That is, literary works, and gradually all the other arts, were to reflect the utopian dreams of a society moving toward "the radiant future" (*svetloe budushchee*). Because the future was configured as bright, so too was literature. Optimistic endings in novels and short stories became the norm. Characters placed devotion to the state above their personal interests. Gray areas, doubts, and long philosophical discourses in the manner of Dostoevsky or Tolstoy were strictly prohibited and branded as "bourgeois." Furthermore, character and plot were meant to be easily accessible to the masses, with clear dividing lines between good and evil. When a Socialist Realist narrative drew to its end, the new Soviet men and women presented on its pages would join hands and march into the future, sure of their goals and even surer in their belief that their true belonging was to the "Great Soviet Family" whose *paterfamilias* was Joseph Stalin.

This doctrine resulted in a spate of production novels that extolled the glories of industrialization, the fulfilling and "overfulfilling" of the Five-Year Plans, and the building of the new state. Socialist Realism was anything but realistic. It was also an aesthetic that by its nature militated against anything of lasting literary value. This literary house of cards created under Stalin, whose chief architect was the writer Maxim Gorky, was built on shaky foundations. Writers were forced to create conformist works extolling a nonexistent reality at a time when the country endured terrible suffering from the combined effects of industrialization, the forced collectivization of farmland, and the purges. Writers of conscience had difficulty bringing themselves to write the kind of prescriptive literature the party demanded. Thus, in the 1930s a deep gulf separated those who produced the literature the party wanted in return for perks and privileges and those who became increasingly disaffected with Stalinist society.

That disaffection took various forms. In some cases, writers stopped writing altogether. Others wrote for the drawer, hoping that a time would come when their works could see the light of day. Mikhail Bulgakov worked on what he called his "sunset novel," *The Master and Margarita,* from 1928 until his death twelve years later, knowing that he would be unable to get it published. His novel was a stunning indictment of a system that rejected true artistic creativity, rewarded mediocrity, and, for all its pretensions to creating a new Soviet man and woman, had progressed little. His satire, aimed brilliantly at everything from the Soviet Writers' Union and the secret police to the country's mental institutions, guaranteed that the manuscript would stay in the drawer well into de-Stalinization, not appearing until 1966–1967 in serial form.

Still others attempted to write honestly within the parameters of what was allowed. Writers such as Vera Panova, whose novels *The Train (Sputniki,* 1945) and *The Factory (Kruzhilikha,* 1947) won her the coveted Stalin Prize, continued to publish but in a way that did not violate their own personal ethics. Some found themselves simultaneously both inside and outside the official camp. The beloved poet and essayist Olga Bergholts delivered impassioned radio broadcasts to the people of Leningrad throughout the nine-hundred-day siege during World War II, becoming for many the voice of the city. Nevertheless, her poetry written in prison (1937–1939), which recorded her anguish over the injustices she and her friends had suffered at the hands of the state, was published only in 1972 (Hodgson 2003, 20). Many writers, such as the poets Anna Akhmatova and Boris Pasternak, found themselves without any material means of support because their works were not deemed publishable by the authorities. As early as the 1920s, Gorky set up translation projects to provide income for writers who otherwise could not support themselves.

There were also many cases of writers not surviving at all. The poet Osip Mandelstam died in a transit camp outside of Vladivostok, having been arrested and sentenced during the purges for some poems he had written that were critical of Stalin. Others languished either in the Gulag (the penal system of the USSR, consisting of a network of labor camps) or in internal exile for years. For instance, novelist Alexander Solzhenitsyn, about whom more is written below, was sentenced to eleven years for making disparaging remarks about Stalin and the Soviet leadership in a personal letter. Some became victims in other ways. One of Russia's more brilliant poets, Marina Tsvetaeva, was caught in the multiple catastrophes of her times. Even before the Stalin era she was forced to leave Russia with her husband, Sergei Efron, a White Army officer (a member of the outlawed political parties who participated in a disconnected series of "White" army fronts against the Communist "Reds" during the Russian Civil War). Unable to find an audience receptive to her poetry in Berlin, Prague, or Paris, Tsvetaeva was reduced to poverty. She returned to the Soviet Union just after the Show Trials in 1939. Unknown and unrecognized in her own country, she committed suicide in 1941 just after the German invasion.

Khrushchev and the Thaw

After Stalin's death in 1953 and the subsequent scaling back somewhat of the Soviet police state under Khrushchev, came a "Thaw" (*ottepel*) in the arts. Russian writers are fond of saying that the problem with Russian thaws is that they reveal the sludge and mud (*sliakot*) that lie buried under the pristine snow and ice during the freeze. So it was with the Thaw under Khrushchev, whose "Secret Speech" before the Twentieth Party Congress in 1956, in which he denounced Stalin, his cult of personality, and the excesses of his rule, signaled to writers that they were free to write about topics formerly forbidden: the camps, the purges, anti-Semitism, and the underbelly of collectivization and industrialization.

Perhaps the most sensational of the works to appear during the Thaw of the late 1950s and early 1960s was Solzhenitsyn's novel *One Day in the Life of Ivan Denisovich* (*Odin den Ivana Denisovicha*), published in 1962 with Khrushchev's personal approval in the liberal literary journal *Novyi mir* (*New World*). The novel details life in a camp in the Russian north, over a twenty-four-hour period, as seen through the eyes of one of its prisoners. What made this narrative so powerful was Solzhenitsyn's portrayal of the camp as a microcosm of the entire country. In Solzhenitsyn's view, one was actually freer in the camps than on the outside because in the Gulag one essentially had nothing left to lose.

As was true of much of the liberalization in Soviet letters that took place during the last half of the twentieth century, the Thaw under Khrushchev proceeded in fits and starts. Khrushchev's de-Stalinization speech, which promised reform, was followed in 1957 by the infamous "Pasternak Affair" that arose over the publication in Italy of Boris Pasternak's Nobel Prize-winning novel *Doctor Zhivago*. According to the party, Pasternak had committed the unforgivable sin of having his novel published abroad before it was published at home. There were reasons why the novel probably would not see the light of day in his own country, however, as it was an impassioned defense of a man who simply wanted to live his life apart from the political turmoil into which Russia had been swept up beginning in 1905. Even though the novel was not overtly anti-Soviet, *Novyi mir* declined to publish it. Thirty years earlier Pasternak had made arrangements with the Italian publisher Feltrinelli to have the book published in Italian after it appeared first in the Soviet Union. There remains much debate about Pasternak's role in the publication of his novel abroad and whether he himself gave the go-ahead to Feltrinelli to publish his work. Whatever Pasternak's role or intent, punishment from the Soviet authorities was swift and merciless. He was expelled from the Writers' Union, was forced to decline the Nobel Prize for Literature that he had been awarded for the work, barely escaped being sent into external exile, and died three years later largely as a result of the stress and harassment to which he had been subjected.

During the Thaw, a new generation of poets appeared, the most prominent of whom were Bella Akhmadulina, Yevgeny Yevtushenko, and Andrei Voznesensky. Yevtushenko, in particular, achieved fame for his poems "Babyi Yar" (1961) and "The Heirs of Stalin" ("Nasledniki Stalina" 1962). "Babyi Yar"—about the unmarked graves of Jews outside Kiev who were massacred by the Nazis during World War II—raised the painful issue of Soviet anti-Semitism. "The Heirs of Stalin," which openly criticized Stalin, suggested that the world the now dead dictator created lived on in the post-Stalin era. These younger poets recited their poems in ways that reflected the Russian tradition of poetry as performance. They were also intent on recapturing the personal, the lyrical, and perhaps above all the language itself, which had been subject to such debasement during the Stalin years. Younger prose writers such as Vasily Aksyonov and Andrei Bitov also came to the literary forefront at this time, writing about what under Stalin had been the "nonexistent" problems of youth, namely the desire of young people for Western culture, and their rebellion against the socialist state. Even as this creative activity bespoke a time of liberalization, throughout the Thaw literature remained a target of conservative party ideologues.

The Brezhnev Era and Zastoi

In October 1964, Khrushchev was forced out of power. The Brezhnev era that followed has often been termed a time of *zastoi* (stagnation). In some ways this is a misnomer, as we shall see below, because not all the literary and cultural advances of the Khrushchev era were lost. To be sure, the early years of Leonid Brezhnev's rule were characterized by a backlash, beginning with the 1966 trial of writers Andrei Siniavsky and Yulyi Daniel, who were each sentenced to several years of hard labor for works critical of the Soviet Union that they published abroad under assumed names. The harshness of their sentences, and those of two other dissident writers, Yuri Galanskov and Alexander Ginzburg, led a growing number of writers to conclude that there was little chance of getting their works published through official channels. Their country's invasion of Czechoslovakia in 1968, which crushed a reformist movement there, further darkened their mood by dashing any lingering hopes for genuine political reform at home. The result was the development of a Soviet dissident movement. For many writers this meant seeking alternative means of finding a readership, either through *samizdat* (self-publishing) or *tamizdat* (publishing abroad), that would allow them to circumvent the Soviet censors.

Meanwhile, the pressure to conform and write politically acceptable works increased. By 1967 word had come down from the highest party echelons to editors, such as Alexander Tvardovsky of *Novyi mir,* that enough had been written on the camps and the purges and that these topics were now off-limits. Seeing that his days as editor were numbered, Tvardovsky pushed through as many manuscripts as possible that dealt with these difficult questions before he and the entire editorial board at *Novyi mir* were forced to resign in 1970. He died the following year. During his tenure as editor of *Novyi mir,* Tvardovsky introduced the Soviet reading public to names that would become synonymous with honest writing on a high artistic level: I. Grekova, Viktor Nekrasov, Alexander Solzhenitsyn, and Vladimir Voinovich, to name a few. Furthermore, he allowed those who had been denied a voice during the Stalin years to be read again, making his contribution to Soviet letters during the 1960s incalculable.

As part of the Brezhnev leadership's efforts to rein in Soviet authors, there was a return to the more strictly enforced canons of Socialist Realism. Works such as Alexander Chakovskii's *Blockade* (*Blokada,* 1969–1975) and Ivan Stadniuk's *War* (*Voina,* 1971–1974) rehabilitated Stalin and celebrated his role as a wartime leader. These stood in stark contrast to earlier works that had taken a more critical and pacifist attitude toward the war, such as Grigori Baklanov's masterful *July 1941* (*Iiul 1941 goda,* 1965), which detailed how Stalin's purges negatively affected the Soviet war effort, and *The Dead Feel No Pain* (*Mertvym ne bolno,* 1965) by Vasil Bykov.

Even as the regime promoted Socialist Realism and sought more control over literature, other genres began to make their way into Soviet letters, heralding a movement away from the revolutionary values propagated under Lenin and Stalin toward a focus on the everyday (*byt*) and personal life, a kind of writing that became known as *bytovaia proza,* or "everyday prose." Of the many voices associated with this style, three stand out: Natalia Baranskaia,

Liudmila Petrushevskaia, and Yury Trifonov. In his novella *The Exchange* (*Obmen,* 1969), Trifonov took on what he saw as the moral decay of the Soviet "middle class," suggesting that the collapse in personal morality in society was linked to the very nature of the Soviet system itself. Baranskaia, in *A Week Like Any Other* (*Nedelia kak nedelia,* 1969), dispensed with the usual varnishing (*lakirovka*) reserved for the portrayal of women in official Soviet literature and instead depicted her female protagonist struggling with the infamous double burden (*dvoinaia nosha*) of work and family. Finally, Liudmila Petrushevskaia, who began writing in the 1970s but did not gain the recognition she deserved until the mid-1980s, introduced a new form of writing called "cruel prose" (*zhestokaia proza*), that exposed the underbelly of Soviet society. Petrushevskaia's prose was and remains an unrelenting examination of cramped and confined communal life, of bleak back alleys and stairwells, and of the despair, hopelessness, and rootlessness of Soviet life that was ignored in official pronouncements.

While *bytovaia proza* was concerned with Russia's urban life, a school of authors known as the *derevenshchiki* (village writers) also came to the fore during the Brezhnev era, represented by such writers as Fyodor Abramov, Vasilii Belov, Valentin Rasputin, Vasilii Shukshin, and Vladimir Soloukhin. These writers deplored the incursion of modern technology into Russia's rural areas and wrote movingly of Russian peasant life as the incarnation and preserver of traditional Russian values. One of the most important of their works was Rasputin's *Farewell to Matyora* (*Proshchanie s Materoi,* 1976), which recounts the construction of a hydroelectric dam in Siberia, and the resulting destruction of an entire way of life that accompanied the flooding of a nearby island.

Gorbachev and Glasnost

Brezhnev's death in November 1982, and the eventual coming to power of Mikhail Gorbachev in March 1985, represented as much a turning point for Soviet literature as it did for Soviet politics and economics. As part of his twin policies of *glasnost* (openness) and *perestroika* (restructuring), Gorbachev promised more openness and candor not just in literature but in all avenues of life. Word went forth that a return to the high literary standards of Russia's past could only be achieved through sincerity and openness. *Glasnost* gave writers permission to explore themes that had been banned under Brezhnev, such as the camps, the Stalin era, and the mistakes and mishaps of Soviet science. Under *glasnost,* literature became more formally experimental, often taking the canon of Socialist Realism and turning it on its head. For writers, filmmakers, and the intelligentsia, it was heady time reminiscent of the Thaw under Khrushchev, but one that held out more promise for real change.

Under *glasnost,* works that either had been published abroad through *tamizdat,* or at home in *samizdat,* had been written for the drawer, or published in the Soviet Union but only selectively distributed to foreigners or the elite, were returned to the reading public. The number of works that fell under these categories was monumental and can only be touched upon here. A sampling included Pasternak's *Doctor Zhivago* and Solzhenitsyn's novels, as well as the poetry of Osip Mandelstam, the memoirs of his widow, Nadezhda Mandelstam, the camp memoirs of Evgeniia Ginzburg, the dystopian novel *We* by Evgeny Zamyatin, Anna Akhmatova's *Requiem,* Lydiia Chukovskaia's memoirs, and Venedikt Erofeev's *Moscow to the End of the Line* (*Moskva-Petushki*). Erofeev's novel, written in 1969–1970, recounts the alcoholic ride of the narrator on a commuter train to Petushki, the end of the line, where he hopes to meet his beloved. Erofeev's narrator suggests that living in an alcoholic stupor was the only way one could survive Soviet reality. The circumstances of this novel's publication illustrated some of limits of *glasnost.* When it was finally published in 1988, it appeared only in the journal *Sobriety and Culture* (*Trezvost i kultura* 12, nos. 1–3, 1988–1989).

Also appearing in the Soviet Union for the first time were works by the émigré writer Vladimir Nabokov, who went into exile with his family in 1919, and the poetry and essays of the young Leningrad poet Joseph Brodsky who, after his forced emigration in 1972, settled in the United States and went on to receive the Nobel Prize for Literature in 1987.

Much of *glasnost* was retrospective in that many of the works published during these years looked back at the past in an attempt to come to terms with it and to set the record straight about the country's Stalinist and Leninist legacy. This retrospective stance of both film and literature derived partly from the fact that many of these works had been produced decades earlier when Stalinism was still fresh in everyone's minds. It was also a function of the spirit of Gorbachev's reforms, which signaled that this time, unlike during the Thaw, there could be no turning back.

Some of the most important of the so-called retrospective works of the *glasnost* era included Anatolii Rybakov's novel *Children of the Arbat* (*Deti Arbata,* written in 1969 but not published until 1987), a thinly fictionalized account of Stalin's purges that examines how the machinery of terror worked in the 1930s and how it affected the lives of ordinary citizens who were caught in its cogs through no fault of their own. Another was Vladimir Dudintsev's *The White Robes* (*Belye odezhdy,* originally written in 1962). One of the more interesting novels to appear during the Gorbachev era, it concerned the repressive measures that had been taken against Soviet scientists who refused to bend scientific results to fit Stalinist ideology. Finally, Sergei Zalygin's novel *After the Storm* (*Posle buri,* 1980, 1985) takes us back to the latter years of the NEP in an attempt to find some sort of reconciliation between the Bolshevik Revolution and the Russian national tradition.

At the same time that many writers turned their attention to the Lenin and Stalin years, others explored more current topics that formerly had been off-limits. In his novel *The Executioner's Block* (*Plakha,* 1986), the Kirghiz writer Chingiz Aitmatov was the first to take up the subject of the drug trade in the Soviet Union. In this work Aitmatov spared no energy in attacking drug use, the senseless destruction of the environment that resulted from the trade, and the moral corruption of the system that helped support it. He draws parallels between his main protagonist and the Christ figure, implicitly establishing a link between Stalinism and the Antichrist. Tatiana Tolstaia's collection of short stories *On the Golden Porch* (*Na zolotom kryltse sideli,* 1987) exude gentle irony, humor, and sympathy for the misfits and dreamers who had been completely written out of the great socialist society. Similarly, Sergei Kaledin took his readers into areas traditionally off-limits for Socialist Realism, such as the world of drunks and derelicts in his novella *The Humble Cemetery* (*Smirennoe kladbishche,* 1987).

Viktor Astafiev's novel *The Sad Detective* (*Pechalnyi detektiv,* 1986) was the first in a long line of works to take on the criminal element in Soviet society. Unfortunately, Astafiev's own anti-Semitism casts a shadow over *The Sad Detective,* as does his anti-Georgian sentiment in *Catching Gudgeon in Georgia* (*Lovlia peskarei v Gruzii,* 1986). Such prose revealed a less savory side of *glasnost* as certain pathologies and prejudices, once repressed and hidden by Soviet censorship and ideology, were laid bare once more.

■ Cultural Lament and the Advent of Pop Culture

Glasnost brought about a sea change in other areas of cultural life as well. The easing of censorship, the introduction of market reforms, and the opening up of the Soviet economy to the West introduced a wave of *makulatura* (pulp fiction) to Soviet readers. The classics of Russian literature suddenly seemed to disappear beneath a swell of translated and transplanted Western pulp, from Stephen King and Danielle Steel to Harlequin romances.

This new pulp craze and easy availability of just about anything in print must be seen against the background of the country's traditional print culture in which Russians prided themselves on being the most literate people on earth. Even though the new consumer culture that appeared in the 1990s has driven many away from reading, or has caused them to forsake the classics for romance novels, detective fiction, or Rambo-like thrillers, it is important to know that for much of the twentieth century, Russians were hungry for books and went to great lengths to get their hands on good literature precisely because of its persistent lack of availability. State-owned bookstores of the Soviet era overflowed with production novels and the complete works of party leaders that no one wanted to read. When books by talented writers appeared, they sold out immediately. In a very real sense, the "most reading nation on earth" suffered from pangs of book hunger.

Prior to *perestroika* and *glasnost,* people acquired literature in different ways. One could place a standing order for the complete works of Russia's major writers through the special-order department at stores such as Dom Knigi (the House of Books). Acquiring books that were banned in the Soviet Union, including the works of foreign and Russian writers published abroad, was a more complex affair. We have already discussed *samizdat* as one of the ways dissident literature was disseminated. The book black market (known as the *podpolnyi* or underground book market, which was located in Moscow near the Kuznetskii Most metro station) provided an alternative venue. There, one could purchase not only books from private sellers, but also lists of books that one could order. Because these books frequently sold for hugely inflated prices, groups of people would pool their resources to buy one copy of a book to share. Books often came in via the diplomatic pouch. Others were printed abroad in editions made expressly for smuggling. Les Editeurs Reunis (YMCA Press) in Paris, for example, published pocket-sized editions of banned books in Russia, designed to fit into a jacket pocket to circumvent customs officials. It was chiefly because of these underground venues that a large number of Soviet citizens living in the major cities had already read much of their own literature by the time it was returned to them under Gorbachev.

If literature was disseminated in ways that were often unpredictable and puzzling, so too did the censorship apparatus function in ways that often seemed random yet almost always related to the political climate. Censorship served as an ideological watchdog of the party and was ubiquitous. Each publishing house had its own in-house censor as did any enterprise or institute where printing was involved, from articles in scholarly journals to directions on how to use your vacuum cleaner.

Forbidding the publication of a work was only one way in which the censorship apparatus operated. Indeed, manuscripts were frequently published after being "reworked" by the infamous red pen of the censor. At other times, a work might be published without significant cuts or alterations but in such a limited *tirazh* (circulation) that it literally sold out overnight. Distribution could also function as a form of censorship. For instance, Tatiana Tolstaia, who began her writing career during the late Soviet era, recounted in a March 1999 conversation with the author how her first collection of short stories sold out immediately in Moscow and St. Petersburg where she was known, but went unsold and unread in provincial towns where no one had heard of her. So attuned were Soviet writers to the prevalence of censorship that even during the relaxed air of the Gorbachev era, the literary atmosphere was redolent with charges that censorship was still in effect through the paper allocation allotted to various publishing houses.

The availability of foreign literature was another matter altogether. What was translated and published shifted with the political winds. Foreign works deemed ideologically acceptable were regularly translated either by the Foreign Language Publishing House or Progress Publishers in Moscow. Works by James Baldwin, John Dos Passos, Jack London, and Upton Sinclair were easily available in Russian translation because their texts propounded a vision of the West as a place of racial and economic injustice that was in line with that put forward by the Soviet government to its people. Gaining access to other foreign literature was more challenging and necessitated a trip to Moscow's Library for Foreign Literature where one could read the work, but only on site in the library's Readers Hall. The transition prompted by *glasnost,* from a complete scarcity of what people wanted to read and an excess of what they did not, to the heavy consumption of pulp fiction at the expense of genuine literature, is one of the hallmarks of the cultural shift from Soviet to post-Soviet Russia.

One genre that suffered greatly during the Soviet era was the romance novel. For Soviet authorities, the plots of such works symbolized "bourgeois moral decadence" and thus were strictly off-limits. Mariia Cherniak (2005, 152) notes that from the late 1950s to the end of the Soviet period, romantic/erotic novels circulated among young women through *samizdat,* and that the hand-copied novels became one of the few ways that Soviet women could procure information about sexuality and the opposite sex that was not available in schools. When the 1990s ushered in the possibility of freer choice in reading material, many women began to devour the Harlequin romances that quickly appeared in translation and were second in popularity only to translated and homegrown detective fiction.

The genre of the detective novel is neither new to post-Soviet Russia, nor was it unknown in prerevolutionary times. In fact, two of Dostoyevsky's most famous novels, *Crime and Punishment* and *The Brothers Karamazov,* can easily be read as early examples of the whodunit, Russian style. Even so, when Russia enjoyed a "detective boom" a century ago, as a result of the easing of political constraints on literature, it was primarily a Western import. From that time on, into the 1920s, such characters in Western detective fiction as Sherlock Holmes, Nat Pinkerton, and Nick Carter enjoyed enormous popularity in Russia (Stites 1992, 24, 42–43). While detective fiction came to a precipitous halt under Stalin, having been removed from library and bookstore shelves for being overly "bourgeois" and "decadent," the genre experienced an almost immediate rebirth after Stalin's death. Soviet writers began to experiment with their own versions of this genre. Writers such as Arkady Adamov, Iulian Semenov, and Arkady and Grigory Vainer wrote within the bounds of what was considered officially acceptable, yet in ways that provided Soviet readers with welcome relief from the official literature of the day.

While Soviet letters produced its own brand of detective fiction in the post-Stalin years, foreign practitioners of the genre also appeared on the shelves. Agatha Christie remains one of the most loved of foreign detective writers, read as widely today as she was in the 1960s and 1970s. Similarly, the French writer Georges Simenon still enjoys enormous popularity through his Inspector Maigret novels. So popular was the Maigret series that in 1974 when the Soviet paper industry was trying to convince people to collect wastepaper to offset a paper shortage, it lured them into doing so by offering them free books, one of which was the *Maigret Stories* (Mehnert 1983, 97).

More recently, detective fiction in Russia has served as a form of catharsis, to say nothing of escape, at a time when there are few easy answers and even fewer crimes being solved. Among the most popular detective writers today are Boris Akunin, Polina Dashkova, Daria Dontsova, and Alexandra Marinina. Since 1998, Akunin (the pen name of Grigory Chkhartishvili, a critic and scholar of Japanese, English, and US literature) has achieved literary stardom with his series of historical detective novels set in the nineteenth century and featuring his super sleuth, Erast Fandorin. More recently, Akunin has produced a trilogy of nineteenth-century detective fiction featuring a nun, Sister Pelagia, as his chief detective and a series devoted to Nicholas Fandorin, the grandson of Erast Fandorin. Among the other prominent representatives of the detective genre, Marinina has also enjoyed phenomenal success, to date producing twenty-eight novels, most of which feature Anastasiia (Nastia) Kamenskaia, a crime analyst in Moscow's central police headquarters. Much of Marinina's popularity is undoubtedly linked to the likeable but somewhat unorthodox personality of Kamenskaia herself, who solves crimes by sitting endless hours at her computer, chain smoking, and drinking innumerable cups of coffee. Completely incompetent at anything remotely resembling "women's work," she leaves such details to her boyfriend. Similarly unconcerned about her appearance, she is pathologically lazy about the details of everyday life. Her spare time is given over to translating Western detective fiction into Russian. So exceedingly popular are Marinina's novels that several have been made into TV serials (Nepomnyashchy 1999). Also of interest in Marinina's work is its discomfort with the role of technology in the world today, coupled with a restrained nostalgia for the norms and values of the Soviet era. For such writers as Marinina and Akunin, the question of identity is never far beneath the surface.

Another genre, that of the *boevik* or Rambo-like action thriller, has made its way into post-Soviet popular culture by appealing to a predominantly male audience. The *boeviki* serve up the expected violence, car chases, and gun battles, the presence of which, alas, in post-Soviet society is not confined to the pages of fiction. It is also a genre, however, that has taken on the fundamental question of the fate of the hero in a society in which deeds are no longer accomplished for the collective good.

The most articulate representative of this new post-Soviet genre is Viktor Dotsenko, whose *Beshenyi* series recounts the exploits of his eponymous hero, hardened by combat in both Afghanistan and Chechnya. Like the heroes of Russia's early oral epics, the *byliny,* Dotsenko's hero is able to perform superhuman feats at a moment's notice. He is also a loner, however, a man for whom allegiances to state and society are meaningless. Much of Dotsenko's work, and that of other writers of the genre, such as Fyodor Butyrsky and Danil Koretsky, suggests an underlying philosophical bent. In their musings on such questions as the Chechen war, the end of empire, and the death penalty, the heroes of these authors contemplate the morass into which Russia has fallen and their part in helping to bring about a moral renewal of the country they have temporarily lost (Dubin 2005).

In one sense the *boeviki* and *detektivy* are nothing more than the latest wave of popular culture in Russia. By the same token, that these books are so widely read suggests more than the simple desire on the part of Russians to read escapist literature. There is, in fact, nothing particularly escapist in reading fiction that addresses the country's most pressing social and political concerns. If on the pages of these works crime and corruption are dealt with in ways unlike in real life, it is also here that a genuine dialogue is taking place on the many challenges facing contemporary Russia.

■ Soviet and Russian Film

No discussion of the cultural scene in Russia today can afford to ignore the role that film has played in Russian life since 1917. During seventy-five years of Soviet rule, cinema had a long and rich, although sometimes battered, history. Like literature, it often served as a vehicle for Communist Party propaganda, yet, particularly after Stalin's death, was often remarkable for its integrity and artistic experimentation.

The Cinema of the Revolution and New Economic Policy

Even before the 1917 Bolshevik Revolution, Russian cinema had begun to flourish. It was Lenin, however, who dramatically elevated its status by recognizing its potential for conveying the Bolsheviks' message to the people. In harnessing it to the administrative machinery of the new Soviet state, Lenin declared film "the most important art" (Zorkaya 1989, 38). The directors working in the immediate postrevolutionary era, although not true Bolsheviks, were nevertheless enormously attracted by the prospect of breaking from the old order and creating a cinema that could be seen and appreciated by the emerging proletariat. Lev Kuleshov, for example, experimented with founding a new aesthetic reality, termed "the Kuleshov effect," by utilizing montage in the editing of shots. Likewise, director Dziga Vertov attempted to create what he termed "revolutionary cinema," which would reflect the ideals and aspirations of the new order by employing radical new cinematic techniques to overturn traditional "bourgeois" narrative. His film *Man with a Movie Camera* (*Chelovek s kinoapparatom,* 1929) placed the viewer and the cameraman in the thick of the everyday, documenting Soviet reality from sunrise to sunset, incorporating into it the passages in human life. Vertov dismissed traditional cinematographers as a "bunch of junk dealers." For him the only true genre worthy of the era was the documentary, which would document and record only the facts as the chronicler of the revolution (Zorkaya 1989, 57).

By the 1920s, experimentation with the technique of montage came to characterize the work of the most important directors: Alexander Dovzhenko, Sergei Eisenstein, and Vsevolod Pudovkin. The best known of the group was Eisenstein, an author of numerous theoretical writings on film, who further developed the technique of montage first worked out by Kuleshov. Although not of working-class origins, Eisenstein was taken with the notion of a revolutionary art. His four silent films, *Strike* (*Stachka,* 1925), *The Battleship Potemkin* (*Bronenosets Potemkin,* 1926), *October* (*Oktiabr,* 1928), and *The Old and the New* (*Staroe i novoe,* 1929), depict the violence and inequities he saw in capitalism, the stirrings of rebellion among the masses, and the coming of revolution. Ironically, the films of these directors never really reached the common people for whom they were intended, as many were simply too experimental in form to find a willing audience among any but the intelligentsia. Experimentation was allowed, however, provided the films were ideologically correct.

The Stalin Era

With the rise of Stalin, however, artists increasingly came under attack for their work. Vertov, who in the opinion of many was the most experimental of the revolutionary directors, ended his career doing newsreels. Eisenstein's fate was more complicated, as he managed to continue producing feature films well into the Stalin era. His film *Alexander Nevsky* (1938) takes as its central character the eponymous thirteenth-century prince of Novgorod. Set to music composed by Sergei Prokofiev, the film depicts Alexander Nevsky's defeat of the invading Teutonic Knights in the famous "Battle of the Ice" on Lake Peipus in 1242. Despite its strongly patriotic content, the Soviet censors banned the film because its direct references to the threat of German aggression (not only during Alexander's life but also their own) were in conflict with Stalin's desire to buy time through the August 1939 signing of a nonaggression pact with Hitler. Only after Nazi Germany's invasion of the Soviet Union, less than two years later, was the film finally shown. Eisenstein encountered problems with censorship again in the release of his last film, the two-part *Ivan the Terrible* (*Ivan Groznyi*, 1943–1946). Part one of the film won Eisenstein the Stalin Prize for its depiction of Ivan as a strong leader who united his people. Part two, however, was neither shown nor acknowledged until 1958, five years after Stalin's death and ten years after Eisenstein's, because of the obvious negative parallels it draws between Ivan the Terrible and Stalin.

By the early 1930s, Stalin had turned Soviet film into one of his more important ideological trump cards. The propaganda regularly ground out by the party sought to convey to a country that had gone through a civil war, forced collectivization, industrialization, man-made famines, and soon, purges, that "life (was) getting better, more joyous, comrades." Life and art, in short, had become completely ideologized. Certain genres, plot types, characters, and conflicts became canonical in Soviet cinema, and any deviation from these standards could leave a film director branded as a "formalist," a "wrecker," or worse. During this period, the film studios produced party-mandated films on the revolution and civil war, such as the Vasiliev brothers' *Chapaev* (1934), Alexander Zarkhi and Josef Heifitz's *Baltic Deputy* (*Deputat Baltiki,* 1937), or Efim Dzigan's *We from Kronstadt* (*My iz Kronshtadta,* 1936). Films were to be heroic in order to raise the consciousness of the masses. There were limits to how "heroic" adventure films could be, however, as party ideologues feared that their action sequences might spark interest in renewed revolutionary activity. Thus after *Chapaev,* an adventure film par excellence, action on the screen became more circumscribed and as a result less interesting (Youngblood 1992, 175).

The 1930s also witnessed the birth of the Stalinist musical, the most famous producers of which were Grigori Aleksandrov and Ivan Pyriev. Pyriev focused on rural life and socialist labor in such films as *The Rich Bride* (*Bogataia nevesta,* 1938), *Tractor Drivers* (*Traktoristy,* 1939), and *The Swineherd and the Shepherd* (*Svinarka i pastukh,* 1941). In films such as *Jolly Fellows* (*Veselye rebiata,* 1934), *Circus* (*Tsirk,* 1936), *Volga-Volga* (1938), and *The Radiant Path* (*Svetlyi put,* 1940), Aleksandrov extolled the virtues of the Soviet system, often at the expense of the West, even as he emulated Hollywood musicals in lavish spectacles, replete with music and dancing. Aleksandrov's films were typical of this era in their reliance on spectacle. Whether through lavish production numbers or Soviet heroes performing superhuman feats, the Soviet viewer in the 1930s was treated to historical, propagandistic entertainment, featuring everything from national heroes from bygone days, who predicted and extolled the coming revolution, to the contemporary hero as explorer, pilot, or geologist, who was engineering the new society and perfecting Soviet science.

The films of the Stalin era closely conformed to the canons of Socialist Realism, according to which individual characters on the screen were either good or evil. The Soviet audience was continually exhorted to be vigilant about the presence of enemies. Just who those enemies were, however, changed with the political tides. During the 1930s, the focus was on the enemy within, namely those among the masses who were accused of sabotaging the Soviet economy, and those among the party elite who were charged with conspiring against Stalin and the Soviet state (Leyda 1960, 344).

By the early 1940s, a different kind of film began to appear as the enemy at home that had been depicted on the Soviet screen gave way to the enemy from abroad. Contrary to what one might expect, World War II did not halt Soviet cinema production but rather increased it by creating an atmosphere in which it became imperative to make highly propagandistic films about the war that exhorted the people onward to victory.

In the early days of the war, newsreels supplanted feature-length films. The first newsreels appeared on June 25, 1941, just three days after the Nazi invasion. From then on updated versions appeared every three days (Kenez 2001, 169). The first months of the war, however, produced little documentary footage of the fighting, both for security reasons and because the Germans were running roughshod over the Soviets. Thus, Soviet citizens who remained at home initially saw little film footage of what was actually taking place on the battlefront. Documentaries instead concentrated on the war effort on the home front and on the quiet heroism of the Soviet people (Kenez 1995, 163). However, as the war progressed, Soviet viewers were increasingly allowed to see the shocking footage of the war's devastation, a fact that contributed enormously to a desire for revenge. The war broke down the usual distinction between the feature-length film and the documentary. Indeed, feature-length films often functioned as documentaries by employing newsreel footage to show Nazi atrocities, as well as the valiant patriotism and heroic sacrifices of the Soviet people.

The immediate postwar period saw a creative decline for the major filmmakers as Stalin took increasing control of the film industry with the result that iconic images of him and panegyrics to his military leadership became the order of the day. Suffering from "film hunger," the country was regularly fed such monumental Stalinist productions as Vladimir Petrov's *Battle of Stalingrad* (*Stalingradskaia bitva,* 1950) and Mikhail Chiaureli's *The Fall of Berlin* (*Padenie Berlina,* 1949). In Chiaureli's film Stalin is depicted as the wise father who calmly directs his troops from the Kremlin as he would players on a chessboard. His image stands in direct contrast to that of Hitler who is portrayed as a mentally deranged leader who is completely unable to command his own forces as the Soviets take Berlin.

Stifled by ideological controls, Soviet directors also began working on the latest genre to receive Stalin's blessing, the biographical film. Under the watchful eye of the censors, directors dutifully produced films that mythologized the Russian and Soviet pasts, such as Vsevolod Pudovkin's *Admiral*

Nakhimov (1946), Grigori Roshal's *Academician Ivan Pavlov* (*Akademik Ivan Pavlov,* 1949), and Chiaureli's film about Stalin's youth, *The Vow* (*Kliatva,* 1946).

The Cinema of the Thaw

After Stalin's death in 1953, the state's insistence on the strict observance of official ideology and Socialist Realism gave way to a more relaxed atmosphere under Khrushchev that allowed directors to experiment in their work. They were now allowed to explore the emotional worlds and psychological complexity of their characters. Even though the Thaw proceeded in fits and starts, sometimes backtracking on its promises of greater freedom, Soviet cinema during this time made impressive advances. Even after Khrushchev was deposed in 1964, much of the easing of control that characterized his tenure as party first secretary continued through the late 1960s. Under Khrushchev, attention turned to increased production of feature-length films, prompting people to return to movie theaters in large numbers. One of the more popular films of the period was *The Cranes Are Flying* (*Letiat zhuravli,* 1957), directed by Mikhail Kalatozov. Drawing an audience of 28.3 million during the first year of its release, the film's honest portrayal of how real people coped with suffering and loss during World War II was a welcome departure from the official ideology of the Stalin era. Contrary to the stock image of the faithful Soviet woman who waits for her beloved to return from the war, Kalatozov's female protagonist, Veronika, betrays her fiancé while he is at the front and marries his cousin out of loneliness and fear. The film also suggests a much more ambivalent attitude toward the war than Soviet viewers had seen previously. The director's camera moves inward, revealing a world whose moral values are no longer defined in terms of black and white but in shades of gray. The film makes the traditional happy ending ever so slightly more complicated while still paying homage to the tenets of Socialist Realism.

Out of the Thaw came other films that were a clear departure from the Stalinist norm, among them Grigori Chukhrai's *Ballad of a Soldier* (*Ballada o soldate,* 1959). Chukhrai took the traditional Soviet war narrative and transformed it by taking it off the battlefield. Chukhrai's male protagonist, the soldier Alyosha, becomes an accidental hero, not through his actions at the front but through his everyday acts of selflessness as he travels home to his village on leave to see his mother.

The cinema of the Thaw also produced films about children, a trend that began in the late 1950s when children began to assume central roles in Soviet feature films. Films such as *Seryozha* (also known as *A Summer to Remember,* 1960), directed by Georgi Danelia and Igor Talankin, and *Ivan's Childhood* (*Ivanovo detstvo,* 1962), directed by Andrey Tarkovsky, brought a fresh vision of Soviet life to the screen by depicting it through the un-spoiled and untutored eyes of children. Entering into the world of a child who "misperceives" what is going on, Soviet viewers were implicitly en-couraged to question the official version of Soviet reality.

On the whole, most film directors from the Stalin era failed to make a successful transition into the new political and artistic climate. There were, of course, exceptions such as Mikhail Kalatozov. Even so, many of the more important films of the Thaw were the works of a newer generation of direc-tors. Among these was Andrey Tarkovsky, who deserves special mention be-cause his films come closest to the European notion of *auteur* cinema in which the director is seen as the main creative force in a film. Tarkovsky made seven films in his lifetime: *The Steamroller and the Violin* (*Katok i skrypka*, 1960), *Ivan's Childhood* (*Ivanovo detstvo*, 1962), *Andrei Rublev* (1966), *Solaris* (*Soliaris*, 1972), *The Mirror* (*Zerkalo*, 1974), *Nostalgia* (*Nos-talghia*, 1983), and *The Sacrifice* (*Offret/Zhertvoprinoshenie*, 1986), the last of which was completed shortly before his death. The canons of Socialist Re-alism were completely anathema to Tarkovsky. His vision of cinema was based on his belief that an artist was responsible not to the state but to a higher calling. For Tarkovsky, art was nothing less than a form of religion. His understanding of the artist drew on the Russian romantic notion of the artist as a martyr to his art, willing to suffer and sacrifice for his cause. For an audience spoon-fed on literature and film that was designed to be easily ac-cessible to the masses, Tarkovsky's films breathed the fresh air of complex-ity, which often made them difficult to interpret. Images appear on the screen that are left unexplained. More important than interpretation for Tarkovksy was the emotional experience that resonates within the viewer, even if it de-fies rational explanation (Tarkovsky 1989).

Tarkovsky ran into trouble, however, with the tightening of ideological controls under Brezhnev. The fate of his third film, *Andrei Rublev*, is a case in point. The story of a fifteenth-century monk who became Russia's most renowned icon painter, the film was completed in 1966. Because of Tarkov-sky's particular approach to his subject, however, the film would not be re-leased until 1971. Instead of portraying Rublev as a national hero living in tumultuous times, Tarkovsky cast him as an artist who chose to withdraw from the world instead of embracing it. Such a telling of the tale ran con-trary to the official Soviet narrative of Russia's glorious medieval past (Johnson and Petrie 1994, 79–85).

Other directors experienced similar difficulties. Among the most hounded during the late 1960s and 1970s was Sergo Paradzhanov, an Armenian raised in Georgia who subsequently studied and worked in the Ukrainian capital, Kiev. In each of his major films he celebrated the national traditions of the people among whom he lived and worked. In *Shadows of Forgotten Ances-tors* (*Teni zabytykh predkov*, 1964) he featured the Ukrainian and Carpathian traditions; in *The Color of Pomegranates* (*Tsvet granata,* also known as *Sayat Nova,* 1969), Armenian national heritage; and in *The Legend of Suram Fortress* (*Legenda o Suramskoi kreposti* 1984/1986) and *Ashik Kerib* (1988), Paradzhanov depicted the Georgian tradition. The Soviet leadership's negative reaction to Paradzhanov's films was symptomatic of the tension that existed between party ideology and the traditions and national aspirations of the country's many ethnic minorities. As Katherine Graney explains in Chapter 7, although the CPSU encouraged the expression of national and artistic traditions, the actual practice and observance of such threatened to undermine the notion that the USSR was based on a "Friendship of Peoples" that transcended any particular ethnic identity. The challenge for the party was how to celebrate ethnic diversity without celebrating it too much and risk the rise of what it viewed as harmful nationalistic tendencies. Such was the perceived threat posed by Paradzhanov's films that in 1974 he was arrested on a number of trumped-up charges ranging from homosexuality to foreign currency dealings. This harassment on the part of the Soviet government largely accounts for the fact that Paradzhanov made only four films in twenty-five years.

The Era of Stagnation

Despite experiences such as those of Tarkovsky and Paradzhanov, Soviet artists during the Brezhnev era did not lose all the gains they had made under Khrushchev. While it is true that some of the shabby and decrepit urban and rural landscapes that were shown on the screen during the Thaw were cleaned up and given a new shine under Brezhnev, Soviet directors still sought to present an honest and convincing portrait of everyday life (*byt*) within the narrower parameters of the day. One of the classic *bytovoi* films of the Brezhnev era was *The Irony of Fate, or Have a Good Sauna!* (*Ironiia sudby, ili s legkim parom!* 1975) directed by Eldar Riazanov. Initially made for television and first broadcast on New Year's Eve 1975, the film became an immediate hit. It tells the story of the accidental meeting of a man and a woman, each engaged to someone else, and the resulting comedy of errors that finally brings them together. Aside from the story it tells, the film represents a social satire of the standardization of Soviet life during the 1960s and 1970s, in which neighborhoods, apartment buildings, and stores looked the same all over the country. Such is the enduring popularity of this film that it continues to be shown on at least two Russian television channels every New Year's Eve. Riazanov's films invariably dealt not with the heroic past but with the everyday, and with regular people who otherwise would have passed unnoticed into the pages of Soviet history.

Other directors similarly used the frustrations and complexities of daily life as ways of exploring larger philosophical questions. Georgi Danelia, for instance, in his film *Autumn Marathon* (*Osennii marafon,* 1979), focuses on a university professor who in trying to please everyone and do the right thing completely loses control of his life. Unlike Soviet films of an earlier era, Danelia's male protagonist resigns himself to what comes his way, with the result that the film's conclusion brings no satisfying solution or change to his circumstances.

Perhaps the most important of the *bytovoi* films released during the Brezhnev era was *Moscow Does Not Believe in Tears* (*Moskva slezam ne verit,* 1979), which won the Academy Award for Best Foreign Film in 1981. The movie, directed by Vladimir Menshov, attracted eighty million domestic viewers and was part of a trend of the *zhenskie filmy,* or women's films, that began in the 1970s. Menshov follows the life of his female protagonist Katya over the course of fifteen years, beginning in 1958. The film was Menshov's take on an issue that was first aired publicly with the publication of Natalia Baranskaia's story "A Week Like Any Other" ("Nedelia kak nedelia") in 1969: Soviet women were tired. They were suffering from "equality." They were tired of having full-time jobs outside the home, yet simultaneously functioning as the providers, nurturers, caretakers, and shoppers in the family, where each task acquired the particular stamp of difficulty and exasperation unique to Soviet life in the 1960s and 1970s. Menshov's film takes on the issues of gender relations, single parenthood, and power struggles between men and women at home and at work. The film ends on an ambiguous note, as Katya, in a surprising gesture, relinquishes her control over the home front to her partner, Gosha, in return for her increased stature in her place of work. Is personal happiness at home her reward for the sacrifices she has made at the workplace, as some have suggested (Taylor et al. 2000, 157), or is her capitulation to Gosha's need to be the head of the household the necessary price she must pay for the relationship to continue? Menshov leaves the question open.

In addition to the *bytovoi* theme, several important films of the 1970s dealt with the problems of Soviet youth. In focusing on young people who felt alienated by the realities of Soviet life, these films became venues through which the public's declining confidence in the party could be displayed. Dinara Asanova, in particular, focused on the problems of teenagers in her film *The Nontransferable Key* (*Kliuch bez prava peredachi,* 1977), which takes as its subject a group of tenth graders at a Soviet high school and explores the relationship between teachers and students. Her subsequent films, *Tough Kids* (*Patsany,* 1983) and *My Sweet, My Dear, My Love, My Only One . . .* (*Milyi, dorogoi, liubimyi, edinstvennyi . . . ,* 1984), are similarly devoted to problems among Soviet youth.

Asanova was one of several female directors who began to make their marks on Soviet cinema in the 1970s. Among these was the Georgian director Lana Gogoberidze, whose *Several Interviews on Personal Matters*

(*Neskolko interviu po lichnym voprosam,* 1979) takes as its heroine the journalist Sofiko, who, like many Soviet women, found herself unable to reconcile the demands of everything that Soviet society asked her to be—loyal citizen, worker, wife, mother, activist—with her life as she actually lived it. How this situation evolved, and who is ultimately to blame for it, are the questions Gogoberidze raises in her film.

Among other prominent female directors of the 1960s and 1970s was Larisa Shepitko, whose first feature-length film, *Wings* (*Krylia,* 1966), took up the question of generational conflict, as a middle-aged woman looks back on her service as a pilot during World War II, at the same time as she tries to come to terms with her daughter's generation. Shepitko made several more films before her untimely death in 1979, notably *Homeland of Electricity* (*Rodina elektrichestva,* 1967), which was banned for twenty years before being shown for the first time in 1987. Perhaps Shepitko's most memorable film, however, is *The Ascent* (*Voskhozhdenie,* 1976), set in German-occupied Belorussia in 1942. The film is a stunning example of what could be accomplished artistically even under Brezhnev as she draws parallels between the partisans who are the focus of her story and the figures of Christ and Judas. At the same time she explores the connection between Marxism and Christianity.

No discussion of Soviet and post-Soviet women film directors is complete without mention of Kira Muratova, who over a forty-two-year span produced sixteen films, many of which were initially shelved only to be publicly screened during the *glasnost* era. Muratova was frequently at odds with the censors because of her films' unromanticized view of Soviet reality and depiction of the dark and difficult relations of family life. One of her films, *Among the Grey Stones* (*Sredi serykh kamnei,* 1983), was so heavily cut prior to its release that Muratova removed her name from its credits.

Although her films are difficult to categorize, many clearly fall within the genre of *chernukha* (from the word "black" and referring to films or literature that depict a bleak reality). With her characters ever at odds with anything remotely resembling mainstream Soviet society, her films offer a powerful critique of the moral, political, and economic state of the Soviet system (Roberts 1999, 144–160). Moreover, the often grim psychological realism in her films frequently extends to the settings in which many of her characters find themselves. In *Getting to Know the Wide World* (*Poznavaia belyi svet,* 1978), Muratova set a deceptively simple love story amidst the concrete, dirt, and bricks of a construction site whose deeper significance was not lost on the Soviet viewer. She is a highly experimental director, often filming from unconventional angles in ways that keep her audience on edge. Among the most important of her works are *Brief Encounters* (*Korotkie vstrechi,* 1967/ 1987) and *Long Goodbyes* (*Dolgie provody,* 1971/1987), which represent the genre of provincial melodrama that was popular in Soviet cinema. *Brief Encounters* tells the story of two women who are in love with the same man.

Between the lines of the plot, Muratova explores the lack of basic amenities in the consumer sector of Soviet society: problems with the water supply, the lack of housing in Soviet cities, and shortages in the retail trade. Her experimental film techniques curried her little favor with the authorities during the Soviet era. As a result, just five copies of *Brief Encounters* were released. *The Asthenic Syndrome* (*Asticheskii sindrom,* 1989), released during *glasnost,* had the distinction of being the only film to be banned during that era because of its profanity and its powerful moral indictment of socialism in the late 1980s (Janumyan 2003). It was released in the Soviet Union only after it was awarded a special jury prize at Berlin in 1990. Her subsequent films, *The Sensitive Policeman* (*Chuvstvitelnyi militsioner,* 1992), *Enthusiasms* (*Uvlechenia,* 1994), *Three Stories* (*Tri istorii,* 1997), *Chekhovian Motifs* (*Chekhovskie motivy,* 2002), and most recently *The Tuner* (*Nastroishchik,* 2004), continue her experimentation with plotless narratives that frequently border on the absurd and the surreal.

Film Under Glasnost

Even before the advent of *glasnost,* literary and artistic production in the Soviet Union had already turned a corner. Many of the films that appeared just prior to *glasnost* had already been in production during Brezhnev's last years, suggesting that cinema had begun to tackle the social and economic problems that were eating away at Soviet society even before official permission was given to discuss them in public. The films of this era dealt with questions ranging from the second economy and alienation to the retreat into private life, all issues that people faced daily but that had not been directly addressed before in cinema. The character of the swindler and the person making a little extra on the side as the economy struggled were enormously popular during this period in films, such as Vladimir Bortko's *The Blonde Girl Around the Corner* (*Blondinka za uglom,* 1984), Viktor Tregubovich's *A Rogue's Saga* (*Prokhindiada,* 1984), and Eldar Riazanov and Emil Braginsky's *Train Station for Two* (*Vokzal dlia dvoikh,* 1983).

Other films made just prior to *glasnost* similarly reflected the crisis of confidence in Soviet values. Rolan Bykov's film *Scarecrow* (*Chuchelo,* 1983), for instance, tells a frightening tale about Soviet youth "gone bad." That the film was seen by about fifty-five million viewers suggests that it touched a raw nerve in Soviet society. Set in provincial Russia, the film was both lavishly praised and harshly criticized for the way it portrayed the "collective mentality" in Soviet society and its suggestion of what can happen when such logic is pushed to the extreme. Bykov's use of Stalinist-era imagery suggested to viewers that the structure of life and social consciousness that had characterized the 1930s was still prevalent in the 1980s.

When *glasnost* became official policy in 1986, the results of the new freedoms were manifested somewhat differently in film and literature. As explained earlier, many of the works of Russian and Soviet literature that previously had been banned by the party but now saw the light of day under *glasnost* had in fact already been available through underground channels. With cinema the situation was different. When a film was denied release, it was put in a canister and shelved, and that was that. There were no extra copies to be purchased through the black market. Thus, when such films were made available to Soviet audiences in the mid-1980s, they had not been previously seen. For this reason, one might argue that the effect of the new openness was more pronounced in film than it was in literature.

One of the most important changes to affect cinema under Gorbachev was the complete restructuring of the Film Makers' Union as old-guard *apparatchiki* were replaced with younger, forward-looking people who were supportive of artistic expression. The late 1980s were a heady time for Soviet cinema. Censorship restrictions were all but abolished, and the studios moved toward self-financing. While this meant that they had more freedom to decide on scripts, schedules, and the like, it also meant that for the first time in seventy-five years they had to be financially self-sustaining.

The first films released under *glasnost* were those that had been made earlier but had been banned by the censors. Chief among these were Alexei German's *Trial on the Road* (*Proverka na doroge,* 1971/1986) and *My Friend Ivan Lapshin* (*Moi drug Ivan Lapshin 1982/1984*), Tengiz Abuladze's *Repentance* (*Pokaianie,* 1984/1986), Alexander Askoldov's *The Commissar* (*Komissar,* 1967/1987), Andrei Konchalovsky's *The Story of Asya Klyachina, Who Loved but Did Not Get Married* (*Istoriia Asi Kliachinoi, kotoraia liubila da ne vyshla zamuzh*), and several films by Kira Muratova.

Many of these films were retrospective, revisiting the war and the Stalin era. German's *Trial on the Road* takes the viewer back to the winter of 1942 but without the heroics that characterized previous war films. Instead, German takes up the sensitive topic of Stalinist ideology during the war, specifically in regard to Russian prisoners of war who were branded traitors to their country because they allowed themselves to be taken alive by the Nazis. His second film, *My Friend Ivan Lapshin,* although difficult to understand and sometimes inaccessible to non-Russian audiences, was voted in 1989 by Soviet film critics as the best Russian film ever made (Taylor et al. 2000, 84). Set in a distant, provincial town in 1935, it narrates the life of a police detective through the eyes of a nine-year-old boy. The film was unique in the way German managed to juxtapose the optimistic, bombastic slogans of the time with the bleak, almost unimaginable hardships of daily life. Hunger, famine, criminality, and even cannibalism were horrifying realities that German captures with his camera, never before documented in Soviet film.

German's movie about Lapshin was just one of several once-banned films released under *glasnost* that dealt with the Stalin theme. The sheer dimensions of the terror, the need to understand the man and the times, and the effect of Stalinism on subsequent generations lay behind such films as Tengiz Abuladze's *Repentance*. The film concerns a small-town Georgian dictator, Varlam Aravidze, who is portrayed as a composite of Stalin, Hitler, Mussolini, and Lavrenti Beria, the former head of Stalin's secret police. Beria, like Stalin, was a Georgian. Although set in Georgia, the film explores the nature of fascism in general and the ways in which the sins of the fathers are visited upon the children. The character most deeply affected by the tyranny of Varlam is, interestingly, not his son but his grandson, whose suicide finally prompts his own father to rethink Varlam's legacy and his role as the inheritor of that legacy. That the film spans three generations seems to suggest that it was made not for those who personally experienced Stalinism, but for the younger generation that, even though it has no memory of the times, also can be counted among its victims.

A number of films actually produced under *glasnost* also focused on the Stalin theme. Chief among these was *The Cold Summer of '53* (*Kholodnoe leto '53,* 1988), which deals with Stalin obliquely through its portrayal of a confrontation between two political exiles living in a small village in northern Russia and a gang of criminals who, in the wake of the general amnesty that was granted for prisoners after Stalin's death, descend upon the village and terrorize it. *Defense Counsel Sedov* (*Zashchitnik Sedov,* 1988), a chilling tale that cuts right to the heart of Stalinism, narrates the story of an unassuming lawyer who is asked to defend four agronomists who have been sentenced to death on fabricated charges. Sedov procures the release and rehabilitation of the prisoners but finds that his actions have set into motion a new wave of arrests, this time of the officials who were originally responsible for the wrongful arrest of the agronomists. Directed by Evgenii Tsymbal, the film is a study of the randomness by which guilt and responsibility, and survival and arrest, were apportioned during the purges. Other notable films that returned to the Stalin theme were Yuri Kara's *The Feast of Balthazar, or A Night with Stalin* (*Piry Valtasara, ili noch so Stalinym,* 1989), Valerii Ogorodnikov's *Prishvin's Paper Eyes* (*Bumazhnye glaza Prishvina,* 1989), Mark Zakhorov's *To Kill the Dragon* (*Ubit drakona,* 1988), and Alexander Kaidanovsky's *The Wife of the Kerosene Seller* (*Zhena kerosinshchika,* 1988).

Vasily Pichul and Maria Khmelik's *Little Vera* (*Malenkaia Vera,* 1988) was the last big film of the Soviet era, attracting fifty million viewers. The film's success was due to the fact that it broke so many taboos at once and played to an audience that had an intimate understanding of the fabric of life lived by Vera and her parents. The film marked the beginning of the sexual revolution in Soviet and post-Soviet cinema and horrified many Soviet viewers who accused it of indecency, immorality, and obscenity. It was also a bitingly honest portrayal of Soviet youth, for whom the dream of communism was a sham but who had no dreams of their own to replace it. The film showed in graphic, no-nonsense terms the despair and disenchantment not only of Vera's generation but that of her parents who had sacrificed for a new order that had rewarded them with hard work, a difficult life, and broken dreams. This family's drama is played out against the backdrop of a decaying economy and a polluted environment, in a system in which unbridled industrialization has brought no discernible improvement to their lives and an apartment filled with memorabilia from countries they will never visit. As its title, *Little Vera* (Little Faith), implies, this is a film that speaks movingly about the failure of the Soviet system and those who have lost faith in it.

Post-Soviet Cinema

Since the demise of the USSR in 1991, Russian cinema has witnessed not only the euphoria and excitement but also the perils and pitfalls of the new era. The challenges the industry faced were many. First, by the early 1990s, movie attendance had fallen considerably as a result of the rise in inflation (including the price of movie tickets), the decline in the number of films being made, and the increase in video sales and home viewing (Larsen 1999, 192–194). Second, film production in the new Russia would no longer be state supported. Instead, studios were privatized, forcing directors to seek their own financial backing. In this new setting, the need for sponsors and an audience prompted Russian film directors to seek closer ties with production companies in the West.

As a result, a number of Russian films have been made in the post-Soviet era with the help of foreign financial backing, the most notable of which is *Burnt by the Sun* (*Utomlennye solntsem* 1994), directed by Nikita Mikhalkov and a coproduction of Russia's Studio TriTe and France's Camera One, with the participation of the Russian State Committee for Cinema, the Russian Club, and France's Canal+ (Beumers 2000). An instant international success, *Burnt by the Sun* won the 1994 Cannes Film Festival's Grand Jury Prize and the 1995 Academy Award for Best Foreign Language Film, making it the third Russian film to win an Oscar. Another Mikhalkov work with substantial foreign backing was *Barber of Siberia* (*Sibirskii tsiriulnik,* 1999). Although not nearly as critically acclaimed as *Burnt by the Sun,* it set a record as the most expensive film in Russian history, costing forty-three million dollars to produce, thirty-three million of which was provided by European backers.

In addition to relying on new forms of financial support, post-Soviet cinema is experimenting with two genres unknown during the communist era: mob movies and suspense thrillers. Two post-Soviet thrillers, *The Recluse* (*Zatvornik,* 2001), directed by Egor Mikhalkov-Konchalovskii, and *The*

The Barber of Siberia, directed by Nikita Mikhalkov.

Admirer (*Poklonnik,* 1999), directed by Nikolai Lebedeev, both show the influence of Alfred Hitchcock in shot selection and the creation of suspense. One also feels the influence of Hollywood in a growing reliance on the star system to sell a film. Soviet cinema never had a star system anything like the one created in Hollywood. Now, the names of such actors in the film credits as Sergei Makovetsky (who starred in Muratova's *Three Stories*) and Oleg Menshikov (who starred in *Burnt by the Sun*) are enough to virtually guarantee a movie's success. Significantly, no women actors are as yet on the list.

Although Russian cinema has in some respects become more a part of the international scene, it is also trying to find its own way, often independent of Hollywood. For instance, the Russian film industry has established its own award, the Nika. Certain trends in Russian cinema are also discernible.

Perhaps not surprisingly, questions of national identity and "Russianness" are predominant in many of the country's films. If Russians under the Soviet regime had their official identity constructed for them by the state, what does it mean now that their primary identity is no longer Soviet, but Russian? Furthermore, what does it mean to be Russian now that their ideological center as a part of the Soviet system has been taken away? It seems that film rather than literature has become the primary medium through which questions of identity are being explored.

Take for example, the extraordinarily popular films *Brother* (*Brat,* 1997) and *Brother 2* (*Brat 2,* 1999) by Alexei Balabanov. Balabanov's hero in both films, Danila Bagrov (played by the late Sergei Bodrov Jr.), is a war veteran, probably from the war in Chechnya, who sets off for St. Petersburg where his ne'er-do-well brother lives and works as a hit man. Danila takes up the life of a killer, on the one hand, and a defender of the poor, on the other. The first film explores the loss of Russia's ideological center, depicting a world in which there is no clear moral framework. Nor is there psychological depth to the characters (Beumers 1999b, 83–87). Danila seems to be nothing more than an empty vessel who as easily replicates the instructions on how to kill as he absorbs the latest in popular culture fads (Borenstein 2004, 477–478). In the movie's last scene, he heads down a snowy road in a truck toward Moscow where he will ply his trade as a killer and continue to look for CDs of his favorite rock band, Nautilus Pompilius. Director Balabanov, in a trademark move, steps back, refusing to take an overtly moral stand or to cast judgment on what he shows so clearly through the lens of his camera.

The search for identity has also spawned films dealing with the country's wars in Afghanistan and Chechnya, focusing on the question of what Russians are fighting for. Sergei Bodrov's *Prisoner of the Mountains* (*Kavkazskii plennik,* 1996), a refashioning of Tolstoy's and Lermontov's poems of the same name (albeit with a change in locale to modern-day Chechnya), is a

Prisoner of the Mountains, directed by Sergei Bodrov.

hard-hitting critique of the Russian army's presence in Chechnya and its treatment of nonethnic Russians. In a slightly different vein, Vladimir Khotinenko's *The Muslim* (*Musulmanin,* 1995) describes a Russian soldier, now a
Muslim, who returns to his village after years in captivity. Khotinenko subtly
highlights the corruption and inadequacy of Russian traditions by comparing
them to those of the people they have occupied. Other films explore relations between the Russians and the non-Russian peoples of the former
USSR. Gennady Sidorov's *Little Old Ladies* (*Starukhi,* 2003) charts the developing relationship between a village made up primarily of old women
and one village idiot, as a family of Uzbek refugees arrive and settle there.
The film provides a slightly different perspective on the relationship between the former empire and its subject nations, as now it is the Uzbeks who
initiate progress (in this case a simple electric power station) without which
the Russian village would continue to decay.

For some directors the question of identity is uniquely tied to that of the
father figure. One of the more skillful treatments of this theme is the film *The
Return* (*Vozvrashchenie,* 2003) directed by Andrei Zviagintsev. The film concerns the sudden and inexplicable return of a father who has been absent
from his family for twelve years. Wishing to reclaim his role as *paterfamilias,*
he takes his two young sons on a fishing trip during the course of which he
dies while trying to save one of them. The film explores the death of the father not only in the personal life of the two boys but implicitly in the larger

Birgit Beumers archive; used courtesy of the Press Service of the Open Russian Film Festival, 2003

Little Old Ladies, directed by Gennady Sidorov.

life of the nation. Zviagintsev's portrayal of this complicated man, who is both a tyrant and a devoted father unable to express his love, suggests the larger tyrant and father figure that perpetually ruled over Soviet life and is still a fixture in the post-Soviet imagination. The film is one of the more haunting of post-Soviet attempts to put the past to rest, as it suggests that such trauma and loss can best be dealt with through poetry and panegyric.

For other directors the past is nostalgically reconfigured and celebrated, as in Alexander Sokurov's monumental *Russian Ark* (*Russkii kovcheg,* 2002). Sokurov treats the viewer to a three-hundred-year historical romp through the Winter Palace and the Hermitage Museum beginning in the time of Peter the Great, and culminating in the last ball held in the palace in 1913 under Nicholas II, in the longest one-shot take in the history of cinema. Framed by a dialogue between the director and the Marquis de Custine, the nineteenth-century French traveler who visited Russia and declared the country a profoundly unhappy one, the film weaves in and out of the rooms of the Hermitage through which pass figures from Russian history, sometimes catching them unawares, sometimes watching them engaged in official business. Sokurov's film is a nostalgic farewell not to the Soviet past but to the prerevolutionary one it supplanted, as well as a celebration of a museum that has been a sustaining presence throughout Russian history.

In the ongoing attempt to rethink the country's national identity and Russianness, past and present are woven neatly together in three films by director Alexander Rogozhkin: *Peculiarities of the National Hunt* (*Osobennosti natsionalnoi okhoty,* 1995), *Peculiarities of National Fishing* (*Osobennosti natsionalnoi rybalki,* 1998), and *Peculiarities of the National Hunt in Wintertime* (*Osobennosti natsionalnoi okhoty v zimnii period,* 2000). At a time when the Russian market might be oversaturated with the search for meaning, with mob violence, and with elegies for a world long gone, Rogozhkin's three films poke lighthearted fun at clichés of the Russian character, noted for its proclivity toward hard drinking, endless saunas, and its love for nature. Rogozhkin takes each of these stereotypical images and creates narratives about a group of Russian men whose goals of hunting and fishing get deflected into an endless *zapoi* (or binge) of vodka drinking. In the first of the movies, they are accompanied on their hunt by a Finnish scholar who wishes to observe Russian national hunting practices and stands nonplussed as the Russians proceed to embark on the most Russian of all Russian practices. Rogozhkin intersperses the modern-day hunt with the Finn's dream sequences of an imagined nineteenth-century Russian hunt, complete with fur-clad, French-speaking nobility, borzoi hounds, and colorful exuberance. At the end of the film, the Finn, who here speaks Russian for the first time, says "It was a good hunt." Indeed, both hunts were good—the imagined one from the past and the one from the present, in which the dreams of what Russia should be in the foreigner's imagination devolve into drunken comradery mixed with no small amount of madness. The film seems to suggest that this as much validates what it means to be Russian as do the brilliant technicolor dreams of Russia's imagined and glorious past.

■ Conclusion: The New Texture of Cultural Life

In assessing cultural life in today's Russia, it is important to bear in mind that the culture now being fashioned did not take shape overnight but is the product of a long process of reform that is at odds with the more conservative ideological cultural policies that characterized much of the Soviet era. Whether one views the contemporary cultural scene as part of an evolutionary process or as a complete turning away from what once had been Russian high culture depends to a large extent on where one stands in relation to the culture of Russia's past.

Indeed, much of the cultural debate today in Russia revolves around the question of what has happened to the glories of the country's prerevolutionary past in the wake of the Westernization that has accelerated since the advent of reform in the mid-1980s. This is an old debate, with origins dating at least as far back as Peter the Great, as one generation after another has struggled with the question of Russia's identity with respect to the West. Today's debate takes place in the wake of the collapse of an empire and in the midst of a rising tide of globalization. In Russia, questions of identity historically have been worked out through the cultural tradition. Regardless of the great changes afoot in contemporary Russia, culture is still the arena where the larger questions of what it means to be Russian will be played out.

■ Note

I would like to give enormous thanks to Birgit Beumers, Eliot Borenstein, and Ekaterina Stetsenko who provided me with materials and answered all sorts of questions. Special thanks go to Michael Brewer, Slavic Reference Librarian at the University of Arizona, for procuring materials at a moment's notice and whose breadth of knowledge remains an inspiration.

■ Bibliography

Representative Anthologies of Russian, Soviet, and Post-Soviet Writing in English

Aksyonov, Vasily, et al., eds. 1982. *Metropol: Literary Almanac.* New York: Norton.
Brown, Clarence, ed. 1993. *The Portable Twentieth-Century Russian Reader.* Rev. and updated ed. New York: Penguin Books.

Chukhontsev, Oleg, ed. 1991. *Dissonant Voices: The New Russian Fiction.* London: Harvill.

Erofeyev, Victor, and Andrew Reynolds, ed. 1995. *The Penguin Book of New Russian Writing: Russia's Fleurs du Mal.* London: Penguin Books.

Gessen, Masha, ed. and trans. 1995. *Half a Revolution: Contemporary Fiction by Russian Women.* Pittsburgh: Cleis Press.

Gibian, George, ed. 1993. *The Portable Nineteenth-Century Russian Reader.* New York: Viking.

Glad, John, and Daniel Weissbort, eds. 1992. *Twentieth-Century Russian Poetry.* Iowa City: University of Iowa Press.

Glas: New Russian Writing. Birmingham, UK: University of Birmingham, Department of Russian.

Goscilo, Helena, ed. 1989. *Balancing Acts: Contemporary Stories by Russian Women.* Bloomington: Indiana University Press.

———, ed. 1995. *Lives in Transit: A Collection of Recent Russian Women's Writing.* Ann Arbor, MI: Ardis.

Goscilo, Helena, and Byron Lindsey, eds. 1990. *Glasnost: An Anthology of Russian Literature Under Gorbachev.* Ann Arbor, MI: Ardis.

———, eds. 1991. *The Wild Beach and Other Stories.* Ann Arbor, MI: Ardis.

Kagal, Ayesha, and Natasha Perova, eds. 1996. *Present Imperfect: Stories by Russian Women.* Boulder, CO: Westview Press.

Kelly, Catriona, ed. and trans. 1994. *An Anthology of Russian Women's Writing, 1777–1992.* Oxford, UK: Oxford University Press.

Markov, Vladimir, and Merrill Sparks, eds. 1967. *Modern Russian Poetry: An Anthology with Verse Translations.* Indianapolis: Bobbs-Merrill.

Milner-Gulland, Robin, and Martin Dewhirst, eds. 1977. *Russian Writing Today.* Harmondsworth, UK: Penguin.

Moss, Kevin, ed. 1997. *Out of the Blue: Russia's Hidden Gay Literature: An Anthology.* San Francisco: Gay Sunshine Press.

Pachmuss, Temira, ed. and trans. 1981. *A Russian Cultural Revival: A Critical Anthology of Émigré Literature Before 1939.* Knoxville: University of Tennessee Press.

Proffer, Carl R., ed. and trans. 1969. *From Karamzin to Bunin: An Anthology of Russian Short Stories.* Bloomington: Indiana University Press.

Proffer, Carl R., and Ellendea Proffer, eds. 1982. *Contemporary Russian Prose.* Ann Arbor, MI: Ardis.

———, eds. 1984. *The Barsukov Triangle, The Two-Toned Blond and Other Stories.* Ann Arbor, MI: Ardis.

Proffer, Carl. R., et al. 1987. *Russian Literature of The Twenties: An Anthology.* Ann Arbor, MI: Ardis.

Rzhevsky, Nicholas, ed. 2005. *An Anthology of Russian Literature from Earliest Writings to Modern Fiction.* Armonk, NY: M. E. Sharpe.

Smith, Gerald S., comp. and trans. 1993. *Contemporary Russian Poetry: A Bilingual Anthology.* Bloomington: Indiana University Press.

Von Geldern, James, and Richard Stites, eds. 1995. *Mass Culture in Soviet Russia: Tales, Poems, Songs, Movies, Plays, and Folklore, 1917–1953.* Bloomington: Indiana University Press.

Yevtushenko, Yevgeny, comp., Albert C. Todd, and Max Hayward, eds. 1993. *Twentieth Century Russian Poetry: Silver and Steel: An Anthology.* New York: Doubleday.

Zenkovsky, Serge A., ed. and trans. 1963. *Medieval Russia's Epics, Chronicles, and Tales.* New York: Dutton.

Representative Studies of Russian, Soviet, and Post-Soviet Literature and Popular Culture

Aiken, Susan Hardy, et al. 1994. *Dialogues/Dialogi: Literary and Cultural Exchanges Between (ex)Soviet and American Women.* Durham, NC: Duke University Press.

Barker, Adele Marie, ed. 1999. *Consuming Russia: Popular Culture, Sex, and Society Since Gorbachev.* Durham, NC: Duke University Press.

Barker, Adele Marie, and Jehanne M. Gheith, eds. 2002. *A History of Women's Writing in Russia.* Cambridge, UK: Cambridge University Press.

Borenstein, Eliot. 2004. "Survival of the Catchiest: Memes and Postmodern Russia." *Slavic and East European Journal* 48(3): 462–483.

———. 2000. *Men Without Women: Masculinity and Revolution in Russian Fiction, 1917–1929.* Durham, NC: Duke University Press.

———. 2007. *Overkill: Sex and Violence in Contemporary Russian Popular Culture.* Ithaca, NY: Cornell University Press.

Boym, Svetlana. 1994. *Common Places: Mythologies of Everyday Life in Russia.* Cambridge, MA: Harvard University Press.

Brintlinger, Angela. 2004. "The Hero in the Madhouse: The Post-Soviet Novel Confronts the Soviet Past." *Slavic Review* 63(1): 43–65.

Brown, Deming. 1978. *Soviet Russian Literature Since Stalin.* Cambridge, UK: Cambridge University Press.

———. 1993. *The Last Years of Soviet Russian Literature: Prose Fiction, 1975–1991.* Cambridge, UK: Cambridge University Press.

Brown, Edward J. 1982. *Russian Literature Since the Revolution.* Rev. and enl. ed. Cambridge, MA: Harvard University Press.

Cherniak, Mariia. 2005. "Russian Romantic Fiction." In *Reading for Entertainment in Contemporary Russia: Post-Soviet Popular Literature in Historical Perspective,* ed. Stephen Lovell and Birgit Menzel. Munich: Sagner.

Clark, Katerina. 1981. *The Soviet Novel: History as Ritual.* Chicago: University of Chicago Press.

Clyman, Toby W., and Diana Greene, eds. 1994. *Women Writers in Russian Literature.* Westport, CT: Greenwood Press.

Condee, Nancy, and Vladimir Padunov. 1988. *The Frontiers of Soviet Culture: Reaching Its Limits?* Harriman Institute Forum 1/5. New York: W. Averell Harriman Institute for Advanced Study of the Soviet Union.

———. 1995. "The ABC of Russian Consumer Culture: Readings, Ratings, and Real Estate." In *Soviet Hieroglyphics: Visual Culture in Late Twentieth-Century Russia,* ed. Nancy Condee. Bloomington: Indiana University Press.

Debreczeny, Paul. 1993. "'Zhitie Aleksandra Boldinskogo': Pushkin's Elevation to Sainthood in Soviet Culture." In *Late Soviet Culture: From Perestroika to Novostroika,* ed. Thomas Lahusen with Gene Kuperman. Durham, NC: Duke University Press.

Dobrenko, Evgeny. 1997. *The Making of the State Reader: Social and Aesthetic Contexts of the Reception of Soviet Literature.* Trans. Jesse M. Savage. Stanford, CA: Stanford University Press.

Dubin, Boris. 2005. "The Action Thriller (Boevik) in Contemporary Russia." In *Reading for Entertainment in Contemporary Russia: Post-Soviet Popular Literature in Historical Perspective,* ed. Stephen Lovell and Birgit Menzel. Munich: Sagner.

Dunham, Vera S. 1990. *In Stalin's Time: Middleclass Values in Soviet Fiction.* Enl. and updated ed. Durham, NC: Duke University Press.

Figes, Orlando. 2002. *Natasha's Dance: A Cultural History of Russia.* New York: Metropolitan Books.

Garrard, John, and Carol Garrard. 1990. *Inside the Soviet Writers' Union.* New York: Free Press.

Goscilo, Helena, ed. 1993. *Fruits of Her Plume: Essays on Contemporary Russian Woman's Culture.* Armonk, NY: M. E. Sharpe.

———, guest ed. 2000. *Russian Culture of the 1990s.* A Special Issue of *Studies in 20th Century Literature* 24(1).

Goscilo, Helena, and Beth Holmgren, eds. 1996. *Russia—Women—Culture.* Bloomington: Indiana University Press.

Günther, Hans. 1990. *The Culture of the Stalin Period.* London: Macmillan.

Heldt, Barbara. 1987. *Terrible Perfection: Women and Russian Literature.* Bloomington: Indiana University Press.

Hingley, Ronald. 1979. *Russian Writers and Soviet Society, 1917–1978.* New York: Random House.

Hodgson, Katharine. 2003. *Voicing the Soviet Experience: The Poetry of Ol'ga Berggol'ts.* Oxford, UK: Oxford University Press.

Holmgren, Beth. 1993. *Women's Works in Stalin's Time: On Lidiia Chukovskaia and Nadezhda Mandelstam.* Bloomington and Indianapolis: Indiana University Press.

Hosking, Geoffrey. 1980. *Beyond Socialist Realism: Soviet Fiction Since Ivan Denisovich.* London: Granada.

Jones, Malcolm V., and Robin Feuer Miller, eds. 1998. *The Cambridge Companion to the Classic Russian Novel.* New York: Cambridge University Press.

Kelly, Catriona. 1994. *A History of Russian Women's Writing, 1820–1992.* Oxford, UK: Clarendon Press.

Kelly, Catriona, and David Shepherd, eds. 1998. *Russian Cultural Studies: An Introduction.* Oxford, UK: Oxford University Press.

Lovell, Stephen, and Birgit Menzel, eds. 2005. *Reading for Entertainment in Contemporary Russia: Post-Soviet Popular Literature in Historical Perspective.* Munich: Sagner.

Mandelstam, Nadezhda. 1970. *Hope Against Hope: A Memoir.* Trans. Max Hayward. New York: Atheneum.

Marsh, Rosalind J. 1986. *Soviet Fiction Since Stalin: Science, Politics, and Literature.* London: Croom Helm.

———. 1995. *History and Literature in Contemporary Russia.* London: Macmillan.

McReynolds, Louise. 1998. "Reading the Russian Romance: What Did the Keys to Happiness Unlock?" *Journal of Popular Culture* 31(4): 95–108.

Mehnert, Klaus. 1983. *The Russians and Their Favorite Books.* Stanford, CA: Stanford University Press.

Nepomnyashchy, Catharine Theimer. 1999, "Markets, Mirrors, and Mayhem: Aleksandra Marinina and the Rise of the New Russian Detektiv." In *Consuming Russia: Popular Culture, Sex, and Society Since Gorbachev,* ed. Adele Marie Barker. Durham, NC: Duke University Press.

Olcott, Anthony. 2001. *Russian Pulp: The Detektiv and the Russian Way of Crime.* Lanham, MD: Rowman & Littlefield.

Porter, Robert. 1994. *Russia's Alternative Prose.* Oxford, UK: Berg.

Sandler, Stephanie, ed. 1999. *Rereading Russian Poetry.* New Haven, CT: Yale University Press.

———. 2004. *Commemorating Pushkin: Russia's Myth of a National Poet.* Stanford, CA: Stanford University Press.

Shepherd, David. 1989. "Canon Fodder? Problems in the Reading of a Soviet Production Novel." In *Discontinuous Discourses in Modern Russian Literature*, ed. Catriona Kelly, Michael Makin, and David Shepherd. Basingstoke, UK: Macmillan.

Shneidman, N. N. 1979. *Soviet Literature in the 1970s: Artistic Diversity and Ideological Conformity*. Toronto: University of Toronto Press.

———. 1989. *Soviet Literature in the 1980s: Decade of Transition*. Toronto: University of Toronto Press.

———. 1995. *Russian Literature, 1988–1994: The End of an Era*. Toronto: University of Toronto Press.

Smith, Gerald Stanton. 1984. *Songs to Seven Strings: Russian Guitar Poetry and Soviet "Mass Song."* Bloomington: Indiana University Press.

Solzhenitsyn, Aleksandr I. 1980. *The Oak and the Calf: Sketches of Literary Life in the Soviet Union*. Trans. Harry Willetts. New York: Harper & Row.

Stites, Richard. 1992. *Russian Popular Culture: Entertainment and Society Since 1900*. Cambridge, UK: Cambridge University Press.

———, ed. 1995. *Culture and Entertainment in Wartime Russia*. Bloomington: Indiana University Press.

Thompson, Terry L., and Richard Sheldon, eds. 1988. *Soviet Society and Culture: Essays in Honor of Vera S. Dunham*. Boulder, CO: Westview Press.

Selected Studies of Soviet and Post-Soviet Film and Television

The following is a selection of works on Soviet and post-Soviet film in English. For those wishing Russian sources, see the Russian film journal *Iskusstvo kino* (www .kinoart.ru). I. B. Tauris publishes studies of individual films under the title KINOfiles Film Companions. For additional sources, see the excellent bibliography compiled by University of Pittsburgh professor Vladimir Padunov (www.pitt.edu/~ slavic/video). Other excellent websites are www.film.ru and www.ntvprofit.ru.

Attwood, Lynne, ed. 1993. *Red Women on the Silver Screen: Soviet Women and Cinema from the Beginning to the End of the Communist Era*. London: Pandora.

Beumers, Birgit, ed. 1999a. *Russia on Reels: The Russian Idea in Post-Soviet Cinema*. London: I. B. Tauris.

———. 1999b. "To Moscow! To Moscow? The Russian Hero and the Loss of the Centre." In *Russia on Reels: The Russian Idea in Post-Soviet Cinema*, ed. Birgit Beumers. London: I. B. Tauris.

———. 2000. *Burnt by the Sun*. London: I. B. Tauris.

———. 2003. "Soviet and Russian Blockbusters: A Question of Genre?" *Slavic Review* 62(3): 441–454.

———. 2005. *Pop Culture Russia!: Media, Arts, and Lifestyle*. Santa Barbara, CA: ABC-CLIO.

Brashinsky, Michael, and Andrew Horton, eds. 1994. *Russian Critics on the Cinema of Glasnost*. New York: Cambridge University Press.

Gillespie, David. 2003. *Russian Cinema*. New York: Longman.

Golovskoy, Val S., with John Rimberg. 1986. *Behind the Soviet Screen: The Motion-Picture Industry in the USSR, 1972–1982*. Ann Arbor, MI: Ardis.

Horton, Andrew, and Michael Brashinsky. 1992. *The Zero Hour: Glasnost and Soviet Cinema in Transition*. Princeton, NJ: Princeton University Press.

Janumyan, Ruslan. 2003. "Kira Muratova." *Senses of Cinema*. http://www.sensesof cinema.com/contents/directors/03/muratova.html.

Johnson, Vida T., and Graham Petrie. 1994. *The Films of Andrei Tarkovsky: A Visual Fugue.* Bloomington: Indiana University Press.

Kenez, Peter. 1995. "Black and White: The War on Film." In *Culture and Entertainment in Wartime Russia,* ed. Richard Stites. Bloomington: Indiana University Press.

———. 2001. *Cinema and Soviet Society from the Revolution to the Death of Stalin.* New and updated ed. London: I. B. Tauris.

Kepley, Vance, Jr., guest ed. 1990. *Contemporary Soviet Cinema.* In *Wide Angle* 12(4).

Larsen, Susan. 1999. "In Search of an Audience: The New Russian Cinema of Reconciliation." In *Consuming Russia: Popular Culture, Sex, and Society Since Gorbachev,* ed. Adele Marie Barker. Durham, NC: Duke University Press.

———. 2000. "Melodramatic Masculinity, National Identity, and the Stalinist Past in Postsoviet Cinema." *Studies in 20th Century Literature* 24(1): 85–120.

———. 2003. "National Identity, Cultural Authority, and the Post-Soviet Blockbuster: Nikita Mikhalkov and Aleksei Balabanov." *Slavic Review* 62(3): 491–511.

Lawton, Anna. 1989. "Toward a New Openness in Soviet Cinema, 1976–1987." In *Post New Wave Cinema in the Soviet Union and Eastern Europe,* ed. Daniel J. Goulding. Bloomington: Indiana University Press.

———, ed. 1992. *The Red Screen: Politics, Society, Art in Soviet Cinema.* London: Routledge.

———. 1992. *Kinoglasnost: Soviet Cinema in Our Time.* Cambridge, UK: Cambridge University Press.

———. 1993 "The Ghost That Does Return: Exorcising Stalin." In *Stalinism and Soviet Cinema,* ed. Richard Taylor and Derek Spring. London: Routledge.

———. 2002. *Before the Fall: Soviet Cinema in the Gorbachev Years.* Xlibris.

———. 2004. *Imaging Russia 2000: Film and Facts.* Washington, D.C.: New Academia.

Leyda, Jay. 1960. *Kino: A History of the Russian and Soviet Film.* New York: Collier Books.

Liehm, Mira, and Antonin J. Liehm. 1980. *The Most Important Art: Soviet and Eastern European Film After 1945.* Berkeley: University of California Press.

Roberts, Graham. 1999. "The Meaning of Death: Kira Muratova's Cinema of the Absurd." In *Russia on Reels: The Russian Idea in Post-Soviet Cinema,* ed. Birgit Beumers. London: I. B. Tauris.

Tarkovsky, Andrey. 1989. *Sculpting in Time: Reflections on the Cinema.* Rev. ed. Trans. Kitty Hunter-Blair. London: Faber and Faber.

Taylor, Richard. 1998. *Film Propaganda: Soviet Russia and Nazi Germany.* 2nd rev. ed. London: I. B. Tauris.

Taylor, Richard, and Derek Spring, ed. 1993. *Stalinism and Soviet Cinema.* London: Routledge.

Taylor, Richard, et al. 2000. *The BFI Companion to Eastern European and Russian Cinema.* London: British Film Institute.

Turovskaya, Maya. 1993. "The 1930s and 1940s: Cinema in Context." In *Stalinism and Soviet Cinema,* ed. Richard Taylor and Derek Spring. London: Routledge.

Vertov, Dziga. 1984. *Kino-Eye: The Writings of Dziga Vertov,* ed. Annette Michelson. Trans. Kevin O'Brien. Berkeley: University of California Press.

Woll, Josephine. 2000. *Real Images: Soviet Cinema and the Thaw.* London: I. B. Tauris.

Youngblood, Denise J. 1992. *Movies for the Masses: Popular Cinema and Soviet Society in the 1920s.* Cambridge, UK: Cambridge University Press.

———. 2007. *Russian War Films: On the Cinema Front, 1914–2005.* Lawrence: University Press of Kansas.

Zorkaya, Neya. 1989. *The Illustrated History of the Soviet Cinema.* New York: Hippocrene Books.

13

Trends and Prospects

Michael L. Bressler

As our journey through Russia's past and present comes to an end, what might be said of the future? The question, *Kuda idet Rossiia?* ("Where is Russia going?"), is not a new one. First posed during the nineteenth century by Russian intellectuals when so much in the world around them was changing, it is one of Russia's so-called cursed questions. One of many who have asked this question is Yegor Gaidar, the architect of Boris Yeltsin's "shock therapy," the sweeping and audacious plan that both men hoped would transform Russia. Reflecting on the "revolution of the 1990s," Gaidar (2003, xi) wonders, "Was it a hard but salutary road toward the creation of a workable democracy with workable markets, the path to the twenty-first century? Or was it the prologue to another closed, stultified regime marching to the music of old myths and anthems?" As the 2007–2008 election season drew near, the answer to Gaidar's question seemed clear: Russia was heading in the wrong direction. As most Western and some Russian observers saw it, policies intended by Putin to strengthen and stabilize Russia through the construction of a managed, sovereign democracy, were producing not "a workable democracy with workable markets," but instead a system that was more oligarchic and autocratic than it was democratic and free.

For its part, the Kremlin could point to the economic success and relative stability Russia had enjoyed under Putin. On the face of things it seems that Putin has been good for the Russian economy. Annual growth in gross domestic product (GDP) has been strong, averaging over 6.6 percent through 2007. By the end of 2006, in fact, Russia's GDP had recovered to its pre–shock therapy levels (Nikolayev 2007). In that year, too, the rate of inflation fell below 10 percent for the first time in the post-Soviet era, although in

2007 it increased again to almost 12 percent (see Table 5.1). Real incomes were also up, moderately outpacing inflation, and the number of Russians living in poverty was half that of 1998, the year of Russia's last great financial crisis (ITAR-TASS 2007; World Bank 2006).

Much of Russia's economic success since 2003 has been the result of the high price of oil and natural gas in international markets. These higher prices are also largely responsible for Russia's renewed geopolitical clout. Whereas under Yeltsin Russia was often ignored by all but its closest neighbors, the world's increasing thirst for oil and gas has allowed the Kremlin to speak in a more strident and assertive voice in international affairs. Ranking number one in natural gas reserves and potentially possessing the world's largest reserves of oil (see World Bank 2006), Russia can expect to be listened to as long as energy prices remain high.

On occasion, Russia has turned this economic clout to its advantage by interrupting (or threatening to interrupt) the flow of energy to Ukraine, the Baltic states, Georgia, and Belarus. Such behavior creates great anxiety in the European Union (EU), many of the members of which are dependent on Russian energy. While not reliant on Russian oil and gas, the United States is alarmed, too, at Russia's apparent willingness to employ energy as a political and economic weapon. Although Russia has gone to great lengths to reassure the EU and the United States that it is a reliable supplier of energy, the two remain skeptical of Russia's intentions. Moscow's use of military force against Georgia in August 2008 has only increased the unease felt in Europe, the United States, and many former Soviet republics over the direction of Russian foreign policy.

As confident and assertive as Russia's leaders are now in their foreign policy, they continue to face a number of problems at home. Among the challenges chronicled in this volume are an aging population, an accelerating HIV/AIDS crisis, high levels of premature deaths, gender inequality, ethnic tension, and environmental degradation. Two other issues also loom large: the lack of accountability in the political system and the negative influence of Russia's resource-based economy on the country's political and economic development.

To the extent that the oil-and-gas boom has given a boost to the Russian economy—accounting for as much as 40 percent of the country's economic growth (Wolf 2007)—many economists argue that possessing vast energy reserves is more a curse than it is a blessing. As a major exporter of energy, Russia is at risk of contracting what is known as "Dutch disease." The problem is that when energy prices are high, the resulting influx of foreign cash increases the value of the domestic currency, making imported goods more affordable for domestic consumers, which in turn dampens the demand for domestic manufacturing. Although rapidly growing consumer demand has thus far allowed Russia to avoid contracting a full-blown case of Dutch disease, the long-term threat of resource dependency to the rest of the economy remains. Another problem facing resource-based economies is that a large share of their growth is dependent on a factor that is largely out of their control: price. Russia's leaders are aware of this problem and have set as a goal the diversification of the Russian economy (see Putin 2007). Diversification will not be accomplished easily, however. As long as energy prices remain high, the logic of Dutch disease remains operative.

At the same time, increased revenues from the sale of oil and gas can produce a false sense of security. Such was the case when an energy boom during the 1970s allowed the Kremlin to postpone consideration of the fundamental reform of an economy that appeared to be prospering, but in truth was ailing. When the price of oil fell in the 1980s, the Soviet leaders finally had to confront the underlying inefficiencies in their system (see Kotkin 2001).

If high prices for natural resources in the international marketplace can produce bad economic policy, so too can it encourage bad behavior on the part of illiberal elites. Economist Vladimir Mau sees a tendency on the part of some Russian political elites to fight over who will control the country's natural wealth, instead of trying to find ways to diversify and modernize the economy (Babich 2005). In the process, these elites have extended the state's control over the "commanding heights" of the economy. Despite claims by high-ranking officials that state control over certain sectors of the economy is the only option open to Russia at present (see Interfax 2007), the inefficiencies inherent in such an approach more than likely will hinder the economy's long-term development. Increased corruption is also an issue as the state increases its control over the most lucrative sectors of the economy, especially oil, gas, and minerals.

Corruption and mismangement are not the only negative effects of Russia's economic dependence on natural resources. Such dependence also can greatly hamper a country's political development. The problem is this: if a government can raise sufficient revenue from the export of natural resources, it need not rely as much on public taxation to support the state budget. The result, Mau argues, is "a kind of a negative social contract" between the state and society: "We [the ruling class] won't require any taxes from you" and in return "you won't demand any political rights" (Babich 2005). In short, if the state expects nothing of its citizens, citizens can expect nothing of the state. If the state, however, must turn to entrepreneurs and the country at large to support its spending, those who are taxed will expect to be able to hold the state accountable for its actions.

The question of accountability is central to Russia's future. How this question is answered in the years and decades ahead not only will affect Russia but also much of the world. Historically, Russia's leaders have relied on the bureaucratic state to solve the country's problems. This was true not only of the tsars and the Soviets but also of Yeltsin and Putin. For Yegor

Gaidar (2003, 116), the bureaucratic state is a "tremendously powerful magnet. . . . Its force field has always determined the trajectory of Russian history, [and] has deformed the face of Russia; it has consumed and destroyed its own society and destroyed itself in the process." Gaidar asks, "Will we be able, at last, to break free of this orbit?"

If Russia is to break free, its ruling elites eventually will have to accept the notion that state strength is not a function of the centralization of political and economic power but is rather a product of a form of government in which elites are accountable not only to the people but to each other. Higher levels of accountability will increase, not decrease, the capacity of the state to govern by making it more difficult for elites to behave carelessly and capriciously in their exercise of power. The more accountable elites are, the stronger the state will be. Of course, those with political power will have to think and behave differently. Important, too, is active and constant public involvement in the policy process. The problem, of course, is that Russia currently lacks the political and constitutional mechanisms (starting with an effective and reliable system of checks and balances) that could allow the public as a part of the normal course of events to press elected and nonelected officials to serve the public interest. The absence of such mechanisms, combined with the country's illiberal turn under Putin, has strengthened, not weakened, the bureaucracy's grip on the system.

As easy as it is to become discouraged by the direction Russia seems to be taking, however, it is important to realize that the country is nevertheless changing. Although some observers claim that Putin's popularity has been in large part a product of an innate desire on the part of the Russian people for a strong leader, the reality is more complex. At the same time that Russians surely want stability in their lives (as most people do), a majority also embrace and endorse the fundamental precepts of democratic government. And even though the commanding heights of the economy are coming increasingly under state control, economic growth, however uneven, is encouraging the growth of a Russian middle class. Although the creation of such a social class, in and of itself, does not guarantee the eventual consolidation of democracy, under the right circumstances (especially with the development of an economically independent entrepreneurial elite) it can serve as an engine for change. Such indeed was the case in tsarist Russia a century ago, and as the Russian economy continues to develop and as Russian society continues to evolve, such may yet be the case in the years and decades ahead.

Indeed, Russian society already seems to be in the midst of such a transformation. According to Vladimir Petukhov (2007), research director of the All-Russia Center for the Study of Public Opinion, VTsIOM, the achievement of economic stability under Putin has given rise to new expectations about life and living within the rapidly forming "middle layer" of Russian society. These expectations are running ahead of the country's social and economic realities, and are reaching beyond the state's ability to deliver services. Members of this emerging middle class want more out of their lives than simply "a good living." They also want space to develop their "creative and professional potential." And even as their interest in parties and party politics wanes ("big-time politics" as Petukhov calls it), middle-class Russians are becoming more interested in what is going on in their communities. Another significant change Petukhov sees is that "these days, it's very difficult to get Russian citizens really scared about anything, or to impose any agenda in which they aren't really interested." As this middle class continues to develop and grow, one could expect that it eventually will put pressure on Russia's political elite to be more attentive to its needs, especially if inflation becomes a problem. The fact that a middle layer exists at all suggests that Russia is changing, even if those who favor democratic development are losing ground at the moment. In focusing as we often do on how far Russia and the Russians have yet to go, it is easy to forget how far the country and its people have already come.

◼ Bibliography

Babich, Dmitry. 2005. "Some Transatlantic Similarities." *Russia Profile,* July 27.

Gaidar, Yegor. 2003. *State and Evolution: Russia's Search for a Free Market.* Trans. Jane Ann Miller. Seattle: University of Washington Press.

Interfax. 2007. "Medvedev: State Share in Russia's Economy Not Excessive," January 31. In *Johnson's Russia List,* no. 24, February 1. http://www.cdi.org/russia/johnson/2007-24-22.cfm

ITAR-TASS. 2007. "Fradkov Praises Government's Work in 2006," January 1.

Kotkin, Stephen. 2001. *Armageddon Averted: The Soviet Collapse, 1970–2000.* Oxford, UK: Oxford University Press.

Nikolayev, Igor. 2007. "Russia's Economy in 2006." *RIA Novosti,* January 2. http://en.rian.ru/analysis/20070102/58297658.html.

Petukhov, Vladimir. 2007. "The Moral Majority: Seven Years On." *Profil,* no. 3, January 29. Trans. Elena Leonova. http://www.russiaprofile.org/cdi/2007/1/31/5141.wbp.

Putin, Vladimir. 2007. Opening Address at the Meeting with Representatives from the Russian Union of Industrialists and Entrepreneurs, February 6. http://www.kremlin.ru/eng/speeches/2007/02/06/2314_type82912type84779_117945.shtml.

Wolf, Charles. 2007. "Where Does Russia's Economy Lie on the Spectrum of 'Transition'?" *Taipei Times,* January 8. http://www.taipeitimes.com/News/editorials/archives/2007/01/08/2003343907.

World Bank. 2006. *Russian Federation—Country Brief 2006–2007.* http://web.worldbank.org/WBSITE/EXTERNAL/COUNTRIES/ECAEXT/RUSSIANFEDERATION EXTN/0,,contentMDK:21054807~menuPK:517666~pagePK:1497618~piPK: 217854~theSitePK:305600,00.html.

Acronyms

ABM	anti-ballistic missile
AIDS	acquired immune deficiency syndrome
CEDAW	Convention on the Elimination of All Forms of Discrimination Against Women
CEIP	Carnegie Endowment for International Peace
CIS	Commonwealth of Independent States
CITES	Convention on International Trade in Endangered Species
Comintern	Communist International
CPR	contraceptive prevalence rate
CPRF	Communist Party of the Russian Federation
CPSU	Communist Party of the Soviet Union
DOTS	Directly Observed Treatment, Short-Course
EBRD	European Bank for Reconstruction and Development
EU	European Union
FDI	foreign direct investment
FIG	financial industrial group
FSB	Federal Security Service of the Russian Federation
FSU	Former Soviet Union
G-7	Group of Seven
G-8	Group of Eight
GDP	gross domestic product
GKO	short-term state securities
GNP	gross national product
Gosplan	State Planning Committee of the USSR
HIV	human immunodeficiency virus
HNP	Health, Nutrition, and Population Database (of the World Bank)

ICF	International Crane Foundation
IDU	injecting drug user
IMF	International Monetary Fund
INF	intermediate-range nuclear forces
KGB	State Security Committee of the USSR
LDPR	Liberal Democratic Party of Russia
LMFBR	liquid metal fast-breeder reactor
LWGR	light water–cooled graphite reactor
MW	megawatts
NATO	North Atlantic Treaty Organization
NEP	New Economic Policy
NGO	nongovernmental organization
ODIHR	Office for Democratic Institutions and Human Rights (of the OSCE)
OECD	Organization for Economic Cooperation and Development
OSCE	Organization for Security and Cooperation in Europe
OVR	Fatherland-All Russia
PPP	purchasing power parity
PR	proportional representation
RBMK	graphite-moderated reactor
RSFSR	Russian Soviet Federated Socialist Republic
SDI	Strategic Defense Initiative, also known as "Star Wars"
SDR	standardized death rates
SMD	single-member district
SPS	Union of Rightist Forces
STD	sexually transmitted disease
TB	tuberculosis
TFR	total fertility rate
TsIK	Central Election Commission of the Russian Federation
UNAIDS	Joint United Nations Program on HIV/AIDS
UNDP	United Nations Development Programme
UNESCO	United Nations Educational, Scientific, and Cultural Organization
UNICEF	United Nations International Children's Emergency Fund
USAID	United States Agency for International Development
USSR	Union of Soviet Socialist Republics
VTsIOM	All-Russia Center for the Study of Public Opinion
VVER	pressurized-water reactor
WHO	World Health Organization
WMD	weapons of mass destruction
WTO	World Trade Organization

The Contributors

Adele Barker is professor of Russian and Slavic studies at the University of Arizona.

Michael L. Bressler is professor of political science at Furman University, in South Carolina.

Katherine E. Graney is associate professor of government at Skidmore College, in New York State.

Timothy Heleniak, formerly of the World Bank and UNICEF, is a doctoral student in the Department of Geography at the University of Maryland.

Sarah L. Henderson is associate professor of political science at Oregon State University.

Olga Kazmina is associate professor of ethnology at Moscow State University.

Allen C. Lynch is Cummings Professor of International Affairs and director of the Center for Russian and East European Studies at the University of Virginia.

Steven G. Marks is professor of history at Clemson University.

James R. Millar is professor emeritus of economics and international affairs at George Washington University.

Philip R. Pryde is professor emeritus of geography at San Diego State University.

Denis J. B. Shaw is reader in Russian geography at the University of Birmingham, in England.

Index

About the Book

*U*nderstanding *Contemporary Russia* provides a thorough introduction to a country currently in the midst of political, economic, and social transformation. Interdisciplinary in design, the book is intended for use as a core text in introductory survey and politics courses and also as a supplement in a variety of discipline-oriented courses.

The authors draw on the best scholarship in their fields to provide sophisticated yet accessible treatments of subjects ranging from geography and history, to politics, economics, and international relations, to ethnicity, population, health, the environment, the role of women, religion, and literature and film. Numerous maps, photographs, and suggestions for further reading enhance the text.

Michael L. Bressler is professor of political science at Furman University.